W9-CQI-324

Journey to the Eastern Hemisphere

Copyright © 2016 by Avyx, Inc.

Avyx, Inc.
8032 South Grant Way
Littleton, CO 80122
(303) 483-0140 FAX (303) 483-0141
info@avyx.com

Library of Congress Control Number: 2016935064

ISBN 978-1-935570-32-5

Table of Contents

ASIA | JAPAN

ASIA | RUSSIA

SOUTHEAST ASIA

SOUTHEAST ASIA | VIETNAM

JOURNEY TO THE

EASTERN
HEMISPHERE

CHINA

CHINA: THE BIG PICTURE

Did you know that more people live in China than any other country on Earth? With a population of 1.3 billion, the People's Republic of China is home to 20% of the world's population. China is one of the oldest continuous civilizations, with roots going back roughly 7,000 years. It is also one of world's largest countries. With such vast size, population, and history, China has developed a rich and fascinating culture.

China is a land of contrasts: ancient and modern, rural and urban, and prosperous and poor. Most of the population lives in the eastern third of the country in sprawling rural villages or huge, modern cities. In the west, various people groups make their homes in desert and mountain regions. Farming is the dominant occupation, though workers are increasingly moving to cities to find jobs in manufacturing and services. Although the nation generates huge economic output and has vast resources, the people as a whole are not wealthy.

Much of China's government, education, and daily life are based on the ancient belief systems and philosophies of Confucianism, Daoism, and Buddhism.

China's oldest written records, dating to about 1,500 BCE, tell us that the nation began as a collection of independent kingdoms that frequently warred with one another. In 221 BCE, China's first emperor, Qin Shi Huangdi, united the country under one central government and founded a dynasty.

Dynastic rule continued for many centuries, and China became one of the world's most advanced civilizations. Inventors, artists, philosophers, and traders spread Chinese influence throughout the world.

In 1912, the dynasties came to an end as the Nationalist Party established a republic in China. Just 37 years later, the Communists took control of the country, and continue to rule to this day. Communists placed strict controls on China's economy, industry, finance, and everyday life. Today, China is slowly allowing more freedom in industry, the media, and everyday life.

CHINA'S HISTORY

As one of the world's oldest civilizations, China has a long and rich history. The first evidence of human settlements in China date back to somewhere between 10,000 and 5,000 BCE. During this time, Chinese civilization grew from two main cultures—the Yangshao and the Longshan. The Yangshao farmed the central valley of the Yellow River, while the Longshan, who lived in walled communities, raised rice, cattle, and sheep.

As early as the 1500's BCE, early forms of writing emerged, allowing Chinese culture to develop quickly. The first major written history of China dates back to 100 BCE and was written by a historian named Sima Qian. Civilization flourished

Fast Facts

Capital:
Beijing

Size:
4th in the world

Area:
5,963,274 sq miles
(15,444,809 sq km)

Coastline:
9,010 miles (14,500 km)

Highest Point:
Mount Everest 29,035 feet (8,850 meters)

Lowest Point:
Turpan Pendi -505 feet (-154 m)

Population:
1.3 billion

Official Languages:
Standard Chinese
(Mandarin)

Currency:
Yuan (or renminbi)

National Anthem:
"The March of the Volunteers"

National Symbol:
dragon

in China, giving rise to many inventions, philosophies, and other cultural developments.

Ancient Chinese history is divided into dynasties, or rule by families. Beginning in 221 BCE, rival kingdoms became united under an emperor to form one massive kingdom. This form of government lasted through several dynasties for thousands of years. In 1912, Chinese citizens overthrew the emperor and formed a republic. Then, in 1949, civil war resulted in a Communist government coming to power. Today, China is a truly "modern" nation that is changing rapidly.

Xia Culture

Xia culture started during the 2100's BCE. Although it was traditionally considered the first dynasty, some scholars suggested this claim was a myth. Archaeologists have uncovered sites that may support the theory of the Xia culture as the first dynasty. Now scholars question how much of the written record is truth and how much is fiction.

Shang Dynasty (1766–1045 BCE)

The Shang created a highly developed society in the eastern valley of the Yellow River. Arising from the Longshan and Xia cultures, the Shang dynasty lasted several hundred years. Archaeologists have discovered bronze vessels, war chariots, and written records they attribute to the Shang people.

Zhou Dynasty (1045–221 BCE)

The Zhou came out from the west, overthrew the Shang, and established a new dynasty. Though they ruled the western part of China, they allowed some followers to create semi-independent states in the east. The most famous individual from the Zhou Dynasty is the philosopher Confucius. He inspired people to live according to moral principles, including respecting others and leading a family-focused life.

The Zhou dynasty was weakened by battles with foreign invaders and the increasing independence of the seven eastern states. Ultimately, the Qin state took control and began a long-lasting period of a united China.

Map of China

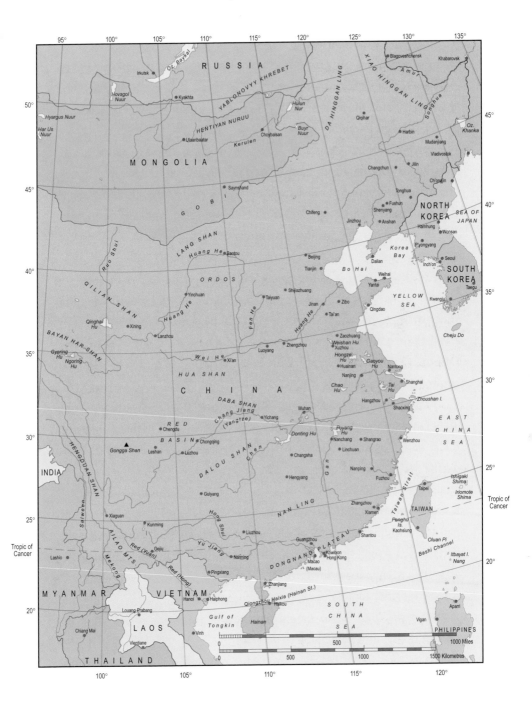

CONFUCIANISM

The gentleman does not seek to satiate himself in eating, does not seek ease in living, is quick in his dealings and prudent in speech, and keeps to the correctness of those with the way. He can be considered as devoted to learning.[1] These words of wisdom are just as powerful today as when Confucius first spoke them over 2500 years ago.

The philosopher Confucius was born in China in 551 BCE, during the Zhou dynasty. At that time, many separate states were at war and the Chinese people began to abandon social traditions of the past. Confucius encouraged others to live peaceful, respectful lives. He taught that *junzi,* or the superior man, should behave according to strong morals. By working hard, respecting others, and contributing to society, junzi would save Chinese culture.

Confucius promoted the golden rule, or treating others the way you would want to be treated. He taught his students to practice self-examination in order to become the best they could be. Junzi respected authority, served their community, and honored their parents. Confucius believed that leaders should rule by virtuous example, which is more effective than laws and punishments.

Part philosophy, part religion, and part social code, Confucianism is a belief system based on the teachings of Confucius. It focuses on moral, ethical behavior, or doing what is right. It does not speak to gods or an afterlife, though it makes mention of heaven. It involves some ceremonial rituals, but Confucianism has no clergy. When Confucius died in 479 BCE, his followers continued spreading and adding to his teachings.

The popularity and focus of Confucianism have changed somewhat over the years, but the basic principles have remained the same. In the 300's BCE, Mencius put forth the belief that people are intrinsically good-hearted and that this natural tendency needed to be preserved. However, just 100 years later, Xunzi taught that people are born neither good nor bad, but that goodness needed to be taught.

In its early years, rulers embraced Confucianism's stance on respect for authority and contribution to the public good. Government officials were trained in Confucian ideals at the Imperial University. They studied a set of books known as the *Five Classics,* which contain teachings of Confucius as well as his early followers. Later, Buddhist and Daoist beliefs influenced Confucianism. For example, Confucianism once focused mainly on the needs of society. Daoist influence encouraged greater awareness of living in harmony with nature.

In the late 1100's CE, a major shift in Confucian thought led to a branch called Neo-Confucianism, which placed more emphasis on the beliefs in Li and Qi, the source of energy in the world, and several hundred years later, taught that people can rely on their own moral mind when making decisions or understanding something new.

Statue of Confucius

Confucianism has influenced almost every aspect of Chinese life. Principles of Confucianism show up frequently in art, music, government, education, literature, and social norms. Koreans, Japanese, and Vietnamese also follow Confucianism in great numbers.

[1]Lun yu, chapter 1 verse 14

THE KINGDOM OF ANCIENT CHINA
221 BCE–1912 CE

Qin Dynasty (221–206 BCE)

The Qin (pronounced "chin") established a strong central government that combined the morality of Confucianism with the strict tenets of Legalism. This philosophy embraced strict laws, clear authority, and efficient administration. Though Emperor Qin Shi Huangdi ruled for only a short time, he made a great impact on China's history. Qin unified the kingdom by getting rid of separate states and standardized the writing system, currency, weights, and measures. He mandated large canal, road, and irrigation projects that improved transportation and farming. He also began construction of the Great Wall of China in an effort to keep out invaders. With later dynasties adding to its construction, the wall eventually stretched about 13,000 miles (20,900 km). The Great Wall of China still stands today and is a popular tourist destination.

Terracotta warriors guard the tomb of Emperor Qin

The Qin dynasty ended after a civil war that followed the emperor's death in 210 BCE. His tomb is one of the most famous in the world, with its army of thousands of life-size terracotta figures. The first emperor spurred great progress, but it cost the Chinese people in the form of high taxes, slavery, and strict laws. This harsh ruler established a kingdom that would last more than 2,000 years. In fact, the name "China" comes from the word *Qin*.

Han Dynasty (206 BCE–220 CE)

When the Han gained control of China, the government became even more dependent on Confucian philosophies. China experienced a brief change in power when Wang Mang took control and established the Xin dynasty from 9-25 CE. After regaining the throne, the Han dynasty initiated great cultural growth. Writers produced many new works, including dictionaries, and preserved classic literature from earlier times. Science, art, and education also flourished. Scientist Zhang Heng invented the first earthquake detection instrument—a bronze vessel that dropped small beads when it experienced tremors. For the first time, China used overland routes to trade with Europe. The

The ruins of Jiaohe, an ancient city along the Silk Road

most famous of these was the Silk Road, named after China's most popular export. People used groups of camels, called caravans, to travel and trade goods with the West. The Chinese traded silk, tea, spices, lacquered wooden objects, and other goods. Chinese culture spread in and out of China as they influenced their neighbors and learned from them in return. One major influence of this period was that of Buddhism, which was introduced from India.

The Han dynasty fell after a century of political turmoil. Dishonesty among rulers and mistreatment of peasants prompted a rebellion that ended the dynasty. For a time, China was divided between competing kingdoms and invading northern forces. China split into northern and southern dynasties. One ongoing, uniting factor was the spread of Buddhism, which impacted all aspects of daily life.

Sui Dynasty (581–618)

Eventually, the Sui dynasty reunited China. They built the Grand Canal in 610, which allowed easier transport between the Yangtze Valley and Northern China. Now, the government could better control the north and protect against invaders.

Tang Dynasty (618–907)

The Tang dynasty saw their capital, Chang'an, become the largest city in the world. This drew scholars, traders, and politicians from all over Asia and led to great cultural accomplishments. One of these was the invention of woodblock printing. By printing full pages of text at a time, rather than hand-painting each character, woodblock printing made books quicker, easier, and cheaper to print. This led to the mass production and distribution of books throughout the nation. The famous poets Li Bo and Du Fu lived during this period. In addition to literature, the Tang dynasty advanced painting, sculpture, and poetry. It also developed more "Chinese" versions of Buddhism, including Zen. The Tang dynasty is known as the golden age of Chinese history.

The Tang gradually lost power after a series of rebellions beginning in 755. Eventually, the Song dynasty reunified the nation in 960.

Song Dynasty (960–1127)

The population of China reached 100 million during the Song dynasty. Rulers solidified the practice of civil service examinations that the Han had begun hundreds of years before. Workers were hired based on ability rather than social status. The Song also adopted Neo-Confucianism as its official philosophy. This school of thought, created mainly by philosopher Zhu Xi, drew from traditional Confucianism along with Buddhism and Daoism.

During this time, Chinese merchants began using paper currency rather than heavy coins. This Chinese invention of paper money spread throughout the world. The Song dynasty also invented the astronomical clock. Built by an official named Su Song, it showed the time of day as well as the position of the planets and stars. Farmers discovered a type of rice that grew more quickly, allowing them to plant several crops per year and feed the growing population. Other developments in art and literature during this period included movable type for printing, hard-glazed porcelains, and landscape paintings.

The Song dynasty moved its capital south after losing part of northern China to a rival dynasty in 1127. For the rest of its reign, it was called the Southern Song, while the dynasty that ruled before 1127 was known as the Northern Song.

Mongol Rule (1279–1368)

After centuries of clashing with civilizations to the north, China finally fell to Mongol invaders in 1279. Leader Kublai Khan established the Yuan dynasty, which put China completely under foreign rule for the first time. During this period, Italian explorer Marco Polo traveled throughout China, bringing back reports that excited Europeans.

Ming Dynasty (1368–1644)

The Chinese endured almost a century of harsh rule at the hands of the Mongols. In the mid-1300's, the people rebelled and established the Ming dynasty. Once again, Chinese culture thrived. However, they saw the rise of European influence in the late 1500's and the 1600's as a threat. The Chinese worried that European traders and Roman Catholic missionaries would threaten the stability of the nation.

The Ming dynasty is famous for building the Chinese imperial palace in the Forbidden City of Beijing. This collection of buildings within a walled city was the seat of Chinese government until 1912. Now, it is a museum recognized as a World Her-

Stone archway leading
to the Ming Dynasty Tombs

itage Site and home to the world's largest collection of preserved ancient wooden structures.

During the 13th to 15th centuries, the Chinese built the largest and most advanced ships in the world. These ships, called junks, were made of wood and had huge canvas or silk sails. They were the first ships to use a rudder for easy steering. Chinese merchants and traders used junks to

The Hall of Supreme Harmony and inner courtyard of the Forbidden City in Beijing

travel the inland rivers and seas. Pirates also used junks to chase down Chinese and foreign traders and steal their goods. Although more modern ships have been developed, some sailors throughout Southeast Asia still use junks today.

Manchus (Qing) (1644–1912)

The Manchus came to power after invading China from the northeast and overthrowing the Ming. Though the Manchus originated outside the Great Wall, they had been greatly influenced by Chinese culture. They based their government on Neo-Confucianism and the model of the Ming. Their Qing dynasty was a time of prosperity in China. The population doubled to 300 million between 1700 and 1800, and Chinese influence spread throughout Asia.

By the late 1700's, China had two closely controlled ports open to trading with European merchants. However, China mainly exported tea and silk, while importing very little in return. They were determined to limit interaction with foreigners. Europeans attempted to balance trade with China by importing opium, a destructive and highly addictive drug. When China outlawed opium, Europeans continued to smuggle it into the country. Opium began to negatively affect China's economy, as addicts spent money on the drug instead of other goods. In 1839, Chinese officials fought back against British smugglers by seizing 20,000 chests of opium in Guangzhou. This led to the first of two Opium Wars, the first from 1839 to 1842, and the second from 1856 to 1860. The United Kingdom, with its superior weapons and technology, easily beat the Chinese both times.

By the mid-1800's, Europe and the United States had taken advantage of China through a series of unfair treaties. The first was the Treaty of Nanjing, which ended the First Opium War. It gave the United Kingdom ownership of the island of Hong Kong and opened more ports to the British, who exercised increasing power over China. British officials were granted the right to deal with Chinese officials on equal terms and to try any criminal cases involving their own citizens. Further treaties with the U.S. and France extended these rights to them as well. China

Chinese junk in Hong Kong

12

tried once again to fight back against European powers, but lost the Second Opium War. Another round of oppressive treaties granted more land to the United Kingdom and some to Russia. They also allowed for traders and missionaries to move further into China's interior.

During this same period, conditions worsened when Chinese agriculture became unable to keep pace with the growing population. Political dishonesty and rebellions weakened the Qing dynasty further.

Taiping Rebellion (1850–1864)

The Taipings believed in a blend of Christianity and intolerance of traditional Chinese culture. Led by Hong Xiuquan, who believed himself to be the younger brother of Jesus, they clashed with the Qing leadership over land distribution and Confucianism. The Taipings thought land should be divided equally among all people. They also demanded equal rights for women. Their rebellion was one of the most deadly in history, with 20 million people killed. The Qing dynasty organized new armies to defeat the uprising and also received military aid from the countries that wanted to maintain their unfair treaties with the Qing leadership.

Open Door Policy (1899)

From 1894 to 1895, China fought in the first Sino-Japanese War against the Japanese. As a result, China lost control of Taiwan and its claim on Korea. It appeared that China, weakened by foreign wars and internal rebellions, would fall to Western countries, each attempting to grab their own slice of the country. However, the threat from foreign powers stirred strong feelings of Chinese nationalism, drawing the people together. Ultimately, China and several other countries agreed to the U.S.'s Open Door policy. It granted equal rights to all countries seeking to use Chinese ports for trade.

Boxer Rebellion (1900)

Growing opposition to Western and Christian influences in China led to the formation of secret societies. One of the most popular was the Boxers, nicknamed for their exercises that resembled shadowboxing. Many of the members were poor farmers, angry and desperate for change. They were eager to join the Boxers after years of annual flooding followed by a drought. They fought against Christianity, killing foreign missionaries and Christian converts, and burning churches. Manchu leadership at first ignored the activity of the Boxers, and then supported the rebellion. At one point, Empress Dowager Tzu Hsi declared war against all foreigners. However, Western forces eventually intervened and ended the rebellion. They put measures into place that ensured foreigners would have access to China, which further hurt China's chances for independence.

Greatly weakened by foreign controls and internal unrest, the Manchu dynasty began to lose its hold on the country. Attempts to reform the government and economy were not enough to appease the many people demanding a republic. Rebels rallied around Dr. Sun Yat-sen, a physician who had been educated in Hawaii and Hong Kong. His anti-dynasty ideas for reform appealed to revolutionaries, who fought against the Manchu for several years.

Dynasties End (1911)

Big changes occurred in China when Empress Dowager Tzu Hsi died in 1908. She was succeeded by Pu Yi, an infant at the time. This led to a nationwide rebellion under Dr. Sun Yat-sen. Sun worked to unify young intellectual revolutionaries with less-cultured rebels belonging to secret

A section of the Great Wall of China and watchtowers

societies. He proposed the Three Principles of the People—nationalism, democracy, and socialism. After overthrowing the Manchus, Sun became the first president of the Provisional Chinese Republic in 1911.

China as a Republic (1912)

China then experienced a period of instability and rapid transfer of power. The Manchus called Yuan Shikai, a military leader, out of retirement to defeat Sun and his republic. Instead, Yuan made a secret deal supporting Sun. The six-year-old emperor Pu Yi stepped down and the era of dynasties ended. Sun resigned and was succeeded by Yuan, who promised a republic. However, Yuan became a dictator and tried to take control and become emperor. In 1912, the Kuomintang regime formed the Nationalist Party and attempted to overthrow Yuan. They were unsuccessful and fled to Japan. Civil war broke out between Republicans, who followed Sun, and rival militarists. In 1916, Yuan died, leading to a period of control by local military leaders.

In 1919, Sun reorganized his Nationalist Party with the help of Russian advisers. They merged with Chinese Communists and built an army. When Sun died in 1925, General Chiang Kai-shek took over the Nationalist Party. He fought to control China and united the nation under one government. After internal conflict, Chiang severed ties with the Communists, causing them to flee to the hills of southern China.

Beginning in 1931, the Nationalist government faced ongoing conflict with Japan, in addition to resistance from Chinese Communists. The Japanese invaded Manchuria and took control of many ports and railways in the east. The Chinese were forced to consent to Japanese demands for land because they were weakened by wars against the Communists. These common enemies rekindled feelings of unity in China and some of the people rallied behind Chiang. Others protested against his giving in to the Japanese. They kidnapped Chiang and only released him once he agreed to give up fighting against the Chinese Communists and focus on the war with Japan.

In 1937, Japan attacked China outright and took control of most of eastern China. Four years later, China joined the Allies in World War II.

The Allies (led by the United Kingdom, the United States, and the Soviet Union) fought against the Axis powers (led by Germany and Japan). Although the Allies helped China in its fight against Japan, China was severely weakened.

During this time, Communists in northern China grew stronger. They trained soldiers and spread Communist thinking. Their army of nearly 1 million took control of areas formerly held by Japan. Leaders redistributed land to peasant farmers according to socialist ideals. Communism became a very real threat to the Nationalist Party.

Communists Win Control (1949)

With the end of World War II in 1945, Japan surrendered to the Allied forces. This left China in a state of civil war as Chiang's Nationalist forces battled for control of China against Mao Zedong's Communist forces. In 1949, Mao successfully established the People's Republic of China with Zhou Enlai as premier. Chiang and his followers fled to Taiwan, where they established Nationalist China.

Meanwhile, Mao's new government went to work immediately, rebuilding the economy and recovering from the war. They seized land from landlords and redistributed it to peasant farmers. In the process, resentful peasants retaliated against their former landlords, killing hundreds of thousands. In 1953, Mao began China's First Five-Year Plan, a set of economic goals. His government supported North Korea in the Korean War in 1950, and annexed Tibet by adding its territory to China. Tibet later tried, and failed, to fight against Chinese occupation. Under the direction of their Buddhist spiritual leader, the Dalai Lama, about 100,000 Tibetans fled to India.

The Great Leap Forward (1958)

Mao envisioned a nation where vast numbers of farmers who worked in rural communes would do what other countries did in factories. His Great Leap Forward attempted to reorganize industry and agriculture by installing small steel furnaces in every village. He believed that a great number of diligent workers could overcome the setbacks of having few resources and little technology. Instead, it forced farmers to abandon their crops and work long hours at machines, leading to a devastating famine. Over 20 million people died of starvation or malnutrition during this failed campaign. People began to question Mao's Communist ideals, with some supporting a classless society of communal workers and others arguing for the division of labor.

During this time, China also severed its ties with the Soviet Union. The Soviet Union strove for "peaceful coexistence" with the West, while China anticipated war. Thus, when China engaged in a border war with India, the Soviet Union failed to send support.

The Cultural Revolution (1966)

After the failure of the Great Leap Forward, members of the Communist Party in China divided support between Mao and factional leader Deng Xiaoping. Consequently, Mao moved to Shanghai and launched the Cultural Revolution. This campaign closed schools and created Red Guard units consisting of young people. The Red Guards carried out violent attacks against ideas of the past. Mao's goal was to erase any differences between peasants and workers, rural and urban, and manual and mental work. During this attempt to wipe out China's traditional culture, beliefs, and customs, millions of people were killed. Most of them were intellectuals,

Mao's body can be seen in a crystal casket at Chairman Mao Memorial Hall in Beijing

artists, and the elderly. Mao also removed many top officials from office for not adhering to Communist ideals. Communist thinking took over China, and Mao emerged as the undisputed leader. During the early 1970's, China began repairing diplomatic relationships with Japan and the United States.

In 1976, both Premier Zhou and Mao died, leaving China in a state of instability. Mao's widow, Jiang Qing, led a group of radicals against Deng Xiaoping's more moderate followers. Deng took office, was quickly replaced, and then reinstated as premier. Jiang and other radical leaders were imprisoned as a more moderate Communist Party took control. This new government recognized the mistakes of Mao's Cultural Revolution and made widespread changes to China's Communist beliefs. They also built stronger ties with the United States and began adopting Western technology and practices to modernize the country.

Tiananmen Square Massacre (1989)

In 1987, Hu Yaobang was removed from his role as general secretary of the Communist Party. Hu was a well-loved leader who stood for the reformation of China. Zhao Ziyang, his replacement, angered many who feared a return to extreme Communist thought and leadership. When Hu

Great Hall of the People in Tiananmen Square in Beijing

died in 1989, student demonstrators filled Tiananmen Square in Beijing to demand democratic reforms. The students wanted greater freedom of speech and more say in the election of officials. They also wanted the leaders to reevaluate Hu, who had stood for freedom of expression. The protests continued for weeks until military forces, armed with guns and tanks, entered the square and killed several hundred protesters. The government also removed Zhao from his post as general secretary because of his failure to stop the pro-democracy movement. Jiang Zemin took over as general secretary in his place.

China Today

China has improved diplomatic relationships with several countries, including the former Soviet republics after the collapse of the Soviet Union in 1991. In addition, the United Kingdom returned Hong Kong to China in 1997. As part of that agreement, China agreed to let Hong Kong

Three Gorges Dam

remain autonomous. In 1999, China also regained the peninsula of Macau from Portuguese rule.

From 1994 to 2010, China undertook the building of the world's largest dam—the Three Gorges Dam on the Yangtze River. In addition to controlling flooding, the dam provides electric power and a usable waterway. Unfortunately, its reservoir flooded a huge area of historical sites and farmland. Over 1 million people had to resettle due to the construction of the dam.

Although Tibet became a self-governing region of China in 1965, Tibetans have faced ongoing religious and cultural persecution at the hands of China. In 2008, protests erupted into riots and required the Chinese military to restore order. Since then, people across the globe lobby for Tibetan independence.

China has worked to move its economy out from under total government control and to build relationships with foreign countries. In 2001, it joined the World Trade Organization in an effort to increase international trade. In 2008, China hosted the Summer Olympic Games in Beijing. This prompted the construction of stadiums and a performance hall, as well as improvements to the airport. The Chinese were proud to host such a prestigious event and even prouder when their country won the most gold medals.

The National Museum of China educates visitors about the arts and history of China

MEET THE PEOPLE OF CHINA

No country in the world has more people than China. With 1.3 billion citizens, China is home to one out of every five people on Earth. A population this size creates an enormous workforce, but also drains the country's resources. One billion people require a lot of food, housing, education, and jobs. In order to control population growth, the Chinese government decreed that men can't marry until age 22, and women can't marry until age 20. Couples are encouraged to wait even longer for marriage, and then may have no more than two children. In large cities, China often enforces a "one-child policy," meaning that a family can only have a single offspring. This has helped slow the population growth, but it has also resulted in more males than females in the population, as many families only give birth when sons are expected and put unwanted daughters up for adoption in the hopes of having a son. In China, a son carries on the family name and inherits property.

Most of China's population (94%) lives on just one-third of the land in the eastern part of the country. Here, they are crowded into large cities or spread out through rural

The Grand Theater and Tomorrow Square in Shanghai, China's largest city

towns and villages. The largest cities are Shanghai and Beijing. About 100 other Chinese cities have populations of one million or more. The number of people migrating out of China is about equal to the number immigrating in from other countries. Along a northern border with Korea, many North Koreans have moved into China to farm.

The Chinese speak a variety of languages and dialects, with Standard Chinese (or Mandarin) spoken in Beijing being the official language for most of the country. While dialects differ in their pronunciation of words, the writing is the same. A few cities or regions have a different official language. For example, the official language of Tibet is Tibetan, and Yue is the official language of the Guangdong province.

The Chinese government officially recognizes 56 different ethnic groups, though 92% of the population is Han Chinese. Most ethnic minorities live scattered throughout the western part of the country, where they

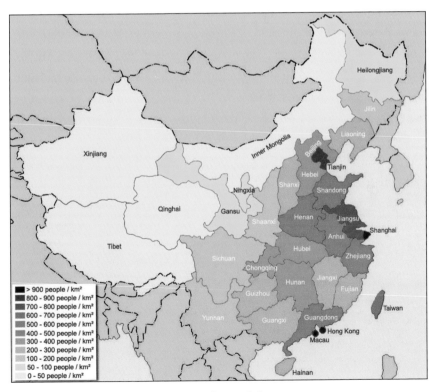

Population density of China

live a nomadic lifestyle, traveling from place to place grazing sheep or goats. Living in relative isolation, they have maintained their own traditional languages and cultures. These minority groups include the Mongols in the north, the Kazakhs in the northwest, and the Tibetans in the southwest.

Because China stretches over 3,107 miles (5,000 km) from west to east, it crosses through five time zones. However, in 1949 China switched from using five time zones to one standard time zone known as Beijing Time or China Standard Time (CST). This means that at 8:00 pm, people in eastern China could be experiencing a beautiful sunset, while those in western China are simultaneously enjoying warm afternoon sunshine.

LAND, WATER, AND CLIMATE IN CHINA

China is generally considered the world's fourth largest country based on area. Some sources, however, list it third, just ahead of the United States. Its total land area is about 5,963,274 square miles (15,444,809 square km). China is located in Eastern Asia, between Vietnam and Mongolia, though it borders 14 other countries, including Russia, North Korea, Kazakhstan, and India. It has approximately 9,010 miles (14,500 km) of coastline, mainly along the East China Sea. The Yangtze and the Yellow Rivers are the

View of the Himalayas from the International Space Station

Tiger Leaping Gorge on the Yangtze

largest of China's thousands of rivers. China is the largest country located entirely in Asia.

Because of its large area, China has a variety of climate zones, from the tropical south to the subarctic north. It experiences frequent typhoons along the southern and eastern coasts, along with floods, tsunamis, and earthquakes. The land in the west is mainly mountains, high plateaus, and deserts. For this reason, most of China's large cities are located in the plains and deltas of the east. China is home to the world's highest peak—Mount Everest, which straddles the border with Nepal, at 29,035 feet (8,850 meters) above sea level. In fact, mountains cover one-third of the land area in China, with the largest mountain range being the Himalayas.

Land

The three major land regions of China are the mountains in the southwest, deserts and plateaus in the northwest, and plains in the east.

In southwestern China, the Tibetan Highlands contain a large, high plateau surrounded by mountains, including Mount Everest. The Yellow River and the Yangtze River both begin in this region and flow east. This region was once the independent state of Tibet. It became part of China in the 1950's, but has remained fairly isolated because of its mountainous terrain and cold, windy climate. Tibet experiences snowstorms, but is otherwise very dry. Few people or animals can survive this rocky, icy wasteland, which has little land suitable for growing crops or grazing. The Tibetan people obtain some of their food, clothing, and transportation from the yaks that inhabit the region.

Northwestern China is a desert region with a small population. It contains the Ordos Desert, the Taklimakan Desert, and part of the Gobi Desert. It also contains mountains, including the Tian Shan range, as well as China's lowest point—the Turpan Depression, which is 505 feet (154 meters) below sea level. This area has a harsh climate and is isolated from the more populous eastern part of China.

The mountainous south and desert-like north in western China are separated by the Qin Ling Mountains. This mountain range runs east to west, forming a border that keeps warm, moist air to the south and cool, dry air to the north. This creates conditions good for growing wheat and millet north of the mountains and rice south of the mountains. The Sichuan Basin just south of the Qin Ling Mountains is one of the main agricultural regions in China. Here, farmers cut unique terraced fields into the hillsides.

The northeastern part of China has some of the best land for farming, along with rich natural resources. A fertile, yellow soil called *loess* is carried by the wind and deposited on the plateaus. Rivers carve valleys into the soft ground and provide irrigation for farming. To keep the valleys from flooding and destroying crops, the Chinese people have built dams and reservoirs to control the flow of rivers. The North China Plain is home to the

Oasis in the Singing Sands Mountains

Terraced farming

world's longest artificial waterway, the Grand Canal, which stretches 1,000 miles (1,610 km). Using water for irrigation also helps control flooding. China's Fertile Triangle is an area between Nanjing, Shanghai, and Hangzhou. It has an ideal combination of level ground, rainfall, and fertile soil that makes it perfect for agriculture. Coal, iron ore, forests, and harbors also make the northeastern region an important source of industry and transportation.

Water

Eastern China has a long coastline along the Pacific Ocean. It borders the Bohai Sea and Korea Bay in the north, the East China Sea along the central coastline, and the South China Sea in the south. The East China Sea and South China Sea are separated by the Taiwan Strait, a 112 mile (180 km) stretch of water that separates Taiwan from mainland China.

The Yangtze River is the largest river in Asia and the third largest river in the world. People also refer to it as the Chang Jiang or the Yangzi. It stretches 3,915 miles (6,300 km) from the Tibetan Highlands of the southwest, across the country to the East China Sea at Shanghai. It contains several dams and locks that help control flooding, allow for transportation, and provide hydroelectric power. In 2006, construction of the Three Gorges Dam was completed, making it the world's largest electricity-generating plant. This required the relocation of more than one million people, as 13 cities and 1,300 villages were flooded when created.

Gezhouba Dam locks on the Yangtze River

The Yellow River, or Huang He, is named for the silt carried by the water that gives it a yellow appearance. It begins in the western highlands and winds across China, first to the far north and then dipping to the south, until it ends at the Bohai Sea in the east.

China's third-longest river system, the Pearl River, flows from west to east through southern China. It empties into the South China Sea near Macau. The Pearl River is named for the pearly shells that are found along the river bottom near the city of Guangzhou.

Climate

China has a greatly varying climate due to its great size and variety of land and water features. The deserts of the north can reach temperatures

Tour boat on a tributary of the Yangtze River

greater than 100 °F in the summer and below −30 °F in the winter. Tibet and areas of northeast China have long, cold winters, while the coastal areas in the south have a tropical climate.

China receives most of its rainfall in the summer, due to seasonal winds called monsoons. The monsoons blow cold, dry air from west to east in the winter, and warm, moist air from east to west during the summer. The northern deserts receive little precipitation, while the southeastern coast can receive up to 80 inches (203 cm) per year.

In late summer, China experiences typhoon season (*typhoon* is the name for a hurricane in the southern hemisphere). Huge windstorms that begin over the Pacific Ocean or South China Sea blow in toward the coastline and hundreds of miles inland. The strong winds and heavy rainfall cause flooding, damage to roads and buildings, and loss of life. In 2013, China was hit by Typhoon Haiyan, one of the most powerful storms ever observed. Regular monsoons and typhoons cause rivers to swell and low-lying areas to flood. A deadly flood occurred in 1998 around the Yangtze River, causing more than 4,000 deaths.

Located close to the infamous Ring of Fire, China also experiences regular earthquakes. The Ring of Fire circles the Pacific Ocean where Earth's shifting crust causes volcanic and earthquake activity. Some of history's deadliest earthquakes have occurred in China, including the 1920 Haiyuan earthquake (more than 234,000 killed), the 1976 Tangshan earthquake (more than 242,000 killed), and the 2008 Sichuan earthquake (more than 68,000 killed). In addition to loss of life, earthquakes cause extensive and costly damage to buildings, roads, dams, and other infrastructure.

EVERYDAY LIFE IN CHINA

Family Life

Traditional Chinese families included several generations living together in one home. Grandparents, parents, and children all helped one another and learned from each other. The oldest male was the head of the household, but the oldest son was responsible for taking care of the family. Girls were expected to obey their fathers, and when they grew up and married to obey their husbands. Oftentimes, parents arranged marriages for their children. Confucian and Daoist philosophies emphasize loyalty to family and harmony within the home.

When Communists came to power in the mid-1900's, they tried to shift loyalty from the family unit to the work group. Economic changes and Western influences also led to a breakdown of traditional family values. For a long time, Chinese families placed more value on sons than daughters. Sons could inherit land and care for their parents in old age. If a woman failed to have sons, her husband could divorce her. Occasionally, newborn daughters were killed in an effort to save resources for sons.

Today, parents no longer expect unquestioning obedience from their children and arranged marriages are rare. Families are urged to value sons and daughters equally and women are encouraged to work outside the home. Families in small rural villages tend to be more traditional than those in big cities.

City Life

Developments in manufacturing, transportation, and communications have led to changes in China's cities. Many cities have grown rapidly since the 1950's and other new cities have sprung up around industrial and mining centers. Over 50% of China's population now lives in these crowded urban areas.

Some older urban homes reflect the traditional style of the countryside. Other homes are in large apartment buildings built by city governments or businesses. Families usually rent, but sometimes buy, apartment homes. Neighborhood committees, consisting of elected residents, work to deter crime and handle day-to-day needs. They might plan after-school activities for children or night classes for adults, set up day-care facilities, and address minor crimes.

The standard of living is generally higher in cities than in rural areas. Most people own a television, household appliances, and a bike or motor scooter. Some own a car or computer. Although wages are low compared with other countries, the cost of living is also low. That means workers can afford food, housing, and other necessities. City life also offers more opportunities for education and entertainment. Most big cities have theaters, museums, and sports facilities.

Country Life

Except for mountainous regions, rural life is centered in compact villages. This is largely due to water supply and defense. Historically, people settled around areas where they could dig deep wells and could easily defend against bandits. Many of these rural villages have since grown to

A family enjoying a walk

populations of several thousand, but they have not developed an urban atmosphere.

Many villages consist of simple homes made from sun-dried brick, but building materials depend on geography. Homes often have several rooms and may even have a few amenities like a television, refrigerator, and sewing machine. Almost all areas have electricity. In some remote areas, rural Chinese live in caves, which are cool in the summer and warm in the winter. Some villages are connected to one another by footpaths and cart tracks. Peasant farmers meet up at markets to exchange goods with those from other villages. The standard of living has been improving in rural areas so that most families have enough food, clothing, and time for leisure.

Traditionally, families in rural areas owned and worked on their own land. However, others rented as tenants or worked as laborers on large farms owned by wealthy families. Communist rule changed land distribution in rural areas. Farmers shared land, tools, and animals in large communes, or organized groups of collective owners. Individual families owned just enough land for a home and raising crops and animals for their own use. In 1979, the government abolished communes and has since allowed farmers more freedom. Communes failed to produce adequate food. However, farmers must abide by contracts that dictate the portion of crops and livestock they must sell to the government and the price. Those who specialize in a single crop or provide services such as machine repair pay a set amount to the government and keep the rest of whatever profit they make on the free market.

Farmers work long hours, especially during times of planting and harvest. They might also attend night classes to learn reading and writing or farming techniques. Rural areas often have a village library, recreation center, or sports facility. Villagers can get together there to watch a movie or theatrical performance, play sports, or use computers.

Recreation

The Chinese enjoy many of the same free-time activities as people in other countries. Favorite pastimes include watching television or movies, reading, going to the theater, and shopping. Friends get together to share meals at a home or out at a restaurant. People play card games, xiang qi (a game like chess), and mah-jongg, a game that uses engraved tiles. Karaoke is especially popular in China. People visit karaoke clubs to sing along to recorded music. Recently, Internet cafes, where people can enjoy a drink and use computers, have cropped up in cities.

Exercise is an important part of everyday life in China. Millions of people rise at dawn to practice martial arts in public parks, such as tai chi. Others play sports imported from Western culture, especially baseball, soccer, and basketball. Dance and acrobatics are also popular forms of exercise and entertainment. In the Olympic Games, China has dominated badminton, diving, table tennis, and weightlifting.

The most important holiday in China is the Chinese New Year, held in spring. To prepare for the new year, families do a thorough spring cleaning of the home. Hundreds of millions of people travel to be with family. The festival involves feasting on foods like steamed fish, considered a lucky food, and steamed dumplings. Families also exchange gifts and give red envelopes of money, especially to children. Cities hold parades, in which people dress up in bright costumes as lions or dragons, symbols of good luck. At midnight, families set off fireworks and light paper lanterns in celebration.

Education

Education is highly valued in China and scholars are respected. Chinese education incorporates elements of Confucianism and moral teaching with academics. It also includes Communist political values. Communist leaders, in an effort to improve education and advance Communism, created literacy programs in rural areas. They also revised the written language to be simpler. Today, over 96% of the population over age 15 can read and write.

The Chinese government encourages all children to attend school for at least nine years. They attend elementary school from about age 6 to age 12 where they learn Chinese, math, science, history, music, art, and physical education. They also take classes in English and politics. Junior middle school and senior middle school last another five or six years. Here, students continue learning academic subjects or receive training in trades such as agriculture and industry. Students who excel on national exams attend key schools, where they receive advanced education.

China does not have enough room in its 2,000 colleges and universities for all who want to attend. Students who score well on exams, or those who can pay private school tuition, attend universities. Others choose from a variety of options for higher education. Technical and vocational schools teach job skills. Some factories run their own "workers' colleges." Adults can study part-time in the evenings or take classes by radio, television, or the Internet.

Religion

Officially, China is an atheist country, meaning it does not recognize any god or religion. More than half of the citizens do not identify themselves with a major religion. However, about 22% follow a folk religion, 18% are Buddhist, 5% are Christian, and 2% are Muslim.

China is the birthplace of Confucianism and Daoism, which are philosophies more than religions. Confucianism is a way of life based on the moral teachings of Confucius. Daoism, or Taoism, teaches people to live in harmony with nature. Based on the book *Tao Te Ching*, it is not as strict as Confucianism and incorporates many gods of Chinese folk religions. These belief systems are widespread throughout Chinese culture and have formed the basis of Chinese government for centuries. Buddhism, which later came to China from India, has also grown popular. It consists of the belief in many gods and reincarnation, or rebirth and life after death.

Communist leaders in the mid-1900's attempted to restrict religious practices in favor of Communist thinking. They destroyed churches and temples, persecuted religious believers, and expelled foreign missionaries. Since the 1970's, the government has become more tolerant of religion but still maintains control over the growth of some organizations.

In the 1990's, a new spiritual movement called Falun Gong emerged. Millions of followers practiced meditation exercises to improve health and spirituality. When 10,000 members demonstrated in Beijing in 1999, the Chinese government took steps to suppress Falun Gong and arrested its founder.

Health Care

The Chinese developed medicine over 4,000 years ago. Traditionally, they used a combination of medicinal herbs and healthy lifestyles. The practice of acupuncture began over 2,000 years ago and continues today. It involves inserting thin needles at key points along the body to treat illnesses like headaches and arthritis. Traditional beliefs state that a person's natural energies, called yin and yang, must be in balance for good health. Doctors use acupuncture and herbal medicines to bring these forces into balance.

Today, health care providers combine traditional practices with modern medicine. Big cities have large publicly or privately owned hospitals. Doctors perform surgeries and use advanced technology to treat patients. In rural areas, a village doctor with less training might prescribe drugs and treat simple illnesses and injuries. However, for more thorough care villagers may have to travel a long way to a more modern health care facility. Patients must pay for a large portion of their health care expenses. Those in urban areas are better able to do so than poorer rural residents.

CHINA'S GOVERNMENT

China is officially named the People's Republic of China, or PRC for short. It is a Communist state with its capital in Beijing. China consists of 23 provinces, or sheng, as well as other regions that fall under slightly different classifications, such as Tibet, Taiwan, and Hong Kong. Until 221 BCE, China was ruled by separate kingdoms. It was then unified under the Qin dynasty. In 1912, dynasty rule was replaced by the Republic of China. In 1949, Communist leaders established the People's Republic of China. The Chinese celebrate National Day every October 1st to commemorate that event.

Citizens 18 years of age or older are allowed to vote in elections. The government follows a constitution that has been amended several times, most recently in 2005. China's top leaders are the president, who is elected every five years, and a premier nominated by the president and approved by the National People's Congress. They serve as the head of the executive branch, or State Council. The president is more of a figurehead, while the premier carries out the day-to-day duties of government.

China's highest decision-making body is the National Party Congress. Serving as the legislative branch of the government, it consists of 2,200 representatives elected by popular vote up to the county level, and by delegates at higher levels. However, the Party Congress only meets once every five years, so a Central Committee, consisting of about 200 members, acts in their name when the Party Congress isn't in session. Other main administrative bodies include the Politburo and the Secretariat, both small groups of powerful leaders. The head of the Secretariat is the general secretary, the highest position in the Chinese Communist Party (CCP).

The judicial branch consists of courts that follow the policies of the Communist Party. The Supreme People's Court, the highest court in the nation, deals with national issues and oversees the lower courts.

The Chinese Communist Party works in parallel with the State Council and is the strongest group in the government. It is responsible for setting major policy directions and establishing Communist values among citizens. The government carries out these policies and handles the day-to-day matters involved in running a huge country. Until recently, there was great overlap between the CCP and the Chinese government, as individuals often held similar positions in both. As representatives of the working class, the CCP traditionally didn't allow business owners to join the party. But that has changed in recent years. Even so, only 5% of China's population belongs to the Communist Party.

China's unified military, the People's Liberation Army (or PLA) consists of an army, navy, and air force. With over two million members, it reports to the joint command of the Central Military Commission. China also has a large militia (a citizens' army) and army reserves. All men must serve in the PLA when they reach 18 years old. Many women serve as well, especially in technical and medical areas.

COMMUNISM

Communism is a political and economic ideology. That means communist beliefs affect all aspects of government, citizens' rights, property, resources, production, and more. It is based on public, rather than private, ownership and government control of most major industries. Communism is related to socialism, a set of beliefs based on communal ownership. However, communism more closely follows the doctrines of Marxism, a worldview developed by German philosopher Karl Marx.

Communist governments are dominated by a single political party that adheres strictly to communist ideals. They own all of a country's means of production—factories, mines, etc.— as well as the land. Although it promises to provide financial security and economic equality for all, communism results in a fairly poor general population with a few extremely wealthy leaders.

Karl Marx

Communism's Roots

As far back as the 300's BCE, ancient Greeks wrote about communal ownership of property. Their early form of communism, based on the Latin word *communis*, proposed ownership of all property and goods by a ruling class. Those rulers would have to put the welfare of the state above that of the individual.

In the 1800's, Karl Marx published his radical ideas about government in *The Communist Manifesto* and *Das Kapital*. These writings criticized capitalism—the economic system in which private citizens own the means of production and set prices. Marx believed that all the problems of history were caused by class struggles. He thought that owners and managers (which he called the bourgeoisie) kept all of the profits of production and treated workers poorly. The workers (or proletariat), on the other hand, labored long hours in unsafe conditions, yet had a lower standard of living. Marx felt sure that a coming revolution would establish common workers as the ruling class. His writing was so inflammatory that he was expelled from his home country of Germany, as well as France and Belgium.

Communism in Practice

In a capitalist economy, private parties (individuals or corporations) own land, factories, and other means of production. They decide what goods or services to provide, how much to produce, what prices to charge, and which workers to hire. In a communist system, on the other hand, the government makes these decisions and more. Central planning means that the government owns all means of production and directs all economic activity. This nationalization, or government control, allowed for the rapid industrialization of Communist countries.

The Chinese Communist Party

Communism came to China in 1921 in the form of the Chinese Communist Party, which still holds power today. Events in Russia influenced Chinese revolutionaries to turn to Marxism. Among the most influential of these revolutionaries was Mao Zedong. Mao began by working with others to organize labor unions in the 1920's, when China's government was unstable. At first, members of the Chinese Communist Party (CCP) formed an alliance with the Nationalist Party government. However, Chiang Kai-shek, leader of the Nationalists, turned the Nationalists against the CCP, suppressing their activity for a time.

Mao and his followers fled the cities and turned their focus to peasant farmers. The CCP had so much support that in 1931 they established the Chinese Soviet Republic, consisting of 10 million people. They elected Mao as chairman. The Nationalist military launched attacks against the Chinese Soviet Republic. Under the leadership of Mao, the Communists defended themselves successfully four separate times. However, Mao was then removed from his position and the new leadership was unable to resist the fifth attack.

Chinese Communist Mao Zedong

After the Nationalist military conquered them, the CCP escaped from southeastern China in the Long March of 1934-35. The Communists marched thousands of miles across 18 mountain ranges and 24 rivers to northwestern China. About 85,000 troops and additional personnel moved secretly at night, carrying all of their weapons and supplies themselves. Unfortunately, tens of thousands of people died due to starvation, fighting, and disease. Mao lost two small children and a younger brother. However, during the year-long trek, Mao rose to the position of undisputed leader of the CCP. The heroism displayed during the march also inspired many young Chinese to join the party.

In 1936, the Nationalists and the CCP set aside their conflict to fight Japanese invaders. For about a decade, the Nationalists put forth little effort while Mao's forces grew stronger by fighting the Japanese, building support, and gaining experience. Once the Japanese were defeated, the Chinese civil war resumed. While the United States supported the Nationalists, Mao's CCP ultimately defeated them in 1949. The Nationalists fled to the island of Taiwan and Mao established the People's Republic of China, a Communist state. With high hopes for a new era, he stated, "The era in which the Chinese were regarded as uncivilized is now over. We will emerge in the world as a highly civilized nation." Mao continued to lead the Communist Party until his death in 1976.

At first, the CCP formed a strong alliance with the Soviet Union, a fellow Communist country. However, the Communist Party of the Soviet Union (CPSU) was much more open to relationships with other foreign countries, including the United States, than the CCP was. These ideological differences caused the CCP to sever ties with the Soviet Union in the 1950's.

The CCP itself experienced a rift in the 1960's when Mao and his more radical followers clashed with more pragmatic Communist leaders Liu Shaoqi and Deng Xiaoping. Mao's Cultural Revolution, a plan for economic and social development, caused others to view him and his ideals as too extreme. However, the Cultural Revolution gained momentum and several of the more pragmatic leaders lost their positions in government. Later, after Mao's death in 1976, Deng Xiaoping took control as head of the CCP. Along with other leaders, Deng put an end to the Cultural Revolution and arrested Mao's widow and other powerful radical leaders.

Deng Xiaoping rose to power when China's economy was greatly weakened. Mao's failed attempt at centralized planning and huge communal farms had left most people very poor. China's economic growth struggled to keep pace with its exploding population. Under Deng's leadership, farmers were once again allowed private land. Others opened private businesses. In special economic zones, foreign investors were allowed to manufacture goods to export. With these changes in place, the economy slowly recovered and the standard of living improved for most people.

Today, the CCP is the largest political party in the world. With over 80 million members, it sets policy for China's central, provincial, and local government. Every five years, a National Party Congress of about 2,000 meets to elect 200 members to a Central Committee. The Central Committee, which meets once a year, elects 25 members to a Politburo. The Politburo leads the CCP and its six to nine top members form a Standing Committee, the highest leadership body in the country. In another branch of the government, the Secretariat handles day-to-day administrative tasks. Its general secretary is the top party official. The CCP partly controls China's military. It also publishes a daily newspaper ("People's Daily") and a biweekly journal ("Seeking Truth").

CHINESE CULTURE

Because Chinese civilization is one of the oldest on Earth and was isolated from the Western world for hundreds of years, it has a rich, unique culture. Traditional Chinese artisans were highly valued for their ability to blend the beauty of nature with functional designs. The various dynasties in China's history each made their own contributions to art, music, and literature.

By the 1800's, European and American influences began to show up in Chinese culture, from food to fashion to theater. After a few hundred years of cultural diffusion, the Communist party took control in 1949. They placed strict limits on Chinese artists, requiring their work to express communist values and ideals. During the Cultural Revolution, the arts were stifled and millions of people were imprisoned or killed, many of them artists and intellectuals. In the 1970's, a change in leadership loosened the reins on artists once again. Now, they have more freedom to express themselves and experiment with different styles.

Pottery

China's vast resources of clay make pottery one of its most well-known and oldest art forms. For hundreds of years, the Chinese have used clay to make porcelain or china objects, like vases and teapots. The Chinese have been using the potter's wheel for over 5,000 years to create pottery. They also developed intricate methods of decorating pottery, including using glazes as far back as the 1300's BCE. Chinese pottery is often decorated with beautiful landscapes, flowers, and calligraphy. Many pieces feature dragons—a symbol of wisdom and goodness. In the 100's CE, the Chinese invented porcelain, a type of delicate china made from very fine clay.

Each life-size terracotta warrior has unique facial features

During the Ming dynasty, a blue and white pattern of decorated porcelain became popular. Upper-class people used pottery to decorate their homes and display their wealth.

Sculpture

China's earliest sculptures were often life-size figures made from clay. Sculptures of people, horses, and even chariots often stood guard around tombs. The most famous of these is the terra-cotta army of China's first emperor. Over 7,500 figures were found guarding his tomb when farmers accidentally discovered them while digging a well in 1974.

As Buddhism spread across China, sculptors turned their attention to decorating shrines with figures of Buddha. They also branched out from clay and stone to begin working with jade, bronze, and other metals. The Chinese were the first to make cast iron by heating iron ore in furnaces and pouring it into molds. However, this metal was used more for tools and weapons than for art.

Paper-Making, Printing, and Writing

The Chinese are credited with being the first to invent paper. This invention came about some time during the Han dynasty, about 200 BCE. The earliest forms of paper used rags, but soon plant material became more popular. Bamboo or other plants would be soaked and turned into a pulp. Then, screens were dipped into the pulp and set out to dry. Government factories mass-produced the paper for civil service workers to use.

Printing was done using wooden blocks with carved symbols. At first, these printing blocks would contain a simple seal that could be stamped onto official documents or personal letters. Later, they were used to print entire pages of books. Carving a wood block for each page of a book was a slow and difficult process, but it caused a rise in literacy across the country.

Chinese writing is an art form all its own. The Chinese language doesn't use an alphabet, because the writing is based on symbols, or characters, instead of sounds. Each word has its own character, which means there are over 40,000 in all. The characters are written and read from the top of the page to the bottom in columns, moving from right to left. A particularly beautiful style of writing invented in China is calligraphy. It is traditionally done with a brush and ink. This ancient art form has been around for thousands of years and is a highly respected skill.

The Forest of Stone Stelae museum is home to over 3,000 inscribed
stone slabs and is called the "Cradle of Calligraphy"

Mural at the Summer Palace in Beijing

Painting

Long before the invention of paper, Chinese artists painted on silk as early as 4,000 BCE. They used the same type of brush used by calligraphers—animal hairs held by a bamboo handle. Artists mainly used black pine soot and glue to make their own ink, but also created colors from plants and minerals. Early on, artists painted a variety of subjects, but by about the 900's CE, landscapes became the most common subject for paintings.

Literature

China has a rich history of writing dating back to 1500 BCE. Scribes carved symbols into bones or turtle shells to record duties of the royal families. With the invention of paper, and the growth of Confucianism, Buddhism, and Daoism, Chinese writing became more beautiful and philosophical. Poetry is an especially valued form of writing that has appeared in paintings, dramas, and novels. Early forms of prose were often religious or philosophical texts, such as the Confucian writings *Five Classics* and the Daoist texts *The Book of the Way and its Virtue* and *The Zhuangzi*.

During the 1200's, fiction and drama became more popular. By 1949, however, Chinese Communists under Mao Zedong restricted all art forms, especially literature. Written works had to represent the working class and had to be accessible to people of all academic abilities. Any criticism of the government was strictly prohibited. Beginning in the 1990's, authors started to have more freedom, but are still forbidden from criticizing government policy.

Theater

Chinese theater combines spoken words, poetry, singing, dialogue, dancing, mime, and acrobatics. Traditional forms date back to the Yuan dynasty of the 1200's, while modern theater has been influenced by Europe and the United States since the late 1800's, often incorporating dialogue, singing, and dancing, a trend that continued through the early 1900's.

Music

Like many other cultures, the Chinese have long used music for ceremonial as well as recreational purposes. They play music at weddings, funerals, and parties. Confucius wrote that "music is the harmony of Heaven and Earth." Musicians in China use a 5-note scale, rather than the 8-note scale used in the West. Although Chinese musicians today play a variety of instruments and musical styles, traditional music used a seven-stringed *qin*, a bamboo mouth organ called a *sheng*, and various types of flutes.

Fashion

One of the oldest textiles, silk, was created in China around 3,000 BCE. Made from the threads of silkworms, the Chinese kept the process of silk-making a secret for thousands of years. Traditional Chinese dress reflected a person's position in society. Emperors, officials, scholars, and other upper-class citizens wore colorful robes made of silk, often decorated with intricate floral patterns. Meanwhile, lower-class workers wore simple cloth garments. Until the 13th century, these were made from a plant fiber called hemp. Then, cotton became more commonplace. For hundreds of years, the Chinese practiced foot binding, in which a young girl's feet were wrapped tightly with a ribbon or cloth. This kept the feet from growing, as small feet were seen as a sign of beauty. Nowadays, Chinese people, especially in urban areas, wear Western-style clothing similar to that of the United States and Europe. In some rural areas, people may wear traditional ethnic or homemade clothing.

Food and Drink

Following the principles of Chinese philosophy, Chinese food is balanced by opposites—hot and cold, spicy and mild, fresh and preserved. A traditional Chinese diet includes lots of grains—wheat in the north and rice in the south. Wheat can be made into noodles and dumplings, which can be stuffed. Vegetables are also a staple, including cabbage, tofu, bamboo shoots, and water chestnuts. Pork, poultry, fish, and eggs provide protein. Some of the more exotic dishes include snake meat or shark's fin. The Chinese traditionally eat with chopsticks and soup spoons. In modern times, Western foods like hamburgers and pizza have become well-loved, especially in China's cities.

Tea is China's favorite traditional drink, but beer and soda have increased in popularity recently. Tea was first grown in China around 200 BCE and has been a major export ever since. Legend has it that tea may have been invented as early as 5,000 years ago by Emperor Shennong. According to one tale, he had ordered that all drinking water be boiled for hygiene purposes. One day, while resting under a bush, dried leaves fell into his boiling water and tea was invented. Whether or not that story is true, tea plays an important part in Chinese culture.

Architecture

Traditional Chinese buildings were typically one-story structures made of wood on a stone platform. Beams supported a tile roof that

The tower of Buddhist Incense at the Summer Palace in Beijing often had a graceful upward-curving shape. Interior walls did not support the roof but provided privacy. Some traditional buildings, called pagodas, had more than one story. They were mainly used as Buddhist temples. Each eight-sided building would have an odd number of stories, with each story slightly smaller than the one below.

Modern Chinese buildings, especially in urban areas, look just like those of any other major city. They are built to withstand frequent earthquakes. Reaching several stories, they help accommodate the large population.

CHINA'S WILDLIFE

The dense population of Eastern China means that there is little room for wildlife there. The harsh mountain climate of the West and deserts of the Northwest also make it difficult for animals to survive. However, some tropical and forest areas are home to an interesting array of animals. Although many are threatened by shrinking habitats, the Chinese government has created over 1,200 reserves where plants and animals are protected.

Panda at the Chongqing Zoo

Forests along the edge of mountainous Tibet are home to pandas, golden monkeys, takins, and other animals. The black and white panda is one of the most recognized symbols of China and is a world-wide symbol of conservation. This bear is endangered due to the loss of its habitat. The world's 1,600 remaining pandas live in the mountain forests of Central China. They spend almost their entire day eating bamboo. However, these forests are being cut down for timber and farmland.

In the tropical regions of the South, elephants and gibbons make their home. Though very few wild elephants live in China, the government is working to protect their habitat. Elephants also need to be protected from poachers and kept away from people and farmland. China is also working to stop the trade of ivory, which has hurt the elephant population worldwide.

The rare Siberian tiger, or Amur tiger, inhabits the Northeast forests. Only about 400 of this endangered species remain, as they were hunted to near extinction in the 1940's. The Siberian tiger endures the harsh winters of Northeast China and Eastern Russia, ranging across a large area in search of prey.

A tough survivor of the Northwest deserts is the Bactrian, or two-humped, camel. Though mostly domesticated, some of this species still live wild in the deserts of Eastern Asia. They are uniquely suited to survive conditions that range from

Bactrian Camels in Asia

above 100°F in the summer to below -20° in the winter. Bactrian camels are also able to drink more than 26 gallons of water at a time, survive on salty water, and walk long distances in search of grass and shrubs to eat.

THE ECONOMY OF CHINA

After a long history of government planning and closely-controlled foreign trade, China became a more open market in the 1970's. Reforms included freedom in setting prices, growth of privately-owned businesses, development of a stock market, and a move away from collective agriculture. However, the national government still controls industries it deems most important to economic stability. These include banks, transportation, and foreign trade.

By 2010, China had become the world's largest exporter of goods. Today, China's economy is one of the world's largest and growing, due in large measure to its large population. However, because of China's huge population, the gross domestic product (GDP—the value of all goods and services a country produces in a year) per person is not high. In fact, it is ranked 113th in the world.

Despite its large economy, China's people have below-average income. They save a lot of their money, which slows economic growth. Other economic problems plague China as well. Population control means that the aging population is growing more rapidly than that of younger workers. Migrants from rural areas are moving to cities in large numbers looking for education and jobs. The huge population and industry are causing environmental damage, such as pollution and deforestation.

China's economy is made up of about 10% agriculture and then a near-even split between industry (44%) and services (46%). Its labor force of 800 million workers is the largest in the world. Workers in China are split almost equally among agriculture, industry, and services. About 4% of the population is unemployed and roughly 6% live below the poverty line.

The Chinese government sets five-year economic plans that establish goals for the economy. Beginning in the 1950's, these plans have recently included huge public works projects to improve roads, subways, bridges, and dams.

China's main exports are electrical machinery, other machinery, clothing, furniture, toys, and textiles. Its largest export partners are Hong Kong, the United States, Germany, and Japan. Its main imports are electrical machinery, other machinery,

The pagoda at Shibaozhai

oil and mineral fuels, nuclear reactor components, medical equipment, metal ores, motor vehicles, and soybeans. China imports goods from all over the world, but mainly from South Korea, Japan, and Taiwan.

Agriculture

Only about 10% of China's land is suitable for farming. Even so, China's farmers produce most of the world's rice. They also grow wheat, corn, tobacco, soybeans, peanuts, tea, sugar beets, potatoes, and cotton. Much of the land lacks irrigation, and farmers face the constant threat of floods, droughts, and erosion. Although modern farming machines are available, many peasant farmers employ simple, traditional methods instead.

Farmers grow rice in special fields called paddies. A rice paddy is a flat area that is flooded to help cultivate rice. Farmers in more hilly areas practice terrace farming. In this practice, long "steps" are cut into hillsides to create flat areas to farm. In the warm south, farmers can harvest two or three rounds of crops per year.

China also raises a great number of livestock. It is the world's leading producer of pigs, chickens, and eggs. Sheep and cattle are also major forms of livestock. Farmers in China raise more domesticated ducks than anywhere else in the world.

Traditionally, most Chinese people lived in rural villages and worked as farmers. Until the late 1970's, the state controlled all agricultural decisions from what to grow and where to what prices to charge. Peasant farmers worked together on communal land. Over the past few decades, policies have changed to allow farmers greater freedom. In modern times, many people are moving away from farms to cities in search of education and jobs.

Forestry and Fishing

Many of China's vast forests are located in the inaccessible central mountain regions. Therefore, most of the country's timber comes from areas in the northeast and south central regions.

With extensive coastlines and inland bodies of water, China leads the world in ocean and freshwater fishing. In addition, raising fish in ponds has been a longstanding practice.

Mineral and Energy Resources

China has some of the world's richest stores of coal, petroleum, and oil. Until recently, however, it has been unable to use these resources due to inadequate production facilities and transportation. Partnering with foreign investors has improved production. China is still working to bring energy resources to places they are most needed — in large cities and industrial areas. It receives 70% of its electrical energy from burning coal, but coal often has to be transported great distances to be used.

China produces more iron ore, aluminum, lead, and zinc than any other country. It is also a leading producer of gold, silver, and copper. Mining in China has been experiencing many problems in recent times. Current reserves of resources are not enough to meet the country's long-term needs. In addition, the process of mining is inefficient, causing much waste and pollution.

Manufacturing

This segment of China's economy has been growing about 10% per year. As the world's number one producer of steel, China engages in much heavy industry. Major manufactured products include automobiles, aircraft, ships, and military equipment. It also produces many consumer goods, especially clothing, electronics, and processed foods. Many foreign companies base their manufacturing in China and export products from there.

Services

With such a large population, Chinese workers must provide many services, including education, health care, banking, transportation, and many others. One of the largest service industries in China is tourism. People from within the country and abroad love to visit the many sights throughout China. This provides many jobs for tour guides, translators, bus drivers, hotel workers, and more.

Transportation

China's great size, population, and economic activity have created a challenge in the area of transportation. Roads, bridges, and railways cannot currently keep up with the need to move people and ship goods. Efforts have been made to extend roads and railways into China's more remote regions. Newer high-speed rail lines have been built to link major cities. Compared to the rest of the world, China is first in the number of navigable waterways, third in the number of roads and railways, and fourteenth in the number of airports.

In rural areas, many people use traditional forms of transportation, such as simple carts or wagons pulled by people or animals. People walk and ride bikes as well. In crowded cities, some people own cars or motor scooters, but most use public transportation like buses, taxis, and trains.

Communication

After the Communists came to power, communication in China came under strict government control. Most newspaper, radio, and television content is limited to the political topics and viewpoints of the Communist party. Since the 1980's, media has included more non-political information and entertainment, though it is still monitored by the government. In 2011, new restrictions set limits on Internet use and media broadcasting. Television stations are limited to two hours of state-approved news each evening and two 90-minute entertainment shows per week.

China has more telephones, cell phones, and Internet users than any other country. Almost all urban areas have modern telephone, radio, television, and Internet services. In rural areas, access to communication varies. Some remote villages have just a single television in a shared location.

Flag of China

NORTH KOREA

NORTH KOREA: THE BIG PICTURE

North Korea, or the Democratic People's Republic of Korea (DPRK), was formed in 1948, though people had been living in this part of the world for as long as recorded history. Korea's ancient history included thousands of years of rule by Korean governments and foreign invaders. In 1392, Korea became united under the Choson dynasty and almost all Koreans worked as farmers in an agricultural society. This kingdom lasted until the Japanese took control from 1910 to 1945. The Japanese shifted Korea's economic focus from agriculture to industry. At the end of World War II, Korea was freed from Japanese rule. The northern half came under Communist rule with help from the Soviet Union.

Communists continued the industrialization of the country and refused to recognize the independent south. The division into North Korea and South Korea led to decades of tension and violence. North Korea attempted but failed to unite both Koreas by force in the Korean War of 1950–1953. Although large-scale fighting stopped, the countries never signed a peace treaty and conflicts continue to this day.

All aspects of North Korean life are dominated by communism. The country is run by a dictator, supported by the powerful Communist party. The government restricts all economic and social activity. The people live austere lives and experience frequent shortages of food and necessities.

MEET THE PEOPLE OF NORTH KOREA

The almost 25 million people of North Korea are overwhelmingly Korean, with just a small number of Chinese and ethnic Japanese. In fact, North Korea is one of the least ethnically diverse countries in the world. The population is growing slowly now, though it doubled between 1953 and 1993. There is very little migration into and out of the country. However, hundreds of thousands of North Koreans have escaped to China and other countries due to political persecution.

All citizens speak Korean, though there are several different dialects, or local forms, that are widely understood by all. About half of the words come from the Chinese language, though there has been an effort to eliminate or replace any words borrowed from Chinese or Western culture. The Korean language uses 10 vowels and 14 consonants.

About 60% of North Koreans live in urban areas, the largest of which is Pyongyang. Other major cities are much smaller in comparison. The rural population is mainly spread out among the western coastal lowlands. Some live in small fishing villages on the east coast. The interior mountains are sparsely settled. Because the government has focused so heavily on industrialization

Fast Facts

Capital:
Pyongyang

Size:
99th in the world

Area:
74,899 sq miles
(194,000 sq km)

Coastline:
1,550 miles (2,494 km)

Highest Point:
Mount Paektu 9,003 feet
(2,744 meters)

Lowest Point:
Sea of Japan 0 feet (0 m)

Population:
25 million

Official Language:
Korean

Currency:
North Korean won (KPW)

National Anthem:
"Aegukka" (Patriotic Song) Although it shares this name with South Korea's anthem, the lyrics are different.

National Symbol:
red star, chollima (winged horse)

since 1945, many Koreans have moved to cities. This has resulted in a shortage of farm workers.

LAND, WATER, WILDLIFE, AND CLIMATE IN NORTH KOREA

Land

North Korea's total land area is about 74,899 square miles (194,000 square km), about the size of the state of Virginia, making it the 99th largest country in the world. In addition to sharing a border with South Korea, North Korea borders China to the north and shares an 11 mile border with Russia. Most of the country is covered by hills and mountains with deep, narrow valleys. The east and west are separated by the Nangnim Mountains, which run from north to south. North Korea's highest peak, Mount Paektu, is an extinct volcano that rises 9,003 feet (2,744 meters) in the northern part of the country. The volcano Changbaishan, on the Chinese border, was active in the past but has not erupted in over one hundred years. Flat coastal plains stretch along the western part of the country and in some parts of the east. Only 20% of North Korea's land is suitable for farming, mainly in the wide, fertile plains of the western coast.

Water

To the east is the East Sea, or Sea of Japan, and to the west is the Korea Bay in the Yellow Sea, giving North Korea a total of 1,550 miles (2,494 km) of coastline. Its longest river, the Yalu, runs approximately 497 miles (800 km) from the southern slope of Mount Paektu westward to the Korea Bay. The Tumen River flows 323 miles (520 km) from the north side of Mount Paektu to the East Sea. The Taedong River flows from north to southwest through the capital of Pyongyang. Most of North Korea's major rivers flow to the Yellow Sea in the west.

Climate

North Korea's climate is generally cool, with long and bitter winters. Average winter temperatures range from 20° F to -10° F. Warm summer

Map of North and South Korea

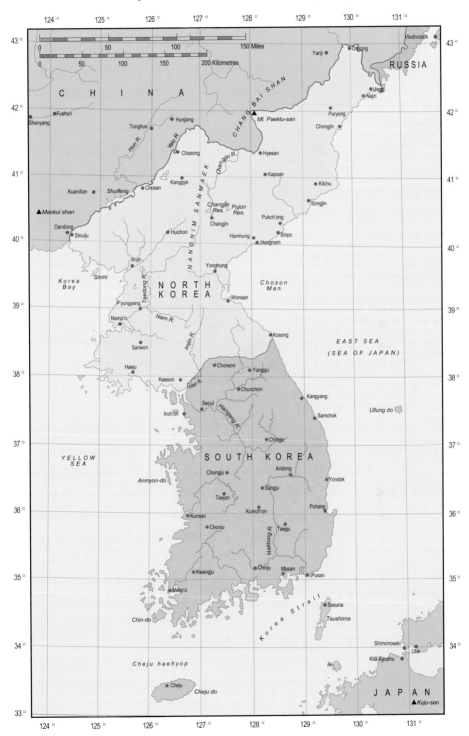

temperatures average 70 to 80° F. Most of the country's 40 inches (101 cm) of annual rainfall occurs in the summer. North Korea experiences some droughts in late spring and typhoons in the early fall. Monsoons, or seasonal winds, bring hot, humid air from the south in the summer and cold, dry air from the north during the winter.

Wildlife

Once home to a variety of large mammals, North Korea has experienced a loss of habitat due to deforestation. Deer, antelope, goat, and leopard populations have dropped greatly. Few, if any, tigers are left. Though the plains are heavily populated by people, they are also home to several bird populations, including pigeons, herons, cranes, and others.

The 784 square mile demilitarized zone has become overtaken by nature since 1953, resulting in a kind of sanctuary. In addition to dozens of birds and fish species, it is also occupied by Asiatic black bears, lynxes, and other mammals.

EVERYDAY LIFE IN NORTH KOREA

Family Life

The overall standard of living in North Korea has improved since World War II. However, the strong focus on industrialization and military growth has hurt the areas of consumer goods and social services. In the 1990's, North Korea experienced extreme economic hardship that led to food shortages, inadequate medical care, and lack of daily necessities. Many North Koreans abandoned their homes and families during this crisis.

City Life

Most urban residents have jobs in factories. North Korea offers housing in urban areas, almost all of which is supported by the government. Working-class families live in small, one room apartments while a few government officials have single-family houses with gardens. Large cities have many newer high-rise buildings, but heat and water systems are

A typical day in Pyongyang, North Korea

inadequate. Streets are typically empty as North Koreans have little leisure time and few own automobiles. Even the largest cities have very few restaurants or theaters where residents can enjoy free time.

Country Life

Communists in North Korea converted small family farms into larger agricultural communes. Farmers work on land they do not own, using some modern machinery. They often live together in government-owned apartment buildings.

Recreation

North Koreans have very little time for leisure. What resources they have are controlled by the government, which operates gyms and runs organized sports. In cities, residents can enjoy state-operated theaters.

Education

North Korea requires 12 years of free primary and secondary education. Students attend preschool for one year, followed by five years of primary school and six years of secondary school. Students learn communist ideology along with work skills. The focus is on science and technology. North Korea boasts a 100% literacy rate—a vast improvement over the less than 50% rate of the 1940's. In addition to academic studies, all students are required to work during the summer. With government approval, North Koreans can continue their education in high school or vocational school. After that, they may attend a two- to six-year college, adult education program, or technical school.

Religion

North Korea has no official religion. It is traditionally a Buddhist and Confucianist country, with some followers of Christianity and Chondogyo (or Religion of the Heavenly Way). The government maintains an illusion of religious freedom by allowing certain state-sponsored groups to exist. However, there is almost no free religious activity independent of the government.

In the past, most Koreans lived according to Confucian ideals, with some influence from Buddhism. Christian missionaries arrived in the 18th and 19th centuries, but were driven out by the end of World War II. In 1860, Confucian teacher Ch'oe Che-u founded Chondogyo, a combination of other major religions, which became quite popular.

Health Care

Although North Koreans enjoy free healthcare, medical resources and personnel are in short supply. Social insurance provides care for injured or disabled workers, care throughout pregnancy and childbirth, homes for the elderly, and funeral benefits.

NORTH KOREA'S GOVERNMENT

The Democratic People's Republic of Korea was formed as a Communist state in 1948. It has been run as a one-man dictatorship since its beginning. It has a Constitution, which has been revised extensively since then. Although the Constitution claims to provide freedoms for religion and speech, people are strictly controlled by the Communist government and have little freedom.

The head of state is no longer called president, since the title "eternal president" was reserved for Kim Il-Sung after his death. Instead, the chairman of the National Defense Commission is the "supreme leader." A Central People's Committee, made up of high-ranking officials of the Communist party, sets policy.

A Supreme People's Assembly consists of 687 members who are seemingly elected to five-year terms by popular vote. In actuality, however, the list of candidates is approved by the ruling Communist party, or the Korean Workers' Party (KWP). The Supreme People's Assembly in turn elects the unopposed premier, who heads the government. They meet only a couple weeks each year, and have little real power. The KWP controls all political activity in the nation, including setting policy and holding elections. All citizens age 17 and older can vote, but there is typically only one candidate per position. Voting is seen as a way to agree with the decisions of the KWP.

The country is divided into nine provinces and four municipalities. The national capital city is Pyongyang. Local governments oversee activity right down to the household level.

Military service is compulsory for men, giving North Korea one of the world's largest military forces, including a 1 million-man army, 110,000-man air force, and 60,000-man navy. Men serve for three to twelve years, and women may volunteer to serve.

NORTH KOREAN CULTURE

Koreans have a distinct identity and culture, despite centuries of foreign influence (especially from China) and attempts by the Japanese to do away with Korean culture. Traditional Korean culture took a blow after World War II when Soviet occupiers destroyed family ties in favor of Communist party loyalty. Under Communism, individual freedoms have been severely limited in North Korea. Westernization, or the adoption of western culture, has occurred slowly and under strict government control. The people live a harsh lifestyle of hard work and obedience to government authority. Scarce cultural activities are generally state-sponsored and group-oriented.

The Arts

North Korea's government supports traditional fine arts as long as they express loyalty to Communist ideals. Most public art celebrates Kim Il-sung and the revolution. Artists and writers promote Communism and nationalism—a belief in the superiority of one's country. They are not allowed to practice or perform independently as every artist, musician, dancer, and writer is assigned to a government institution. Museums and archaeological sites are important cultural attractions as they help strengthen feelings of North Korean pride.

Fashion

Clothing in North Korea is generally basic and functional rather than fashionable. It resembles that worn in other parts of the developed world. On holidays, some North Koreans dress in traditional clothes—long, full skirts for women and loose trousers for men, along with a shirt and jacket.

Food and Drink

The most popular food in North Korea is rice. People also commonly eat fish, barley, beans, potatoes, and some fruits. Korea is famous for *kimchi*—a spicy, sour mix of pickled or fermented vegetables, usually cabbage and radishes. North Koreans eat very little meat or dairy products. Tea and coffee are the most common drinks. Koreans also enjoy a variety of alcoholic drinks, including beer and *sake* (rice wine).

THE ECONOMY OF NORTH KOREA

North Korea's economy has been greatly weakened by its Communist government. As a command economy, the government sets economic goals, determines prices, and controls all means of production. Central planning and the focus on military growth have resulted in chronic economic problems, shortages, and a low standard of living. North Korea is a closed economy, both in terms of interaction with other countries and disclosure about economic activities. National industrialization and the focus on self-reliance have resulted in insufficient agriculture, substandard consumer goods, and lack of foreign investment. North Korea's economy is one of the slowest-growing economies in the world. A disastrous 2009 effort to reform the currency caused severe inflation and economic hardship. North Korea has recently attempted to establish special economic zones to improve trade and cooperation with other countries.

Although North Korea a reasonably large labor force (41st worldwide), with 12.6 million workers, its economic output per person is one of the world's lowest. Roughly 37% of workers partake in agricultural activity and 63% in industry and services. Industry makes up almost half of the nation's economy, with another 33% coming from services and 25% from agriculture. North Korea's exports go overwhelmingly to China (76%) and South Korea (16%), and consist mainly of minerals, metal products, military equipment, fish products, and textiles. It imports mainly petroleum, coal, machinery, and grain. Imports exceed exports.

The capital city of Pyongyang

Agriculture

Less than 20% of North Korea's land is suitable for farming. Farmers grow rice, corn, soybeans, and potatoes and raise cattle and pigs. Farmers' challenges include crop-destroying weather, poor soil, rocky terrain, lack of machinery and fuel, along with the inefficient Communist system of collective farming. North Korea relies on frequent international food aid to avoid famine and starvation. Much of the population suffers from long-term malnutrition. Since 2002, the government has allowed a small increase in freedom for farmers.

Forestry and Fishing

Japanese occupation in the first half of the 1900's greatly depleted North Korea's timber resources. Reforestation efforts have helped replenish the forests. The nation is ideally suited for excellent fishing, with long coastlines, numerous islands, and offshore reefs. A variety of currents bring both warm- and cold-water species.

Mineral and Energy Resources

North Korea is rich in mineral resources, including gold, iron ore, coal, tungsten, and graphite. Mining operations, however, are mainly small-scale. Energy comes primarily from hydroelectric plants and coal-burning plants. Electric power in North Korea falls far short of the country's needs.

Manufacturing

North Korea's major industries are military products, machines, chemicals, textiles, and food processing.

Services

Tourism is greatly restricted in North Korea. Most visitors come from China and all are accompanied by official North Korean guides.

Transportation

After the devastating Korean War of the 1950's, transportation in North Korea has improved greatly. Rail lines, the most important form of transportation, were rebuilt with help from other Communist countries, especially the Soviet Union. However, current growth is limited by scarce energy resources. Paved roads are rare, since few people own automobiles. Citizens are not allowed to travel freely among counties and provinces, though many do so illegally. Air travel is controlled by the government, with one international airport in Pyongyang and a few other domestic airports elsewhere.

Communication

All media outlets in North Korea are strictly state-controlled and heavily censored. The government is responsible for several daily newspapers, periodicals, radio broadcasts, and television programs. These outlets all promote communist ideology and North Korean nationalism. Through extensive government effort, radios are in almost every home and village and almost as many televisions. Government radio broadcasts are often blared through loudspeakers in public places in villages. Foreign broadcasts are banned and the government jams all such signals. Internet use is greatly restricted.

NORTH KOREA'S HISTORY

The history of people on the Korean peninsula dates back thousands of years. The earliest people groups to settle the area were the Tungusic people, who migrated from Manchuria and Siberia. They developed the Korean language, which draws heavily on Chinese. Pyongyang frequently served as a key city or capital during Korea's early history.

Early History

Traditionally, Choson, located near the modern-day capital Pyongyang, formed the first Korean state in 2333 BCE. Around 100 BCE, the Chinese invaded and conquered the northern part of the Korean peninsula. The Koreans, separated into tribes, fought back to regain some of the territory and united themselves into states. The three Korean states of Koguryo, Paekche, and Silla formed the Three Kingdoms of ancient Korea.

Koguryo, in the north, took back control of the Chinese territory in 313 CE. Fighting then broke out among the Three Kingdoms for total control of the Korean peninsula. In the 660's, with the help of the Chinese, Silla conquered the other two states. During the next 200 years of relative stability, Korean culture flourished in the form of arts, education, and Confucian thought.

When Silla collapsed after fighting in the 800's and 900's, the conquerors renamed the area Koryo, which became the modern name Korea. Under new leadership, books and learning became a priority. In 1234, Koreans invented the first printing press to use movable metal type.

After centuries of alternately fighting against and allying with Chinese invaders, war broke out once again in the mid-1200's. A group allied with

Gyeongbokgung royal palace in Seoul was built in 1394

the Chinese Ming dynasty defeated those allied with the Mongol tribes from the north. The victorious General Yi Song-gye became king of the new nation, which he renamed Choson.

Choson Dynasty (1392–1910)

General Yi established an independent kingdom in 1392. He moved the capital to Seoul, now the capital of South Korea, and made Confucianism the national religion. Buddhism, which had continued since the 700's, became less important. During the centuries-long Choson dynasty, Korean culture flourished and the economy grew. Korea resisted invasions by the Japanese and Chinese.

Under the rule of the Choson dynasty, Korea closed itself off to all foreign countries in the 1600's and was known as the Hermit Kingdom for 200 years. Only China and Japan traded with Korea. When Catholic missionaries came from Europe in the 1830's, Korean authorities persecuted them and killed any converts.

Japan Takes Control (1910–1945)

Japan forced Korea into a trade agreement in 1876 that opened ports to foreign trade. Several other countries then signed treaties to trade with

Korea as well. The countries began to fight for control of Korea. When Japan went to war against China and then Russia in the early 1900's, they moved troops through Korea. Even when the wars ended, the troops remained. Japan exerted increasing control over Korea until it formally annexed the country by adding it to Japanese territory in 1910. The Japanese ruled the Koreans harshly, instituting major social and economic changes. They saw Korea as a source of people and industry to fuel their war efforts. They forced Koreans to work in mines, factories, and the military. The Korean language was banned in public and Koreans were assigned Japanese-style names.

Japanese rule came to an end when Japan lost World War II. With Soviet troops in the north and American troops in the south, Korea was divided for what was expected to be a temporary reconstruction period. However, as relations between the U.S. and Soviet Union worsened, the two regions became more separate.

North and South Korea (1948)

By 1948, the U.S. in the south and Soviet Union in the north had helped establish new governments in Korea and began to withdraw their influence. This left the Republic of Korea in the south and the Democratic People's Republic in the north. Neither government recognized the other as an authority in Korea. The south followed more democratic principles while the north maintained Communist rule. North Korea's first premier was Kim Il-Sung, head of the Korean Workers' Party (or KWP), the Communist party in North Korea. He was installed on September 9, 1948, the day North Korea was officially formed. He established himself as the "Great Leader" and ruled harshly until his death in 1994.

Korean War Begins (1950)

With both regions eager to take over the entire Korean peninsula, North Korea struck first with a surprise attack in June of 1950. The ensuing Korean War lasted until 1953 and resulted in devastation and loss of life on both sides. As part of the Cold War between communists and non-communists in other countries, both sides of the Korean War were given foreign aid. China and the Soviet Union gave aid to North Korea, and the United Nations supported South Korea. The war ended with an uneasy truce and a boundary between the two countries called a demilitarized zone (or DMZ). Tensions continued through the 1950's and 1960's. Both countries stationed armed troops along the border, and fighting occasionally erupted.

After the Korean War, Kim Il-Sung strengthened the country's military forces by increasing the number of troops and investing in infrastructure, such as airfields. The government redistributed farmland from the wealthy to the poor and organized collective farms. The Soviet Union, China, and countries in Eastern Europe all aided in North Korea's economic growth. However, Kim soon eliminated the Soviet and Chinese Communist influences. Without foreign aid, and with a strong focus on the military and heavy industry, North Korea continually failed to meet its economic goals. This resulted in food shortages, which were worsened by the rapid population growth. Between 1953 and 1993, North Korea's population tripled.

North Korea's strict travel and trade restrictions, along with complete government control of the press, isolated it from the rest of the world. For decades, the country maintained friendly relations with the Soviet Union and China, while remaining hostile toward the United States. However, the collapse of the Communist party in the Soviet Union and friendly relations between China and South Korea left North Korea with few allies. Even so, North Korea still desired to unify South Korea under its control.

This tension between North and South Korea continued for decades. In 1967-8 North Korean troops ventured into the demilitarized zone, attacked South Korean troops, and entered the South Korean capital city in a failed assassination attempt against the South Korean president. North Korea also took aggressive actions against the United States by seizing a U.S. ship in 1968 and shooting down a U.S. Navy plane in 1969. North Korea was found guilty of a bombing in Burma that killed 17 South Korean officials in 1983. When South Korea hosted the Olympic games in 1988, North Korea refused to participate.

Signed Agreement (1991)

Finally, North Korea gave up its insistence on a single joint Korean seat in the United Nations (UN). North and South Korea were each admitted to the UN as separate and equal members. Around this time, diplomatic relations between the two longtime rivals began to improve. Leaders met for talks and relatives were allowed to cross the DMZ to visit separated family members. The two countries agreed to stop using force against one another, increase trade and communication, and prohibit nuclear weapons. Cooperation stalled in 1993, however, due to controversy over North Korea's nuclear weapons program.

Before Kim Il-Sung's death, he had promoted his son, Kim Jong Il, to several top government posts. Kim Il-Sung was named North Korea's "eternal president" and his son took the title "supreme leader." Kim Jong Il continued his father's cult of personality and focus on "military first politics." He did, however, advance foreign relations by signing a treaty with the United States to stop development of nuclear weapons. In return, the United States helped build two reactors to provide electrical power throughout North Korea. This effort involved cooperation among North Korea, South Korea, Japan, and the United States.

In the 1990's, North Korea was weakened by a devastating food shortage that resulted in hundreds of thousands of deaths due to starvation. The country nearly collapsed economically when a government program aimed at reforming the currency failed. The government acknowledged the failure of the program and executed the official responsible for the change. Unfortunately, North Korea also renewed nuclear weapons activity in the late 1990's and early 2000's, reviving international tensions.

In December 2011, Kim Jong Il died, leaving his youngest son, Kim Jong-Un, as supreme leader. Once again, North Korea agreed to stop nuclear weapons testing in exchange for food and aid from the United States. However, this pledge was short-lived as North Korea denied access to weapons inspectors, tested nuclear devices, and refused to submit reports on weapons activity. Since then, North Korea has engaged in a cycle of alternately denying they have certain nuclear weapons capabilities and threatening to use those nuclear weapon capabilities they have.

THE KOREAN WAR

After World War II, Korea was divided into two parts with two different forms of government: North Korea had a communist form of government and South Korea had a more democratic form of government. The Soviet Union helped establish the Communist government in the north, while the United States helped establish democracy in the south.

In 1950, the North Korean army crossed the dividing line of the two countries in an effort to forcefully unite both parts of Korea under a single communist government. Nations around the world watched and waited to see if the conflict between North and South Korea would grow into a full-scale war between the Soviet Union and the United States, or even erupt into World War III. For the first time, a worldwide organization, the United Nations, played a role in a war. It condemned the aggression by North Korea and called member nations to help support South Korea.

From 1950 to 1953, over 2.5 million people lost their lives in the Korean War. Over 60 years later, the two countries have yet to settle on a peace treaty.

Tensions leading to the war began immediately in 1945 after the end of World War II. Japan lost control of Korea, which it had annexed in 1910. The Korean people were now free and ready to rebuild their nation. In order to aid the reconstruction, the country was divided into the north and the south along the 38th parallel for what was expected to be a short time. The Soviet Union occupied the north and the United States occupied the south. However, political tensions between the Soviet Union and the U.S., World War II allies, entangled their Korean counterparts.

The Soviet Union had become an increasingly powerful Communist nation by the mid-1900's. While the democratic U.S. opposed Soviet growth and ideology, the two countries had only engaged in a "cold war" up to that point. Without fighting one another directly, both the Soviet Union and the U.S. took steps to strengthen and spread their own political systems throughout the world.

In 1947, the newly-formed United Nations declared that the Korean people should hold elections to establish one government. The Soviet Union refused and instead helped establish the Democratic People's Republic of Korea. Meanwhile, South Korea formed its own government, the Republic of Korea, and the United States removed the last of its troops. Thus, one outcome of these warring ideologies was the formation of the separate nations of North Korea and South Korea in 1948.

The two new neighboring countries withstood an uneasy peace as each refused to recognize the independence of the other and both established their opposing forms of government. In North Korea, Communist dictator Kim Il-Sung received the full support of the Soviet Union. In South Korea, president (and sometimes dictator) Sygman Rhee tested the limits of democracy. Before the Korean War even began, constant skirmishes along the border between North and South Korea resulted in almost 10,000 deaths. For the most part, the United States avoided direct intervention in South Korea, but concern over the spread of communism forced the U.S. to remain involved.

The first military action of the Cold War took place on June 25, 1950, when the North Korean People's Army invaded South Korea. This marked the beginning of the Korean War. Under Communist influence, 75,000 North Korean soldiers crossed into South Korea. U.S. troops immediately came to South Korea's aid in fighting the war. Under the leadership of President Harry Truman, Americans saw this as a war not only between North and South Korea, but between democracy and the global threat of communism. "If we let Korea down, the Soviet[s] will keep right on going and swallow up one [place] after another," said Truman. The global community, represented by the United Nations, agreed. The UN condemned the invasion and called upon its members to help South Korea. It placed military forces of 15 other member nations under the command of the United States as Allies in the fight against North Korea. In all, 41 nations contributed aid to South Korea in the form of food, weapons, and supplies.

The beginning of the war did not go well for the Allies. The North Korean army was much more disciplined and better prepared than the South Korean army. They had experience from fighting alongside the Soviets and Chinese during World War II. They advanced rapidly through South Korea. The American troops, parched by the hot, dry summer, drank contaminated water in rice paddies and became sick. By the end of the summer, U.S. General Douglas MacArthur changed the strategy. No longer would the Allies simply attempt to defend South Korea from invasion. Their new goal was to free North Korea from harmful Communist control.

The new strategy was successful at first. A surprise attack by sea at Incheon allowed the Allies to push the invading troops out of Seoul. General MacArthur and his forces chased them north across the border. They captured the North Korean capital of Pyongyang and drove the North Koreans almost to the Chinese border.

This tactic, however, was seen as aggression by Communist China. Chinese dictator Mao Zedong sent troops to North Korea to help defend against the invading Americans. He also warned the U.S. to avoid the Chinese border. Tensions ran high as General MacArthur sought to provoke the Chinese into fighting but President Truman hoped to avoid a larger conflict. Eventually, the Chinese joined the fighting and pushed the Allies back to the south. The hundreds of thousands of Chinese troops were far more than what General MacArthur had predicted. Communists recaptured the South Korean capital of Seoul.

General MacArthur hoped to mount another attack against North Korea. He famously claimed that there was "no substitute for victory" against these Communist forces. Although much of the world hoped to stop the spread of Communism, no one wanted to repeat the recent horrors of World War II. In April of 1951, President Truman fired the aggressive General MacArthur and turned his focus toward peace talks. General Matthew B. Ridgway took over as commander in chief of the U.S. armed forces.

For the next two years, fighting continued as the leaders attempted to come to a peace agreement. Both North and South Korea agreed to stop fighting and maintain the boundary between the countries. However, they disagreed about what to do with prisoners of war. North Korea and

The demilitarized zone between
North and South Korea

the Chinese wanted POWs to be forcibly "repatriated," i.e., to remain in the country which had captured them. South Korea and the United States wanted POWs to be returned to their homelands. Negotiations stalled.

The Korean War was unpopular among Americans. In 1953, they elected former army general Dwight D. Eisenhower as president upon his promise to end the war. Finally, the two sides reached an agreement on July 27, 1953. Prisoners of war would be allowed to decide where they wanted to live. A new boundary would add 1,500 square miles (2,414 square km) to South Korea's territory. The boundary between the two countries would remain a 2-mile wide "demilitarized zone."

A result of the war was that South Korea remained free of communism and the contrast between North and South Korea remains to this day.

The Korean War was relatively short, but it was devastating. Between 2.5 million and 5 million people lost their lives. More than half of these were civilians and almost 40,000 were Americans. Another 100,000 Americans were wounded. The demilitarized zone still exists between North and South Korea decades later. Attempts at reconciliation and peace talks have been interrupted by outbreaks of fighting and suspicions over nuclear weapons development in the north. North and South Korea have never signed a peace treaty and rely on the 1953 armistice agreement. U.S. military troops remain in South Korea to discourage any further hostilities.

Flag of North Korea

SOUTH KOREA

SOUTH KOREA: THE BIG PICTURE

Every August 15th, the people of South Korea celebrate Liberation Day. This was the day in 1945 on which they became independent from Japan. The Republic of Korea (ROK) was formed three years later on this date. Although the nation is fairly new, people have been living in Korea for as long as recorded history.

Although South and North Korea share ancient history, since 1945 their paths have differed. Despite conflicts with its northern neighbor and some internal turmoil, South Korea has flourished under its democratic government. Income and the standard of living have improved greatly, helping make South Korea a considerable economic power.

MEET THE PEOPLE OF SOUTH KOREA

The ethnic makeup of South Korea is almost completely homogeneous, meaning that almost everyone is ethnically Korean. A small population of about 20,000 Chinese also live in the country. The foreign population is increasing, with most immigrants coming from China, Japan, and the United States. The number of people migrating into the country is about equal to the number migrating out. Overall, South Korea's population is growing very slowly, with one of the lowest birth rates in the world.

All citizens speak Korean, and English is taught widely in schools.

Most South Koreans (83%) live in cities. Almost 10 million live in Seoul, the largest city. Six other cities have a population of 1 million or more. Because roughly half of the nation's people live in these seven cities, the population density is very high. In rural areas, people live in villages clustered in river valleys, at the base of hills, or in coastal lowlands. Only a few settlements are scattered throughout the mountains.

LAND, WATER, WILDLIFE, AND CLIMATE IN SOUTH KOREA

Land

South Korea's total land area is about 61,963 square miles (160,483 square km), about the size of the state of Pennsylvania, making it the 109th largest country in the world. South Korea's only adjacent neighbor is the country of North Korea, to the north. It is separated from Japan, to the south, by the Korea Strait. The land is mainly hilly and mountainous, with small valleys throughout and narrow coastal plains. The T'aebaek Mountains run north-south along the eastern coastline. Other mountain ranges branch off from there, including the Sobaek Mountains, but none are very high. The highest point, Mount Halla, is a

Fast Facts

Capital:
Seoul

Size:
109th in the world

Area:
61,963 sq miles
(160,483 sq km)

Coastline:
1,499 miles (2,412 km)

Highest Point:
Mount Halla 6,398 feet
(1,950 m)

Lowest Point:
Sea of Japan 0 feet (0 m)

Population:
49 million

Official Language:
Korean (with English widely spoken)

Currency:
South Korean won (KRW)

National Anthem:
"Aegukga" (Patriotic Song) Although it shares this name with North Korea's anthem, the lyrics are different.

National Symbol:
yin-yang

historically active volcano that has not erupted in centuries. South Korea also consists of several small islands, mainly to the south and west, including the volcanic island of Cheju.

Seoul's residents enjoying Cheonggyecheon

Water

South Korea is bordered by the East Sea, or Sea of Japan, to the east, the Yellow Sea to the west, and the East China Sea to the south. This gives South Korea a total of 1,499 miles (2,412 km) of coastline. Almost all rivers originate in the T'aebaek Mountains and flow south or west. The Han, Kŭm, and Naktong are all important rivers in South Korea. The Naktong River is South Korea's longest, at approximately 325 miles (523 km). Because of South Korea's complex coastline and the shallowness of the Yellow Sea, the west coast experiences tidal variations of up to 30 feet (9 meters)—one of the most pronounced in the world.

Climate

South Korea has a temperate climate with generally cold, dry winters and hot, humid summers. Average winter temperatures range from the mid-30s °F to the low 20s °F with summers averaging in the high 70s °F. Rainfall in South Korea is heavier in summer than in winter and averages about 35–60 inches (89–152 cm) per year. The east coast is the driest and the south coast is the wettest. Winter snowfall is heaviest in the mountains. South Korea's climate is influenced by monsoons, or seasonal winds. Occasional typhoons bring high winds and floods.

Wildlife

Once home to a variety of large mammals, South Korea has experienced a loss of habitat due to deforestation. Overfishing and pollution have also impacted marine habitats. Deer are the most abundant large mammal in South Korea. Populations of tigers, leopards, lynxes, and bears have almost disappeared. Hundreds of bird species migrate to South Korea seasonally.

EVERYDAY LIFE IN SOUTH KOREA

Family Life

Despite recent modernization in many aspects of life, South Koreans still maintain many traditional values of Confucian culture. These include respect for elders and societal seniority based on age, marital status, and economic status. Because traditional beliefs state that spirits do not leave the earth for many years, South Koreans still consider deceased relatives part of the family and honor them on major holidays.

Holidays and celebrations are very important to South Koreans, who mark the major life milestones of a baby's first 100 days of life, marriage, and the 61st birthday. They also celebrate the Lunar New Year (called Sŏllal) and the harvest moon festival (called Chusŏk, or the Korean Thanksgiving). Families wear traditional clothing, prepare special foods, and make formal greetings to elders.

City Life

Although South Korea's population has not grown overall, people have been moving to cities in vast numbers. This rapid urbanization led to a shortage of housing in big cities. Before the 1960's, the capital Seoul had few buildings above 10 stories. Now, high-rise apartment buildings provide over 2.5 million homes. While the government responded quickly to the need for housing, other services, such as water, sewage systems, and transportation, have not kept pace with the need.

Overall, city-dwellers enjoy better job opportunities, education, health care, and entertainment than those living in rural areas. However, they also face increasing crime, traffic, and pollution.

Country Life

Rural homes are usually simple structures made of brick or concrete blocks. Some have a second or third story and almost all have electricity. Traditional ondol floors carry hot air from the kitchen through channels to heat the home. More modern buildings use pipes to carry heated water or electric coils to provide heat from below the floor.

Recreation

South Koreans love to spend leisure time outdoors and exercising. The country offers many national parks where people can hike, camp, or ski. Tae kwon do, a form of martial arts, and wrestling are two of the most popular sports. South Korea has professional leagues for baseball and soccer. They also enjoy a variety of Western sports, such as golf, tennis, table tennis, and boxing.

In 1988, Seoul, South Korea hosted the Summer Olympic Games. Pyeongchang, another city in South Korea, has been chosen to host the 2018 Winter Olympic Games. In 2002, South Korea co-hosted the World Cup soccer finals along with Japan. These international events have boosted sports programs and facilities as well as national pride.

In addition to sports, South Koreans enjoy movies, plays, operas, and musical performances. Reading is popular and television networks offer a wide variety of entertainment.

The night lights in the city of Seoul

Gwangju World Cup Stadium

Education

Almost all of the adults in South Korea can read and write. Children must attend six years of primary school and three years of middle school, both of which are free. After that, most go on to high school or technical school. Since the end of World War II, colleges and universities have increased in number. Now, about 80% of high school graduates go to college. Admission to the best schools, however, is fiercely competitive and high school students must work extensively to prepare for the entrance exams. In recent years, overseas study has grown popular, especially in the United States.

Religion

South Korea has no official religion, but the people are guaranteed freedom of religion. About 43% of South Koreans claim no religion. The rest are about 32% Christian and 24% Buddhist. The nation also has strong historical ties to shamanism (the belief in spirits that respond to a shaman, or priest), Buddhism, Daoism, and Confucianism. As different belief systems came into and fell out of popular practice, none were truly abandoned. This has resulted in a unique mix of beliefs among South Koreans, which influences their culture.

Health Care

Since the end of the Korean War in 1953, health care has improved to the point that most people have health insurance and access to medical care. Sanitation and public health have also improved, leading to fewer epidemics.

SOUTH KOREA'S GOVERNMENT

The Republic of Korea (ROK) is a republic, meaning elected officials represent the people and follow an established set of laws. Its capital is in the northern city of Seoul. The nation is divided into nine provinces, six metropolitan cities, one special city (Seoul), and one special self-governing city (Sejong).

South Korea's Constitution became effective July 17, 1948 and has been amended several times since. It guarantees basic freedoms such as religion and the press, but these can be limited by the government. All citizens age 19 and older have the right to vote, and they elect a president for one five-year term who serves as chief of state and commander of the armed forces. The president appoints a prime minister to serve as the head of the government. These two leaders collaborate to appoint a State Council, a group of advisors. The National Assembly consists of 300 leaders who are elected through a combination of direct and indirect voting to serve four-year terms. They make and carry out the laws of the nation. South Korea has several different political parties as well as several special interest groups, such as Lawyers for a Democratic Society, the National Council of Churches in Korea, and the Federation of Korean Industries.

The nation maintains an army, navy, and air force. Service is mandatory for all males for at least 21 months, and women may volunteer to serve. The armed forces are much smaller than those of North Korea and exist mainly to defend against an attack from this northern neighbor. For this purpose, South Korea also has a large number of U.S. troops stationed in the country.

SOUTH KOREAN CULTURE

Despite recent political and economic changes, South Korea has a long and rich history that forms a unique culture. Several sites have been named UNESCO World Heritage sites, including Buddhist writings at Haein Temple, volcanic caves on the island of Cheju, and burial monuments that are thousands of years old. The National Museum of Korea in Seoul is home to many cultural artifacts and the National Museum of Contemporary Art holds the country's largest collection of contemporary art.

Goryeo Celadon kettle designed like a turtle

The Arts

South Koreans have long enjoyed performances by traveling troupes. They put on puppet shows, do acrobatics, juggle, sing, and dance. The most popular traditional dance is the sandae masked dance, wherein male performers wear large, brightly painted masks made of paper, wood, or gourds. Traditionally, singers and dancers would be accompanied by a 12-stringed zither and an hourglass-shaped drum called a changgo.

Korean painting dates back thousands of years to murals found in ancient royal tombs. Artists also developed several distinct forms of ceramics, including fine celadon (greenish glazed) ware.

Today, South Korea has several national companies for dance, drama, and music.

Fashion

The hanbok is a traditional Korean form of dress, still worn on special occasions. South Koreans wear different hanbok for different occasions, usually involving a long, full skirt and short jacket for women and loose pants and jacket for men. For everyday wear, most Koreans dress in typical Western clothing.

Food and Drink

The Korean diet is based on rice and other grains, along with vegetables and beans. In urban areas, foreign dishes like pizza, hamburgers, and sushi have become popular. Korea is famous for kimchi—a spicy, sour mix of pickled or fermented vegetables, usually cabbage and radishes. In the fall, families or whole villages spend several days preparing the winter supply of kimchi in a festival called kimjang. South Koreans eat a small but increasing amount of meat or dairy products. Tea and coffee are the most common drinks. Koreans also enjoy a variety of alcoholic drinks, including beer, sake (rice wine), and soju (a distilled grain alcohol).

THE ECONOMY OF SOUTH KOREA

South Korea's economy is one of the largest in Asia and ranks 14th in the world. It far surpasses its northern neighbor, North Korea. Most economic growth in South Korea has occurred since the 1950's, after the nation was formed and finished fighting the Korean War. Prior to that time, it had been mainly an agricultural society. Since then, however, it has become more industrialized and modernized.

The work force is one of the largest in the world (25th) but is aging rapidly. About 3% of South Koreans are unemployed and 16% live below the poverty line.

Agriculture

Although agriculture was the primary economic activity in the past, it now makes up just 2% of the nation's economy. Farmers grow rice, barley, vegetables, and fruit. They also raise cattle, pigs, and chickens and provide milk and eggs. South Korea must import many of its food needs. Rapid urbanization has caused the population of farmers to become smaller and older. This problem has been offset by improvements in machinery.

Forestry and Fishing

South Korea has been recovering from deforestation during the Japanese occupation. However, logging remains a small industry and South

Korea imports much of its timber. Fishing, on the other hand, is an important economic resource. The country is ideally suited for deep-sea fishing. It consumes and exports large numbers of fish.

Mineral and Energy Resources

South Korea lacks mineral resources, with just small reserves of coal, iron ore, gold, lead, and other minerals. It imports almost all of its petroleum and metal needs. The nation relies mainly on thermal electric power, with some hydroelectric and nuclear power sources.

Manufacturing

Major industries in South Korea include electronics, automobiles, chemicals, steel, and shipbuilding. Manufacturing and industry account for 39% of the nation's economy. Many of the goods are produced for export, making South Korea the 6th largest exporter in the world. Almost half of these exports go to China, the United States, Japan, and Hong Kong. The rapid growth of cities has led to an increase in construction of buildings, roads, and water and sewage systems.

Port of Busan is the largest port in South Korea

Services

This sector accounts for almost 59% of South Korea's economy. The country has a large tourism industry, catering largely to visitors from other Asian countries. Other major service industries include finance, real estate, insurance, and business services.

Transportation

Most of South Korea's passenger travel and freight transport occurs on roads. It has a well-developed bus network and several railways, which are mainly government-owned. A few large cities have subway systems. South Korea also has several domestic and international airports.

Communication

With freedom of the press, South Korea has many public and private newspapers, radio stations, and television networks.

SOUTH KOREA'S HISTORY

Both North and South Korea share their past history. (To read about that history, see North Korea's History.) The two countries' histories diverge after World War II. Once the Japanese had been forced to leave, South Korea needed to be rebuilt.

North and South Korea (1948)

By 1948, the U.S. in the South and Soviet Union in the North had helped establish new governments in Korea and began to withdraw their influence. This left the Republic of Korea in the south and the Democratic People's Republic in the north. Neither government

Once surrounded by walls, Seoul is still home to the "Great Southern Gate"

recognized the other as an authority in Korea. The north followed communist principles while the south maintained democratic rule. South Koreans elected Syngman Rhee as their first president.

After the Korean War

The Korean War (1950–1953) amplified tensions between President Rhee and his National Assembly. Rhee ran for four terms as president, instead of two, and pushed through laws that allowed him to be elected by the popular vote. Legislators and student demonstrators opposed his level of control over the government. Under intense pressure, Rhee resigned in 1960 and fled to Hawaii. His time as president is known as the First Republic.

For a few months thereafter, a parliamentary cabinet ruled South Korea with Prime Minister Chang Myŏn elected as a figurehead. During this Second Republic, South Korea suffered from social and economic problems and its government was hobbled by opposing factions. In 1961, General Park Chung-Hee overthrew the government in a military coup.

Park ruled South Korea under martial law and dissolved the National Assembly. However, pressure from non-military leaders as well as foreign powers forced him to run for president in a democratic election. In 1963, Park was elected by a narrow margin to become president during the Third Republic. Like Rhee before him, Park took political action to extend his presidency beyond two four-year terms. After being elected for a third term, Rhee went so far as to declare a national state of emergency in which he suspended the constitution and dissolved the legislature. Beginning in 1972, the Fourth Republic began with Park serving unlimited six-year terms. He had almost unlimited power and worked to suppress anyone who opposed him. Under Park's leadership, the government greatly limited freedom of speech and of the press. They also jailed many of Park's opponents. After two more re-elections, Park was assassinated by his friend, and leader of the Korean Central Intelligence Agency, Kim Jae-Kyu.

Throughout this time of political turmoil in the late 1900's, tensions with North Korea continued. During Park's presidency, North Korean troops ventured into the demilitarized zone, attacked South Korean troops, and entered the South Korean capital city in a failed assassination attempt against him. North Korea was also found guilty of a bombing in Burma that killed 17 South Korean officials in 1983. When South Korea hosted the Olympic games in 1988, North Korea refused to participate.

After Park's assassination, South Korea experienced a brief period of military rule. Clashes between demonstrators and the military occurred frequently and were often violent. The government was finally restored with the election of President Chun Doo-Hwan in 1980. Beginning with this Fifth Republic, the president would be limited to one seven-year term. Chun ruled until 1988, when Roh Tae-Woo took office in the nation's first peaceful transfer of power. Under his leadership, which began the Sixth Republic, South Korea hosted the Summer Olympic Games. Political parties became more unified and ties with foreign nations were strengthened. Legislation was changed to limit the president's term to five years instead of seven.

Signed Agreement (1991)

Finally, North Korea gave up its insistence on a single joint Korean seat in the United Nations (UN). North and South Korea were each admitted to the UN as separate and equal members. Around this time, diplomatic relations between the two longtime rivals began to improve. Leaders met for talks and relatives were allowed to cross the DMZ to visit separated family members. The two countries agreed to stop using force against one another, increase trade and communication, and prohibit nuclear weapons. Cooperation stalled, however, in 1993 due to controversy over North Korea's nuclear weapons program.

In 1993, President Kim Young-Sam took office. He was a civilian, rather than a military leader. He took action to end government corruption and removed thousands of officials from their positions. Kim's own son was arrested for bribery and tax evasion. Previous presidents Chun and Roh were also convicted of serious crimes involving finances.

The next president, Kim Dae-Jung, extended pardons to Chun and Roh as an act of goodwill. Kim improved the nation's relations with North Korea and was awarded the Nobel Prize for Peace for this "sunshine" policy.

In 2013, South Korea's first female leader, Park Geun-hye, took office as president. She is the daughter of former President Park Chung-hee.

Flag of South Korea

JAPAN

JAPAN: THE BIG PICTURE

The Japanese name for their nation, *Nippon* or *Nihon*, means *source of the sun*. According to legend, the sun goddess created Nippon and the emperors were her descendants. The tradition of an emperor, or imperial house, continues to this day, though official doctrine no longer claims that the emperor is deity. The name *Japan* likely comes from a mispronunciation of *Zipangu*, the name given to the country in the late 1200's by Italian explorer Marco Polo, who only heard about the country from the Chinese, but never visited himself.

Japan consists of a string of volcanic islands in the North Pacific Ocean. Most of the population lives crowded into cities on the main islands of Hokkaido, Honshu, Kyushu, and Shikoku, though thousands of smaller islands also make up Japan. With no immediate neighbors, Japan is closest to Russia, Korea, and China.

The extensive mountains and forests of Japan's interior make for beautiful scenery, but difficult habitation and farming. As a result, most people live along narrow strips of coastal plains where they have developed farms and built huge cities. Today, these cities, including the capital of Tokyo, are modern, bustling centers of culture, commerce, and industry.

Despite having few natural resources, Japan has become one of the world's top economic powers. Its manufacturing centers import raw materials to convert into finished goods such as automobiles, computers, electronics, processed foods, chemicals, and textiles. Japan is one of the largest importers and exporters in the world.

Combining Japan's long history of developing its own traditions in isolation from other countries with a recent embrace of all things Western, Japan enjoys a rich culture. Chinese culture heavily influenced Japanese art, government, language, religion, and technology from about 400 to 800 CE. Another wave of influence came from Europe beginning in the mid-1500's. Soon after, however, Japanese leaders cut ties with foreign nations and sought to isolate Japan from outside influence. This isolation continued until 1853, when the United States encouraged Japan to open its ports to foreign trade.

Nowadays, evidence of modern and traditional culture abound. The Japanese people wear modern Western clothing, but don traditional *kimonos* for festivals and special occasions. Sports fans enjoy baseball as well as the ancient form of Japanese wrestling called *sumo*. People watch modern movies and listen to rock music, but also continue to enjoy centuries-old *noh* and *kabuki* theater.

Japan's incredible economic and military growth of the late 1800's and early 1900's was cut short by the devastation of World War II. Despite some early victories, Japan surrendered to the United States and Allied nations after the atomic bombing of Hiroshima and Nagasaki in 1945. The war left

Fast Facts

Capital:
Tokyo

Size:
62nd in the world

Area:
234,825 sq miles
(608,000 sq km)

Coastline:
18,486 miles (29,750 km)

Highest Point:
Mount Fuji 12,388 feet
(3,776 m)

Lowest Point:
Hachiro-gata -13 feet
(-4 m)

Population:
127 million

Official Language:
Japanese

Currency:
yen

National Anthem:
"Kimigayo"
(The Emperor's Reign)

National Symbol:
red sun disc

Japan in a state of economic, social, and political ruin. However, the nation rebuilt itself quickly under the guidance and help of occupying Allied forces.

Today, Japan has returned to its status as a great industrial nation. Under a new Constitution, a democratic form of government has flourished. The standard of living of the Japanese people is one of the highest in the world.

MEET THE PEOPLE OF JAPAN

With over 127 million people, Japan is the 11th most populous nation in the world. Almost 100% of its citizens are ethnically Japanese, with small populations of Koreans, Chinese, and Brazilians. In the northernmost islands live the indigenous Ainu, who have a unique ethnicity and culture. The Japanese descended from mainly northeastern Asian immigrants who traveled to the Japanese islands sometime around 10,000 BCE. These early people, called *Jomon* (meaning *cord-marked*), made pottery bearing the impressions of ropes or cords. By about 300 BCE, the *Yayoi* people replaced the Jomon, settling in the area around modern-day Tokyo. They developed villages, agriculture, and cast bronze into tools and weapons. The Yayoi closely resembled today's Japanese in appearance and language.

Many of the Koreans in Japan descend from the hundreds of thousands who were forced to migrate to Japan under imperial rule in the early 1900's. They lack full citizenship to this day and face discrimination. Other ethnic groups considered "resident aliens" in Japan are the indigenous Ainu people of Hokkaido and the people of Okinawa.

About 80% of the Japanese people live on the largest island, Honshu. Settlement throughout the mountains has always been sparse, with most of the population settling along the coastal lowlands. In fact, about 90% of Japanese live on just 20% of the land, making these areas among the world's most crowded. Japan's largest urban area, Tokyo, is the most populous in the world with over 37 million people. Osaka-Kobe, Nagoya, and three other cities have populations over 2.5 million.

Since the industrialization of the late 1800's and beyond, Japan's population grew and moved into urban centers. After 100 years of explosive population growth, Japan's birth rate dropped to almost the lowest in the

Map of Japan

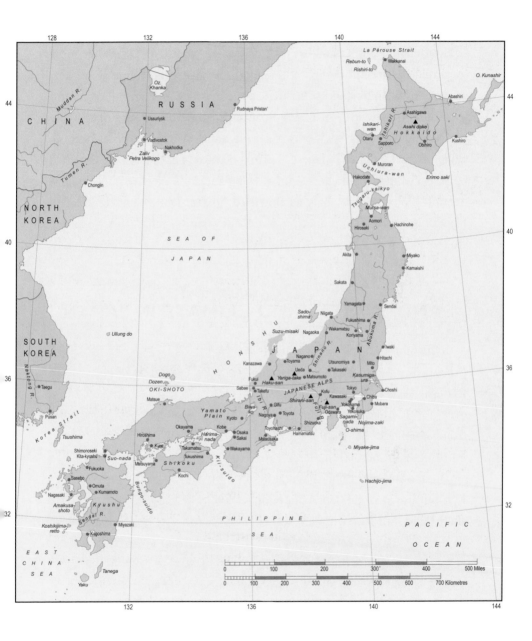

world. Combined with high life expectancy, the result is a shrinking and aging Japanese population.

The Japanese language has various dialects, including the major ones of Hondo and Nantō, as well as the one spoken by Okinawans. While most local dialects are not understood among different people groups, all Japanese people understand standard Japanese that is spoken in Tokyo and used in schools, television, and radio. Many people also speak English. The native language once spoken by the indigenous Ainu people has become nearly extinct. Spoken Japanese is akin to Korean, but the writing system is based on Chinese characters along with Japanese phonetic symbols. Before the mid 1900's, this system of writing used 5,000 different characters, called *kanji*. It has since been reduced to about 2,000 simpler characters. Japanese students learn this complex writing system, along with a system of spelling Japanese words using the Roman alphabet.

LAND, WATER, AND CLIMATE IN JAPAN

The nation of Japan is an archipelago, or island chain, located in Eastern Asia. It stretches in an arc over 1,491 miles (2,400 km) long from northeast to southwest. The four main islands, from largest to smallest, are Honshu, Hokkaido, Kyushu, and Shikoku. Japan does not share land borders with any other countries. Its nearest neighbor is South Korea, across the Korea Strait, as well as North Korea and Russia across the Sea of Japan to the west.

Japan is roughly the size of California

Land

A great underwater mountain range rises out of the Pacific Ocean to create the islands of Japan. As a result, the land is mostly rugged, with over 70% covered in mountains. Hills, valleys, gorges, waterfalls, and dense

Mount Fuji as seen from the space shuttle

forests all add to the natural beauty. In addition to the four largest islands, Japan consists of several smaller island groups, including the Ryukyu Islands, the Izu Islands, the Bonin Islands, and the Volcano Islands. The large island of Honshu has three main mountain ranges, including the Japanese Alps, which are the country's tallest mountains. The largest flat lowland in Japan, the Kanto Plain, lies along the east coast of Honshu, where Tokyo is located.

Japan is home to over 150 volcanoes, of which 60 are active. This includes Mount Fuji, or Fujiyama, Japan's highest peak at 12,388 feet (3,776 meters), an active volcano which last erupted in 1707. More recent eruptions include Mount O in 1983, Mount Mihara in 1986, and the Izu Islands and Mount Unzen in 1991. Scientists keep a close watch on Unzen and Sakura-jima, as these volcanoes are located close to densely populated areas. Every year, Japan experiences over a thousand seismic events—mainly tremors but occasionally severe earthquakes. Japan's volcano and earthquake activity is due to its location along the Ring of Fire—an area circling the Pacific Ocean where Earth's shifting crust causes violent changes. This activity results in many hot springs throughout Japan. Violent earthquakes can also produce destructive tsunamis—huge waves caused by underwater earthquakes.

Water

Surrounded by water in all directions, Japan has 18,641 miles (30,000 km) of coastline. To the west, the Sea of Japan separates the nation from North and South Korea and Russia. The La Perouse Strait to the north separates it from the Russian island Sakhalin. To the east lies the North Pacific Ocean and to the south the Philippine Sea. Japan is separated from China by the East China Sea to the southwest.

Japan's rivers are mostly short and swift-running, due to the mountainous terrain. This makes many of them impossible to navigate by boat. However, they are useful for irrigation and hydroelectric power. Some rivers in volcanic areas are too acidic to use for drinking or irrigation. The major rivers are the Teshio, Ishikari, Kitakami, and Chikugo. Some of Japan's lakes, such as Kutcharo, Towada, and Ashi, are actually calderas (large, basin-shaped depressions in the peak of volcanoes) filled with water. Others are valleys that filled with water when the mouth of a river became dammed by sand. The largest lake, Lake Biwa, covers 416 square miles (1077 square km) of central Honshu.

Climate

Many factors greatly affect the climate in Japan. The Pacific Ocean and the large Asian landmass create monsoons (seasonal winds) that bring wet or dry weather depending on the season. Strong Pacific currents—the warm Kuroshio and the cold Oyashio—influence the climate. The vast latitudinal stretch from north to south creates differences in temperature, and the mountainous terrain creates local variations in climate.

Overall, the climate is tropical in the south and cool to temperate in the north. Average winter temperatures range from 18-46 °F and average summer temperatures range from 70-82 °F. The coasts are warmer and wetter than the mountainous interior. Typhoons (tropical cyclones that form over the ocean) and tsunamis occur frequently, especially in the southwest.

Rainfall is heaviest in the summer and exceeds 40 inches (101 cm) per year in most areas. Central Honshu can receive more than 160 inches (406 cm) annually. The Japanese call the rainy season the *baiu*, or plum rain, because it occurs during the time when plums are ripe. Many areas, especially the Sea of Japan coast, receive snowfall in the winter.

EVERYDAY LIFE IN JAPAN

Family Life

Hundreds of years ago, Japanese society was divided into social classes. The most prestigious group was the peer class, followed by the four working classes—warrior, farmer, craftsman, and merchant. The lowest social class, called the outcast class or *burakumin*, handled tasks considered "unclean," such as slaughtering cattle and executing criminals. They lived in slum areas of cities or specially segregated villages. Their descendants, who make up about 2% of the population, still face discrimination to some extent today.

Today, Japanese home life revolves around work and school. The traditional roles of men as breadwinners and women as homemakers are slowly changing. However, women still earn lower wages than men and have fewer employment benefits. Many women work outside the home before marriage and, to a lesser degree, while raising children. In general, society expects women to marry, have children, and stay home to care for their families. Meanwhile, men work to support the family and are paid a "family allowance" by employers. In the past, marriages were arranged by families, but now love matches have become more popular. A Japanese wedding may consist of a traditional Shinto ceremony followed by a Christian- or Western-style observance.

The Japanese love to celebrate. In addition to 15 national holidays, they also celebrate many festivals throughout the year. December 23rd marks the birthday of Emperor Akihito, followed by a large New Year's celebration beginning December 31st. For this event, families spend three days visiting shrines, temples, and homes of friends and family. In general, however, the Japanese rarely entertain guests in their homes because the homes are small and many of the meetings are business-like.

City Life

Approximately 90% of the Japanese live in Japan's crowded urban areas. The large cities reflect Japan's economic success with expensive cars, fashionable stores, and expensive apartments. Most people enjoy a high standard of living and have good jobs. They have access to many restaurants, stores, and types of entertainment. They live mainly in high-rise apartment buildings, but small single homes are also scattered throughout the cities. Land prices in Tokyo are among the highest in the world. Therefore, it makes more sense to build a tall apartment building on a plot of land rather than a single house. This way, the high cost of living is divided among many families rather than just one.

Despite the many benefits of city life, the nation has struggled to keep pace with the growing urban population. In addition to housing, large cities need infrastructure such as roads, public transportation, utilities, and sewers to meet the needs of the people. Housing in Japan is quite expensive, which has forced people further and further from city centers. As a result, many Japanese workers have very long commutes. The lack of zoning laws in Japanese cities results in a unique mix of stores, homes, factories, and even agricultural land in some urban districts. While overcrowding in cities has led to pollution, crime and poverty are generally low in Japan.

More and more people now live in apartments or homes they own themselves, rather than units owned by corporations or the government. In addition, the amount of living space per person has increased. A traditional Japanese home uses sliding paper screens to separate rooms. People sit on floor cushions rather than chairs and sleep on a padded quilt called a *futon*. Modern homes may contain some Western-style furniture as well as carpets instead of *tatami* (straw mats) on the floors.

Country Life

A small number of Japanese, about 10–15% of the population, live in rural areas. They earn their living by farming, fishing, and harvesting edible seaweed. Many rural villages have maintained the traditional system of cooperative agriculture called *aza* or *mura*, which consists of 30 to 50 households that work together and assist one another to form an independent unit. They combine traditional practices along with modern equipment and farming techniques.

Wooden homes are similar to those in the cities. Rural land is less expensive than that in urban areas, but it is still high compared to other nations. Most rural villages have close ties to nearby cities, with workers often traveling to the city for seasonal work in the winter. In fact, very few rural families live on farming income alone. By working two or even three jobs, farmers average a slightly higher income than those working in cities. However, rural populations are declining as many people leave the countryside permanently to live and work in the cities.

Recreation

The Japanese love sports. As Western culture influenced Japan in the early 1900's, sports such as basketball, soccer, golf, and tennis became popular. Baseball, introduced to Japan in the 1870's, has become a favorite national sport. Professional baseball players are well-known celebrities and many have found success playing Major League Baseball in the United States. Since 1993, Japan has had a popular professional football league. Both schools and the military emphasize participation in sports.

The practice of martial arts in Japan can be traced to the 8th century. It includes competitive *kendo, judo,* and *karate* as well as non-competitive *jujitsu* and *aikido. Sumo* wrestling is perhaps the oldest and most popular national sport in Japan.

Japan hosted the Summer Olympic Games of 1964 in Tokyo and the Winter Games in Sapporo (1972) and Nagano (1998). The nation's most dominant Olympic sports are gymnastics and *judo.*

In addition to sports, the Japanese love travel. The country's many parks and institutions support the enjoyment of nature. In the spring, travelers follow the progression of the cherry blossoms from south to north. In the fall, this trend reverses as they follow the coloring leaves of maple trees from north to south. Japanese also enjoy visiting temples, shrines, hot springs, and historical sites. Wealthier families travel abroad to major cities in Europe, the west coast of the United States, South Korea, and Australia.

At home, the Japanese enjoy card games and board games. *Shogi* and *go* both resemble chess. *Mah-jongg* is a popular game played with rectangular tiles. Women in particular participate in a traditional tea-serving ceremony, chant ballads, or practice the art of flower arranging, called *ikebana.* Men often meet up together after work to enjoy a drink of *sake* (wine made from rice) or beer at a local restaurant or bar.

Education

The Japanese value education so highly that fierce academic competition results in problems like bullying. From a very young age, students are screened and selected for schools based on academic achievement. Schools are ranked strictly and students work very hard to be accepted into the "best" ones.

All Japanese children must attend school for at least nine years, but almost everyone completes more schooling. Kindergarten, which is optional, can last one to three years. It is followed by a six-year elementary school, three-year middle school, and three-year high school. Extracurricular "cram" schools, called *juku*, exist for children as young as preschool. There, students spend several hours each day after school preparing for exams. Until the 1990's, schools held classes on Saturdays, a practice which is slowly fading out.

In Japan, public elementary and middle schools are free but high school requires tuition. Students attend from April through March with a vacation break in August. They study typical subjects such as language, math, art, music, physical education, science, and social studies. The Japanese also study homemaking, moral education, and English. Although the Japanese language is particularly difficult to learn, almost all adults are literate. Japanese students score very well on exams compared with other nations, but many complain that the educational system is too demanding. They believe students should do less memorization, spend less time in school, and learn in a more creative fashion.

University education is highly desirable and serves as the means to achieve social status and income potential. Males in particular measure their success by the reputation of the university they attend. The two most prestigious and competitive universities are Tokyo and Kyōto. Once a year, students take very difficult entrance examinations to determine their eligibility for the universities. The rigorous high school curriculum, combined with extracurricular "cram" schools, attempt to prepare students for the examinations. Once they get past this hurdle, almost all students succeed in universities, which are more lenient than high schools. Male students are more likely to attend universities, while females are more likely to attend junior colleges or technical schools.

Education beyond a university occurs regularly throughout Japan. Adults can take classes in technology, arts, vocational training, homemaking, physical education, and other areas. Many adults take foreign language classes.

Religion

Japan does not have an official religion. Most of the people observe a combination of spiritual practices without intense religious beliefs. About 80% of Japanese observe Shintoism, overlapping with 67% who observe Buddhism. Christianity, ancient shamanism, and some new religions also have some followers. Families do not formally train children in religion, but often observe religious practices in the home.

At one time, Shintoism was a state-supported religion, with the Japanese emperor considered a divine being. Although that support ended after World War II, Shintoism remains Japan's most popular religion. The word Shinto means *the way of the gods*. Shintoism is polytheistic, meaning it includes many gods (called *kami*) including people, natural objects like rocks and trees, Hindu gods, and Chinese spirits. It also involves the practice of ancestor worship. Shrines are popular Shinto structures throughout the nation.

Buddhism, which came from Korea and China in the 500's, was also adopted as the national religion at one point. Several sects remain influential throughout Japan today and Buddhist temples exist throughout the country. Buddhism is a more structured belief system than Shintoism. It focuses on living a virtuous life in order to obtain perfect peace and happiness.

In the late 1500's, Jesuit and Franciscan missionaries brought Christianity to Japan. At first, it was well-received and seen as a symbol of European culture. However, in the 1600's it was banned and Christians were persecuted. Many continued to practice Christianity in hiding until the ban was lifted in 1873. Today, the Japanese widely celebrate Christmas, though more as a folk tradition than a religious observation.

A small temple near Mount Fuji

SHINTO

Indigenous Japanese developed the Shinto religion thousands of years ago. Unlike many other religious belief systems, Shinto has no single god, no founder, and no official texts. Rather, it is a set of guiding beliefs that has shaped Japanese thought throughout the ages. In the sixth century CE, this set of beliefs was given the name Shinto to distinguish it from the increasingly popular Buddhist religion.

The word Shinto means "the way of kami," with kami meaning "the gods" or "spirits." This polytheistic religion includes many deities in the form of people, natural objects like rocks and trees, and gods and spirits borrowed from Buddhism and Chinese beliefs. The spirits provide the driving force behind growth, creativity, and healing. Shinto is wholly focused on life in this world, rather than an afterlife. It lays out ethical principles for life, but does not include a set of commandments or laws. Because Shintoism is based more on ritual than specific spiritual beliefs, it readily coexists with other religions, such as Buddhism. Since Shinto is fully an ethnic or cultural way of life, the Japanese do not attempt to spread Shintoism to other countries and few people outside Japan practice it.

The practice of Shintoism, to which about 80% of Japanese adhere, involves devotion to shrines and rituals that allow people to communicate with kami. Followers of Shinto believe that spirits enjoy attention from them and, if made happy, will intervene in their lives to bring love, happiness, and success. Shrines can be found in almost every Japanese community as well as in private homes. Devotees focus on their own local shrine more than on a unified religion as a whole. Such local shrines have become popular tourist destinations throughout the country.

Shinto festivals, called matsuri, combine solemn worship and joyful reverie. Each festival celebrates a particular kami as guest of honor and might include a parade, theatrical performance, or sumo wrestling match along with feasting. Worshippers offer flowers, money, or food at the shrine. Most festivals follow the ancient farming calendar and major life events. The more private rituals at home might consist of prayers for blessings or thanksgiving.

According to Shinto belief, Japan was created by the sun goddess, from whom the emperors descended. Therefore, the emperor was long considered a divine being. Eventually, the Japanese government made Shintoism official policy, called State Shinto, placing more emphasis on national goals such as patriotism and Japanese nationalism. Japan's new Constitution, developed after World War II, abolished State Shinto and denied the deity of the emperor. However, the personal practice of Shintoism continues to permeate Japanese culture.

Shinto shrine in Kyoto

Health Care

The high standard of living in Japan, along with national health insurance for all citizens, contributes to the good health of its people. Japan's obesity rate is one of the lowest in the industrialized world. The leading cause of death is cancer, which has increased significantly in the past 50 years.

Employers and workers contribute to the costs of health care and pensions, while government entities pay for other social welfare programs. Japan's health costs are rising due to health complications from a more Westernized diet and the aging population. To compensate for the low birth rate and long life expectancy that created this elderly population, Japan's government has changed nursing-care laws and raised the age for full pension benefits.

JAPAN'S GOVERNMENT

The nation of Japan has a parliamentary government with a constitutional monarchy. That means it is a democracy in which the legislative branch holds the most power and an emperor serves as a figurehead.

Several dates mark important advancements in establishing Japan's government. The traditional date of the nation's founding by Emperor Jimmu is 660 BCE. In 1890, the Meiji Constitution established a constitutional monarchy. The current Constitution was adopted in 1946 as an amendment to the Meiji Constitution, downgrading the emperor from the supreme sovereign authority to a figurehead who represents the unity of the people. Sovereignty, along with fundamental human rights, now legally belongs to the people. Japanese enjoy freedom of religion, speech, and the press. All citizens 20 years of age and older can vote in elections.

The Japanese modeled their legal system after Germany's, with influences from England, the United States, and Japanese traditions. The government separates power between legislative, executive, and judicial branches. In addition to an emperor who mainly performs formalities, Japan's prime minister is head of the executive branch and Cabinet. The legislative branch of the government, called the Diet, consists of a House of Councillors and a House of Representatives, each with a few hundred seats. Candidates from several different political parties vie for seats in the government. The judicial branch consists of a chief justice, a Supreme Court, and several lower courts.

The country is divided into eight regions called *chihō* that run from northeast to southwest. They are further divided into 47 prefectures. The prefectures vary greatly in size and serve as an intermediate governing body between towns and the central government. Japan's capital city is Tokyo, whose Kasumigaseki district houses most government offices.

Japan's constitution "forever renounces war." Therefore, the country can only maintain military forces for the purpose of defense. From 1945 to 1950, this meant that Japan only had a police force. However, after the Korean War began, Japan started to rebuild its armed forces in order to preserve peace and security. Service in Japan's army, navy, and air force is voluntary. The Ministry of Defense maintains close ties with the United States military, which has many military bases in Japan. Japan's first deployment of troops outside the country, in 2009, took action against Somalian pirates who interfered with Japanese shipping.

Tokyo's Metropolitan Government Building

JAPANESE CULTURE

Japanese culture has been strongly influenced by China (in ancient times) and the West (in modern times). However, Japan has been able to maintain its own unique culture while embracing foreign influence. Modern Japanese culture is very urban, Westernized, and trendy. Teenagers in particular follow fads in clothing, hairstyles, and music. American and European styles also show up in architecture, art, education, literature, and recreation. The characteristic Japanese fingerprint on many of these cultural expressions is a clean simplicity.

Japan's Agency for Cultural Affairs supports artists and attempts to preserve traditional Japanese art forms. It preserves and promotes historical sites and works with modern museums and research institutes. The agency identifies talented artists and performers as "living national treasures" for practicing traditional art forms. By providing them with stipends, the agency helps these artists continue their craft and train apprentices. Without this work of the Agency for Cultural Affairs, these art forms could be lost forever.

The Arts

Japanese taste in art tends to be more subtle than the lavish Chinese style and more refined than the cumbersome style of the West. Japanese believe that good art expresses the conflicts among individuals, families, and communities. Traditional forms of art include the tea ceremony, gardening and flower arranging, architecture, painting, sculpture, and the artistic handwriting form calligraphy. Artisans work with bamboo, paper, silk, ceramics, ivory, and lacquer.

Small clay figures called *haniwa* date back to the 200's BCE. These sculptures of animals, servants, and everyday objects adorned the graves of

Traditional Japanese architecture

important people. Buddhist temples also contain ancient sculptures made of wood, clay, or bronze. The Great Buddha at Kamakura is the most famous of these.

Theater

A laughing Buddha sculpture

Theater in Japan combines music, dance, and drama. The oldest form of theater, the *noh* play, presents serious subjects, such as history, through movement, masks, and chanting. In the 1600's, *bunraku* became popular. Performances involve a narrator and large puppets controlled by silent handlers. The more light-hearted *kabuki* is famous for its distinct makeup and costumes. The many large cities of Japan have several symphony orchestras, museums, art galleries, and gardens. Cinemas show popular Western movies as well as Japanese films.

Music

Traditional Japanese music relies on drums, flutes, gongs, and stringed instruments such as the *biwa*, *koto*, and *samisen*. Folk music has become rare, but performances are still well-attended. Popular Western music such as jazz, rock, and pop is widespread. Many Japanese songs combine Western instruments, style, and topics with Japanese lyrics. In the 1970's, the Japanese invented *karaoke*, which means "empty orchestra," a popular form of musical entertainment in which people sing along to a backing track and read lyrics from a screen.

Literature

Japan may lay claim to the world's first novel—*The Tale of Genji*, written by Murasaki Shikibu in the early 1000's. This classic is considered by many to be Japan's greatest work of fiction. The ancient poetry form *haiku* also remains popular.

Fashion

Modern Japanese clothing resembles that worn in the United States and Western Europe. Men wear suits and ties to work. Older men stick to dark, conservative colors while younger men might wear brighter colors and patterns. Women wear skirts, blouses, slacks, or dresses. Silk scarves are a favorite accessory. Some people wear expen-

Women wear traditional, colorful kimonos

sive designer clothes and many younger people wear trendier fashions. For school, children wear a uniform consisting of a dark jacket with matching pants, shorts, or skirt.

Traditional Japanese clothing can still be seen on special occasions such as weddings, funerals, or holidays. For women, this includes a long silk *kimono*, which is like a robe. A sash called an *obi* ties around the waist to hold it closed. Sandals called *zori* are the traditional footwear.

Food and Drink

Japanese cuisine is famous for many raw or lightly cooked dishes, such as sushi—a combination of cooked rice, raw seafood, vegetables, and eggs served in various shapes. Tempura is a similar combination of foods served battered and deep-fried. Most meals include some form of rice, tofu (curd made from soybeans), or noodles, such as soba or udon. Fish is traditionally the main form of protein.

Japanese families eat out at restaurants regularly. In addition to typical Japanese food, they can choose from a variety of foreign restaurants, including Denny's and McDonald's. In fact, Japan's rice production has decreased about 50% in the past 50 years because younger people eat a less traditional diet than their elders. In addition to fish, they eat more beef, chicken, and pork. They also consume more fruit, dairy, and breads. As a result of this changing diet, Japanese youth are growing three to four inches (8 to 10 cm) taller than their grandparents did.

The Japanese typically serve tea at every meal. People around the world drink green tea from the region around Mount Fuji. Typical Japanese drinks also include sake (a rice-based alcohol), beer, and whiskey.

JAPAN'S WILDLIFE

Japan's abundant rain and mild temperatures have created lush forests and plant growth throughout the country. The Ryukyu and Bonin Islands contain semitropical rainforests of oaks, ferns, camphor, and mulberries. Kyushu's southern coast is home to mangrove swamps. Vast forests of evergreens stretch throughout the mountains of the central and northern lands. On the high peaks of Yaku Island grow Japanese cedars more than 2,000 years old. Japan is famous for its colorful maple trees in fall and pink cherry blossoms in spring.

The remote forests provide a habitat for a wide variety of animals including bears, wild boars, foxes, deer, antelope, and wild monkeys called macaque. The reptile and amphibian populations include sea turtles, snakes, frogs, toads, and a Japanese giant salamander that can grow to four feet (1.2 meters) or longer. Over 600 bird species live in or migrate through Japan. The abundant waters are home to whales, dolphins, porpoises, and an extensive range of fish and crustaceans. Freshwater fish live in rivers and lakes throughout the country. Koi ponds, home to brightly-colored carp, are popular decorations.

Lotus blossom.

THE ECONOMY OF JAPAN

Since the end of World War II, Japan has made great strides economically. After complete devastation due to the war, Japan rebuilt its economy with help from Allied occupation forces. Land reforms led to more productive agriculture, and the growth of industry created a demand for consumer products. Japan has developed into a top economic power due to the cooperation between government and industry, its mastery of technology, and the strong work ethic among the labor force.

Japan now has the 5th largest economy in the world based on Gross Domestic Product (GDP), a measurement of goods and services produced. It boasts one of the world's lowest unemployment rates. Japan has the 9th largest labor force in the world, with over 65 million workers. It is a world leader (ranked 5th) in both imports and exports, with major ports in Chiba, Kobe, Nagoya, and Yokohama. Japanese families have higher incomes, more assets, and more savings than those in most other countries.

Despite these advantages, Japan faces some serious economic struggles. The national debt is the highest of any country in the world. The aging population, combined with a low birth rate, creates economic concerns—as more people reach old age, there are fewer young workers to support them. Japan has scarce natural resources, which makes it dependent on imports of raw materials. The 2001 earthquake and tsunami disaster increased this need by shutting down Japan's nuclear reactors.

Agriculture

Japan's farmlands, though highly productive, account for a small portion of the economy. Only 12% of the land is useful for agriculture, so the Japanese import almost half of their food needs. Though the mountainous terrain is a disadvantage for farmers, the abundant rain and freshwater rivers make growing rice in wet paddies possible. Farmers increase their crop yields by using advanced seeds, fertilizers, and machinery along with the technique of terraced farming, which involves growing crops along strips of land cut into hillsides. Only 3% of Japan's huge labor force works in agriculture, down from 45% in 1950. As younger people leave farms for jobs in the city, the average age of Japan's farmers is increasing.

The primary crops are rice, barley, vegetables, tea, fruit, flowers, sugar cane, and wheat. Farmers also raise poultry, pork, and beef. Until 1999, Japan banned the import of rice in order to encourage self-sufficiency. However, consumers now want less government interference in food prices and import taxes in order to make food less expensive.

Forestry and Fishing

Although forests cover 69% of Japan's land, much of these lumber resources grow in mountainous areas that can't be reached. In addition, logging in Japan is expensive and inefficient. As a result, the country imports lumber to meet most of its needs.

With its extensive coastline, Japan has abundant fishing resources. Fishing provides much of the nation's food as well as exports. Fishing workers engage in deep-sea fishing, raising clams and oysters, and farming freshwater pearls. Although many species of whales are endangered, Japan continues to practice whaling. As with agriculture, the age of fishing workers is increasing as younger workers seek jobs in cities.

Japan's waters suffer from over-fishing as well as pollution.

Mineral and Energy Resources

Japan severely lacks mineral resources and has almost no energy resources of its own. Therefore, Japan is the world's largest importer of coal and natural gas and the second-largest importer of oil. The many factories, businesses, and homes require a vast amount of energy that mainly comes from coal, natural gas, and petroleum. Until 2011, Japan got about 25% of its power from nuclear plants. However, an earthquake and tsunami in March of that year caused extensive damage to a nuclear power plant, releasing dangerous radioactivity into the environment. Since then, Japan has shut down all nuclear power plants.

Japan has only small reserves of coal, iron ore, zinc, lead, copper, and other minerals. Its infrastructure does not allow for efficient large-scale mining, so Japan imports these resources more cheaply than mining them.

Manufacturing

Japan's great economic growth comes through its manufacturing. Since World War II, Japan has produced greater numbers, better quality, and more variety of goods, and has done so more and more efficiently than before. Japan's industrial plants rank among the world's largest and most advanced. Japan is home to major brands like Honda, Nissan, and Toyota (all automobiles), Panasonic, and Sony. Japan manufactures technologically advanced motor vehicles, electronics, and tools, as well as ships, chemicals, textiles, and processed foods. A large portion of these goods are exported to other countries. Manufacturing plants typically import components, or pieces, and then assemble them into cars, computers, cameras, televisions, and other goods to sell at a large mark-up.

For a long time, Japan experienced trade surpluses with many other nations. That means the other nations bought more goods from Japan than Japan bought in return. Mainly wealthy countries in North America, Western Europe, and East Asia purchased consumer goods like cars and electronics. When these wealthy nations experienced economic slowdowns, they became uneasy with Japan's surpluses. As a result, the Japanese government eased restrictions on imported goods.

Construction

As Japan rebuilt after the devastation of World War II, construction became an important sector of the economy. Roads, bridges, homes, factories, and buildings needed to be rebuilt. As the population soared, the demand for apartment buildings, offices, and shops increased. By the 1990's, Japan's large construction companies began to expand into other parts of the world, building large projects throughout Asia, the United Kingdom, and the United States.

Services

Over 70% of Japanese workers are employed in the service industry, and this sector accounts for about 70% of the economy. Japan's large population relies on many service workers such as bankers, accountants, teachers, doctors, lawyers, and managers. Many service jobs that require higher education provide good pay and benefits. Workers in small retail shops, theaters, and restaurants earn lower pay and have less job security.

Transportation

Traditionally, the Japanese people traveled mainly on foot, sometimes using small wagons to transport goods. Beginning in the late 1800's, however, railways and iron ships became important means for transporting people and goods. In fact, the development of roads lagged behind car production and resulted in confusing and congested traffic patterns in the growing cities. Today, the huge number of automobiles clogging Japan's urban areas causes problems with pollution, noise, and traffic.

Tunnels and bridges connect all of Japan's major islands, and every major metropolitan area has an airport. The world's first undersea railway tunnel runs between Kyushu and Honshu. Japan is also home to the world's longest suspension bridge—the Akashi Kaikyo Bridge that spans 6,529 feet (1,990 meters) between Honshu and Awaji Island.

Communication

Japan's postal and communication networks are among the best in the world. Almost all citizens have access to the Internet, satellite television and radio, and cellular phones. Every day, Japan publishes about 120 newspapers and every year it publishes tens of thousands of new books. *Manga*, popular comic books for adults and children, have even become popular in the United States. Japanese families that own television sets pay a yearly license fee to the government, which controls broadcasting.

JAPAN'S HISTORY

Japan's long history is quite decisively split into "before" and "after" World War II. For thousands of years before the war, Japan was a very isolated and politically turbulent nation, experiencing periods of war and social stagnation punctuated by periods of peaceful cultural growth. Since the end of the war, Japan has made significant political, social, and economic reforms and has strengthened ties with other nations.

Jomon Period (10,000–300 BCE)

Until fairly recently, historians and archaeologists knew almost nothing about prehistoric Japan. Since World War II, however, thousands of archeological sites have revealed stone tools crafted by the nation's earliest occupants. These people most likely migrated from mainland Asia across land straits that once connected Japan to the Korean peninsula. Around 10,000 BCE this ancient civilization used fire, hunted, and lived in pits or caves in villages of about 50 people. Without any evidence of pottery use, this period has been dubbed the Pre-Ceramic era.

From this early civilization arose the Jomon culture, which left more thorough records of their existence. Their use of pottery and creation of polished tools resemble typical cultures from around the world during this same era. However, the Jomon did not adopt the common practices of agriculture, weaving, or erecting stone monuments. Their highly developed pottery bore the impressions of ropes, giving rise to the name *jomon,* meaning "cord-marked." The Jomon wore clothing made mainly of bark, and jewelry made of seashells, stones, bones, horns, and clay.

Yayoi Era (300 BCE–300 CE)

While the Jomon culture continued to develop, another culture called the Yayoi arose in Kyushu. The more advanced Yayoi spread eastward and eventually overtook the Jomon. Incorporating new technologies from China and Korea, the Yayoi learned to cultivate and irrigate rice in wet paddies. They also used clay, fired at higher temperatures to increase strength, to make wheels. Bronze and iron tools and weapons also came into use during this period. The Yayoi used looms to weave vegetable fibers into cloth for clothing. Ancient burial sites indicate that Yayoi society included class divisions, as some graves are set apart from the others and surrounded by swords, beads, and mirrors.

Kofun Era (300 CE–622 CE)

After the decline of the Yayoi culture around 300 CE, a centuries-long period called the Tumulus, or Tomb, period began. During this time, the Yamato culture arose and united the nation under a king. Their influence spread throughout the Yamato Plain, located southeast of modern Kyoto. They engaged in warfare with Korean kingdoms, erected religious shrines, and exchanged ideas with the Chinese. The Yamato built huge keyhole-shaped tombs, some over 1,000 feet (305 meters) tall, called *kofun* in which to bury their dead. As a result, the era is often known as the Kofun era. Swords, armor, arrowheads, and small clay sculptures called *haniwa* often surround the tombs.

During the 6th century, Yamato royalty began to lose power to various clans. As part of the struggle to reform the government, Prince Shotoku worked to spread Confucian and Buddhist ideals. However, his reforms did not last. After Prince Shotoku's death in 622, a rival family killed his son and the nation fell into a period of turmoil. Reports of the powerful new Tang dynasty in China caused many Japanese to desire a similar powerful central government.

Taika Reforms (645)

This desire was fulfilled in 645 when Japan experienced a complete coup d'état—a violent overthrow of the government. The head of the new imperial household, Kotoku, established himself as emperor and wiped out any forces that opposed the imperial family. Under the emperor, Japanese citizens could no longer own private land. Instead, most people worked as farmers on government land and paid taxes to the government. The emperor also established capital cities and a unified military. These reforms are called the Taika Reforms and they marked a new era of Japan as an independent nation. Most of the influence behind these reforms came from China, which had established systems for organizing society, managing land, and running the government.

Under various emperors, Japan's capital city shifted from Asuka to Nara, with a few other cities in between. Buddhism became more and more important in government and culture. Emperor Shomu, in particular, worked to spread Buddhism throughout the nation and incorporate its ideals into the government. He founded several Buddhist temples, called *kokubunji*, to house monks and nuns who would attend to peoples' spiritual needs. However, the monks became more wealthy and powerful than anticipated, causing problems for the government. Later emperors cut ties with the temples and lessened the influence of Buddhism in matters of state.

Heian Period (794)

In 794, Emperor Kammu again moved the capital to Heian-kyo, modern day Kyoto, giving rise to a period called the Heian Period that lasted several hundred years. A male head of the imperial family ruled as emperor while male heads of noble families filled other government roles. Noble women, who could not hold government positions, often spent time observing nature and writing poetry. This was a largely peaceful time of cultural growth and also indulgence by the wealthy imperial family. Japanese writing developed during this time and the warrior class known as *samurai* also arose. Toward the end of this era, powerful noble families, some of whom intermarried with the imperial family, weakened the emperor and his government.

The crumbling imperial government allowed for the creation of private estates. At first, these were Buddhist temples that functioned independently of the government. Later, they grew to include private citizens who owned land without paying taxes or submitting to government interference. Some estates grew to be huge, requiring the employment of samurai to protect them and maintain order.

First Shogun (Late 1100's)

In the late 1100's, two rival clans, both descended from noble families, clashed over control of the nation. Emperor Kiyomori, of the Taira clan, ruled in a particularly dominant manner. Enemies of his, led by passed-over prince Yoritomo of the Minamoto clan, mounted an uprising. This Gempei War erupted into the largest conflict in Japan to date. After years of fighting, Japan's monarchy ended in the 1180's. In its place, a military government called a *shogunate* began. The capital was relocated to Kamakura in eastern Japan. Yoritomo became the

A statue of famous samurai
Kusunoki Masashige

first *shogun*, or military leader, under the emperor. He put his younger brothers in charge of suppressing the Taira while he increased his own power by taking control of both private estates and public lands. He awarded positions over these estates to nobles who swore their loyalty to him.

The shogunate, however, was an unstable form of government. Over the next 200 years, the imperial government lost influence while private estate owners lost property and power to the shogun's supporters. The Minamoto family lost control to a clan called Hojo and the government in Kamakura fell to the Ashikaga clan. The Ashikaga established a new central government in Kyoto that lasted just over 100 years.

By the 1460's, Japan was reduced to a collection of warring clans with no central authority. Peasant farmers, private estate owners, and Buddhist monks all had to provide for their own protection. Some hired traveling samurai to form small private armies. Other samurai became powerful lords, called *daimyo*, controlling large areas of farmland and armies of warriors. The daimyo fought one another, leading to a long period of civil war in Japan.

During this time in the 1500's, a Christian missionary, Saint Francis Xavier, came to Japan from Portugal. In addition to sharing Christianity, he introduced the Japanese to luxury goods from Portuguese traders. The Japanese had little interest in converting to Christianity, but they eagerly bought European goods. The daimyo, especially, took interest in the advanced weapons and added firearms to aid them in war.

With the new advantage of European guns, a regional lord named Nobunaga brought the capital of Kyoto under his control. By commanding a large military force, he began to bring order to other areas of Japan. After Nobunaga's murder in 1582, Toyotomi Hideyoshi continued his efforts. Hideyoshi made several effective reforms to return order to the nation. He disarmed the peasant farmers, restored control to the disorderly samurai, and reorganized farmlands. With conditions improving in Japan, Hideyoshi even tried twice to invade Korea, but was unsuccessful.

Tokugawa House (1603)

Another noble who had served under Nobunaga, Tokugawa Ieyasu, succeeded Hideyoshi in governing Japan. Given the title of shogun by the emperor, Tokugawa and his family ruled for the next 265 years. Under this system, the shogun carefully shared authority with the daimyo. The shogun controlled about one-fourth of the farmland and oversaw foreign trade, mining, and major cities, including his capital of Edo (now Tokyo). He also maintained a large military and the sole right to issue currency. Approximately 270 daimyo controlled the other three-fourths of the farmland. They ruled over their own domains, known as *han*, where they established laws and collected taxes.

Seclusion Edicts (1630's)

During this time, groups of foreigners began to grow in Japan. Immigrants from Portugal, Spain, England, the Netherlands, and China brought with them their own religious beliefs and economic needs. The shogun saw their presence as a threat, both due to their largely Christian religion and their potential to trade and make individual daimyo more wealthy and powerful. Ieyasu thought that Christians would take sides with Hideyoshi's heir against him, and so took steps to prohibit Christianity.

The policy of outlawing Christianity continued under the following shoguns, even to the point of sacrificing foreign trade. In order to prevent foreign influence from toppling the delicate power structure in Japan, the shogun issued *seclusion edicts* - orders that expelled most foreigners. This policy of *sakoku* (or "closed country") allowed only a few Dutch and Chinese traders to remain, but they were confined to the city of Nagasaki. From this remote location, Japan maintained limited interaction with the European world until the mid-1800's. Even Japanese traders were prohibited from traveling overseas.

A period of isolation and internal growth followed. Japan had cut off most contact with the rest of the world and entered a time of peace after so many centuries of civil war. Japan's economy developed as workers focused on their trades rather than fighting. Farmers and merchants alike learned to save and invest money. Financial firms developed and conducted trade and management operations. In the cities, arts and culture flourished. This period saw the development of distinctly new Japanese art and theater forms, such as *kabuki* (stage drama) and *bunraku* (puppet theater). Edo grew to become one of the largest cities in the world. As urban centers developed, communication and transportation also improved.

The Tokugawa era was not without its problems, however. The strict government discouraged individual freedoms. Its financial problems led to slow development of commercial entities. The feudal system that developed in Japan during this period was among the most rigid in world history. Society was divided into strict classes of warriors, farmers, artisans, and merchants. Women had especially low status, even within their own households. Peasant farmers, suffering poor harvests and harsh lords, joined together to protest. Meanwhile, the samurai became dissatisfied with declining incomes and the inability to improve their social standing.

Japan Opened (1854)

Around 1845, British traders began putting pressure on Japan to open its ports for trade. The Dutch merchants, Japan's only European trading partner at that point, became nervous that the British would cut into their profits. In response, diplomats from the Netherlands made efforts to control the opening of Japanese trade ports. However, the Japanese rulers refused. Over the next few years, British and French warships visited Japan to request trade relationships. Japan increased its defenses, but did not drive away the foreign ships as it had done in the past.

Pressure to open Japan's ports to foreign trade increased with the arrival of U.S. ships in 1846 and 1853. On the latter of these visits, Commodore Matthew C. Perry of the U.S. navy was rebuffed by the shogun. When he returned a year later, negotiations for trade began. By 1858, they succeeded in signing a trade treaty between Japan and the U.S. that opened five Japanese ports to international trade. In addition, it allowed for American citizens to fall under U.S. law while on Japanese soil.

Throughout Japan, the samurai and daimyo held divided opinions about the treaty. Many felt that the agreement was unfair because it granted Americans rights that the Japanese did not receive in return. Some became so enraged that they attacked and killed foreign officials. Others plotted, but failed, to overthrow the shogun government.

Meiji Era (1868–1912)

Sweeping political changes came to Japan in 1868 when imperial rule again replaced the shogunate government. That year, a group of samurai convinced the shogun to resign and restored power to the imperial house. Without the consent of the Japanese people, they acted on the belief that Japan needed to become more secure and competitive with Western powers. A boy emperor named Meiji, or "Enlightened Rule," became the head of the government in a revolution known as the Meiji Restoration. In reality, the leaders who masterminded the revolution ruled the country more so than the young emperor.

As the feudal system of the Tokugawa house crumbled under the combined stresses of foreign influence and internal strife, the new emperor shifted the nation's focus from isolation to unification. He moved into the Tokugawa castle in Edo and changed the city's name to Tokyo. Powerful nations of the West served as Japan's new model for constitutional unity, industrial power, and military strength. The slogan "Enriching the Nation and Strengthening the Military" became Japan's new motto. The

Narita's Gaku-do Hall, erected in 1861

government invested in economic development of the nation, including the development of mines, shipyards, and factories. Eventually, the government was unable to run these industries efficiently. It sold many ventures to private groups typically owned and run by a family. These *zaibatsu*, as they became known, grew to be very large and wealthy while helping the government reach its goals of enriching the nation.

The imperial government persuaded lords to return their extensive lands to control under the throne. The daimyo became governors over newly established prefectures, or were removed from political positions entirely. The samurai were reduced to commoners, and their distinct hairstyle and privilege of carrying swords were abolished. At first, the government paid former samurai an annual pension, but this practice ended in 1876 due to financial strains.

Some samurai found work leading the newly enriched military force. As part of the nation's strategy to increase defenses, the Meiji leadership recruited former farmers to serve as soldiers. It also invested in shipbuilding and weapons. After just two decades, Japan became the top military power in East Asia.

Political changes occurred as a result of the Meiji Restoration. Government leaders established the nation's first Constitution. It set the emperor as the official head of government along with prime ministers, Cabinet members, and a legislature with two houses. It also organized the court system and identified the rights of citizens. While Japanese people gained more freedom to pursue an occupation of their own choosing, they had little power or influence in government. By law, males became head of the household and women's rights were even more limited than they had been in the past.

The final facet of Japan's enrichment was the development of national pride. Toward this end, the government established a public school system, which allowed people to improve their social and economic status. It also served to build a sense of superiority among the people. The government also used religious ideology to build national unity, replacing Buddhism as the top religion with Shinto—a system of beliefs that supported the throne.

The Imperial Palace in Tokyo

Imperialism Begins (1895)

After the Meiji Restoration, the Japanese became strong enough to expand their influence into Taiwan, Korea, and Manchuria by military force. Following the example of other powerful empires, such as Britain, Japan's sense of superiority and desire for growth led to war and imperialism—the rule over a foreign land by force.

Their first victory came against China in 1895, when Japan won a short war to take control of Taiwan. They used this new land acquisition as an agricultural colony, providing the nation with rice and sugar. Then, in 1905, Japan entered into a five-year war against Russia to gain control of Korea. During this time, they also gained ground in Manchuria. Once again, they exploited the new conquest for rice, industry, and workers. The Japanese treated the Koreans poorly and the Koreans resented their colonization.

Japan Enters World War I (1914)

World War I provided further opportunities for Japan to extend its influence. In 1914, Japan took sides with Britain and the Allies against

Germany. As the war effort drew the attention of Western nations away from trade and investment in the East, Japan capitalized on new opportunities. Exporters and manufacturers moved into newly deserted markets in India and other parts of Asia. As Japan's economy boomed, the *zaibatsu* (family businesses) became even larger.

Military Takes Control of Government (1930)

The boom times were short lived. The end of the war brought a renewal of Western trade in India and Asia, cutting into Japan's commercial ventures. Combined with the worldwide economic depression of the late 1920's, Japan's economy suffered. The situation became worse when a massive earthquake struck Tokyo, killing over 140,000 people and causing extensive damage. Meanwhile, strengthened Chinese forces threatened Japan's holdings in Manchuria.

By the 1930's, Japan's leaders could no longer handle the many problems facing the nation. As the prime minister and other officials struggled to maintain control, the military became more powerful and aggressive. In 1931, they took back control of Manchuria. Officials who opposed the army faced threats from nationalist groups—those who sought to build up the nation again. The following year, a group of nationalists assassinated the prime minister and the military took control of the government.

Under new military leadership, Japan sought to increase its territory and influence. As Japanese armies marched through China and Southeast Asia, world powers became concerned. At that time, Nazi Germany and Fascist Italy were causing trouble in the West. Japan's pacts with these two countries set them squarely against the United States and other Allied nations.

World War II (1941–1945)

Japan did not immediately enter into World War II at its start in 1939. Instead, it slowly sent troops into French Indochina. By 1941, Japanese troops had moved further south, causing the United States to take action. When the U.S. cut off exports to Japan, newly instituted Prime Minister General Hideki Tojo prepared for war.

War came suddenly and by surprise in the form of an air strike against U.S. military bases at Pearl Harbor in Hawaii. The Japanese also bombed U.S. bases in other areas of the Pacific, including Guam and the Philippines. Spurred into action by these attacks, the United States entered into war against Japan and its allies, Germany and Italy.

At first, the war with Japan seemed evenly matched. Japan gained ground with victories in Southeast Asia and the South Pacific. The Battle of the Coral Sea, which pitted U.S. and Australian navies against Japan, resulted in somewhat of a draw. Then the U.S. won a decisive victory at the Battle of Midway. Suffering a string of defeats, the Japanese government began to crumble in 1944.

At that point, the United States went after the Japanese homeland, bombing cities and industrial targets, and blocking imports of vital supplies. On August 6, 1945, the United States dropped an atomic bomb on the city of Hiroshima, causing complete devastation. Days later, the United States bombed Nagasaki with an even larger atomic bomb. Meanwhile, Russia jumped on the weakened nation by invading Manchuria and Korea.

Facing inevitable defeat, Emperor Hirohito agreed to surrender on August 14. As the sole condition, he requested that the Allies respect the wishes of the Japanese people to preserve the imperial position of emperor. With that settled, Japanese officials boarded an American battleship and agreed to the terms set forth by the Allies. This included surrender of all Japanese territory in mainland Asia and islands in the Pacific. It reduced Japan to just four main islands and a few smaller surrounding ones. It wasn't until decades later that the United States turned over control of the Bonin Islands, Iwo Jima, and the Ryukyu Islands to Japan. Russia still occupies the Kuril Islands, once Japan's territory.

Japanese Constitution (1946)

After the war, U.S. forces, under the direction of General Douglas MacArthur, occupied Japan to oversee its reforms. The Japanese government remained, but only to carry out the ideals of the American-inspired changes. As part of these changes, more than 5 million Japanese troops were disarmed. Thousands of military leaders and soldiers were tried for war crimes and more than 900 were executed. Others were imprisoned.

MacArthur and his advisors established a new Constitution for Japan. It removed power from the emperor, maintaining him only as a figurehead. A new two-part legislature became the new lawmaking body, and a prime minister, elected by the legislature, became the head of the government. The Constitution also expanded the rights of citizens, especially those of women and children. Occupying forces worked to reorganize and rebuild Japan's social and economic structures. They redistributed farmlands, changed the educational system, and legalized labor unions. With the support of the emperor, the new Constitution was well-received by most Japanese.

Allied occupation continued until April 28, 1952, when Japan signed a peace treaty with 48 nations.

Postwar Period

Despite optimistic reforms, Japan was in bad shape after the war. Bombing had destroyed most large cities and many industrial resources. Most Japanese lost their jobs and lived in poverty. They faced inflation and

Gardens surround Tokyo's Imperial Palace

famine, living in poor conditions in rural villages. With so many trading ships destroyed, Japan was unable to renew trade with foreign partners. In addition, the currency was worth so little it couldn't purchase as much from other nations.

After about a decade of concentrated effort and financial assistance from the United States, Japan began to recover. The nation's strong work ethic, along with wise money management, helped it return to prewar economic levels by the mid-1950's. People began moving back to cities, leaving farming for service and industry jobs. Even the imperial house eased into modern times with Crown Prince Akihito marrying a commoner in 1959 and Emperor Hirohito leaving the country in 1971 for a first-ever royal visit to Western Europe.

Modern Challenges

In 1989, Emperor Akihito began his reign in a time of political and economic turmoil. The Liberal Democratic Party (LDP), which had been the ruling political party since the 1950's, became corrupt. The next decade saw several changes with respect to party influence and coalitions.

Meanwhile, Japan's strong currency, high labor costs, and high real estate values made its manufactured goods expensive for foreign trade partners. Consumers began to favor low-priced goods from developing nations over Japan's exports. In addition, the banking system suffered from loans that defaulted due to a drop in real estate prices in the 1990's. Like many other nations at the time, Japan entered an economic recession. Unemployment rose, spending declined, and incomes stopped growing.

In 2001, dynamic leader Junichiro Koizumi became prime minister, promising economic reforms that would revive the nation. He was succeeded by Shinzo Abe in 2006, who resigned shortly thereafter due to a series of scandals. After several changes in leadership, including 11 different prime ministers in 13 years, Abe again rose to the position of prime minister in 2012. He has continued working for economic reform in Japan.

In March of 2011, Japan suffered the devastating effects of the most powerful earthquake to ever hit the nation, just off the coast of Honshu. It triggered a tsunami—a 23-foot ocean wave—that flooded cities and rural areas. It swept away homes, trains, cars, and people, leaving a path of complete destruction. As a result of the tsunami, a nuclear power plant leaked dangerous radioactivity into the environment. In addition, some 16,000 people were killed and thousands of others went missing.

Flag of Japan

RUSSIA: THE BIG PICTURE

As the world's largest country, Russia spans Eastern Europe and all of northern Asia. It stretches from the Baltic Sea in the west to the Pacific Ocean in the east, and from the Arctic Ocean in the north to the Black Sea in the south. This huge expanse of land provides an abundant source of crops and materials, but its extreme climate makes daily life difficult. Vast stores of petroleum, natural gas, coal, and iron ore lie spread out across the country, but are often far from populated areas or difficult to access due to cold weather.

The capital city of Moscow, located in the far west, is Russia's largest city. Further north, on the Baltic Sea coast, Saint Petersburg is the nation's largest seaport. Russia's cities are crowded with three-fourths of the population. Urban dwellers enjoy better education and health care than those in rural areas, but also experience greater problems with crime, pollution, and overcrowding.

Most Russians descended from a group of early Slavic people called the Russians, though the nation is also home to many minority ethnic groups. The East Slavs formed a Russian state in Europe in the 800's. This state eventually gained huge amounts of territory and various people groups. For centuries, *czars*, or emperors, ruled the people. The czars controlled almost every aspect of Russian life, resulting in a time of slow economic development among a poor, uneducated population. By the

sia

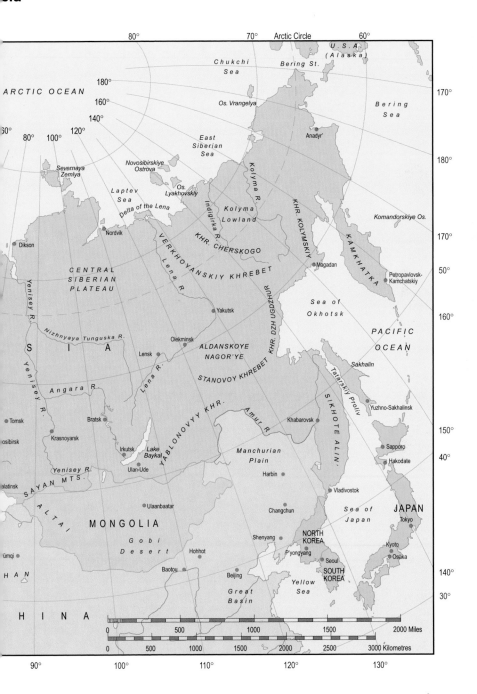

ARCTIC OCEAN

80°   70°   Arctic Circle   60°

Chukchi
Sea

Bering St.

U.S.A.
(A l a s k a)

180°
160°
140°
120°

Os. Vrangelya

Bering
Sea

170°

80°   100°

East
Siberian
Sea

Anadyr'

180°

Severnaya
Zemlya

Novosibirskiye
Ostrova

Komandorskiye Os.

170°

Laptev
Sea

Os.
Lyakhovskiy

Kolyma
Lowland

KHR. KOLYMSKIY

Delta of the Lena

Nordvik

Kolyma R.

Indigirka R.

KHR. CHERSKOGO

K A M C H A T K A

50°

Dikson

CENTRAL
SIBERIAN
PLATEAU

VERKHOYANSKIY KHREBET

Lena R.

Magadan

Petropavlovsk-
Kamchatskiy

160°

Yenisey R.

Yakutsk

Sea of
Okhotsk

PACIFIC

Nizhnyaya Tunguska R.

Olekminsk

ALDANSKOYE
NAGOR'YE

KHR. DZH UGDZHUR

OCEAN

S   I   A

Lensk

Lena R.

Sakhalin

Yenisey R.

Angara R.

STANOVOY KHREBET

Tatarskiy Proliv

Tomsk

Bratsk

YABLONOVYY KHR.

Amur R.

Khabarovsk

Yuzhno-Sakhalinsk

150°

osibirsk

Krasnoyarsk

Irkutsk   *Lake*
          Baykal

Manchurian
Plain

S I K H O T E   A L I N'

Sapporo

40°

Ulan-Ude

Harbin

Hakodate

alatinsk

Yenisey R.

SAYAN MTS.

Vladivostok

Sea of
Japan

JAPAN

A L T A I

Ulaanbaatar

Changchun

Tokyo

úmqi

MONGOLIA

Shenyang

NORTH
KOREA

Kyoto

H A N

Gobi
Desert

Hohhot

P'yongyang

Osaka

Baotou

Seoul

H I N A

Beijing

Yellow
Sea

SOUTH
KOREA

140°

Great
Basin

30°

0   500   1000   1500   2000 Miles

0   500   1000   1500   2000   2500   3000 Kilometres

90°   100°   110°   120°   130°

early 1900's, revolutionaries, fed up with the imbalance of power, overthrew the czars. Russia became the largest and most influential nation of the Russian Soviet Federative Socialist Republic (R.S.F.S.R.) and later the Union of Soviet Socialist Republics (U.S.S.R.), or Soviet Union.

Russia became independent on August 24, 1991 after the fall of the Soviet Union. The recent downfall of Soviet-style Communism has brought economic, political, and legal changes. Russia's middle-class is now growing after a long and difficult history of a powerful few ruling over the poor masses. The nation has worked to transition from an economy controlled by the state to one based on private enterprise. It now belongs to a federation of republics called the Commonwealth of Independent States.

MEET THE PEOPLE OF RUSSIA

More than three quarters of the people of Russia are ethnic Russians. Other ethnic groups, which number more than 190, include Tatar (3.7%), Ukrainian (1.4%), Bashkir (1.1%), Chuvash (1%), and Chechen (1%). In Russia, Jews are considered a nationality group rather than a religious group. Having faced historic discrimination, many Jews now live in self-governing regions of Russia, or have moved out of the country. Some minority groups of

Fast Facts

Capital:
Moscow

Size:
1st in the world

Area:
6,592,735 sq miles
(10,610,000 sq km)

Coastline:
23,396 miles (37,652 km)

Highest Point:
Mount Elbrus 18,481 feet
(5,633 m)

Lowest Point:
Caspian Sea -92 feet
(-28 m)

Population:
142 million

Official Language:
Russian

Currency:
Russian rubles

National Anthem:
"Gimm Rossiyskoy Federatsii" (National Anthem of the Russian Federation)

National Symbol:
bear, double-headed eagle

indigenous peoples live in remote parts of the far north, where they have forged a way of life in the extreme cold.

Historically, Slavs lived in Eastern Europe thousands of years ago. They split into three groups based on migration patterns, with the East Slavs settling around present-day Moscow in the 800's. Since then, Moscow has been at the heart of Russia's growth and activity. Beginning in the 1500's, Russia began to expand and colonize other areas, adding ethnic groups. Today, most Russians live in the European portion of the country, especially in the area around Moscow. In the last century, however, many Russians have migrated from the west to Siberia in the east. Although Siberia makes up three-fourths of Russia's area, it is home to only about one-fifth of the nation's population.

Russians primarily speak Russian, with just 4% of the population speaking other primary languages such as Dolgang, German, Chechen, or Tatar. The Russian language is the same throughout the country, though different regions have slightly different accents. It is written in the Cyrillic alphabet, which has 33 characters.

Despite being the world's largest nation, Russia's population is only the 10th largest in the world. The low population is likely due to the fact that Russia has one of the lowest birth rates and highest death rates in the world.

LAND, WATER, AND CLIMATE IN RUSSIA

The massive country of Russia covers all of northern Asia and part of Europe. At just over 6,592,735 square miles (10,610,000 square km), it is nearly twice the size of Canada, the world's next largest country. Such a vast expanse of land incorporates a variety of terrain and climates, from tall mountains to flat plains and from deserts to deep forests and Arctic tundra.

Northern Russia has a long coastline along the Arctic Ocean. Its eastern coast borders the North Pacific Ocean. To the west and south, Russia shares over 13,670 miles (22,000 km) of land boundaries with 14 countries, including Kazakhstan, China, Mongolia, and Ukraine. The nation also includes a small detached portion of land, called Kaliningrad, located near

Poland. The European portion of Russia is divided from the Asian portion by the Ural Mountains that run north to south.

Land

At its widest point, Russia spans 5,592 miles (9,000 km) from east to west. To cross by train takes a full week. The nation's 9 time zones mean that Russians on the east coast go to bed while those in the west enjoy lunch. This huge area gives Russia a variety of landforms.

West of the Ural Mountains lies a broad plain with low hills known as the European Plain. Most of the European part of Russia, along with most of the country's population, lies in this region. It is home to much industrial activity, though it has fewer natural resources than other regions. The north is heavily forested while the south has largely been cleared for agriculture. Overall, the European Plain averages 590 feet (180 meters) above sea level. At the southern edge, the Caucasus Mountains span the border with Georgia between the Black Sea and Caspian Sea. Europe's tallest peak, Mount Elbrus at 18,481 feet (5,633 meters), is part of this mountain range.

The Ural Mountains separate the European part of Russia from the Asian part. They contain rich deposits of natural resources, including iron, copper, and other metals. Large cities like Yekaterinburg and Chelyabinsk have developed around industries in the middle section of this mountainous region.

East of the Ural Mountains lies the massive area of Siberia, which is separated into a western plain, a central plateau, and an eastern upland. The West Siberian Plain is the world's largest (1 million square miles) (2,590,000 square km) flat region (no higher than 500 feet [152 meters] above sea level). Though it tends to be marshy due to poor drainage, crops grow in the south. It also contains rich deposits of oil and natural gas. The Central Siberian Plateau averages 2,000 feet (610 meters) above sea level, with higher mountain ranges in the south. It experiences extreme temperatures, both high and low. The East Siberian Uplands stretch across the easternmost part of the nation and include some islands in the Pacific Ocean. Here, mountains rise to 10,000 feet (3,048 meters) and, along with the harsh climate, make mining the valuable mineral resources difficult.

Russia experiences some volcanic activity in the Kuril Islands, a chain of over 50 islands in the Pacific Ocean. The Kamchatka Peninsula, just north of the Kuril Islands, also experiences volcanic activity and earthquakes. Among its 29 historically active volcanoes is Kliuchevskoi, which erupted in 2007 and 2010. Spring floods, along with summer and autumn forest fires, occur regularly throughout Siberia and parts of European Russia.

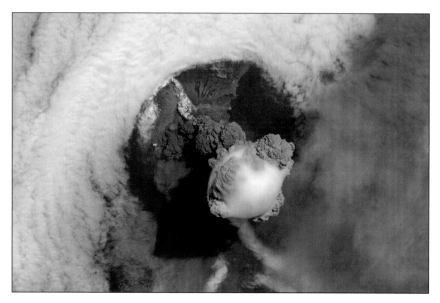

In 2009, Sarychev Peak in the Kuril Islands erupted

Water

Russia is home to approximately 2 million saltwater and freshwater lakes. Lake Baikal, the deepest lake in the world, holds approximately one fifth of the world's fresh water. Lake Ladoga, near Saint Petersburg, is Europe's largest lake. Russia's southern border touches the Caspian Sea, the world's largest inland body of water.

Russia also has many extensive river systems. The Volga River, which runs north to south through central Russia, is Europe's longest river. It carries more than half of Russia's waterway traffic. The Lena River, Russia's longest river, stretches 2,734 miles (4,400 km) to the Arctic Ocean. Though

Russia's rivers, lakes, and canals are important avenues of transportation, many are frozen for much of the year.

Climate

From north to south, Russia measures up to 2,500 miles (4,000 km). This creates a series of wide climate bands that stretch horizontally across the country and give Russia the widest range of temperatures in the world. The northernmost zone is Arctic desert, followed by tundra, a treeless plain with short summers and very cold, long winters. Further south lies a large area of forest. The colder forest area, known as the taiga, consists of coniferous, or cone-bearing, trees such as pine, fir, spruce, and cedar. It is home to some forest animals, but its poor soil makes the taiga unsuitable for farming. South of the taiga, forests contain more deciduous trees, or those that lose their leaves in the winter. Here, the climate is milder and the soil is better for farming. The southern half of the nation consists of wooded steppe, large flatlands, mountains, and semidesert. Steppes are grassy plains that contain Russia's most fertile soil, called *chernozem*. The mountains and semidesert of the far south range from dry lowlands to dense vegetation, depending on the elevation.

Winters in Russia vary from cool along the Black Sea coast to frigid in Siberia while summers vary from warm in the steppes to cool along the Arctic coast. Spring and autumn are very short seasons of rapid change from one extreme to another. Russia recorded the world's lowest temperature outside of Antarctica when Oymyakon reached -96° F. This intense cold creates permafrost, a layer of subsoil that remains frozen year-round, covering almost 4 million square miles (6,437,380 square km) of the country. Permafrost makes construction difficult and leads to spring flooding because melting snow cannot seep into the frozen soil. The cold also means that evaporation occurs slowly, so moisture accumulates, creating abundant rivers, lakes, and swamps. High temperatures above 100° F have also occurred in the summer.

Precipitation is generally low across the country, except in a few areas. The Pacific coast experiences summer monsoons—moisture-rich winds that bring heavy rains. Some mountain regions also receive over 40 inches (101 cm) of precipitation per year. Most of Russia is covered in snow between 40 and 250 days per year.

EVERYDAY LIFE IN RUSSIA

Family Life

Everyday life in Russia has changed greatly since the 1990's. Under Soviet rule, the government controlled almost every aspect of life, including work, education, religion, and the arts. Today, people have more freedom and more options to choose from in almost all areas of life.

City Life

Most Russians (74%) live in urban areas, the largest of which is Moscow, with a population of over 12 million. Five other cities have populations over a million, including Saint Petersburg at almost 5 million. The largest cities are closely congregated around industrial areas, while smaller cities are spread out through mining areas and smaller industrial areas.

Private ownership of property in Russian cities is a fairly new development that is spreading slowly. Under Soviet rule, the state owned all urban housing and property. People lived mainly in plain, high-rise apartments. In these small apartments, families often shared kitchens and bathrooms with other tenants. Rents were very low, so the government did not keep up with maintenance. As a result, many buildings became run-down. After the bombings of World War II, Russia experienced a severe shortage of housing, and apartments became even more crowded.

Once ownership transferred from the state to individuals, conditions began to improve. Apartment sizes increased, many new homes were built, and buildings were maintained in better condition. Some cities remain crowded, with people living in plain apartments. In other areas, wealthy Russians have begun building luxury apartments and large homes. Despite the shift from total communism to some capitalism, urban-dwellers in Russia still face shortages. Food, services, and consumer goods are often in short supply or too expensive for most people to afford. People in cities also face problems of crime and pollution.

Urban life in modern Moscow

Country Life

As young people move from rural areas to cities, the rural areas are left with a population of mostly elderly people. Villagers usually live near collective farms where people work together, though individual farms have increased since the end of Soviet rule.

During the Soviet era, some people in rural areas could own their own homes, but the size was strictly limited. Today, some single-family homes in small towns still lack indoor plumbing, gas, or electricity. In the country, education, health care, and cultural life is also of lower quality than in the city.

Recreation

Since World War II, Russians have increased their involvement and achievements in sports. Soviet athletes first participated in the Olympic Games in the 1950's, dominating in ice hockey, volleyball, wrestling, boxing, weightlifting, and gymnastics. Soccer has also become very popular in Russia, with three professional men's divisions and growing participation among women. During the Soviet era, its ice hockey team won 20 world championships from 1954-1991. Today, many of Russia's top hockey players play for the North American National Hockey League (NHL), though Russia's professional league is also popular.

Average citizens in Russia often lack facilities and equipment to participate in sports, but enjoy active lives outdoors. Many people enjoy jogging, fishing, hiking, and bicycling. Some have country cottages, or *dachas*, where they can get away from the city and enjoy the outdoors. In the summer, some Russians vacation at resorts along the Black Sea, Baltic Sea, Volga River, and in Siberia.

Outside of sports, Russia dominates the world in competitive chess. Beginning in the early 1900's, the state identified and trained promising children to become professional chess champions. Russians also enjoy reading, watching television and movies, walking, and visiting museums.

Education

In Soviet-era Russia, state-controlled education was very rigid and focused on Communist ideals. Students crowded into run-down school buildings with few resources. Today, the federal government still controls the licensing of teachers, distribution of textbooks, and awarding of diplomas. In addition, it oversees requirements for language, math, and science education. Smaller regional offices control school finances as well as other educational areas, such as history, humanities, and social sciences. New private schools, once banned by the Soviet government, are now opening in Russia. The nation also has many special schools for students who are gifted, or who have physical or learning disabilities.

Russia has a very high literacy rate, due to free public education and the high value placed on learning. Most students attend preschool and kindergarten. After that, they must complete nine years of education and receive a general education certificate. Almost all students continue on for two or three years of secondary education and beyond. Others attend vocational schools to learn a trade. Students who do not speak Russian can learn in their own language at the primary level. However, Russian is required at the secondary level and degrees are only awarded in Russian, Bashkir, and Tatar. The most popular foreign language taught in Russia is English.

Students compete to enter highly-selective schools of higher education where a degree usually takes five years. Russia has a long history of top-level math and science education. Its Moscow State University began in 1755. Along with universities in Saint Petersburg and Kazan, Moscow State University produced world-class mathematicians and scientists. Since the fall of communism, the number of universities has grown, and these schools offer a wider variety of subject matter than before. However, universities are often expensive and suffer from funding shortages.

Outside of school, Russians can learn at the hundreds of museums and thousands of libraries. Moscow is home to the State Historical Museum, the nation's main collection of historical artifacts, and the State Central Museum of Contemporary History of Russia, which focuses on the Russian Revolution. Saint Petersburg houses one of the world's largest collections of art in the Hermitage Museum. Public libraries exist in almost every town, and private organizations such as schools, labor unions, and civic organizations also have libraries.

Religion

With no official religion, the nation is not very religious. About 15–20% of the population are Russian Orthodox and roughly 10–15% are Muslim. However, these estimates count only believers who actively practice their faith. Because Russia experienced over 70 years of Soviet rule which banned religious freedom, many believers are non-practicing.

The Russian Orthodox Church formed in the 10th century, when Prince Vladimir I converted to Christianity. It remained dominant for almost 1,000 years until Communists took power and restricted religion. Since the 1980's, Russians have regained much religious freedom

A Russian Orthodox church in Moscow

131

and the Russian Orthodox Church continues as the major religious organization. Christmas is celebrated by the Russian Orthodox Church on January 7, which is a national holiday.

Religions that were recognized by the Soviet Union continue to have freedom in Russia. These include Buddhism, Islam, Judaism, and some Christian denominations. Other religions or denominations that did not register before the fall of the Soviet Union cannot publish religious literature or operate religious schools. These groups include Baptists, Mormons, and Roman Catholics. They must register every year for 15 years before the government grants them more freedoms. Although laws exist restricting these religions, the government has not enforced them strictly.

Health Care

Russia uses public funds to pay for the health and welfare needs of its people. Under communism, these programs were funded by the central government. Today, employers, state governments, and trade unions contribute to the costs. Citizens receive free health care, along with job training, pensions, and scholarships. Workers receive up to a month of paid vacation time annually.

Compared to the rest of the world, Russia has fairly low rates of obesity, but high infant mortality. The life expectancy dropped sharply in the 1990's, after the fall of Communist controls. This drop was largely due to poor nutrition, inadequate health care, smoking, alcoholism, and pollution. Infectious diseases that had been wiped out in the past returned. Cancer, tuberculosis, and heart disease reached all-time highs as hospitals suffered from the lack of funding, training, and resources. A low birth rate also contributed to an aging population, which brings with it health concerns.

Today, Russia's life expectancy and the state of its health care are improving. However, alcoholism remains a major problem, especially among men. An estimated one-third of men and one-sixth of women in Russia have an alcohol addiction. The problem can be traced back decades to when Soviet-era Russia used vodka, a strong alcohol, as a form of currency. When food, money, and consumer goods became scarce, people traded vodka because it was easy to transport and didn't spoil. The government is now working to combat the alcohol problem.

RUSSIA'S GOVERNMENT

The Russian Federation, formed in 1991, grew out of the Russian Empire and Russian Soviet Federative Socialist Republic (R.S.F.S.R.). It is a federation in which partially self-governing states fall under a central government. The United States does not recognize Russia's annexation of Ukraine's Autonomous Republic of Crimea, which occurred in 2014. After the Soviet Union dissolved in 1991, Russia formed a loose partnership with other former Soviet republics called the Commonwealth of Independent States (C.I.S.).

Prior to the formation of the Russian Federation, the R.S.F.S.R. completely dominated Russian politics. The Communist Party of the Soviet Union, the only legal political party, held all governmental power and chose all leaders. In the late 1980's, President Mikhail Gorbachev began a series of changes known as *perestroika*, or "restructuring." These changes gradually gave greater freedoms to individuals and reduced government control of the economy. In 1990, other political groups began to form, including the Democratic Russia Movement—a collection of political parties that supported democracy over Communism.

In 1988, citizens voted for a Congress of People's Deputies in an election that involved real choice, rather than only candidates chosen by the Communist Party. In 1991, Boris Yeltsin became the first democratically elected president as the Soviet Union dissolved into independent countries. He continued to lead the country through its transition until 1999. With the end of the Soviet Union, the Democratic Russia Movement broke off into many separate political parties. Despite new freedoms, the Communist Party remained popular and won many seats in government.

Russia's new Constitution, adopted in 1993, calls for a president to serve no more than two consecutive four-year terms. The president appoints the prime minister, some judges, and cabinet members. The legislature consists of a Federal Assembly, made up of the Federation Council and the State Duma. The Federation Council is made up of local government officials who are elected or appointed by local government bodies. The 450 members of the State Duma are elected by the people, with the most popular political parties receiving the most seats. All laws must pass through the State Duma before going before the Federation Council. The Federation Council also approves the president's appointments to office. The Russian Constitution provides citizens with welfare, social security, pensions, free health care, and affordable housing. In addition, all citizens 18 and older have the right to vote.

In Russia, smaller regional governments work under the central government. However, they tend to lack the tax revenue to support basic services like wages for teachers and police. Adding to their challenges, huge portions of regional budgets go toward pensions.

The Russian president is commander in chief of the armed forces, which include an army, navy, air force, and strategic rocket force. All men over age 18 must serve in the military, though many avoid service, and women may volunteer to serve. Russia has one of the largest armed forces in the world, at 750,000 active servicemen, and possesses nuclear weapons. In 2010, President Vladimir Putin began efforts to strengthen the military by increasing spending. Russia also has intelligence agencies, a government security service, a Federal Border Service, and many private security forces. These organizations help combat crimes across borders and within Russia, where organized crime increased greatly after the fall of communism.

COMMUNISM

Communism is a political and economic ideology. That means communist beliefs affect all aspects of government, citizens' rights, property, resources, production, and more. It is based on public, rather than private, ownership and government control of most major industries.

Communist governments are dominated by a single political party that adheres strictly to communist ideals. They own all of a country's means of production—factories, mines, etc.—as well as the land. Although it promises to provide financial security and economic equality for all, communism generally results in a fairly poor population with a few extremely wealthy leaders.

In the 1800's, Karl Marx published his radical ideas about government in *The Communist Manifesto* and *Das Kapital*. These writings criticized capitalism—the economic system in which private citizens own the means of production and set prices.

Russian revolutionary leader Vladimir Lenin developed Marx's ideas further. He claimed that European capitalists were only successful because of imperialism—the unfair exertion of

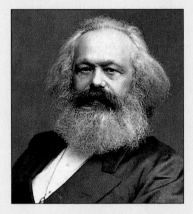

Karl Marx

power over other countries. Europeans practiced imperialism by producing goods cheaply in African and Asian colonies. By taking advantage of low-wage workers, capitalists kept prices low in Europe. In 1917, Lenin's Bolshevik party overthrew the Russian government and established the world's first Communist state. In the years after Lenin's death, the Union of Soviet Socialist Republics (U.S.S.R) grew in size and power. It helped establish Communist governments throughout Eastern Europe and in China.

Under communism, the Soviet Union built up a huge military, created more jobs, and improved education. Income disparity—the difference between earnings of the rich and the poor—was lower than in capitalist countries. However, communism also had its downsides. Factories produced low-quality goods that did not reflect changing tastes of consumers. Prices

Vladimir Lenin

set by the government did not accurately relate to costs, which resulted in waste. Workers, paid equally regardless of skill or effort, had no reason to innovate or increase production. This led to shortages in food, housing, and other goods. While average citizens experienced a low standard of living, government officials enjoyed perks that let them live above the level of their comparable income. These included government cars, better health care, a variety of abundant food, and more luxurious housing.

Communism also led to restrictions of personal freedoms. In the single-party system, opposition to communist ideals is often strictly forbidden. Citizens are not allowed to express criticism of the government or form organizations to resist communism. Religion is also frowned upon as a possible threat to communism.

The Decline of Communism

This rapid growth of communism through the 1940's alarmed non-communist countries. Many, including the United States, took steps to prevent its spread. The Cold War—a tense but largely non-violent conflict between Communist and non-communist countries—continued until the early 1990's. It involved forming alliances and providing aid to countries to either help spread or resist communism.

The Cold War ended when Communist governments in Eastern Europe and the Soviet Union collapsed, as a consequence of the huge middle class becoming disappointed by the failed promises of communism. Political corruption and slow economic growth also contributed to the weakening of Communist governments. Capitalist economies in Japan, the United States, and much of Europe, had become the dominant industrial powers. The Soviet Union and Communist countries in Eastern Europe could no longer compete.

This left China, Cuba, North Korea, Vietnam, and just a few other countries with Communist governments.

Communism in Russia

Russia instituted a Communist form of government before any other country. Its agriculture-based system differed from Marx's vision of a highly industrialized nation focused on manufacturing. However, after experiencing widespread starvation due to bad harvests, unhappy Russians began to embrace Marx's radical ideas about government.

Interest in Marxism grew with the formation of the Russian Social Democratic Labor Party in 1898. Within five years, the organization split in two over political disagreements. The Mensheviks favored more democratic methods and a large membership. The Bolsheviks, who followed Lenin, supported a smaller revolutionary-led Communist party.

Amid the problems caused by World War I (1914-1918), Russians overthrew their czar and established a temporary democratic government in 1917. That same year, Lenin and his Bolsheviks seized power, even though they were relatively small in number. Lenin established a Communist government, withdrew the nation from World War I, and made immediate changes to all aspects of Russian life.

Under Lenin, the government took control of most agricultural production, all industry, and factories. The government's secret police, known as the Cheka, helped enforce the adoption of the Communist system. These changes were not readily accepted, and Russia entered a period of civil war as non-communists fought against Communists for control of government. Though Lenin defeated his rivals, after all of the fighting and economic changes, the nation was a disaster .

Facing possible economic collapse, Lenin relented in his use of force and terror and presented his New Economic Policy (NEP) in 1921. Under the NEP, the state cooperated more fully with business owners and others. Though the economy began to recover, the government continued to have just one political party—the Communists—which controlled all public organizations, such as labor unions. In 1922, Russia and other Communist countries formed the Union of Soviet Socialist Republics (U.S.S.R.), or the Soviet Union.

After Lenin's death in 1924, Joseph Stalin rose to power as head of the Communist Party and the Soviet government. His 25-year reign was even harsher than Lenin's and he became known as the leader who ruled with an iron fist. Stalin's economic plans included combining small farms owned by peasants into large government-controlled collectives.

Millions of farmers who resisted this change were either exiled or murdered. Although the Soviet Union's economy and power grew under Stalin, life became extremely difficult for citizens, who began to protest. Stalin responded to such opposition with the Great Purge, which consisted of arresting and executing anyone suspected of being "enemies of the people." From 1936-1938, Stalin's secret police helped carry out this program of terror, effectively removing all political opponents.

Nikita Khrushchev became head of the Soviet Communist Party and of the Soviet government after Stalin's death in 1953. He opposed Stalin's use of terror and force. He eased government control over writers, artists, and scholars. He attempted to reform the economy, but made little impact. In 1964, the Communist Party replaced Khrushchev with Leonid Brezhnev, who once again increased government control over the economy and culture. His changes remained in place through two more brief changes in leadership.

In 1985, Mikhail Gorbachev took over as leader of the Soviet Union. At this point, Russia's economy continued to suffer and the nation fell behind other world powers. The government had trouble maintaining its huge military, and the people had become very dissatisfied with communism. In response, Gorbachev began to restructure Soviet political and economic systems via a program called *perestroika* or restructuring. People enjoyed greater freedom and choice, relations with the West improved, and the economy began to recover.

In 1990, voters chose Gorbachev as president of the U.S.S.R. and he suspended all activities of the Communist Party. Over the next few years, most republics of the U.S.S.R., including Russia, declared independence. The Soviet Union collapsed and Communism in that area came to an end.

RUSSIAN CULTURE

Russia consists of a huge territory that has included a wide variety of cultures over the course of its long history. As a result, its culture borrows from many foreign influences. The earliest of these were the Slavs, Byzantines, and Mongols. By the 1700's, European influence became stronger and Russia started to make contributions to art and culture that were recognized and honored around the world.

Under the reign of Peter I (Peter the Great), Russia experienced a cultural renaissance, or reawakening, due to an inflow of Western ideas. This led to great advancements and achievements in many artistic areas. Today, Russia is known for its contributions to classical music, ballet, drama, and literature. It is home to many world-renowned museums, operas, orchestras, and dance companies.

The famous architecture and artwork of Saints Peter and Paul Cathedral in Saint Petersburg

Painting

One of history's most famous icons, *Old Testament Trinity* by Andrei Rublev, has remained in Moscow since 1410. An icon is a religious painting that Eastern Orthodox Christians consider sacred. Icons must follow strict style guidelines. Artists broke from this mold after the Renaissance of the 1700's to produce a wider variety of visual arts. Among the most famous of these artists is Marc Chagall, who painted whimsical images that defy logic. Under communism, however, artists were mainly restricted to producing portraits of Russian Communist Party leader Vladimir Lenin throughout the 1900's.

Literature

Before the modern era, Russia's first full autobiography *The Life of the Archpriest Avvakum, by Himself,* was published around 1672. In the early 1700's, poets developed classical meters that continue to be popular today. Authors wrote the first tragedies, comedies, and works of fiction based on the European style. In the 1800's, Aleksandr Pushkin arose as Russia's national poet. Novels by Fyodor Dostoyevsky and Leo Tolstoy, published around this same time period, have remained classic works of literature around the world. Later authors attempted to comment on social and political problems of communism, but were strictly censored by the government.

Performing Arts

Russia's first school of ballet began in 1734 and was heavily influenced by French and Italian styles. Until the 1900's, all dancers and actors worked for the government and received harsh treatment. Nevertheless, Russian ballet became the gold standard of dance, drawing many dancers and choreographers to work for Russian Imperial Theaters. Throughout Soviet rule, Russian ballet continued to thrive, producing international stars such as Rudolf Nureyev and Mikhail Baryshnikov. Puppet theater and circus performances also became popular and continue to draw crowds and international acclaim.

Music

Russian music broke away from folk and religious styles in the 1700's, when Empress Anna Ivanovna welcomed an Italian opera troupe to entertain her. Over the next 200 years, Russian musicians and composers developed a rich musical tradition. The most famous of these, Peter Tchaikovsky, composed *Swan Lake*, *The Nutcracker*, and *The Sleeping Beauty* in the late 1800's. Shortly after that, Sergei Rachmaninoff and Igor Stravinsky also became famous for classical music and ballet scores.

Fashion

Traditional Russian clothing is rarely seen anymore, except during some special occasions in rural areas. It consists of brightly embroidered shirts, blouses, and headwear. Shoes were woven from *bast*, a fiber that comes from tree bark.

Under Soviet rule, Russians had few options for clothing. Most wore plain clothing in limited styles and owned only a few outfits. Since the 1970's, Russia's markets have opened to imported clothing of higher quality and more varied styles, and Russian manufacturers have worked to keep up. Now, people dress fashionably, though their choices are restricted by the high cost of clothing and the cold winters.

Food and Drink

Traditional Russian cuisine centers on cabbage, potatoes, carrots, sour cream, and apples. The famous Russian soup *borsch* is made from beets. Another popular soup, *okroshka*, is made from stale black bread, cucumbers, boiled eggs, and sausage. Main dishes based on beef, chicken, pork, and fish round out the traditional hearty Russian diet. Dishes such as *Beef Stroganoff* (beef sautéed with onions, mushrooms, and sour cream sauces) and *blinis* (salmon and sour cream pancakes) have become popular around the world. Foods are often fried and prepared with lots of sugar. Recently, packaged, processed foods and Western "fast foods" have become increasingly popular. Russians tend to eat a breakfast of eggs, sausage, porridge, bread, and jam followed by a large midday meal and a light supper.

Russians enjoy drinking tea or coffee with their meals, and the nation is famous for its vodka, a strong alcohol. In Russia, a swig of straight vodka is usually followed by a salty piece of fish, a sour cucumber, a pickled mushroom, or a piece of rye bread with butter. In summer, Russians often drink *kvass*, a type of beer made from fermented black bread. Although Russians frown upon public intoxication, alcohol abuse has long been a major social problem.

Saint Basil's Cathedral in Moscow

Peterhof Palace was once the summer palace of Peter I

Architecture

On Moscow's Red Square stands the famous Cathedral of St. Basil the Blessed, a combination of Byzantine and Asian architectural influences easily identified by its onion-shaped domes. Built in the mid-1500's by Czar Ivan IV (the Terrible), it commemorates the Russian capture of the Tatar capital.

Saint Isaac's Cathedral in Saint Petersburg

The Cathedral of the Resurrection of Christ in Saint Petersburg

142

In 1703, Czar Peter I founded the city of Saint Petersburg and had Italian and French architects design it. The Great Palace at Peterhof is an example of this Western European style.

Though Russia boasts many famous churches and cathedrals, its tradition of beautiful architecture also shows up in the railway terminals of the late 1800's. The Kremlin, a collection of buildings in Moscow, includes famous churches, palaces, and museums built between the late 1400's and mid-1900's.

The Lena River Delta is Russia's largest protected wilderness area

RUSSIA'S WILDLIFE

Animal life and vegetation vary throughout Russia depending on latitude (northern or southern) and elevation. Northern tundra areas are generally swampy and barren, with just a few mosses and shrubs growing. Indigenous people herd reindeer in the tundra, and other animals, including Arctic foxes, musk oxen, beavers, and owls, also survive there. In summer, waterfowl live near the Arctic Ocean. Further south, the taiga is home to dense forests and squirrels, foxes, ermines, elks, bears, muskrat, and wolves. The warmer deciduous forests and wooded steppe have been cleared somewhat for agriculture, but some provide homes for forest animals. Open

143

areas of the steppe provide little shelter for animals, but burrowing rodents survive there, along with skunks, foxes, wolves, and antelope.

THE ECONOMY OF RUSSIA

Although Russia is the largest country in the world, its location in relation to major sea lanes of the world is unfavorable. In addition, much of the country lacks proper soils and climates (either too cold or too dry) for agriculture. Even the nation's rich stores of valuable natural resources are often difficult to extract and ship due to their location and the harsh climate. These factors, combined with Russia's Communist past, have made it 7th in the world in Gross Domestic Product (GDP), a measurement of goods and services produced in a country. Its economy is growing slowly compared to other industrialized countries.

Russia's labor force of 75 million is the 8th largest in the world. The nation has 5% unemployment, though an aging population is causing concerns over possible labor shortages in the future. Approximately 11% of the population live below the poverty line.

Russia is the world's 10th largest exporter, providing other countries with petroleum and petroleum products, natural gas, metals, wood and wood products, chemicals, and a wide variety of manufactured goods. It is also the 19th largest importer, purchasing machinery, vehicles, pharmaceutical products, plastic, semi-finished metal products, meat, fruits and nuts, optical and medical instruments, iron, and steel from other countries. Its primary trade partners are Germany, the United States, Belarus, Ukraine, and Kazakhstan. Russia joined the World Trade Organization (WTO), a group that promotes trade between nations, in 2012.

Under Soviet rule, Russia's government controlled every aspect of the economy. It owned all of the land, farms, and factories. It told workers what to produce, how much to produce, how much to charge, and to whom to sell. Communist leaders shifted the country's efforts from farming to heavy industries like steel, chemicals, machines, and construction. As a result, industry grew quickly but other areas suffered.

Since the 1991 collapse of the Soviet Union, Russia has taken steps to reform its economy. Once state-owned and controlled, the economy is now mostly market-driven. This shift includes private ownership of industries and resources. Private ownership of land has not yet been implemented fully. At first, the reforms had a terrible impact on the economy. The value of currency fell while prices rose, banks collapsed, people lost their life savings, and necessary goods were in short supply. Industrial environmental disasters such as the nuclear power accident in Chernobyl also hurt the economy.

Agriculture

Although Russia has plenty of land, only 13% is used for agriculture. This is because much of Russia is either too mountainous, too dry, or too often frozen to farm. The nation also has a very short growing season. As a result of these challenges, agriculture contributes only 4% of Russia's GDP and employs only 10% of its workers. Russia's most productive farming region is the Black Earth Belt, between the Ukrainian border and southwestern Siberia. The area is named for its dark, rich soil, known as *chernozem* (black earth).

Grain crops, such as wheat, barley, rye, and oats, take up more than half of Russia's farmland. Other primary crops include sugar beets, sunflower seeds, vegetables, and fruits, along with fodder crops (food for animals) of grass and corn. Farmers also raise cows for beef and milk. Although the state no longer controls collective farms, many farmers still follow the tradition of working together in large cooperatives.

Forestry and Fishing

About 50% of Russia's land is covered in forest, making it one of the world's great timber suppliers. This abundance leads to thriving industries in timber, pulp, paper, and woodworking. However, Russia has had to work to protect its forests from disappearing. Because of the cold, harsh climate, new trees cannot grow fast enough to replace those being cut down.

Russia's extensive coastlines along the Atlantic and Pacific Oceans contribute to a strong fishing industry. About one-third of the world's canned fish and one-fourth of the world's fresh and frozen fish come from Russia. In order to process huge numbers of fish far from industrialized areas, Russian fishermen use factory ships to do the work at sea. Russia's lakes and rivers also provide fish, but suffer from pollution. Sturgeon from the Caspian Sea provide the world's best *caviar*, a delicacy made from salted fish eggs.

Mineral and Energy Resources

Russia is home to major deposits of oil, natural gas, coal, and many strategic minerals. It also has reserves of rare earth elements, which are naturally occurring elements of the periodic table. As a result, the nation has almost all the resources it needs for modern industry. Coal is especially abundant, but the industry has had trouble transitioning from state ownership to private enterprise. Many mines have closed as a result. Natural gas and oil are also plentiful, carried across the country through a huge system of pipelines.

Russia's power comes from some 600 thermal power plants, 100 hydroelectric stations, and several nuclear power plants. In 1986, an accident at the Chernobyl nuclear power plant in Ukraine released radioactive particles into the atmosphere. Since then, nuclear power production has grown slowly.

Manufacturing

Manufacturing accounts for 36% of Russia's GDP but new production grows slowly. Approximately 28% of Russian workers help produce goods for sale or export. Mining and extractive industries produce coal, oil, gas, chemicals, and metals. Also popular are all forms of machine building, from rolling mills to high-performance aircraft and space vehicles, defense industries (including radar, missile production, advanced electronic components), shipbuilding, road and rail transportation equipment, communications equipment, agricultural machinery, tractors, construction equipment, electric power equipment, medical and scientific instruments, consumer goods, textiles, foodstuffs, and handicrafts. The Moscow area is home to much of Russia's manufacturing activity.

Services

As Russia's largest sector of the economy, services account for 60% of the GDP and employ 63% of the nation's workers. Under Soviet rule, services suffered as the state made no effort to meet consumer demands. Citizens had to put up with poor service because they had no other options. Though this sector is improving, public services such as police, schools, and hospitals still struggle to meet the needs of citizens.

Transportation

Russia has over 1,000 airports and over 621,000 miles (999,400 km) of roadways. Its railways and waterways rank 2nd in the world based on distance covered. The nation's primary seaports are Kaliningrad, Nakhodka, Novorossiysk, Primorsk, and Vostochny. The city of Saint Petersburg, on the Neva River, is the primary river port. However, many of Russia's waterways are frozen for much of the year.

The percentage of Russians who own automobiles is small, but automobile ownership is a growing symbol of middle-class status. Roads, however, are underdeveloped and transporting goods by truck is slow and expensive. Russia's large cities have modern subways, high-speed commuter trains, buses, trams, and trolleys. In rural areas, traditional horse and buggy transportation still exists.

Communication

Russia's national television stations are mainly controlled by the government. The nation is 7th in the world in its use of telephones, cellular phones, and Internet. This is a great improvement since the early 1990's, when only about one-third of households had a telephone.

RUSSIA'S HISTORY

Due to its vast size and its location, Russia has been described in many ways over the years. It is European and it is Asian. It includes numerous and varied people groups. Its name and political affiliation have changed several times. As a result, even historians and Russian scholars struggle to define Russia's development and impact on world history.

Ancient Russia (1200 BCE–1300's CE)

The Cimmerians are the first people group known to have lived in Russia. Originating in southeast Europe, they settled north of the Black Sea (now Ukraine) around 1200 BCE. About 500 years later, an Iranian people group called the Scythians conquered the Cimmerians and pushed them to the south. The Scythians incorporated many Greek and Roman influences by trading with and marrying among these neighbors. In about 200 BCE, another Iranian people group called the Sarmatians took control of the area but kept up relations with the Greeks and Romans.

In 200 CE, various foreign tribes began fighting for control of the region. First the Goths from Germany ruled, then Huns from Asia. They were followed by Avars and Khazars who expanded the conquered area and brought new foreign influences. Finally, Slavic groups from unknown origins came to the area in the 800's. They established towns in the European part of Russia and developed trade with neighboring regions.

The *Primary Chronicle*, written in Kiev around 1111, contains the earliest written history of Russia. It states that the Slavic groups asked a Viking tribe to rule their town of Novgorod, which had become politically unstable. The Vikings, called *Varangian Russes*, arrived in 862 to bring order to an area they called the "land of the Rus." Some historians, however, doubt the reliability of the *Primary Chronicle*. They believe the Vikings invaded the area.

Under the rule of the Vikings, Kiev became an important city. It had been established by East Slavs as the state of Kievan Rus and was captured by Vikings in 882. Its location on a main trade route between the Baltic Sea, the Black Sea, and the Byzantine Empire made it a desirable seat of government and economic activity. Under the rule of Prince Oleg, Kiev's army fought off invaders from the south and east.

Kiev became so important that its ruler became *grand prince* above all the other princes of Kievan Rus. Around 988, Vladimir I became grand prince. He converted to Christianity and changed the state religion from nature worship to Christianity. Later, the Russian Orthodox Church made Vladimir I a saint.

By the mid-1000's, civil war among Kievan Rus rulers led to the state's demise. In its weakened condition, Kiev fell to invading Mongol, or Tatar, armies from Asia during the 1200's. The Mongols were led by Genghis Khan's grandson, Batu, in a very destructive invasion. After destroying the city of Kiev in 1240, they moved the capital to Sarai, near modern-day Volgograd. Russia became part of the Mongol Empire known as the Golden Horde. The Mongols ruled harshly, but were mainly concerned with collecting taxes and maintaining strong armies. Otherwise, they kept from interfering with Russian life.

Gradually, power began to shift from Mongols to Russians, and the center of power shifted to Moscow. There, Prince Yuri married the Mongol ruler's sister and became the Russian grand prince in 1318. Mongols began fighting to protect the Russian grand prince and later paid him taxes. Rich and powerful Russians began to hold positions in Moscow's government and army. The chief bishop of the Russian Orthodox Church stayed in Moscow rather than moving to Kiev. By the late 1400's, Moscow had become the most powerful city in Russia. Meanwhile, the Golden Horde grew weaker. Russians defeated the Mongols in several battles and later refused to pay taxes to the Golden Horde.

Ivan the Terrible (1533–1584)

In 1547, Moscow's grand prince, Ivan IV, became the first czar, or ruler, over all of Russia. Ivan became known as Ivan the Terrible due to his brutal and sometimes insane actions. He had hundreds of upper-class landowners arrested and murdered, giving their property to lower-class soldiers and government officials as payment. He burned villages, killed church leaders, and kept strict control over citizens' contributions to his army. In a fit of rage, he killed his own son. Although he added to Russia's territory by conquering lands to the west and southeast, Ivan IV's leadership was harmful to the nation's development. He instituted *serfdom*, which bound poor farm workers to estates as virtual slaves.

False Dmitriy (1605)

A time of unrest, known as the Time of Troubles, followed the death of Ivan IV. His first son was dead and his second son, Fedor I, was not fit to rule. Fedor had no male heirs and his younger brother, Dmitriy, died in 1591. Without a clear ruler, the nation's land council elected Fedor's brother-in-law, Boris, as czar. Boris made some positive changes to Russia in his time as czar. However, a person posing as Dmitriy showed up in 1604 claiming that he had not died but had fled to Lithuania. This False Dmitriy, believed to be a former monk named Gregory Otrepiev, invaded Russia with an army of Polish troops and unhappy Russians.

A time of unrest, invasion, and civil war continued until 1613. False Dmitriy became czar in 1605 but was killed one year later. Another False Dmitriy rose up and tried to take the throne. Peasants revolted against landowners. Polish armies invaded Moscow. Finally, Russia regained control of Moscow in 1612. In the absence of any royal person to take the throne, the land council elected Michael Romanov as czar. The Romanovs ruled Russia as czars for 300 years.

Peter the Great (1682–1725)

Odd circumstances in 1682 led to the crowning of two co-czars, both children. Half-brothers Peter I and Ivan V were too young to rule,

The former Imperial Winter Palace in Saint Petersburg

so Ivan's sister Sophia ruled in their place. As Peter grew, he learned much from Western European influence. In 1696, when Ivan died, Peter's followers forced Sophia to retire and Peter emerged as a powerful new leader.

Peter, who became known as Peter the Great, made military improvements and increased Russia's size by conquering new territories. He moved the capital to newly-founded Saint Petersburg in 1712. Under Peter's rule, Russia adopted Western influences in education, economics, and culture. Peter improved the organization and efficiency of Russia's government. However, he also increased his own power over other officials and let the condition of serfs worsen.

Catherine the Great (1762–1796)

A power struggle followed Peter's 1725 death, with Empress Catherine II finally coming to power in 1762. Known as Catherine the Great, this new leader embraced Western culture and promoted arts, education, fashion, and extravagant parties. While the upper-class enjoyed these new diversions, most Russians remained very poor. Catherine's efforts to bring Western ideas of freedom and equality to government had little impact.

Meanwhile, Russia continued to conquer nearby territories, gaining most of Belarus, Lithuania, and Ukraine from Poland along with Crimea and other lands once ruled by the Ottoman Empire. Russia had grown to become a major world power. Catherine ruled until her death in 1796, after which her son, Paul, took the throne.

Alexander I (1801–1825)

Paul ruled for just five years before he was murdered. His son, Alexander I, became czar and ushered in a time of great political, military, and cultural advancement in Russia. Alexander valued education and Western thought. He spoke of freeing the serfs and turning Russia into a republic, though he did neither. Under his rule Russia gained territory from Persia, Sweden, and the Ottoman Empire. The army successfully fought off an invasion of Moscow by Napoleon Bonaparte's Grand Army of France.

However, much of Moscow was destroyed, possibly by fires set by Russians themselves, and Napoleon's troops suffered as much from cold and lack of food as from Russian defenses. Nevertheless, Russia played a major part in defeating Napoleon in his efforts to conquer Europe.

Although Alexander had spoken of reforms, his reign as czar was harsh and Russia's social and political problems continued. Revolutionaries, including a group called the *Decembrists*, began protesting, calling for change, and revolting against Russia's government. Nicholas I, who followed Alexander as czar, feared these revolts. He placed military officers in government positions and further increased control over Russian government and everyday life. His military defended Eastern Orthodox Churches against the Muslim Ottoman Empire and gained territory around the Black Sea. Despite tight controls, Russian literature flourished during Nicholas' reign.

The General Staff Building in Saint Petersburg's Palace Square
commemorates the victory over Napoleon

Crimean War (1853–1856)

In addition to gaining territory around the Black Sea, Russia also obtained the use of the Ottoman straits, allowing ships to pass from the Black Sea to the Mediterranean Sea. European countries, like the United Kingdom and France, however, objected to these developments. They helped the Ottomans fight against Russia in the Crimean War. They defeated Russia in 1856, with Russia signing the Treaty of Paris to end the war.

The defeat didn't stop Russia from expanding in other directions. From 1858 through 1867, Russia won territories in China, the Caucasus Mountain area, and central Asia. Although Russia owned part of North America, it sold the Alaskan territory to the United States in 1867.

Nicholas' son, Alexander II, came to power during the Crimean War. He learned that Russia would have to make improvements in order to keep up with major Western powers. He made reforms to economics, government, and education. Finally realizing that serfdom was hurting the nation, he set the serfs free and gave them land of their own. Despite making major changes, Alexander could not please everyone. Revolutionaries complained that his reforms were too little and made attempts on his life. In 1881, terrorists killed Alexander in a bombing. His son, Alexander III, became czar and reversed many of the reforms made by his father.

Nicholas II (1894–1917)

In 1894, Russia's final czar, Nicholas II, took the throne during a very difficult time. Several bad harvests caused widespread starvation among peasants. Middle-class urban workers grew discontent with the increasing industrialization. Russia suffered a 1905 defeat in the unpopular Russo-Japanese war. Under these circumstances, Russians began looking to other political movements, including socialism and Marxism. They formed political and labor parties, protested, and held strikes. Vladimir Lenin became the leader of a group called the *Bolsheviks*, a majority party that later became the Communist Party.

During a 1905 strike, thousands of workers marched to the czar's Winter Palace in Saint Petersburg intending to ask for reforms. Instead, government troops fired on the unarmed protesters, killing hundreds in a slaughter known as *Bloody Sunday*.

Afterward, the revolution gained much momentum and protests continued. Nicholas attempted to appease unhappy Russians by forming an elected government body, called the Duma, but many remained unsatisfied.

The Duma did not fairly represent peasants and workers and Nicholas broke established laws in order to make the selection of officers less democratic.

World War I (1914)

By 1914, Russia, France, and the United Kingdom had signed agreements to defend one another against attacks, forming the Triple Entente. They anticipated attacks from the Triple Alliance, a coalition formed by Germany, Italy, and Austria-Hungary.

On August 1, tensions turned to fighting, as Germany declared war on Russia. Fighting continued back and forth on many fronts, with Russia experiencing some victories and some losses. The war took a great toll on the Russian people, who suffered shortages of food, housing, fuel, and transportation. Increasingly, they opposed the czar and the war. They grew suspicious of Grigori Rasputin, a monk who served as close advisor to Nicholas and his wife.

Revolutionary Period (1917)

In December 1916, unhappy Russian nobles murdered Rasputin. The following February, the people of Russia revolted in the February Revolution. The Duma defied Nicholas' orders by setting up a temporary government. Nicholas lost all political support and gave up the throne in March. He and his family were imprisoned and later killed by Bolshevik revolutionaries.

The Cruiser Aurora began the assault on the Winter Palace to begin the October 1917 Revolution

Later that year, Bolsheviks led the October Revolution, in which they seized the Winter Palace, overthrew the temporary government, and established Lenin as head of a new government.

Russia under Lenin (1917–1924)

Lenin quickly made huge changes to Russian life. He withdrew the nation from World War I, put government in control of all industry, and seized agricultural goods from peasant farmers. In 1918, Lenin and the Bolsheviks moved the capital to Moscow and established the Russian Communist Party (later called the Communist Party of the Soviet Union).

Russian Civil War (1918–1920)

At first, anti-communists resisted Communist control. They fought for control of Russia in a civil war that spanned three years. Anti-communist countries, including Canada, France, Japan, the United Kingdom, and the United States, gave their support, but the Communists were victorious. They spread communism through Russia and into Georgia, Ukraine, Armenia, Belarus, and central Asia.

Lenin responded to peasant uprisings and labor strikes by introducing a New Economic Policy. It allowed small businesses to run their own operations and peasants to maintain their farms, but it kept government control over important areas of banking, foreign trade, heavy industry, and transportation. Lenin's Communist government also formed the Union of Soviet Socialist Republics, or U.S.S.R. This new nation included many satellites, including Belarus, Ukraine, Armenia, Georgia, Lithuania, Kazakhstan, and others.

The Great Purge (1930's)

Upon Lenin's death in 1924, Communist Party General Secretary Joseph Stalin became dictator. Against the wishes of many citizens, he moved the economy further into socialism. His policies combined small, private farms into huge collectives run by the government. He put much focus on developing heavy industry as well.

To help prevent political rivals from rising up against him, Stalin instituted the Great Purge. In the mid-1930's, his secret police arrested millions of people, sending some to labor camps and killing others. Stalin established himself as a harsh dictator with complete control over the Soviet Union.

World War II (1941)

As Stalin rose to power in the Soviet Union, Adolf Hitler rose to power as dictator of Germany. Hitler began efforts to conquer Europe, but Germany and the Soviet Union signed a treaty agreeing not to attack one another. In September, both countries invaded Poland from opposite sides. The following June, Germany broke the treaty by invading the Soviet Union.

At first, the German army advanced quickly through Russia. However, the Russians won an important victory in the Battle of Stalingrad (now the city of Volgograd), and drove the Germans out. The Soviet army continued its pursuit of the Germans across Eastern Europe and into Germany, where they gained control of Berlin, the German capital, in 1945. Five days later, the Germans surrendered and World War II came to an end. Although the Soviet Union played an important part in the war, it suffered more losses than all the other Allied countries combined. Today, Russians remember their fight against Germany as the Great Patriotic War.

The Cold War (1948–1980's)

After the end of World War II, the Soviet Union resumed its spread of communism under Stalin. It extended Soviet control over Bulgaria, Czechoslovakia, Hungary, Poland, Romania, and East Germany. Communist countries cut contact with Western democracies, leading to a period of distrust and suspicion known as the Cold War. While the Cold War didn't involve direct fighting, nations competed to support the spread of their government ideals to developing areas of the world.

In 1953, Stalin died and was succeeded by Nikita Khrushchev as premier of the Soviet Union. Khrushchev continued spreading communism, but also relaxed some of Stalin's restrictions on interactions with the West. Under his leadership, Soviet people's standard of living improved, as did relations with the West.

Khrushchev's leadership came to an end in 1964 when other Communist leaders seized control from him. Leonid Brezhnev became head of the Communist Party, while Aleksei Kosygin became premier. Together, they oversaw Communist expansion into Africa. They also directed the economy toward making more consumer goods and constructing housing. However, attempts to reconcile with the West failed. The United States disagreed with the Soviet Union's invasion of Afghanistan and its violations of human rights. Both the Soviet Union and the United States increased their arsenals of nuclear weapons, creating great tension around the world.

Tensions began to decrease in 1985, when Mikhail Gorbachev became head of the Communist Party. He improved relations with Western nations and reduced government control of the Soviet economy. Citizens enjoyed greater freedoms and fewer restrictions in politics, literature, and the arts. In 1989, they voted in the nation's first real election—one that was not controlled by the Communist Party. They elected members of the newly formed Congress of People's Deputies, which later chose Gorbachev as president of the Soviet Union.

Soviet Union Dissolves (1991)

In 1991, the leaders of Soviet republics, including Gorbachev, decided that the regional governments should have more power than the central government of the Soviet Union. While the leaders worked to sign a treaty to this effect, Gorbachev and his family were attacked and imprisoned in their vacation home by conservative Communist Party forces. Russia's president, Boris Yeltsin, opposed the coup, which collapsed after just two days. Gorbachev returned as president of the Soviet Union but gave up his position as head of the Communist Party.

A short period of instability and change followed, as Yeltsin and other leaders formed the Commonwealth of Independent States (C.I.S.) and declared the end of the Soviet Union. Toward the end of 1991, Gorbachev resigned and the Soviet Union ended, with Yeltsin taking control of the Kremlin, the seat of central government in Moscow.

Russia Today

The breakup of the Soviet Union helped end many remaining tensions from the Cold War. Russia reduced the size of its army and other former Soviet republics turned over nuclear weapons to Russia. The C.I.S. has worked to balance Russia's leadership with concerns about it becoming dominant over smaller states.

Some of Russia's economic changes have had mixed results. Dropping government price controls led to rapid price increases and a lower standard of living for many Russians. Transitioning businesses to private ownership led to a small number of wealthy owners controlling many large companies. Some Russians, led by Vice President Alexander Rutskoi, opposed Yeltsin and his economic changes. Political unrest followed, with Yeltsin suspending Rutskoi when he attempted to dissolve the parliament and remove Yeltsin from office. The situation culminated with Rutskoi and his followers barricading themselves in the parliament building and anti-Yeltsin crowds rioting in Moscow. Finally, the military arrested Rutskoi and other leaders, and Yeltsin returned to power.

In 1993, voters elected a new parliament and approved a new Constitution. They elected Yeltsin to a second term as president in 1996. Facing economic crisis in the following years, Yeltsin made many changes to government, conflicting with his cabinet and with parliament. Suffering poor health, Yeltsin turned over most of his duties in 1998. One of his final government changes involved appointing Vladimir Putin as prime minister.

Putin had formerly been in charge of Russia's domestic intelligence service. He now took on the formidable task of solving Russia's many problems as prime minister. One of these problems involved the region of Chechnya, in southwestern Russia. In 1991, the Chechen government had demanded independence from Russia, while many of its residents wanted to remain part of Russia. Violence broke out in 1992, and Yeltsin sent troops to regain control of the region in 1994. After years of serious fighting, Yeltsin and the Chechen leader signed a peace treaty. However, trouble arose again in 1999, when Islamic militants seized several towns in a nearby republic.

Yeltsin resigned in 1999, appointing Putin as acting president. Under Putin, Russia invaded Chechnya and engaged in a costly and destructive war in which many civilians were killed. Many Russians and people from other countries disagreed with Russia's handling of the conflict.

The following March, voters officially elected Putin as president of Russia and reelected him in 2004. During his presidency, Putin faced continued conflicts with Chechen terrorists. In 2002, they seized a Moscow theater and held hundreds of civilians hostage. Russian forces overcame the terrorists, but over 100 hostages died from inhaling gas used by the Russians. In 2004, Chechen terrorists seized a school in Beslan and held over 1,000 hostages, including children. After a three-day standoff, a bomb exploded in the school and Russian forces ended the attack. In all, over 300 civilians died.

Putin also faced economic challenges. He once again increased the power of the central government and limited freedom of expression. He had wealthy individuals arrested for financial crimes and stripped of power. Even when Putin's presidency ended in 2008, he continued controlling the nation as prime minister under President Dmitry Medvedev. In the next election, in 2012, Putin was again elected president under suspicions of ballot tampering, and he appointed Medvedev as his prime minister.

In 2014, Russia continued to draw criticism by seizing the Crimean Peninsula in Ukraine. Among tensions and fighting in the area, other countries imposed sanctions on Russia. The United States and other countries refused to acknowledge Russia's annexation of Crimea. They put economic restrictions on Russia's oil and gas industries as a type of punishment. The sanctions weakened Russia's economy even further, though conflict over Crimea continued.

Flag of Russia

SOUTHEAST ASIA

SOUTHEAST ASIA

SOUTHEAST ASIA: THE BIG PICTURE

Southeast Asia spans the peninsula and islands between the Pacific Ocean and the Indian Ocean, including Brunei, Cambodia, East Timor, Laos, Malaysia, Myanmar, the Philippines, Singapore, Thailand, Vietnam, and most of Indonesia. The term "Southeast Asia" came into use after World War II to describe this region east of India and south of China.

Since these countries are so close together, they share similar geography, climate, history, economies, and people groups. Individually, these nations have unique governments, languages, customs, and lifestyles.

MEET THE PEOPLE OF SOUTHEAST ASIA

Roughly 620 million people, many of Chinese or Malay descent, call Southeast Asia home. Just over 250 million live in Southeast Asia's largest and most populous nation, Indonesia. Another 100 million live in the Philippines. The smallest populations reside in Brunei, Laos, and Singapore. Almost half of Southeast Asians live in rural areas. Others live crowded into big cities like Jakarta, Indonesia; Bangkok, Thailand; and Manila, the Philippines.

The major religions in this region are Buddhism and Islam. In the Philippines over 80% of the population practice Catholicism. In more

A typical floating house in Cambodia

isolated areas, some people groups practice animism, or the belief that spirits inhabit ordinary objects.

LAND, WATER, AND CLIMATE IN SOUTHEAST ASIA

With an area of about 2,796,170 square miles (7,242,047 square km), Southeast Asia consists of the mainland peninsula and separate archipelagos, or chains of volcanic islands. The mainland portion, formerly called Indochina, includes Cambodia, Laos, Myanmar, Thailand, Vietnam, and the western part of Malaysia. The island nations are Indonesia, Singapore, the Philippines, East Timor, Brunei, and the eastern part of Malaysia. The largest of these nations is Indonesia, with an area of 1,183,444 square miles (3,065,105 square km). The smallest is Singapore, with an area of 433 square miles (1,121 square km).

The land is a rugged mix of volcanic mountains and dense tropical forests. The region's hot, humid climate is affected by heavy rains and seasonal monsoons—strong winds that bring changes in the weather.

Bangkok, Thailand

THE ECONOMY OF SOUTHEAST ASIA

Agriculture thrives in Southeast Asia due to the rich, fertile soil. Southeast Asian farmers supply much of the world with tea, spices, rubber, and especially rice. Extensive forests provide most of the world's teak, and coastal waters supply an abundant variety of fish. Some areas have rich deposits of petroleum, tin, and gems. Manufacturing goods for export has become a growing industry in many countries.

A water village in Brunei, backed by dense forests, rugged mountains, and an Islamic mosque

SOUTHEAST ASIA'S HISTORY

China and India influenced the earliest civilizations in Southeast Asia. The Khmers and Malays were two of these early people groups. For a time, Islam was the dominant influence in the region, but waned during European colonial occupation.

Beginning in the 1500's, European merchants discovered Southeast Asia's wealth of resources and began taking over the region. Except for Thailand, the countries all fell under the control of the United Kingdom, France, the Netherlands, Portugal, Spain, and the United States.

Since the end of World War II, Southeast Asian nations have gained their independence. For decades, many of the newly independent nations

struggled through political and economic problems. In the 1950's, newly
formed Communist North Vietnam
invaded South Vietnam, beginning
the long and bitter Vietnam War.
Laos and Cambodia also experienced
conflict between Communist and
non-communist factions. After years

A Buddhist temple in Singapore

of fighting, the victorious Communist forces united North Vietnam and
South Vietnam into one nation in 1975. Today, Vietnam and Laos are two
of only five Communist countries in the world.

Several of the Southeast Asian nations (Indonesia, Malaysia, the
Philippines, Singapore, and Thailand) created an organization in 1967
to help improve the political, economic, and
social stability of the region. This Association of Southeast Asian Nations (ASEAN) has
since grown to include Brunei, Vietnam, Laos,
Myanmar, and Cambodia.

Flag of Philippines

Flag of Brunei

Flag of East Timor

Flag of Malaysia

Flag of Cambodia

Flag of Myanmar

Flag of Laos

Flag of Singapore

Flag of Thailand

Flag of Indonesia

SOUTHEAST ASIA

VIETNAM

VIETNAM: THE BIG PICTURE

For millennia, Vietnam has been shaped by Chinese influence, European colonialism, and war. This medium-sized nation in Southeast Asia was once split in two—Communist North Vietnam and non-communist South Vietnam. Since 1975, the nation has been unified as a socialist republic. Its capital, Hanoi, lies in the north, and its largest city, Ho Chi Minh City, is in the south.

Vietnam's first civilizations occupied the Red River delta sometime between 5,000 and 3,000 BCE. Over many centuries, they developed agricultural societies and fought off foreign invaders, mainly those from China. In the mid-1800's, the French ruled over Vietnam, an outgrowth of European colonialism. This continued until World War II, when Japanese forces took control. In 1945, with Japan's defeat in WWII, Vietnamese leader Ho Chi Minh resisted French attempts to regain control.

Vietnam's recent history includes the division of the country, a devastating war between North and South (with heavy involvement from the United States), a drawn-out war against forces in neighboring Cambodia, and finally, reunification in 1975. Today, Vietnam is growing politically, economically, and culturally, even as they maintain their traditions while adapting to foreign and modern influences.

MEET THE PEOPLE OF VIETNAM

Most of Vietnam's population (86%) identify ethnically as Viet, or Kinh. Several smaller ethnic groups, mainly scattered through the mountains, are linked to either China or Cambodia. These groups have maintained unique cultures and languages due to the distinct regions and isolation created by Vietnam's geography. Even under French rule, the nation was divided into northern, central, and southern regions.

Vietnamese is the official language, though many citizens speak English. French and Chinese are popular second languages, while many ethnic groups speak traditional languages.

Although Vietnam is ranked 66th in the world in land area, it has the 15th largest population. The nation experienced a "baby boom," or time of increased birth rate, in the 1970's and 80's. At the same time, life expectancy increased greatly. The result is that Vietnam has a large aging population. After the partition of Vietnam in 1954, many people moved from north to south. Once the nation reunified in 1975, hundreds of thousands of Vietnamese left the country.

Fast Facts

Capital:
Hanoi

Size:
66th in the world

Area:
205,804 sq miles
(533,029 sq km)

Coastline:
2,140 miles (3,444 km)

Highest Point:
Fan Si Pan 10,315 feet
(3,144 m)

Lowest Point:
South China Sea 0 feet
(0 m)

Population:
94 million

Official Language:
Vietnamese

Currency:
dong

National Anthem:
"Tien quan ca" (The Song of the Marching Troops)

National Symbol:
lotus blossom

LAND, WATER, AND CLIMATE IN VIETNAM

S-shaped Vietnam extends 1,025 miles (1,650 km) from north to south in Southeastern Asia on a landmass called the Indochinese Peninsula. It shares 806 miles (1,297 km) of border with China to the north. To the west, it shares a 1,343 mile (2,161 km) border with Laos and a 720 mile (1,159 km) border with Cambodia. At its narrowest point, Vietnam is only 31 miles (50 km) across. Its coastlines border the Gulf of Thailand, Gulf of Tonkin, and the South China Sea.

Halong Bay in north Vietnam

Land

Vietnam's major land features are the Red River delta in the north, the Mekong River delta in the south, and a long, narrow coastal plain in between. These three regions have distinct geography. The far north has hills and mountains tapering toward the Red River delta, a triangular region of dense population and extensive agriculture. The central region is dominated by the Annamite Range, or Truong Son mountains. Except for narrow strips along the coast, the soil is generally poor for farming in central Vietnam. In the south, the Mekong delta has earned the nickname "the rice bowl" of the nation for its vast plains that allow for rice farming. Vietnam's largest city, Hi Chi Minh City, serves as this region's urban center and hub of economic activity.

Water

The nation's coastline wraps along the east and south for 2,140 miles (3,444 km). It is often interrupted by rocky peaks that jut out into the South China Sea, isolating areas from one another.

Map of Vietnam

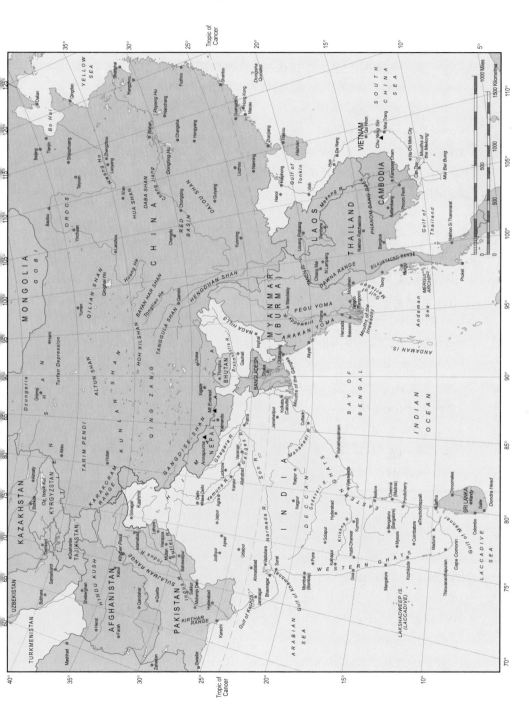

Climate

Vietnam's climate is generally hot, wet, and humid. Seasonal winds called monsoons bring heavy rain in the summer and cooler temperatures in the winter. Northern Vietnam experiences slightly cooler temperatures than the tropical south. The capital city of Hanoi in the north averages 85° F in summer and 63° F in winter while Ho Chi Minh City in the south averages 81° F year-round. From May to September, the country has a hot, rainy summer with occasional typhoons and extensive flooding. The winter months are drier, but still warm. Areas of Vietnam can receive more than 70 inches (178 cm) of rainfall per year.

EVERYDAY LIFE IN VIETNAM

Family life

The Vietnamese place great importance on family due to their Confucian heritage. In the workplace, many people work from early in the morning until evening with a period of rest during the hot midday. About a fifth of Vietnamese children ages 5–14 have jobs.

City life

About a third of the Vietnamese people live in cities, but that number is growing as many move to urban areas for better work and life opportunities. Ho Chi Minh City (formerly Saigon) has a population over 7 million, and Hanoi (the capital) has a population of about 3.5 million. Other large cities include Can Tho, Haiphong, Da Nang, and Bien Hoa, with populations around 1 million each. In general, city-dwellers enjoy a higher standard of

One Pillar Pagoda Buddhist Temple

living than those in the country, though many families in the cities live in crowded conditions due to a shortage of housing.

City streets are crowded with bicyclists, motorcyclists, and a variety of road-side stands that sell food and other items. Many people travel by *cyclo* taxi—a pedaled vehicle with three wheels and a seat for passengers.

Country life

Most Vietnamese live and work in small country villages where life revolves around growing rice or other crops. In rural areas, groups of homes are often surrounded by a bamboo hedge. Other homes stand above the ground on pilings.

Recreation

Vietnam has participated in the Olympic Games since 1952, focusing on water sports, martial arts, weightlifting, table tennis, and track. Soccer is the most popular sport among the Vietnamese, who also enjoy volleyball, badminton, wrestling, and bicycling. A uniquely Asian sport, called *sepak takraw*, is like a combination of soccer and volleyball. The nation's many lakes and rivers provide swimming spots for the people. The Vietnamese also play games of chess, dominoes, and billiards.

Education

By placing great importance on education, Vietnam has attained a high (95%) literacy rate. All children attend school from age 6 to 14. The government mandates five years of primary school and four years of lower-secondary school. Schools focus on teaching science, technology, economics, and business. Study abroad programs are common, with students traveling to the Soviet Union, Eastern Europe, Japan, and, more recently, the United States and Western Europe.

Many students continue on to higher education in universities, agricultural colleges, technical or vocational schools, and private business academies. Hanoi University of Science and Technology, Vietnam National University, and Can Tho University are the nation's largest universities.

Although these and other universities are expanding, they are not keeping pace with the growing number of students.

Religion

Vietnam has no official religion. Anywhere from 10 to 50% of the population practice a blend of Confucianism, Daoism, and Mahayana Buddhism. Developed over many years, this religion is referred to as the Three Teachings. Catholicism was brought to Vietnam in the 1500's and spread quickly after the French took control in the mid-1800's. However, the government banned all foreign clergy in 1954 and has exerted control over clergy and churches to this day, even though the 1992 constitution guarantees freedom of religion. Today, about 6% of the Vietnamese are Catholic. The nation also has a small percentage of followers of Islam, Protestantism, and local traditional religions. Spirit worship and nature worship exist in some rural villages.

Health care

Until Vietnam reunified, those living in the north enjoyed much better health care than those living in the rural south. After 1975, extensive health care spread throughout the nation. The government struggled to keep up with the growing population and inadequate water and sewage systems. Increased health care spending helped improve access to clean water, controlled the spread of malaria, expanded the number of doctors, and reduced the infant mortality rate. More recently, the nation has worked to combat the spread of tuberculosis, bird flu, and HIV/AIDS, though many victims of HIV/AIDS do not report their condition because of discrimination.

VIETNAM'S GOVERNMENT

The Socialist Republic of Vietnam adopted its first constitution in 1980. It established a Council of State and Council of Ministers as government leaders. A revised constitution in 1992 replaced the Council of State

with an elected president and the Council of Ministers with a cabinet. This revision also allowed for more economic freedoms, such as private ownership of businesses.

Currently, the highest legislative body is the National Assembly. The members are elected by popular vote, serve five-year terms, and choose one of their own to serve as president. The president appoints other officials, including the prime minister who acts as the head of state and commands the armed forces.

All citizens over age 18 have the right to vote. In practice, the Communist Party of Vietnam (CPV) leads the government. The Party makes overall policy decisions, while elected officials, such as the president, carry out the day-to-day tasks of running the government. Under this system of *democratic centralism*, authority flows down from the CPV.

Vietnam is a Communist state divided into more than 64 provinces. The People's Armed Forces includes an army, navy, air force, border defense, and coast guard. All male citizens must serve at least 18 months in the armed forces; service is voluntary for women.

VIETNAMESE CULTURE

Vietnam celebrates its diverse culture throughout the country. Hanoi is home to ancient structures like the 11th-century Temple of Literature and the One Pillar Pagoda. Ho Chi Minh City includes national museums, galleries, libraries, and a museum devoted to the lives of Vietnamese women and one that celebrates the country's ethnic diversity. Many towns have Buddhist pagodas, ancient tombs, and other historical sites.

A popular sport called Sepak Takraw

The Arts

Today, Vietnamese artists under the *doi moi* policy (economic changes that allowed for private ownership of businesses) enjoy limited freedom of expression. They often create art by putting a modern twist on traditional themes. They are heavily influenced by the Chinese and French. Only rarely does the government censor pieces that they consider harmful to the culture.

Traditional crafts such as weaving, basket-making, painting, carving, and lacquer work remain popular. Artists practice embroidery or ceramics. Under French rule, artists adopted the Impressionist style of oil painting on canvas. They often used their art to express dissatisfaction with French rule. Later, under Communist rule, art was used for political and social purposes.

In the world of cinema, Vietnam's first motion pictures were government-made propaganda films and cheap kung fu or romance movies. Since censorship became more lenient in 2002, private studios have released more critically acclaimed films.

Theater

For many years, Communist control stifled the theater in Vietnam, with all productions controlled by the government and all performers employed by the state. Over the past two decades, freedom has increased and censorship has decreased. Private theater companies have grown and new forms of theater, such as comedies, operas, and circus, have become popular. In *mua roi nuoc*, puppeteers perform in water while musicians and singers provide dialogue and sound effects.

Music

Vietnamese music traditionally involves a combination of instruments. Traditional string instruments include a variety of lutes, zithers, fiddles, and even a three-stringed banjo called a *dan tam*. The main wind instrument is a bamboo flute called a *sáo trúc*. Musicians also bang on barrel-shaped drums called *trong com* or gongs.

Vietnam's Communist government long tried to suppress the spread of many modern musical genres. It forbade anything Western, rock-inspired, or depressing. Despite strict controls, many Vietnamese shared illegal recordings. More recently, the government has loosened restrictions on music, allowing for jazz, rock, and other Western influences. The new "traditional but modern" blend of Vietnamese music is called *cai bien*.

Literature

Until the late 1200's, the Vietnamese did not have their own script and so authors wrote in Chinese. They later developed a unique form of writing using the Roman alphabet. Early writings include long, narrative poems. Nguyen Trai became famous writing in the transitional style of modified Chinese characters called *chu nom*. Later, Nguyen Du wrote his famous poem *The Tale of Kieu* in Vietnamese. As writers began publishing novels and short stories, they avoided controversial topics such as politics.

Fashion

In most areas of Vietnam, especially in big cities, people wear Western-style clothing. Most blouses, trousers, and dresses are simple and loose-fitting, made from lightweight fabrics. Women occasionally wear a traditional *ao dai*, which is a long tunic worn over pants. Some members of the Hmong minority group wear a unique style of baggy skirts or shorts, embroidered belts and aprons, and a turban or head cloth.

Food and Drink

Vietnam's signature dish is *pho*—a noodle soup made from broth, fresh vegetables, long rice noodles, and meat or seafood. Most meals include rice, along with tofu, seafood, chicken, pork, or duck. The Vietnamese drink green tea, sugar cane juice, coconut milk, and soft drinks. Some French foods, like coffee and long loaves of bread called baguettes, remain popular as well.

VIETNAM'S WILDLIFE

Malayan Tapir

Vietnam's broad range of climate and landscape supports a variety of plant and animal life. The extensive forests are home to many different species. However, chemical deforestation by the U.S. during the Vietnam War killed large areas of forest in the south. Today, illegal logging and human settlements have prevented these forests from growing back.

Several large mammals live in Vietnam's central highlands, including elephants, tapirs, tigers, leopards, wild oxen, and bears. The forests are also home to deer, wild pigs, porcupines, jackals, otters, skunks, and several types of primates. Vietnam is home to about 600 species of birds as well as many crocodiles, pythons, and cobras.

THE ECONOMY OF VIETNAM

After reunification in 1975, Vietnam's economy slowed down due to poor infrastructure and high population growth. The nation suffered high unemployment and poverty under government ownership of banks and factories. However, beginning in 1986, economic changes called *doi moi* (renovation) helped improve conditions by allowing for private ownership of businesses. The economy surged to the world's 37th largest based on Gross Domestic Product (GDP), a measure of goods and services produced. This is due, in part, to a huge workforce that is the 12th largest in the world. Of this population, about half work in agriculture, a fifth work in industry, and just less than a third work in services.

Vietnam is a major world exporter (34th) and importer (32nd). It exports clothes, shoes, electronics, seafood, rice, and coffee to the United States, China, Japan, and other countries. It imports products like machinery, steel, plastics, and automobiles, mainly from China and

South Korea. Vietnam joined the international World Trade Organization (WTO) in 2007.

Agriculture

About 35% of Vietnam's land is used for agriculture, which makes up almost a fifth of the overall economy. Though agriculture employs more workers than any other sector, it has decreased in importance over the past few decades. Vietnamese farmers produce rice, coffee, rubber, tea, pepper, soybeans, cashews, sugar cane, peanuts, bananas, and poultry. The Red River delta, Mekong River delta, and the southern terrace region produce most of the nation's agricultural products. Rice is by far the most important crop.

Forestry and Fishing

Forests cover about 45% of the land in Vietnam. The lumber industry produces raw materials for furniture, plywood, and paper. Vietnam's extensive coastal waters contribute to a strong fishing industry. Seafood has become one of the nation's top exports, including shrimp, squid, crab, and lobster.

Mineral and Energy Resources

Coal makes up the largest portion of the mining industry in Vietnam. Other minerals include phosphates, manganese, bauxite, chromate, and offshore oil and gas deposits. The country is investing in infrastructure to make the most of their oil and gas resources. The population surge of the 1980's resulted in energy shortages for a decade. Since then, Vietnam has successfully quadrupled its energy output.

Manufacturing

Manufacturing makes up 38% of Vietnam's economy, with food and beverage processing leading the way. This includes the processing of seafood, coffee, tea, and condiments. The nation also produces clothing, shoes, machinery, cement, chemical fertilizer, glass, tires, oil, and mobile phones. Automobile manufacturing is the fastest-growing industry in Vietnam.

Services

Service industries once took a backseat to industrial and military development, but now make up almost 50% of Vietnam's economy. Many service jobs, such as research, design, marketing, finance, and telecommunications, support the robust manufacturing industries. Additionally, jobs in tourism have increased in recent years.

Transportation

Vietnam's rugged interior makes north-south transportation difficult and forces traffic to the narrow coastal lowlands. The government has worked to expanded some rail lines and highways. Nevertheless, roughly half of the nation's roads are unpaved and many paved roads need repair. Few people own automobiles, but many use bicycles, motorcycles, and buses. Many small boats navigate the rivers and canals of the major river deltas while larger ships operate along coastal ports. Many small cities have domestic airports and Ho Chi Minh City and Hanoi have international airports.

Communication

Telecommunications have grown rapidly in the past few decades, with Vietnam currently 8th in the world for cell phone usage. The government's Ministry of Information and Communication controls all media, including television, radio, newspapers, and magazines. It forbids criticism of the government or Marxist ideology in the media.

VIETNAM'S HISTORY

Early History

Although people have lived in the region since the Stone Age, Vietnam was first mentioned by Chinese explorers in the 200's BCE. At that time, Vietnam was a collection of tribes living along the Red River delta. An Duong founded a kingdom called Au Lac in 258. Half a century later, Chinese official Zhao Tuo absorbed Au Lac and others into his own kingdom of Nam Viet. The Chinese Han dynasty conquered Nam Viet in 111, setting off centuries of Chinese rule and Vietnamese rebellion. The Vietnamese finally threw off Chinese rule permanently in 938 CE, after a rebellion led by Ngo Quyen. Despite Vietnam's independence, Chinese influence in government, writing, religion, and other areas remained.

In 944, Ngo Quyen's death left Vietnam unstable. The nation entered a period of rule by sparring warlords and various dynasties. The longest-lasting of these were the Ly dynasty (1009–1225) and the Tran dynasty (1225–1400), which gave the nation some political stability. Throughout the following years, rulers continued expanding Vietnam into the south. The growing nation alternatively cooperated with and fought off invasion from the Chinese. Internal conflicts and a struggle for control divided the country and the government during the 15th through the 18th centuries.

Finally, in 1802, the Nguyen dynasty produced a leader who united the country. Nguyen Anh took the role of emperor and changed his name to Gia Long. He named his new nation Vietnam and established its capital in Hue. Although the Nguyen dynasty formally continued until 1945, the French invasion in 1858 disrupted the Vietnamese government.

Western Conquest

Beginning in the 17th century, Western powers began colonizing areas of Eastern Asia, seeking to capitalize on trade opportunities. The French military began moving into southern Vietnam in 1858, first seizing the city of Da Nang. By the 1890's, France ruled all of Vietnam, along with Cambodia and Laos, in what was called French Indochina. France claimed its conquest was an effort to protect missionaries and Catholic converts, but in reality France wanted a base for trade with China. Once the French discovered the rich mineral resources and agricultural potential of Vietnam, they also sought to build plantations and export goods. Consequently, the French improved the national infrastructure, building roads, railways, and bridges and expanding ports.

The French-Vietnamese ruling class caused increasing dissatisfaction among the Vietnamese population at large. Political parties, such as the Vietnamese Nationalist Party, the Indochinese Communist Party, and the New Vietnamese Revolutionary party resisted French rule. Most Vietnamese were optimistic when, in 1940, the French government allowed Japan to use parts of Vietnam for military operations during World War II. The Vietnamese thought that the Japanese would help free them from French rule. Many eagerly made plans to help the Japanese fight against the French.

However, Japan had no intention of granting Vietnam independence. In 1941, many Vietnamese joined an organization called the Vietminh. Under the leadership of Ho Chi Minh and other Communist party officials, the Vietminh called for unity and independence.

End of Colonialism

In March of 1945, Japan seized control of Vietnam from the French. The victory was short lived, as Japan surrendered to Allied forces in August of that same year. Shortly afterward, Vietnam declared its independence in the August Revolution, establishing the Democratic Republic of Vietnam (DRV). Drawing from the American Declaration of Independence and inspired by the way the United States overthrew European colonialism, Ho and other leaders fully expected the United States to support Vietnam's revolution. However, despite the Vietminh's cooperation with the U.S. during World War II, their communist ideologies prevented U.S. support.

France responded to the Vietminh's declaration of independence by going to war. During this Indochina War, France controlled most of Vietnam's cities while Vietnamese revolutionaries controlled the countryside. In the south, many Vietnamese who opposed communism sided with the French, as did Bao Dai, the Nguyen dynasty's last emperor. Together, they formed the Associated State of Vietnam to fight against the Vietminh. The fighting ended in 1954 when the Vietminh won a victory over the French at Dien Bien Phu.

The outcome of the war was the Geneva Accords, a set of agreements written in Geneva, Switzerland in 1954 by a group of representatives from Cambodia, China, France, Laos, the United Kingdom, the United States, the Soviet Union, the Democratic Republic of Vietnam, and the Associated State of Vietnam. The agreements temporarily divided Vietnam into the Communist-dominated north and the non-communist south. They planned for a 1956 election to unite the country, but the election was continually postponed by the southern Vietnamese (supported by the U.S.), who feared Ho Chi Minh would win.

Vietnam War

After World War II, the United States and other Western nations sought to end the spread of communism. The U.S. aided European countries in rebuilding after the devastation of the war. This aid allowed France to continue fighting in Vietnam. Not only did the U.S. deny support to the Vietminh and aid France, but it also formally recognized the Associated State of Vietnam in the south.

In 1957, Vietnamese rebels in the south revolted against the U.S.-backed government of Ngo Dinh Diem. The United States responded by sending money, military equipment, and troops to aid South Vietnam, beginning the Vietnam War,

A young Ho Chi Minh at the French Communist Party congress in 1921

or, as the Vietnamese call it, the American War. During the fighting, the U.S. military attempted to cut off South Vietnam from northern troops by dropping tons of chemicals on the forests of central Vietnam. Rice fields and villages were destroyed by the war. In addition to these losses, millions of Vietnamese died, many of whom were civilians, along with 58,000 American soldiers. The U.S. withdrew the last of its troops in 1973 and, two years later, the south fell to northern Communist forces. The nation became united as the Socialist Republic of Vietnam.

Khmer Rouge

Just after the Vietnam War ended, Vietnam entered a long war in neighboring Cambodia. There, a Communist government called the

Khmer Rouge refused Vietnam's efforts to create close ties. As a result, Vietnam invaded Cambodia in December of 1978 and overthrew the Khmer Rouge, installing a pro-Vietnamese government while the Khmer Rouge forces retreated to isolated jungles of the country. Years of guerilla warfare followed as the Khmer Rouge fought against Vietnamese rule. Most other Southeast Asian nations opposed Vietnam's invasion, and China even briefly entered the war against Vietnam. The United States and other Western countries imposed a trade embargo, banning trade with Vietnam. In the 1980's, Vietnam began withdrawing troops from Cambodia, but the war continued until 1991.

Vietnam Today

In 1986, a new policy called *doi moi*, or renovation, allowed for more economic freedom and modernized the Vietnamese economy. It also allowed for more foreign investment in the once-isolated nation, improving overall living conditions. In 1995, Vietnam reestablished a diplomatic relationship with the United States. It also joined the Association of Southeast Asian Nations (ASEAN), an organization formed to help improve the political, economic, and social stability of the region. Today, Vietnam and the United States have a trade agreement that has normalized their trade relationship.

THE VIETNAM WAR

The United States' longest war took place in Southeast Asia from 1954–1975. The conflict occurred between Communist North Vietnam (or the Communist Democratic Republic of Vietnam) and non-communist South Vietnam (or the Republic of Vietnam). North Vietnam and some of its allies in the south sought to unite the country as one under communism. South Vietnam fought to remain separate and maintain a democratic government.

The conflict escalated when powerful nations involved in the Cold War took up rival causes. The United States, in an effort to stop the spread of communism, supported the South. The Soviet Union and China supported the North. All three nations provided money, equipment, and military advice, but only the United States sent combat troops. In the end, the United States and South Vietnam were unable to defeat the North Vietnamese.

War Begins

From 1957 to 1963, the war mainly involved soldiers from South Vietnam fighting against the Viet Cong (rebels who supported the North). North Vietnam, while still trying to avoid military conflict, supported the revolt. It did not engage directly in the fighting but sent supplies to the South by way of roads and trails through Cambodia and Laos that became known as the Ho Chi Minh Trail. As the Viet Cong grew in numbers and strength, the U.S., now under the leadership of President John F. Kennedy, increased military and economic aid to South Vietnam.

During this time, Buddhists in South Vietnam complained that Diem, a Roman Catholic, and his government were restricting their religious rights. Many Buddhists protested, but Diem did little to improve the situation. Eventually, South Vietnamese generals, with the support of the U.S., overthrew Diem and murdered him. A period of instability followed, creating an opportunity for North Vietnam to step in and take control.

Intense Fighting

Beginning in 1964, North Vietnam started fighting against the southern forces directly, and quickly gained control of about 75% of South Vietnam. An incident in the Gulf of Tonkin off the coast of North Vietnam brought the first U.S. combat troops into the war. The U.S. destroyer *Maddox* was attacked by the North Vietnamese as it monitored secret naval raids. President Lyndon B. Johnson announced two days later that North Vietnamese torpedo boats had again attacked the *Maddox* and the *C. Turner Joy*, though this second attack was never proven. Although the U.S.

did not declare war against North Vietnam, Johnson began sending troops into Vietnam in 1965.

In addition to the United States, the nations of Australia, New Zealand, the Philippines, South Korea, and Thailand also sent soldiers to support South Vietnam. By 1969, half a million U.S. troops were stationed in Vietnam. Together, those fighting on the side of the South greatly outnumbered the troops of the North. Meanwhile, the Soviet Union and China sent money, equipment, and advisers to the North but did not engage combat troops. The North Vietnamese, in turn, used these resources to fight and to support their allies in the South.

The U.S. strategy relied on superior equipment and a highly-trained military. They used B-52 bombers to make air strikes against North Vietnam and the Viet Cong. Helicopters searched out enemies, delivered supplies, and transported the wounded. The U.S. hoped not to conquer North Vietnam but to wear them down so they would give up the fight. Meanwhile, the North Vietnamese and Viet Cong avoided large battles, instead relying on surprise attacks.

Bombing by the U.S. caused tremendous damage, but did not bring an end to the fighting. In ground battles, the U.S. soldiers often won, but North Vietnam continued to supply replacement troops to the Viet Cong. It also relied on its vast store of materials supplied by the Soviet Union and China. Americans began to voice complaints about the war in Vietnam. Some wanted the military to act more aggressively in attacking the North and forcing an end to the war. Others wanted the U.S. to withdraw completely.

The War Ends

After years of fighting, the U.S. could no longer bear the cost and the casualties of the Vietnam War. President Johnson asked for new taxes to help finance the war and the American people strongly resisted. Around this same time, the North Vietnamese increased their efforts against the capital city of Saigon. They hoped that the South Vietnamese would lose faith in their unstable government and the Americans would negotiate peace. In January of 1968, North Vietnam launched the Tet Offensive, named after the Vietnamese New Year of Tet. Although it did not have the desired effect, the attacks shocked the Americans and led President Johnson to make political changes that led toward peace.

Peace talks began in 1968 in Paris. Although the nations were unable to reach an agreement, the number of American troops in Vietnam began to decline. President Richard M. Nixon planned to help train the South Vietnamese army to take over the war effort so the U.S. could pull out completely.

In 1970, however, U.S. and South Vietnamese soldiers entered Cambodia, where they captured large stores of North Vietnamese weapons. Many Americans protested this campaign because they thought it increased the war effort once again. At Kent State University in Ohio, National Guard soldiers fired on student protesters, killing four and wounding several others. Widespread protests broke out across the country, prompting the government to bring its involvement in Vietnam to an end.

The U.S. withdrew the last of its troops in 1973. Although the nations involved agreed to a ceasefire during this time, the fighting resumed soon after the Americans left. Two years later, the South fell to northern Communist forces. North Vietnam captured the southern capital of Saigon (now Ho Chi Minh City) and the South surrendered. The nation became united as the Socialist Republic of Vietnam.

Around this time, North Vietnam also helped nearby Cambodia and Laos adopt Communist governments. However, Cambodia's Khmer Rouge, a pro-communist group, favored the Chinese over the Vietnamese. Conflicts arose that led to a lengthy fight between Vietnam, Cambodia, and China.

The unified nation of Vietnam finally held an election in April of 1976 to choose its 500-member National Assembly. In an effort to "reeducate" citizens who had supported the non-communist South, the government sent more than a million people to labor camps. Some spent days or weeks, while others spent over a decade. Other changes occurred as northerners migrated to the south, bringing with them their own dialect of Vietnamese which became the standard language. The government relocated many ethnic Kinh to new areas in the highlands and mountains.

Under these changes, many Vietnamese and even Chinese fled the country. Known as *boat people* for the small boats they used for travel, these refugees risked drowning and pirate attacks. Many landed in refugee camps throughout Southeast Asia until they could relocate to the United States, Canada, Australia, Belgium, and France. When the United Nations closed nearly all of the refugee camps in the mid-1990's, many refugees were sent back to Vietnam.

Effects of the War

During the years of fighting, the U.S. military attempted to cut off South Vietnam from northern troops by dropping tons of chemicals on the forests of central Vietnam, causing lasting devastation. Rice fields and villages were also destroyed by the war. In addition to these losses, over 3 million Vietnamese died, about half of whom were civilians, along with 58,000 American soldiers. In addition, about 300,000 American soldiers were wounded.

U.S. involvement in the war was strongly debated at that time and has continued to be debated since. Americans disagree about whether or not military efforts were necessary or effective. Information has surfaced about questionable decisions and secret actions of U.S. military leaders. Many veterans of the Vietnam War had trouble adjusting to civilian life at the war's end and struggled with alcoholism, drug abuse, depression, and homelessness. Because many Americans opposed the war, they treated returning veterans poorly.

In 1982, the United States government dedicated the Vietnam Veterans Memorial in Washington, D.C. Its long stretch of black granite bears the names of those Americans who lost their lives in the war. In 1995, the United States and Vietnam began diplomatic relations once again.

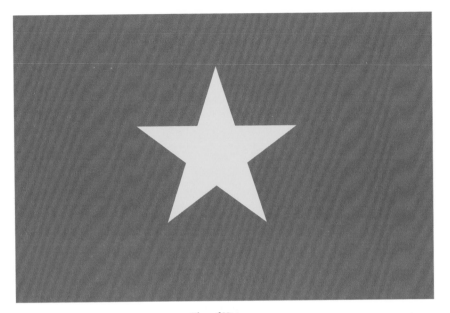

Flag of Vietnam

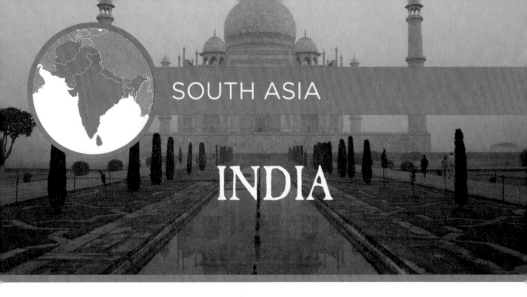

INDIA

INDIA: THE BIG PICTURE

India is the world's 7th largest country in terms of size, but its population is the second-highest in the world. Therefore, the nation is more crowded than almost any other. Nestled into southern Asia, this home to over 1 billion people borders the Arabian Sea and the Bay of Bengal between Burma and Pakistan.

Diversity abounds in India, from its climate to its geography to its people. The land spans snowy mountains in the north, a scorching desert in the west, and wet, tropical forests in the south. The people represent a wide variety of ethnicities and religious groups and they speak over 1,000 different languages and dialects. Many Indians are well-educated and wealthy but millions of others live in poverty and lack basic literacy skills. The ethnic and religious diversity that creates a rich culture in India also leads to ongoing friction between people groups.

Civilization in India began sometime around 2,500 BCE in the Indus Valley. Through the ages, many different empires ruled the area. In the late 1700's, Great Britain took control of India as a colony. Traders exploited the people and resources, which included gold, spices, and textiles. After struggling for independence for almost 200 years, India gained independence in 1947. Since then, the nation has undergone several political, economic, and geographical changes.

MEET THE PEOPLE OF INDIA

India's huge population is almost three-quarters Indo-Aryan. The next largest ethnicity is Dravidian. There are many others. The Indo-Aryans descend from a central Asian people group called the Aryans. They invaded India sometime around 1500 BCE and drove the indigenous Dravidians south. Today, most Indo-Aryans still live in the north while most Dravidians live in the south. Various small tribes live in remote forest and hill areas throughout the country. They include the Bhils, Gonds, Khasis, Mizos, and many others.

India has the widest variety of languages—over 1,000—spoken anywhere in the world. Among the many languages spoken throughout the country, Hindi accounts for 41% of speakers, with Bengali, Telugu, Marathi, Tamil, Urdu, and other languages in lesser amounts. Many of India's modern languages grew out of Sanskrit, an ancient language. Most people also speak English, which officials use for political and commercial communication. All elementary and secondary schools require Hindi, but many English-language schools also exist, especially in large cities.

For a time, the Indian government attempted to unite the country by spreading the Hindi language to all people. However,

Fast Facts

Capital:
New Delhi

Size:
7th in the world

Area:
2,042,611 sq miles
(5,290,338 sq km)

Coastline:
4,350 miles (7,000 km)

Highest Point:
Kanchenjunga 28,209 feet
(8,598 m)

Lowest Point:
Indian Ocean 0 feet (0 m)

Population:
1.3 billion

Official Languages:
Hindi, English, and 14 others

Currency: ₹
Indian rupee

National Anthem:
"Jana-Gana-Mana"
(Thou Art the Ruler of
the Minds of All People)

National Symbol:
Lion Capital of Ashoka,
which depicts
four Asiatic lions
standing back to
back mounted on
a circular abacus

सत्यमेव जयते

many non-Hindi speakers opposed this effort. They feared the loss of their culture and discrimination. Finally, the Indian government gave in to pressure to organize states around language groups. For example, most Telugu speakers live in Andhra Pradesh and Telangana. However, every state still includes a variety of languages and dialects. When drivers travel to and from a different state, the script and language on the signs change.

LAND, WATER, AND CLIMATE IN INDIA

The nation of India, along with Bangladesh and Pakistan, sits on a subcontinent set off from the rest of Asia by mountains. The southern portion juts into the Indian Ocean in a triangular peninsula. The north shares boundaries with Bangladesh, Bhutan, Burma, China, Nepal, and Pakistan. India is slightly more than one-third the size of the United States, making it the seventh-largest nation in the world. India also includes island territories in the Indian Ocean—Lakshadweep in the Arabian Sea and the Andaman and Nicobar Islands in the Bay of Bengal.

Land

India's major land divisions include the Himalayas in the north, flat to rolling plains along the Ganges in the middle of the country, and an upland plain called the Deccan Plateau in the south.

The world's largest mountain system, the Himalayas, forms India's northern border. The peaks stretch approximately 1,500 miles (2,400 km) from Pakistan to Bhutan. A relatively young mountain range, the Himalayas experience frequent earthquakes and landslides as they continue to grow. This activity often causes extensive damage and loss of life. Many deep gorges, raging streams, and glaciers crisscross the Himalayas. The world's highest peak, Mount Everest, lies outside of India along the China-Nepal border, but Kanchenjunga, the third tallest mountain in the world, lies on India's border with Nepal. Snow covers the Himalayas year-round.

The Indo-Gangetic Plain, or the North Indian Plain, occupies the middle portion of India. This flat expanse of land contains the Indus River system in the west and the Ganges River basin in the east. The Ganges delta

Map of India

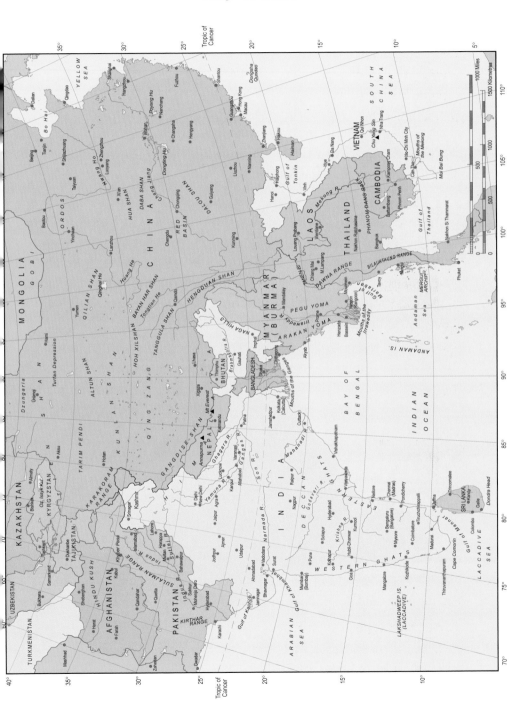

area floods each year with the monsoon rains. The rich, fertile soil has supported farming in the region for centuries. To the far west lies the sparsely populated Thar Desert.

In southern India, the Deccan plateau rises about 1,000 to 2,500 feet (305 to 760 meters) above sea level. It includes mountainous, rainy areas called the Western Ghats along the Arabian Sea and the hilly Eastern Ghats along the Bay of Bengal. The two meet in the southern Nilgiri Hills. While the Western and Eastern Ghats are covered in thick forests, most of the remaining Deccan plateau is farmland.

Water

The Indian Ocean surrounding India's southern peninsula consists of the Arabian Sea to the west and the Bay of Bengal to the east. The southern tip of India, Cape Comorin, divides the two bodies of water.

India's greatest river, the Ganges, begins high in the Himalayas and flows east to the Bay of Bengal. Indians consider its waters sacred, and they often bathe in the river to purify themselves. Important cities such as Allahabad and Varanasi have sprung up along the Ganges River.

Other important rivers include the Indus, Brahmaputra, Narmada, Tapi, Godavari, Krishna, and Mahanadi. India has few natural lakes for such a large country, but it has many reservoirs formed by damming rivers. The nation's largest natural freshwater lake is Wular Lake.

Climate

Overall, India has three main seasons. The hot, dry season lasts from March to June, the hot, wet season lasts from June to September, and the cool season lasts from October to February. Low temperatures reach far below zero in the Himalayas and high temperatures regularly exceed 100° F in the plains and desert. May and June are the hottest months.

India experiences seasonal monsoons, with strong seasonal winds bringing heavy rains. The rains often provide relief from the intense heat and help crops to grow. Other times, they cause flash floods and widespread damage. Monsoons bring approximately three-fourths of India's yearly precipitation. Rainfall in India varies from 450 inches (1143 cm) per year in the northeast to less than 4 inches (10 cm) per year in some desert regions. Before and after monsoon season, India experiences fierce tropical cyclones in the coastal areas. The country also experiences droughts, severe thunderstorms, and earthquakes. Barren Island in the Andaman Sea is a volcano that has been active in recent years.

EVERYDAY LIFE IN INDIA

Communities in India are organized into social groups called *castes.* People follow rules about what job to have, what to eat, and who to marry based on their caste. A person's caste, or *jati,* is determined by birth and never changes. Rules about castes have become less strict, but the social classes still exist. The caste system can be seen more clearly among Hindus than among other religious groups.

In modern times, middle- and upper-class Indians living in cities enjoy a lifestyle similar to that of many European and American city dwellers. Poorer or rural Indians have diverse lifestyles, some of which are isolated and involve traditional work done by hand. Religion and caste dictate much of everyday life for almost all Indians.

Family Life

Almost all Indians consider the family the most important social entity. Traditionally, Indian families included several generations under one roof, sharing living space, chores, and even finances. A woman would move into the home of her husband's family, which might include his parents, his brothers and their wives, his unmarried sisters, and any children. A male is the undisputed head of the household and females are expected to be obedient.

Parents often arrange marriages in order to bring chosen families together. Families of the bride pay a *dowry,* gifts of money or goods given to a husband's family, even though the practice has become illegal. Couples are expected to have children soon after marriage and society prefers sons over daughters because sons take on the responsibilities of working on farms and caring for aging parents. In recent times, families living in one home have grown smaller, with just parents and their young children living together. People can reject an arranged marriage and chose a partner based on love. In India, almost all adults are married and divorce is uncommon.

City Life

Indian cities began as centers of trade, politics, and religion. Varanasi, Patna, and others date back to ancient times. Other cities began as small fishing villages that the British developed into major ports in the 1600's. Among these, Mumbai now boasts a population of 12 million, Kolkata 11 million, and Chennai 9 million. Other major cities include the capital city New Delhi (and its surrounding region of Delhi) with a population of 11 million, Bangalore with 10 million people, and Hyderabad with 9 million people. Despite these high populations, less than one-third of Indians live in urban areas.

Once India gained independence from Britain, many Indians moved to the cities in search of jobs. Cities became overcrowded and people did not have enough housing and resources. Not everyone had electricity or water. Some people lived packed into tiny shacks in slum areas. Today,

Varanasi, one of the world's oldest continually inhabited cities

cities are still tightly packed with people, buildings, vehicles, and even animals. Shops line the crowded city streets and often have living space above or behind. Many Indians still live in poverty, with inadequate housing and resources. They live in extensive slums or are homeless.

Outside of the crowded cities, wealthy businesspeople or high-ranking government and military officers live in *cantonments*. These lovely homes line wide, tree-lined streets and have access to modern shopping areas. British rulers built the cantonments when they ruled India and lived there away from the crowded neighborhoods of the Indians. Today, India's big cities have some of the highest housing prices in the world. The government has done little to provide affordable housing for the many who live in poverty.

Country Life

Because India is so crowded, rural areas are generally made up of villages. There, families live close together and farm the nearby fields. Poorer families live in small huts with mud floors while wealthier families can afford to build homes from brick or concrete. Inside their homes, villagers have few possessions. They have pots for cooking, carrying water, and storing grain. They sleep on woven mats that can be moved outside during warm weather. Some villages have electricity and running water, but many others have only kerosene lanterns for light and a nearby pond or river for water. Most villagers cook over a *chula*, a clay, coal-burning oven.

Narrow, unpaved roads wind through India's rural villages. People gather in open central areas, possibly near a well, grain mill, or temple. There, villagers might also have access to a few shops, a post office, and a loudspeaker that broadcasts public radio.

Recreation

Indians love to play and watch cricket, a British game similar to baseball. They also enjoy field hockey, golf, and soccer. *Kabaddi* is a traditional Indian team sport, some 4,000 years old, that resembles rugby and wrestling. Another traditional game, *kho-kho*, resembles tag.

Outside of athletics, Indians play cards and chess and fly kites. Like people in most countries, they enjoy television, movies, concerts, and plays.

Education

The Indian Constitution provides free, mandatory education for children up to age 14. The literacy rate varies greatly from state to state, from roughly 50% in Bihar to almost 100% in Kerala. In general, literacy of males (81%) is far greater than literacy of females (61%).

Students in India attend primary school for five years (from about age 6 to 11). Many students attend irregularly or stop attending school altogether. By age 11–14, only half of Indian children attend school. Many of them drop out to help at home with farm chores or to watch younger children. The Indian government is working to improve education, especially for girls and those in disadvantaged groups.

In addition to free public school, India has many private and church-run schools. These schools generally use English as a primary language and are very popular among families that can afford the tuition. India also has many government-run universities. However, graduates often have trouble finding jobs and many leave the country, never to return.

Religion

Although India has no official religion, most Indians are very religious. About 80% practice Hinduism and 14% are Muslim. Other religions, such as Christianity, Buddhism, and Sikhism, can be practiced in India. In 1947, Pakistan broke away from India to become an independent, and mainly Muslim, country. Many Muslim Indians moved to Pakistan and many Hindus and Sikhs moved from Pakistan to India.

Hinduism involves a wide variety of beliefs. Among the sacred texts, the Vedas, the Upanishads, and the Puranas outline some beliefs and guide behavior among believers. Hindus worship Brahman, who takes many forms. Among the thousands of gods and goddesses, most Hindus worship Shiva or Vishnu. Another key belief is *reincarnation*, or the belief that the soul is reborn into another body after death. Many Hindus practice *yoga*, which develops physical and mental fitness. They do not eat beef because they consider cows to be sacred. In spring, Hindus celebrate Holi by sprinkling colored powder on one another. In fall, they celebrate Diwali with fireworks. The most popular festival throughout

India, Vasantpanchami, celebrates Sarasvati, the Hindu god of learning, each February.

Around 500 BCE, Siddhartha Gautama founded Buddhism in India. The religion grew and spread to other countries, but has since become less popular in India. In the 700's CE, Islam came to India and many Hindus converted. Today, many of the world's Muslims live in India, mostly in large cities of the north. They mainly fall into the Sunni sect, but Shiite Muslims also exist in small pockets around the country. Around 1500, Europeans brought Christianity to India. Most Indian Christians now live in the northeast and the far south. They are mainly Roman Catholic and have come mostly from the lower castes or from tribal groups.

India is also home to significant populations of Jainists, Sikhs, and Zoroastrians. Jainism began in India in the 500's BCE. Its founder, Mahavira, taught a peaceful existence that values all animal life. Therefore, Jainists are strict vegetarians. Also originated in India, the Sikh religion was founded by Nanak in the late 1400's. This *guru*, or religious teacher, celebrated bravery and renounced the caste system. Today, many Sikhs are farmers, traders, and soldiers. Zoroastrians, also known as Parsis, came to India over 1,000 years ago from Iran. They fled to India to avoid conversion to Islam and now make up the world's largest Zoroastrian population.

Much of India's small Jewish population has moved to Israel. Various tribal peoples practice folk religions, such as those involving animism or spirit worship.

HINDUISM

Hinduism is one of the world's major religions, just behind Christianity and Islam in the number of followers. Although the British gave Hinduism its name in the early 1800's, the religious traditions of Hinduism began around 4,000 years ago in India. Today, approximately 950 million people around the world practice some form of Hinduism. It remains most popular in India. Hinduism is classified as a religion, but many followers consider it more a way of life than a set of religious beliefs.

Some Hindus prefer the title "Vedic religion" for their faith. This term refers to the ancient texts known as the Vedas. This collection of religious poems was originally spoken works that were later written in Sanskrit. The four Vedas each contain four parts that include prayers, hymns, theology, and philosophy. These writings inspired later texts such as the *Puranas*, the *Ramayana*, and the *Mahabharata*. The *Puranas*, stories written in verse, tell about the Hindu deities and heroes. They describe the beginning of the world and the cycle of death and rebirth. The *Ramayana* and the *Mahabharata* are long epic poems that teach Hindu beliefs through adventure stories. In one such story, Prince Rama tries to rescue his wife from the demon king Ravana. In another, a warrior named Arjuna discusses the meaning of life with the god Krishna.

Krishna is just one of many Hindu gods and goddesses. Another god Hindus believe in is Brahman, whose spirit takes many forms, including animals and objects. Most Hindus worship Shiva, the god who destroys the universe and allows for rebirth, or Vishnu, who preserves the universe and also takes human forms called *avatars*. Some Hindus worship gods in animal form, since they believe animals as well as people have souls. Cows are especially sacred, which is why Hindus do not eat beef.

An important Hindu belief is that of *reincarnation*. According to Hindu teaching, the soul never dies but is reborn into a new body after the old body dies. A person can even be reincarnated into an animal. Throughout their lives, Hindus follow the law of *karma*, which states that their actions will determine how they become reincarnated. A good life leads to rebirth into a higher state while an evil life leads to rebirth into a lowly state. The goal of life is to achieve spiritual perfection, which ends the cycle of death and rebirth. Then Hindus enter a new existence called *moksha*. Most Hindus are cremated rather than buried upon death.

Some Hindus achieve special status during their lifetime via spiritual disciplines. A *guru*, or spiritual teacher, develops understanding of spiritual matters. A *yogi* practices yoga and strict self-discipline. Both gurus and yogis are respected during life and after death. Sometimes Hindus disagree about whether a person has become a true guru or yogi.

Hindu beliefs affect almost all areas of life and society. One of the greatest influences is the *caste* system outlined in several Hindu texts. This social class system divides labor in a community and outlines rules of conduct. A person's caste, or *jati*, is determined by birth and never changes. The caste system groups people into four main classes. The highest caste, called Brahmans, includes priests and scholars. The next group, called Kshatriyas, includes rulers and warriors. The Vaishyas include merchants and other professionals, and the Shudras are artisans, laborers, and servants. The caste system has grown to include thousands of sub-categories over time. The lowest class, called *untouchables*, falls outside the caste system. Members of this class handle undesirable jobs, such as those involving garbage, toilets, or dead people or animals. They often live in villages isolated from the rest of society and many Indians refuse to even touch them. Untouchables have equal rights under the Indian Constitution, but they still face discrimination. Hindus follow rules about what job to have, what to eat, and whom to marry based on caste. These rules have become less strict over time, but the social classes still exist.

Hindu worship typically occurs at home or individually rather than in large communities. Most homes contain a shrine to a chosen deity and family members conduct the daily worship. They perform ceremonies and rituals around special events, such as the birth of a child, in order to give thanks or to ask for protection and prosperity. Worship at home often involves five elements: food offered to the gods, another offering for "all beings," water mixed with sesame offered to spirits of the deceased, hospitality in the home, and reciting the Vedas. Other rituals include bathing, prayer, and meditation. Sometimes a Hindu priest visits the home to perform rituals.

At community temples, priests take care of sculpted images of gods and goddesses. Each temple is dedicated to one deity and contains several shrines that portray that deity in different forms. Hindus believe that the deities actually live in the images, so priests wash and dress them and bring them food each day. Temples might be small, simple structures or huge, walled compounds that include bathing pools, courtyards, schools, hospitals, and monasteries.

On special days, temples can become quite crowded as Hindus gather to honor a deity. Some people make a pilgrimage, or journey, to visit a temple on a special occasion. Other festivals are celebrated at home or in the neighborhood. In spring, Hindus celebrate Holi in honor of Kama, the god of love. They dance, build bonfires, and sprinkle colored powder on one another. The Indian new year begins just after Holi, so it is also a time to forgive others, pay debts, and rid oneself of evil. In the fall, Hindus celebrate Diwali in honor of Lakshmi, the goddess of wealth and good fortune. They set off fireworks and participate in gambling. The most popular festival throughout India, Vasantpanchami, celebrates Sarasvati, the Hindu god of learning, each February. Festivals fall on different dates depending on the region and often last several days.

SIKHISM

Perhaps you've heard of a *guru*—a person who is a wise teacher or spiritual guide. The word *guru* is actually a Sanskrit term that has been used by different Indian religions for thousands of years. Even the early Vedas refer to gurus.

In the late 1400's, Guru Nanak, a spiritual teacher, developed the Sikh (pronounced "seek") religion in the Punjab region of northwest India. The word *Sikh* is Sanskrit for *disciple* or *learner*. The Sikhs call their faith *Gurmat*, which is Punjabi for "the Way of the Guru."

At the age of 30, Nanak received a revelation from God. He spent the rest of his life spreading the message of God's oneness and the equality of all humans. Although Guru Nanak was the first leader, Sikhs believe that 10 Gurus in all shared the same spirit. The last of these 10, Guru Gobind Singh, died in 1708. After that, the spirit of the Guru transferred to Sikhism's sacred text, *Guru Granth Sahib* ("The Granth as the Guru").

Sikhism developed under Mughal rule in northern India, which was a time of persecution for Sikhs. Authorities killed the 5th and the 9th gurus. Therefore, the 10th and final guru created a Sikh military, called *Khalsa*, or *brotherhood of the pure*. At this time, Sikh men adopted their signature long hair and added the surname *Singh*, or *lion*, to their name.

Sikhs believe in one God, who is all-powerful but without form. They call the essence of God *Naam,* or the Divine Name. It is this essence that indwelt the ten Gurus and now resides in the Guru Granth Sahib. Sikhs strive to be united with God through selflessness and meditation. By overcoming *humai,* the selfish nature all men are born with, they become freed from life and death. Until then, Sikhs believe in reincarnation, or rebirth, of the soul after death. After a person dies, Sikhism teaches that the soul can be reborn into any one of over 8 million life forms.

Sikhs meet in a *gurdwara,* a place of worship to meditate, listen to scripture readings, and share a meal. In the practice of *langar* (free kitchen), Sikhs prepare a vegetarian meal for the rest of the congregation.

Today, India is home to about 20 million Sikhs who mainly live in the state of Punjab. Sikhs also live around the world, especially in Canada, Malaysia, the United States, the United Kingdom, and countries in East Africa. Many Sikh men continue to observe the tradition of never shaving or cutting their hair. They wear their long hair tied in a knot called a *Joora,* and usually cover it with a turban.

Sikh man in traditional turban

Health Care

Until the country's independence from Great Britain in 1947, Indians experienced a very low life expectancy. Although this measure of health has improved greatly over the past decades, it still falls short of other nations. Starvation is no longer as great a concern as in the past, but many still suffer from malnutrition. India has a very low obesity rate, but it is also second in the world in the number of underweight children.

Many Indians lack access to safe drinking water, which leads to diseases such as bacterial diarrhea, hepatitis A and E, leptospirosis, and typhoid fever. Poor sanitation and sewage disposal contribute to these problems. Overall, the risk of infectious disease in India is very high. It ranks first in the world of people living with HIV/AIDS. Other risks include dengue fever, Japanese encephalitis, malaria, and rabies. More recently, the highly contagious H5N1 avian influenza (bird flu) has become a problem in India. Rates of tuberculosis and blindness due to trachoma (a contagious eye infection) remain high in India as well.

The Indian government has worked to improve overall health and welfare in the nation. Smallpox, which had been a leading cause of death, was wiped out in 1977. Another widespread effort almost freed India of malaria in 1958, but failed to wipe it out completely. The number of hospitals and rural health clinics has grown, though many lack proper equipment, medical supplies, and trained personnel. Efforts to provide welfare services to certain populations (nomadic tribes, lower castes, the disabled) have had little impact.

INDIA'S GOVERNMENT

The Republic of India is a federal republic with 29 states and 7 union territories. One of these territories is the National Capital Territory of Delhi in the nation's capital New Delhi. India won its independence from Great Britain on August 15, 1947. However, Indians celebrate Republic Day on January 26, a national holiday when the first Constitution was adopted in 1950. The government has amended the Constitution many times since then. It now guarantees all citizens equal rights and freedom from discrimination. The Constitution's guidelines also direct the government to promote the people's welfare through education, employment, and public health efforts.

India's central government is a parliamentary system consisting of a president as head of state and a prime minister as head of government. The president and two houses (House of the People and Council of States) make up the Parliament, which is India's main lawmaking body. The president serves a five-year term and appoints the prime minister, who is the most powerful official in the Indian government. The prime minister, along with the Council of Ministers, runs the day-to-day government operations.

In Parliament, the House of the People (or Lok Sabha) consists of 545 members who serve five-year terms. States with larger populations send more representatives to the Lok Sabha than states with smaller populations. The Council of States (or Rajya Sabha) consists of 250 members who serve six-year terms. Twelve of these members are popular academic or cultural figures nominated by the president.

In addition to India's central government, each state also has its own government body. It includes a governor appointed by the president and a chief minister, who is appointed by the governor. Citizens vote for the members of the state legislative body. State governments have little power and little income compared with Parliament. In small villages, elected leaders form a *panchayat*, or council. The panchayat helps solve minor problems by listening to complaints and assigning punishments.

The law system in India is based on the English model, but separate personal codes apply to Muslims, Christians, and Hindus. India's highest court, the Supreme Court, consists of a chief justice and 25 associate justices appointed by the president. Judges can serve until age 65. In general, India's courts are backlogged and suffer corruption. The government has been working since 2011 to solve these problems.

More than one million Indians voluntarily serve in the armed forces, which consist of an army, navy, coast guard, and air force. In addition to one of the world's largest military forces, India also has several police agencies. State governments oversee most police functions, but the central government handles those that involve border security, natural disasters, and central investigation.

INDIAN CULTURE

India has had over 4,000 years of artistic development. As a result, it has a rich and varied heritage of art and culture. Modern global influences have come slowly to India, especially its rural areas. Even in large cities, most Indians opt for traditional Indian fashion, cuisine, and culture. Although Western pop culture is widespread, especially among youths, India produces plenty of its own movies and music that are also popular at home and abroad.

Architecture

India's spectacular architecture dates back to the cave temples of Ajanta, Ellora, and others. Carved out of cliffs of solid rock in the first millennium CE, they contain ancient sculptures and frescoes (painting on plaster walls). Later Hindu temples continued the architectural tradition, including sculptured columns, open porches, gateway towers, and stone steps. Throughout the temples, visitors enjoy the many carvings and sculptures.

Muslim influence came to India in the 1200's, bringing with it unique architectural elements. The most famous example of this is the Taj Mahal in Agra. Built in 1650, the massive building is a tomb built by Emperor Shah Jahan for his favorite wife. Because Islam forbids representing images, the building is decorated in elaborate geometric and floral designs made of precious materials like marble and gems.

India is famous for its unique stepwells—huge depressions dug deep into the ground to reach the fresh water below. Stepwells combine form and function, using beautiful architecture to serve a practical purpose. They are lined all around with flights of steps and often include a Hindu temple. Stepwells were normally built by royal or wealthy Indians to provide villagers access to fresh water.

Decorated columns at Agra Fort

During the 1700's, Europeans brought Western-style architecture to India, mainly in the form of churches. Some of these buildings reflect the ancient architecture of Greece and Rome, while others follow the Gothic style, with tall spires and pointed arches. The British destroyed many of India's stepwells due to hygiene concerns.

Literature

Like many Indian traditions, literature began as a religious and philosophical expression. The Hindu Vedas, sacred texts, date back about 3,000 years. They were originally spoken works that were later written

The Taj Mahal and its long reflecting pool

in Sanskrit, an ancient Indian language. Today, priests and scholars still memorize some of the lengthy writings. Other popular works, originally in Sanskrit, include the *Mahabharata* and *Ramayana*. Both are epic poems that explore human values through fantastic adventures. They have inspired centuries of Indian literature.

Although British rule stifled the production of Indian literature, it has had a recent revival. Some popular authors write in their various regional languages or dialects, but many write in English. Bankim Chandra Chatterjee, who wrote in Bengali, first made the novel a popular genre in India. Modern writers like Salman Rushdie, Arundhati Roy, and Kiran Desai all wrote award-winning books in English.

Music and Dance

India has a long tradition of performing arts. As early as 400 BCE, dancers expressed Hindu themes in *bharata natyam*, the classical dance of southern India. It involves a single dancer performing an intricate sequence of symbolic hand gestures. Traditional dance varies by region and includes *kathak*, *odissi*, and *Manipuri*. These dances involve facial expressions, body movements, and hand gestures to tell stories and convey moods. A popular folk dance, the free-form *bhangra*, is known for its high-leaping dancers.

Traditional Indian music often expresses religious themes or accompanies performances at festivals and celebrations. It uses stringed instruments (sitar, sarod, tamboura, and vina) and percussion instruments (tabla and mridangam). Its distinct sound comes from a musical scale arranged in *ragas*, or patterns of notes. Today, the Symphony Orchestra of India in Mumbai plays Western classical music. Much of India's popular music comes from its movie musicals, which combine traditional, religious, and Western styles.

Theater and Cinema

India often produces more films per year than any other country. The "Bollywood" film industry, centered in Mumbai (formerly called Bombay), is named after its U.S. counterpart, Hollywood. Many of its movies involve vibrant song and dance scenes intermixed with action sequences. Indians closely follow the off-screen lives of favorite actors and actresses.

Indian theater has regained popularity after being pushed aside by cinema for many years. Bengali playwrights, like Nobel Prize winner Rabindranath Tagore, have helped lead the revival.

Fashion

Traditional clothing has remained popular in India, though more current Western-style clothing is widely available in cities. In general, men wear a simple, untailored *dhoti* or *lungi*, both types of loose, wrapped bottoms. Those in rural areas often go without a shirt or wear just a simple shawl in cooler weather. In cities, men wear tailored Western-style shirts and trousers, jackets, and vests. Indian women usually wear a *sari*—a long flowing skirt and short blouse. Women wrap their saris differently from region to region, normally draping a long piece of the fabric over a shoulder or the head. Saris are often brightly colored and embroidered. Women who reserve saris for special occasions dress day-to-day in the *shalwar-kamiz*—loose-fitting trousers with a long tunic. Many Indians do not wear shoes, especially in rural areas. When necessary, most Indians wear simple sandals on their feet. Many students, in and outside of cities, wear

Western-style tailored school uniforms. Jeans are becoming increasingly popular among wealthier Indians in cities.

Food and Drink

Indian cuisine is popular around the world, and it varies throughout India itself. In the north, most meals include flat wheat bread called *chapatti*. In the east and south, the primary grain is rice, and in the west, Indians eat pearl millet bread called *bajra*. In addition to the staple grain of the region, meals usually include a pureed legume called *dal* and vegetables. Wealthier Indians enjoy yogurt with their meals. Meat is rare, and many Indians are vegetarians. Hindus do not eat beef, as they consider cows sacred, and Muslims do not eat pork. Chicken and lamb are expensive and normally reserved for special occasions. Fish, milk, pickles, and fruit round out the Indian diet. A variety of spices add flavor to simple meals. Most dishes include some combination of chilies, coriander, cumin, garlic, ginger, mustard seeds, red pepper, and turmeric. Indians in the north and east drink tea, while those in the south more commonly enjoy coffee.

INDIA'S WILDLIFE

A rich variety of animal life abounds in India. The different climates and habitats have created homes for many different species of mammals, birds, reptiles, and aquatic life. The government and other organizations have created wildlife preserves. Some endangered animals, such as the great Indian bustard (a bird), are protected by laws.

The Indian elephant, the one-horned Indian rhinoceros, primates, and other large mammals roam the jungles and grasslands. All exist in limited numbers today and many are endangered. Wild elephants live in national parks like the Periyar Wildlife Sanctuary in Kerala and Bandipur in Karnataka. The Indian rhinoceros finds refuge at the Kaziranga National Park and the Manas Wildlife Sanctuary in Assam. Rhesus monkeys, gray monkeys, and macaques live in the forests and near human settlements. These clever primates have learned how to obtain food from homes and restaurants, and have become a nuisance in many areas.

Ruminants, a type of grass-eating animal, include wild bison, buffalo, and several varieties of antelope and deer. These populations draw several different predators, like lions, tigers, leopards, foxes, and jackals. The Asiatic lion, the only type found outside of Africa, only remains in Gir National Park in Gujarat. The Bengal tiger, the most numerous of tigers in the world, roams the forests throughout parts of India. Since Project Tiger began establishing reserves, the Bengal tiger has rebounded from the verge of extinction.

The Himalayas have their own variety of wildlife, such as wild sheep and goats, ibex, pandas, and snow leopards. In villages across India, people have domesticated oxen, buffalo, horses, and dromedary camels to help with farming and transportation.

Approximately one-eighth of the world's bird species live in India. The nation supports more than 1,200 species of birds, many living among the extensive rivers and wetlands where they feed upon fish. Flamingos have formed one of their largest breeding colonies in the Rann of Kachchh. Other notable bird species include the peacock, India's national bird, and the Indian crane, which stands as tall as a human.

Crocodiles abound in India's rivers, swamps, and lakes and often reach 20 feet (6 m) or more in length. In addition to these dangerous reptiles, India is also home to nearly 400 types of snake, many of them venomous. Turtles and lizards are common throughout India. Sharks inhibit the coastal waters and even travel inland through waterways. Approximately 2,000 species of fish also live in India's waters. Indians often catch and eat catfish, carp, and the 6-foot long mahseer.

Silkworms and bees produce valuable resources, as does the lac insect. It leaves behind a sticky substance that is used in lacquer and dye. Some pests, such as mosquitoes or flatworms, spread disease or make humans and animals ill.

THE ECONOMY OF INDIA

Gross Domestic Product, or GDP, measures the goods and services produced by a country. India's huge GDP is the fourth-largest in the world. However, because of India's massive population, its GDP per person is actually quite low, making it one of the world's poorest countries. About 30% of Indians live in poverty.

India's diverse economy ranges from traditional village farming to modern agriculture, from handicrafts to a wide range of modern industries, and it includes a multitude of services. Just under half of the work force is in agriculture. Services account for nearly two-thirds of India's output with less than one-third of its labor force. India's large population of educated English-speakers has made it a major exporter of information technology services, business outsourcing services, and software workers. Its labor force is relatively young and, at 502 million strong, is the world's second-largest workforce. Government reforms in the past two decades have helped India move from a centrally-controlled economy to more of a free-market system.

India imports more goods than it exports, with a primary need for petroleum. It also imports raw materials for manufacturing, such as chemicals, iron and steel, and machinery. India exports cotton textiles and clothing, chemicals, machinery, and iron ore. It trades mainly with China, Germany, Japan, Saudi Arabia, the United Arab Emirates, and the United States.

Agriculture

Farming employs about half of India's workers and contributes 18% of its GDP. Over half of the farms are just 3 acres or smaller, providing barely more than what a family needs to live on. The average size is shrinking, as farms are normally divided among a man's sons upon his death. Throughout India, about 61% of the land is used for agriculture, making it one of the most extensively farmed countries in the world. However, irrigation is not always available, so farmers rely heavily on seasonal rains. An unexpected dry season can cause widespread crop failure. Since the mid-1800's, irrigation efforts have increased across the nation. Use of high-yield seed has also helped improve crop production.

Key crops in India include rice, wheat, and other cereal crops, which make up about three-fifths of the farmland. Farmers also grow pulses (beans, lentils, and legumes such as chickpeas), oilseed, cotton, jute, tea, sugarcane, spices, onions, and potatoes. Many crops are grown to produce cooking oils. Despite being a top producer of grains, pulses, bananas, and mangoes, India consumes most of its produce rather than exporting it. Livestock provide dairy products, sheep and goat meat, and poultry. Although Indians eat little meat, cattle are used as work animals and to provide milk, leather, and fertilizer.

Forestry and Fishing

Almost one-fourth of India is covered in forest. The forestry industry is not highly developed, but India manages to cut down more hardwood than almost any other country. Teak, cedar, and other woods provide timber, pulp, and fuel for fire. The Indian government is working to combat deforestation as the huge population strains the available resources.

India's extensive coastline and rivers provide excellent fishing grounds. Fisherman with small, non-mechanized boats bring in small catches of fish close to shore. Newer mechanized boats venture further out to sea and bring in larger catches. Major catches include sardine and mackerel. Inland fishing and aquaculture produce carp, shrimp, and a variety of fish.

Mineral and Energy Resources

India possesses a wealth of mineral and energy resources, including the world's fourth-largest coal reserves. Coal is mined in about 500 mines throughout the country, and produces enough to supply India's needs and export a slight surplus. Although India has abundant natural gas and petroleum reserves, these do not meet the needs of its huge population, so more must be imported. The nation also mines plenty of iron ore, manganese, mica, bauxite, rare earth elements, titanium ore, chromite, diamonds, and limestone. The highest-value metals produced are iron and copper.

India has long been unable to keep up with the population's need for electricity. Therefore, people often experience outages or rationing of electric power. Most electricity comes from coal-powered thermal plants and some hydroelectric plants. India has few nuclear power plants.

Manufacturing

Manufacturing in India is very diverse, from home-based handicrafts like weaving and pottery-making, to large-scale industrial production of machinery and chemicals. The largest portion of manufacturing workers are employed in the textile industries, which include cotton, wool, silk, jute, and synthetic fibers. Almost every large Indian city has a cotton mill. As a top producer of iron and steel, India has many factories that process these raw materials and others that produce aircraft, automobiles, appliances, and other machinery. Overall, manufacturing makes up about a quarter of India's GDP.

Services

Until the 1990's, India's government controlled many services, including banking, finance, and construction. It oversaw building of railroads, highways, harbors, irrigation and power projects, and many government-owned factories and hotels. More recently, the private services sector has grown, led by a thriving computer software and customer service industry. India provides customer service call centers for many international companies. These services, along with thriving tourism, hospitality industries, and other services, contribute 58% of the nation's GDP.

Transportation

India has a well-developed transportation system that ranges from simple ox-drawn carts to modern aircraft. Indians have traditionally used railroads to transport most goods, but the use of automobiles is increasing. The government owns and controls the 39,000 miles (62,800 km) of railroad, which is the world's most extensive and most heavily used system. It also employs more Indians than any other employer in the country. Subway use did not come to India until 1989, but it is growing slowly in large cities.

The central government also manages ports in Mumbai, Kolkata, and Chennai, while state governments manage smaller ports. India only uses about one-third of its waterways for commercial shipping. In 1953, India's government took control of air travel, narrowing it down to just two companies—Air India and Indian Airlines. It has since opened airports to some private and international airlines.

Communication

Central and state governments also control much of India's communication outlets. Overall, phone lines have not kept pace with the growing population and many rural villages have no telephone service. However, cellular service provided by private companies is growing rapidly. The Ministry of Information and Broadcasting dominates television and radio service, though some stations are privately owned and operated. Satellite television and radio is providing Indians with greater selection. Internet access is available in cities, though many computer-owners access the Internet at cybercafés, rather than paying for their own subscription. India also publishes thousands of daily newspapers in a variety of languages.

INDIA'S HISTORY

India is home to one of the world's oldest and most influential civilizations. Seen as a land of riches, India has long been subject to invasions and warring empires. European traders came to India in the late 1400's and the nation fell under British rule in the late 1700's. India gained its independence from Great Britain in 1947.

Indus Valley Civilization (2500 BCE)

The past century has revealed much archaeological information about India's first inhabitants. Though people have lived in the area for thousands of years, the first true civilization is about 4,600 years old. This Indus Valley Civilization, named after the area of western India and Pakistan where it arose, was quite advanced for the time. Farmers cultivated crops and raised livestock, allowing for permanent settlements in the cities of Hrappa and Mohenjo-Daro. The people developed systems of counting, measuring, weighing, and writing. However, scholars have yet to decipher the form of writing, which includes over 500 symbols. The early people of the Indus Valley left behind walled cities, tools, and pottery that archaeologists continue to study and learn from today. The society collapsed sometime between 2000 and 1750 BCE, but scholars still don't know exactly when or why. Popular theories include changes to the environment, such as crop failure, flooding, or disease.

Aryan Invasion (1500 BCE)

After the decline of the Indus Valley Civilization, a group of people called the Dravidians arose throughout India. The Dravidians lived in towns and grew crops. In about 1500 BCE, they were invaded by a group called the Aryans. The Aryans, who came from the area that is now Iran, drove the Dravidians south and ruled most of India. They settled villages where they raised livestock such as sheep, goats, cows, and horses.

During the centuries of Aryan rule, many lasting influences developed in India. The caste system was established, with the Dravidians likely becoming the lowest cast, or Shudras. The highest caste of priests and scholars, the Brahmans, developed the Sanskrit language and many religious rituals. This period saw the composition of the earliest Hindu writings, including the *Vedas*, the *Upanishads*, the *Mahabharata*, and the *Ramayana*. Those who rejected the Brahmans' authority and the Vedas branched off into two religions that grew quickly throughout India in the 500's and 400's BCE. Siddhartha Gautama founded Buddhism and himself became known as Buddha, or the Enlightened One. Mahavira founded Jainism.

Persian and Greek Invasions (518–323 BCE)

India's northwest region of Gandhara (now in Pakistan) fell to Persian invaders in 518 BCE. Two centuries later, Macedonian leader Alexander the Great and his Greek army invaded India. Their efforts to move east to the Ganges River were cut short by disease, exhaustion, and possibly fear of the Nanda army. Alexander's troops refused to go beyond the Beas River. There, Alexander turned his army around, but left generals to rule over conquered provinces as satraps, or governors. Indian forces drove out most of these *satraps* within a few years. However, the Greek influence led to trade and communication between Europe and western Asia. Alexander's campaign is not recorded in any Indian historical source, but was documented by Greek and Roman writers, who likely exaggerated the tale.

Mauryan Empire (324–185 BCE)

Records of Alexander the Great's campaign into India include mention of a prince Chandragupta Maurya. Chandragupta defeated the feared Nanda army of the east. He then rose to become the first ruler to unite an empire across all of India (and parts of Afghanistan) around 324 BCE. Only the southern tip of the peninsula remained outside of the Mauryan Empire.

Chandragupta's grandson Ashoka ruled from about 272 to 232 BCE. At first, he continued to increase the size of the empire by conquering the nearby kingdom of Kalinga. However, he found that violence and bloodshed did not align with his Buddhist beliefs. Ashoka turned his attention from war to spreading Buddhist teachings and nonviolence. He sent missionaries across India and into Sri Lanka to teach Buddhism. He incorporated moral laws into the carvings throughout his kingdom. India's current national symbol, the Lion Capital of Ashoka, comes from this important artwork.

Upon Ashoka's death, the Mauryan Empire began to break apart. Over the following centuries, invaders from other parts of central Asia moved into India and established ruling dynasties. The Scythians and the Kushans were two such groups.

Gupta Dynasty (320–515 CE)

In 320 CE, India was united once again under the Gupta dynasty. Historians view this two hundred year period as a "golden age" in India's history. Art, literature, science, and philosophy flourished during this time. Famous writings, including those of poet Kalidasa, come from this period, along with the famous artwork of the frescoes at Ajanta. Many Hindu temples were built during the Gupta dynasty and India's system of medicine, called Ayurveda, was developed.

Meanwhile, southern India remained outside of the unified empire. From about 50 BCE until the 1000's CE, this area came under the rule of various dynasties, including the Satavahanas, the Cholas, and the Pallavas. The civilization that developed in southern India spread its culture and influence throughout Southeast Asia via traders and voyagers.

Period of Invasions (455–1500's)

Following this brief golden age, India fell subject to several invasions. Beginning in about 455, Huns from central Asia invaded. They were followed in the early 700's by Muslim armies from Arabia. One such army, led by Afghan warrior Mahmud of Ghazni, caused widespread damage as they destroyed temples and looted cities. Later, Muslim general Qutb ub-din Aybak united northern India under the Delhi Sultanate in 1206, establishing himself as sultan. The Delhi Sultanate continued until about 1398, when Timur, a leader from what is now Uzbekistan, conquered the city of Delhi.

European Arrival (1498)

In 1498, European explorers and traders reached India for the first time when Portuguese explorer Vasco da Gama arrived in Kozhikode. They sought to control the trade routes to eastern Asia. At the time, traders from Portugal, Italy, and Turkey all competed for Asian silk, spices, and other goods. In an effort to secure trade routes, the Portuguese took control of parts of India's west coast.

Mughal Empire (1526–mid 1700's)

The last sultan of Delhi, Ibrahim Lodi, fell to invaders in 1526. These armies from central Asia followed the leadership of Babur, a descendent of both Timur and famous Mongol warlord Genghis Khan. Babur's rule began the Mughal Empire, a powerful dynasty that flourished for just over one hundred years , before it began a long decline.

Babur conquered much of northern India during his reign, and his grandson Akbar expanded the empire west to Afghanistan and south to the Godavari River. One of the world's most powerful rulers at the time, Akbar involved Hindus in government and the military, though he himself was Muslim.

Akbar's grandson, Shah Jahan, is perhaps the most famous Mughal emperor, remembered for the great buildings he had erected. One of these, the Taj Mahal at Agra, continues to draw tourists from around the world. The building is a tomb that Shah Jahan had built for his favorite wife.

The Mughal Empire began to fall apart under the rule of Shah Jahan's son, Aurangzeb, who rose to power in 1658. Aurangzeb, a strict Muslim, undid much of the progress made by Akbar. He imposed a tax on Hindus, destroyed temples, and tried to convert Hindus to Islam by force. Hindus revolted, leading to costly wars that hurt the empire.

East India Company (1600's–1858)

With European traders firmly established in India by 1600, England's Queen Elizabeth I approved the formation of the East India Company. The Mughal emperor at the time (Akbar's son Jahangir) approved of the com-

The Taj Mahal in Agra

pany setting up trading posts and forts to facilitate trade between Europe, India, and East Asia. With posts in Bombay (Mumbai), Calcutta (Kolkata), and Madras (Chennai), England became the dominant European power in India.

After the collapse of the Mughal Empire by the mid-1700's, Europeans expanded their influence and became very wealthy. The East India Company imposed taxes on Indians in some regions, which was not well received. Although the Indians protested, the British used force to get their way. In 1757, the East India Company defeated the army of Bengal's Mughal governor. This marked the beginning of the British Empire's rule in India, which continued for the next hundred years. In 1774, the East India Company appointed Warren Hastings as the first governor general of India, firmly establishing British control of the country.

Indian Rebellion (1857–1859)

Indians resented British rule for many reasons. The British taxed farmers and took land from many Indians. They interfered with Indian customs and religion. Facing widespread hunger and oppression, Indians rebelled against British rule. In 1857, the rebellions came to a head in an uprising called the Sepoy Rebellion (or Sepoy Mutiny). At the time, Indian soldiers called *sepoys* served under British officers at an army base in Meerut. The British ordered the sepoys to bite open the cartridges for their rifles. However, the Hindu and Muslim sepoys believed the cartridges to have been greased with cow and hog fat, which they were forbidden to eat. Their refusal to obey orders sparked a rebellion that spread through northern and central India. However, the Indians lacked weapons and organized leadership, and were defeated by the British in 1859.

British India (1858–1947)

During the Indian Rebellion, the British government took direct control of India from the East India Company. The British *Raj* (or administration) appointed a viceroy to rule over British India, along with an executive council appointed by the British monarch and the viceroy. The government divided India into provinces, each of which had its own governor and executive council. However, most areas retained a local prince, who ruled under the advice of a British representative. The prince generally dealt with all local issues while British officials handled defense and foreign affairs.

Only a few small areas of India remained outside of the British Empire, ruled as colonies by France and Portugal.

British rule had great influence on Indian life. The British improved the nation's infrastructure by building railroads, irrigation systems, and telephone and telegraph systems. However, many Indians lived in poverty, and food was often scarce. Indian soldiers fought in British wars in Afghanistan (1878–1881) and Burma (1885). Education was neglected, though the British did establish universities. Little was done to industrialize India.

In an effort to plan a better future for Indians, several educated and professional Indians formed the Indian National Congress in 1885. Their goal was to improve opportunities and equal treatment for Indians, who were unable to advance in government and the military. Although the congress involved people from all regions and many religions, some saw it as a Hindu organization seeking Hindu rule. In 1906, Muslim leaders formed a rival organization for Muslims only. The British encouraged this splintering of India's efforts toward equality.

Throughout the early 1900's, Indians continued to protest unfair treatment and rebelled against British rule. Meanwhile, the British government promised much in the way of reforms but delivered little. Some positive changes were the inclusion of an Indian on the viceroy's executive council and a slight increase in political influence among Indians. However, the British also attempted to divide Bengal into separate sections for Hindus and Muslims, tried to restrict Indian rights, and involved India in the fight against Germany in World War I. The protests turned to disaster on April 13, 1919 in Amritsar. There, British troops entered a meeting place filled with unarmed Indians and blocked the entrance. The soldiers then opened fire, killing 400 and wounding 1,200 in what became known as the Amritsar Massacre.

After the Amritsar Massacre, Indians largely gave up hope of reforms and instead demanded complete independence. Against this background of bloodshed and protest, Mohandas K. Gandhi arose as a leader in the Indian National Congress and the independence movement. Gandhi was a lawyer who had spent years living in England and South Africa. His first major protest came in response to Britain's Rowlatt Acts, the law that denied Indians the right to trial by jury. Gandhi stressed nonviolent forms of protest against unfair treatment, such as refusing to pay taxes and boycotting British goods, services, courts, and schools. This approach, called *civil disobedience*, spread across India and gained millions of followers. Gandhi became known as *Mahatma*, or "Great Soul."

Indian Independence Movement (1930's–1940's)

The Indian Independence Movement, led by Gandhi, gained momentum in the 1930's, with large numbers of participants and media exposure. In one act of nonviolent protest, Gandhi led hundreds of Indians on a 240-mile (386 km) march to the sea, where they made salt. This act directly disobeyed a British law, called the Salt Acts, that prohibited Indians from possessing any salt other than that bought from the government.

Around the same time, Muslim leader Mohammad Ali Jinnah and the Muslim League began resisting Congress. Jinnah and his followers demanded a separate independent area, which they called Pakistan, to be designated a Muslim homeland.

In 1935, the Government of India Act brought a new Constitution to the nation. It included greater concessions for Indian representation in government, but it was a far cry from independence.

World War II (1939–1945)

In 1939, the British went to war against Germany. Once again, it involved all of India in the war, without consulting Indian leaders. The British went as far as to promise independence to India upon the end of the war. However, the Indian National Congress refused to support Great Britain in the war, and demanded immediate self-government.

Despite protests, Indians contributed much to the war effort. Troops fought for Britain in Africa and the Middle East. At home, factories produced supplies for the Allied armies and farmers grew coffee, tea, rice, and wheat to export to Allied nations. In 1943, the British exported so much of India's food resources that a famine occurred in Bengal, killing 3 million Indians.

Japanese involvement in the war in 1941 brought the fighting closer to India. The Japanese army captured Burma and then invaded eastern India. At that point, thousands of Indian troops joined the Japanese in an effort to drive the British out of India. However, this Indian National Army, as they called themselves, was unsuccessful.

Amid the turmoil of World War II, the Indian National Congress continued to talk with British leaders about independence. Gandhi organized another nonviolent movement, called the Quit India Movement, in 1942. This time, however, the British responded by imprisoning all Congress leaders for the remainder of the war. This opened the door for the Muslim League to cooperate with the British, in hopes of receiving land for a separate nation.

Independence and Partition (1947)

In 1945, World War II ended, and the British released Congress leaders from prison and resumed independence talks. The British agreed to grant India independence on the condition that India's leaders agree on a new form of government. With tensions high between the Muslim League and the Indian National Congress, this proved impossible. On August 16, 1946, the Muslim League declared Direct Action Day, a widespread demonstration aimed at preventing the British from dealing with Congress exclusively. Demonstrations became violent in Calcutta and other cities.

With no reasonable alternative in sight, the British agreed to partition Pakistan as a separate Muslim nation and grant India its independence. In August of 1947, millions of Hindus and Sikhs fled Pakistan while Muslims headed for their new homeland in Pakistan. As a result of the chaos and rioting that ensued, between one and two million people died. Additional fighting broke out between India and Pakistan over the state of Kashmir. With a Hindu leader and largely Muslim population, Kashmir initially remained independent but eventually became part of India.

Throughout these tense times, Gandhi continued to preach nonviolence and religious tolerance. On January 30, 1948, he was assassinated by a Hindu who disagreed with his peaceful tactics and tolerance of Muslims.

In 1950, Roman Catholic nun Mother Teresa founded the Missionaries of Charity in Calcutta (now Kolkata). Mother Teresa was sent to India by a religious order, or community, in her home country Macedonia. She began her work as a teacher at a convent in Calcutta. Soon, she left the convent to work among the poor more directly and became an Indian citizen in 1948. Her Missionaries of Charity provided food for the hungry and operated schools, hospitals, shelters, and orphanages. Mother Teresa is known for seeking out and living among the most rejected in society, earning her the nickname *Saint of the Gutters*. She earned the 1979 Nobel Peace Prize and many other accolades for her humanitarian work in India.

Jawaharlal Nehru (1950)

After independence, Gandhi's close friend Jawaharlal Nehru became prime minister. A new constitution became effective January 26, 1950 (now celebrated each year as Republic Day).

Nehru's new government controlled industry and the economy in an attempt to raise India's standard of living. Great improvements were made under the first *five-year plan*, an effort to reform the economy and political system. Women gained more rights, farmers gained ownership of their land, malaria was controlled, and production increased greatly. People had more to eat at lower prices and children attended school in much higher numbers.

In 1954, France turned over the last of its Indian colonies to Nehru's government. After Portugal refused to do the same, Indian troops invaded in 1961 and unified those territories with the rest of the nation. Despite efforts to unify the newly independent nation, India faced difficulties due to diverse people groups, religions, and languages. The state boundaries drawn up by the British did not reflect natural settlement patterns. The new Indian government tried to correct this by giving major language groups their own states. For example, Andhra (now Andhra Pradesh and Telangana) was created for Telugu speakers.

India stayed out of international conflicts, such as the Cold War, relying instead on the UN to settle disputes and maintain peace. However, India's troops were forced into action when China invaded the northeast in 1962. After fighting them off, Nehru decided to direct more funding from health and education toward military spending.

Indira Gandhi (1966)

Nehru died in 1964 while still serving as prime minister. Cabinet member Lal Bahadur Shastri succeeded him in this role, but died just two years later. In 1966, Nehru's daughter Indira Gandhi became India's prime minister.

Fighting between Pakistan and India continued through the 1960's, with both sides violating a UN cease-fire. The two nations fought over Kashmir, and Pakistan experienced its own civil war in 1971. India aided East Pakistan in its fight against West Pakistan and took in many refugees. Ultimately, East Pakistan won and became the independent nation of Bangladesh.

The 1970's saw economic and political turmoil throughout India. The improvements of Nehru's government were reversed, resulting in food shortages, unemployment, and other economic problems. Indira Gandhi fought with the high court, which tried to make her resign in 1975. Declaring a state of emergency, Gandhi jailed her opponents and censored her critics. Two years later, the state of emergency ended and the political prisoners were released. Elections were held and, for the first time, the Congress Party lost. Moraji Desai of the new Janata Party became prime minister until the party fell apart. In 1980, Indira Gandhi was elected once again as prime minister.

In the 1980's, Sikhs in the Punjab area began demonstrating against discrimination and demanding a separate Sikh state. During one demonstration, they occupied a sacred Sikh shrine in Amritsar. Fighting broke out between the Sikhs and the government, resulting in attacks on the temple and the deaths of Sikh leaders. In response, two Sikhs serving on Gandhi's security force assassinated her on October 31, 1984. Riots followed, with thousands of Sikhs killed.

India Today (1984–present)

Gandhi's son Rajiv became prime minister and head of the Congress Party after her death. Longstanding conflicts continued throughout India. Indians, Pakistanis, and Kashmiris clashed over the independence or alliance of Kashmir. Hindus and Muslims fought over claims to holy lands. Various ethnic groups fought for independence from India.

The problems and conflicts carried into politics, with Rajiv and his government accused of corruption. When the Congress-I Party (Indira's political party) lost control of Parliament, Rajiv resigned as prime minister. He was assassinated in 1991.

Recently, India has continued to face conflict with Pakistan, and friction among its own diverse ethnic groups. Amid these problems, India was devastated by an undersea earthquake in 2004 that caused a huge ocean surge, called a *tsunami*, to flood and destroy areas along the Indian Ocean. More than 16,000 Indians lost their lives in the tsunami, and millions more were left homeless.

The Flag of India

THE MIDDLE EAST

MIDDLE EAST: THE BIG PICTURE

The Middle East is a region that includes parts of Asia, Africa, and Europe. The name and its meaning have changed over time, but today it generally includes the countries on and around the Arabian Peninsula. These include Bahrain, Egypt, Iran, Iraq, Israel (plus the West Bank and the Gaza Strip), Jordan, Kuwait, Lebanon, Oman, Qatar, Saudi Arabia, Syria, Turkey, the United Arab Emirates, and Yemen. Together, these 15 countries cover about 2,812,000 square miles (7,283,000 square km), comparable to about one third the size of the United States. It is home to some 396 million people. Some definitions of the Middle East also include Afghanistan, Algeria, Cyprus, Libya, Morocco, Pakistan, Sudan, and Tunisia.

MEET THE PEOPLE OF THE MIDDLE EAST

The people of the Middle East represent a wide variety of backgrounds, religions, languages, and customs. Situated at the convergence of Europe, Africa, and Asia, the Middle East has seen many civilizations rise and fall, and has been influenced by many other regions. Today, most people identify themselves based on national and ethnic groups, language, and religion. The most populous group are Arabs.

Arabs use the common Arabic language in writing and media broadcasts, but spoken Arabic varies from one area to another. Other common languages spoken throughout the Middle East include Persian, also called Farsi (spoken in Iran), Turkish (spoken in Turkey), Hebrew (spoken among Jews in Israel), and Kurdish (spoken among Kurds in several countries).

LAND, WATER, AND CLIMATE IN THE MIDDLE EAST

The Middle East stretches from the Mediterranean Sea to the Indian Ocean. Although the climate is generally quite dry, the region boasts extensive access to waterways. Egypt, Israel, Lebanon, Syria, and Turkey border the Mediterranean Sea. In the north, Turkey also borders the Black Sea and Iran borders the Caspian Sea. The Arabian Peninsula is largely surrounded by the Red Sea, the Arabian Sea, and the Persian Gulf. Two major river systems, the Tigris-Euphrates and the Nile, flow through several countries. Egypt's Suez Canal on the Sinai Peninsula is an important connection between the Mediterranean Sea and the Red Sea. It greatly shortens the journey from Europe to Asia.

Mountains stretch across the northern part of the Middle East, with the Pontic and

Fast Facts

Largest country:
Saudi Arabia

Largest city:
Cairo, Egypt (population 7.8 million)

Primary language:
Arabic

The city of Cairo, Egypt with mosques in the foreground

Taurus Mountains in Turkey and the Elburz and Zagros Mountains in Iran. Elsewhere, the land is flat and dry. In Egypt, the Eastern Desert and Western Desert make up the great Sahara Desert. The Eastern Desert is the section of the Sahara Desert east of the Nile River, between the river and the Red Sea. The Western Desert, also known as the Libyan Desert, covers eastern Libya, western Egypt, and northwestern Sudan. Southern Saudi Arabia is also covered by the rolling dunes of the Rub al Khali Desert.

The Nile River empties into the Mediterranean Sea,
with the Suez Canal immediately to the east

EVERYDAY LIFE IN THE MIDDLE EAST

Middle Eastern civilization arose out of three main groups of people living in the region. Peasant farmers lived in small villages where they raised crops and some livestock. Nomads, or traveling herders, followed their flocks across more remote areas. City-dwellers, comprised of merchants, craftsmen, and officials, congregated in growing cities. All three groups of people depended on one another economically and came together in local markets to trade goods and services.

Map of the Middle East

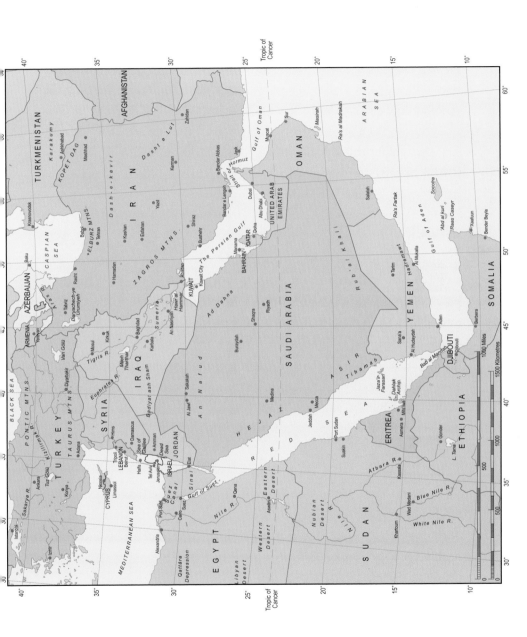

Family Life

Most Middle Easterners marry and have children, though today's adults do so later than their parents and grandparents did and generally have fewer children. Women, in addition to raising children, have always done work on farms, in the home, and in cities. However, during the 1800's it became a sign of wealth to keep women secluded in the home. Over the past hundred years, this practice has disappeared and women pursue education and careers outside the home. However, in many areas women continue to fight for expanded legal rights. Some laws and customs pertaining to women come from religious beliefs. Other than in Turkey, religion dominates family life in every Middle Eastern country.

City Life

Over the past 200 years, cities have become a predominant feature of many Middle Eastern nations. As the population of the region grew, cities became larger and more developed. People in some regions began producing oil from rich natural reserves and became quite wealthy. Except for Israel, most non-oil producing countries in the region are relatively poor. Today, cities are home to more than half of the population of the Middle East. Cities generally offer clean drinking water, access to modern media, health care facilities, and schools. In general, the literacy rate is higher for males than for females.

Country Life

Middle Easterners living in rural villages tend to be poor and have limited access to amenities. Sanitation may be poor and children are less likely to attend school. Access to electricity, clean water, television, and health care vary from one village to another.

Religion

Islam is the dominant religion in the Middle East, with about a 90% Muslim population. The Islamic religion began in the 600's CE when the Prophet Muhammed received revelations from Allah. Islam dictates many facets of everyday life, from what clothing to wear, to prayer times, to food options. After the death of Muhammad, Muslims disagreed about who should become the leader. They broke into two branches—the Shi'ites are the majority in Iran, Iraq, and Lebanon, while the Sunni are the majority in other countries.

In Israel, 80% of the population are Jews, or those who follow Judaism. The ancient Hebrews founded Judaism, the first *monotheistic* (believing in one God) religion. Jews vary in how strictly they observe the principles of Judaism, with Orthodox Jews being the strictest.

Christianity, made up of followers of Jesus, also originated in the Middle East. A variety of Protestant, Catholic, and Greek Orthodox churches exist in all countries outside of the Arabian Peninsula. In Saudi Arabia and surrounding countries, Islam is the official religion and other religions are prohibited. Though some Christians live in these countries, they face persecution from government and society.

Some Middle Easterners follow the Baha'i Faith, which was founded in the 1800's in what is now Iran and Iraq. This monotheistic religion bases its principles on the teachings of Baha'u'llah.

The Sultan Ahmed Mosque in Istanbul, Turkey

THE ECONOMY OF THE MIDDLE EAST

The economy of many Middle Eastern countries changed dramatically in the mid-1900's, when oil deposits were discovered around the Persian Gulf. Since then, countries that were once quite poor have become very wealthy. In addition to supplying much of the world's oil, the Middle East has thriving industries in banking, tourism, and trade. Some workers leave poorer countries to find work elsewhere and send money home to their families.

Agriculture

The dry climate of the Middle East has presented a challenge to farmers. However, some areas (Lebanon and parts of Israel, Syria, Iraq, Turkey, and Iran) receive enough rainfall to grow crops. Other areas depend on seasonal monsoons to bring rain (Yemen and Oman) or tap into river systems for irrigation (Egypt and Iraq). As irrigation systems, dams, and equipment have improved, farming has expanded in the Middle East.

Major crops include wheat, barley, corn, and rice. Farmers also grow fruit, cotton, olives, potatoes, sugarcane, and coffee.

Mining and Manufacturing

Manufacturing in the Middle East centers on oil refining. Almost two-thirds of the world's oil can be found in Saudi Arabia, Iran, Iraq, Kuwait, Oman, Qatar, and the United Arab Emirates. Other major manufactured goods include processed foods, chemicals and fertilizers, construction materials, textiles, and weapons. The textile industry in the Middle East is quite old and the region is known for producing muslin (named after Mosul, Iraq), damask (named after Damascus, Syria), and fine carpets. High-tech industries such as software and recording have grown in some countries.

Trade

Although Israel is one of the world's top arms producers, the Middle East receives many of its weapons from the United States. The region also imports food (wheat, flour, and meat), machinery, and consumer goods. Oil, primarily sent to Europe and Japan, is the region's major export. Other exports include textiles, fruits, and vegetables.

THE MIDDLE EAST'S HISTORY

Ancient History (3,500–600's BCE)

The Middle East is home to the earliest peoples and civilizations in the world. As far back as 25,000 BCE, people inhabited this region. They developed agriculture around 8,000 BCE. Then two of the first civilizations arose between 3,500 and 3,100 BCE. The Sumer civilization (or Sumerians) arose in present-day Iraq. The fertile land between the Tigris and Euphrates Rivers allowed this people group to create permanent settlements around farmlands. The Egyptian civilization arose around the Nile River in Egypt.

Over time, other civilizations arose and disappeared. The Hittites arose in present-day Turkey, and the Babylonians took over the Sumerian civilization around 1100 BCE. Around that same time, the Hebrews developed the world's first monotheistic religion in Israel. In the 800's BCE, the Phoenician civilization arose and created the first alphabet. Other ancient Middle Eastern advances span mathematics, medicine, and astronomy.

The Middle East experienced a period of foreign invasions beginning in the 800's BCE. The Assyrians invaded from northern Iraq, and the Medes invaded from northern Iran. By about 550 BCE, the Persian Empire had spread to include much of the Middle East. This was followed by the *Hellenistic*, or Greek, influence, brought by Alexander the Great in 331 BCE. His domination of the entire region brought with it great advancements in learning and culture.

In 30 BCE, the Roman Empire replaced the Greek Empire throughout the Middle East. During this time, Jesus Christ lived in what is now Israel and Egypt. His followers founded Christianity, which remained the region's major religion for about 600 years.

Islamic Empire (late 600's–early 900's CE)

A new prophet arose in the Middle East about 610 CE, bringing with him a new religion. While living in Mecca, the Prophet Muhammad believed he had received a revelation from Allah and began preaching a monotheistic message. His followers were called Muslims and their religion Islam. After Muhammad's death in 632, Muslims disagreed about who should become *caliph*, or leader. This disagreement led to a split that resulted in two branches of Islam, called the Sunnis and the Shi'ites.

Eventually, Muslim influence spread as far as Morocco and Spain in the west and Central Asia in the east. As Arabs conquered these territories, people under their rule adopted Islam and the Arabic language. The Islamic Empire flourished from the late 600's to the early 900's. The caliph first ruled from Damascus, Syria, but later moved to the new capital of Baghdad in Iraq.

The Islamic Empire began to lose power in the 800's, when the Middle East broke into several separate states. These states often failed to defend against invaders because they were warring with one another. In 1055, Muslim Turks from Central Asia conquered Baghdad and controlled much of the region. Just decades later, Europeans invaded, and established small states around the Mediterranean. The European military expeditions, called *Crusades*, were an effort to provide access for pilgrims to the Holy Land. Their influence lasted from about 1100 to 1300. Meanwhile, Mongol forces from Central Asia invaded the Middle East from the east.

Ottoman Empire (1300's–1800's)

The fractured state of the Middle East in the 1300's and 1400's made it vulnerable to a growing power from the north. The Ottoman Empire, consisting of Turkish Muslims, spread from Asia Minor and southeastern Europe to conquer most of the Middle East. By the 1500's, the Ottoman Empire had become one of the most powerful in the world. It threatened Europe until the 1700's, when Europe began to surge ahead in technology and industry.

As European powers increased, the dominance of the Ottoman Empire in the Middle East decreased. By the early 1900's, France, the United Kingdom, and Italy had taken control of lands in North Africa and the Persian Gulf previously held by the Ottomans.

World War I (1914–1918)

The Allies, made up mostly of European countries, finally defeated the Ottoman Empire completely in World War I. The United Kingdom gained control of several territories, including Egypt and Iraq, while France took Lebanon and Syria. The Turks, however, won their fight for independence and established the Republic of Turkey in 1923. Iran, Yemen, and Saudi Arabia also remained independent.

European colonial control did not last long in the Middle East. Uprisings led to independence for Iraq (1932), Lebanon (1943), Syria (1946), Jordan (1946), and Israel (1948). Egypt, the first country to rise up against British rule, gained partial independence in 1922. Because of Egypt's key shipping route through the Suez Canal, the British continued to control military and foreign affairs there.

During the time of European colonial rule in the Middle East, Muslims developed a strong sense of *nationalism*, or unity as a nation. Their shared religion, language, and customs led to a desire for an Islamic government and Islamic influence in all areas of life. In Egypt, Muslims founded the Muslim Brotherhood in 1928 to promote Islamic values.

Palestinian Conflict (1920's)

The rise of *Islamism*, an ideology based on total adherence to Islam, occurred at the same time as a similar movement in Palestine. There, the desire for a Jewish homeland and complete Jewish culture, called *Zionism*, had been growing for years. The Jews and Arabs clashed over control of Palestine, a country on the east coast of the Mediterranean.

European Jews had migrated to the area since the late 1800's and saw it as their homeland. When German Nazis began persecuting Jews in the 1930's, the number who moved to Palestine increased. The Jews wanted a separate, safe homeland, which they called Israel, the historical name of the region. Arab nationalists also claimed Palestine as their homeland and feared British support of the Zionists. The Arabs revolted from 1936 to 1939 but could not overcome the British forces. The Zionists also revolted against British rule and the Arabs who opposed them after World War II.

In an attempt to solve the conflict, the United Nations (UN) divided Palestine into two states—one Jewish and one Arab. The Jewish state, called Israel, was the larger of the two and Jewish leaders accepted this settlement. Arab leaders did not and Arab armies from Egypt, Iraq, Jordan, Lebanon, and Syria fought Jewish forces in order to control more land. When Jewish forces prevailed, many Arab civilians fled the area.

Israel defeated the Arab forces and ended up with a larger territory than the UN had intended. Jordan took control of an area called the West Bank and Egypt controlled the Gaza Strip. Israelis call this the War of Independence and refused to allow more than 700,000 Palestinian Arab refugees to return to their homes. Palestinian Arabs call the war *al-nakba*, or *the disaster*. Disputes still exist over Israel's borders, the rights of Palestinian refugees, and acceptance of Israel as an independent state by Arab nations.

Cold War Alliances (mid-1940's–early 1990's)

After World War II, much of the world was affected by the Cold War, a period of tension between Communist and non-communist nations. The Soviet Union and its allies attempted to spread communism, while the United States and its allies attempted to stop this effort. Though the nations never fought one another directly, they supported other countries in their fight for or against communism.

Some Arab nationalists opposed European and American influence, preferring to side with the Soviets and embrace *socialism*—a system in which government controls the economy. In Egypt, Iraq, and Syria, military leaders overthrew existing governments to establish socialist systems. Gamal Abdel Nasser overthrew King Faruk of Egypt in 1952. Four years later, his forces seized control of the Suez Canal from the British and French. Although Israel, the United Kingdom, and France responded by attacking Egypt, they withdrew under pressure from the United States and the Soviet Union.

As the Cold War continued, Saudi Arabia, Kuwait, Jordan, Iran and Turkey became aligned with the United States. Israel became especially close with the United States in the 1960's. In response, the Soviet Union supplied weapons to Egypt, Syria, and Iraq to aid their fight against Israel.

Six-Day War/June War (1967)

In 1967, intense fighting broke out between the Egyptians and the Israelis. Nasser had moved troops into the Sinai Peninsula to protect Syria against attack from Israel. He also closed a strait leading to an important Israeli port. As a result, Israel attacked Egypt on June 5. In a war that Israelis call the Six-Day War and Arabs call the June War, Israel seized territories from its Arab neighbors. From Egypt, Israel gained the Sinai Peninsula and Gaza Strip; from Syria it took control of the Golan Heights; and from Jordan it seized the West Bank and East Jerusalem.

In 1969, Palestinian nationalist Yasser Arafat became head of the Palestine Liberation Organization (PLO). He had been leading guerilla attacks against Israel, and now united several groups in an effort to create a Palestinian state. His forces consisted mainly of refugees from the West Bank, the Gaza Strip, Syria, and Lebanon. Their attacks often targeted civilians, and Israel responded with counterattacks.

Yom Kippur War (1973)

As fighting in the Middle East continued, the United States became the main power in the Persian Gulf, supplying arms to Israel. Egypt and Syria attacked Israel in 1973, in an effort to regain the Golan Heights and the Sinai Peninsula. With help from the United States, Israel prevailed. Israelis call this war the Yom Kippur War, while Arabs refer to it as the October War (or Ramadan War). In response to this defeat, many Arab oil-producing states banned the export of oil to the United States. Oil prices rose dramatically, making many Arab states very wealthy.

Egypt, under the new leadership of President Anwar el-Sadat, abandoned socialism and became an ally of the United States. In 1978, Sadat visited Camp David, Maryland to begin peace talks with Israeli Prime Minister Menachem Begin. Israel agreed to return the Sinai Peninsula, and the two nations signed a peace treaty.

In Syria and Lebanon, however, fighting intensified. Christians and Muslims in Lebanon broke into civil war in 1975. The following year, Syria got involved, fearing that a Muslim-PLO victory in Lebanon would bring a response from Israel. Israel did respond, and invaded, defeating the PLO in 1978 and 1982. Israeli forces drove the PLO out of Lebanon completely and sought to take control of the nation. Even with the support of the United States, Israel was unable to overcome Syria and its new ally, the Islamist organization Hezbollah. Lebanon's civil war ended in 1990, and Israeli troops withdrew from Lebanon in 2000. Syrian troops withdrew in 2005.

In Iran, Islamic revolutionaries led by Ayatollah Ruhollah Khomeini (an Ayatollah is a high-ranking Islamic clergyman) overthrew the Shah (or King/Emperor of Iran) and established a republic. Because the United States had supported the Iranian Shah, the new government no longer allied itself with the United States. Iranian revolutionaries held U.S. embassy employees hostage for over a year.

War with the Soviet Union (1979–1989)

Meanwhile, the Soviet Union invaded Afghanistan in 1979 to promote communism there. Thousands of young Muslims from across the Middle East volunteered to fight the Soviet invasion. They saw this as a war defending their Islamic faith and called themselves *mujahideen*, or *warriors for the faith*. The United States, Saudi Arabia, and Pakistan all supported the mujahideen, but after the war some mujahideen turned against the United States and its allies. One such soldier was Osama bin Laden, who later led attacks against the United States.

In 1980, war began between Iran and Iraq. The United States supported Iraq, led by President Saddam Hussein, and helped force a cease-fire in 1988. During this time of conflict in Iran, Iraq, and Afghanistan, the U.S. military established several bases in the Persian Gulf and built up forces there.

In the late 1980's, Palestinians once again rose up against Israel. Called the *intifada*, this uprising lasted until 1993. During the years of conflict, a new Islamist organization called Hamas began to replace the PLO in leading the Palestinian resistance movement. The PLO then renounced terrorism, recognizing Israel as a state and declaring its own state in the West Bank and the Gaza Strip.

The 1990's

In late 1990 and early 1991, 39 nations, led by the United States, came together to protect Saudi Arabia and Kuwait from an Iraqi invasion. This coalition forced Saddam Hussein's Iraqi troops out of Kuwait. The UN tried to limit Hussein's power and protect Iraqi Kurds and Shi'ites who opposed him. The UN forced Hussein to give up all weapons of mass destruction (chemical, biological, and nuclear weapons) and established "no-fly" zones.

While tensions with Iraq increased, Israel and Palestine attempted to move toward peace. Leaders met in Oslo, Norway for peace talks. Israel gave up some areas of the West Bank and the Gaza Strip to the Palestinians, and also signed a peace treaty with Jordan. However, not all Israelis or Palestinians agreed with the outcome of the peace talks. Hamas especially opposed the new agreement. Fighting continued as Jewish settlements spread into the West Bank and the Gaza Strip, and Palestinians sought to force Israel from nearby territory.

Bahrain skyline at night

The 2000's

As Palestinians rose up once again, Israel responded, and back-and-forth attacks continued. Hamas, which does not recognize Israel as a state, gained power in Palestinian elections in 2006. As a result, allies of Israel, including the United States, refused to deal with Hamas. Hamas seized the Gaza Strip while Fatah, a rival Palestinian group, took control of the West Bank. Ongoing violence in Gaza resulted in hundreds of deaths. Israel also fought with Lebanon, when Hezbollah captured two Israeli soldiers in 2006.

Violence in the Middle East spread to the United States in 2001. The militant Islamist organization al-Qaeda, led by Osama bin Laden, launched a terrorist attack against the United States on September 11. Al-Qaeda opposed U.S. presence in Saudi Arabia and considered Americans enemies of Islam. The United States responded with a "war on terrorism" that resulted in overthrowing Afghanistan's Taliban, a ruling group that aided al-Qaeda. U.S. troops killed bin Laden in 2011.

U.S. involvement in the Middle East continued in 2003, when the U.S. waged war against Iraq. The intent of the war was to disarm Hussein's government of any weapons of mass destruction. The U.S. succeeded in overthrowing Hussein and establishing a more democratic government in Iraq, though no weapons of mass destruction were found. Iraq adopted a new Constitution, held elections, and saw a decline of violence. U.S. troops withdrew from the area in 2011.

The Wailing Wall "El Muro de los Lamentos" located in Jerusalem

The Middle East Today

In 2011, protesters across the Middle East clashed with governments in an uprising called the "Arab Spring." Thousands of people were killed as governments tried to control the protests. In Tunisia, President Zine El-Abidine Ben Ali resigned, as did Egyptian President Hosni Mubarak. In Yemen, President Ali Abdullah Salih was wounded in an attack. Syrian protests against President Bashar al-Assad and his government led to nearly 200,000 deaths. In Libya, protesters took up arms against leader Muammar Gaddafi with the support of the UN and the North Atlantic Treaty Organization (NATO). Gaddafi went into hiding and was later killed as a new transitional government was established.

Today, protests, violence, and political changes continue in many countries of the Middle East. In Palestine, Hamas and Fatah have formed a joint government, but continue to clash with Israel. Yemen's government was overthrown by a Muslim rebel group and now different factions are fighting for control. A radical Islamic group called the Islamic State (or ISIS or ISIL) has recently emerged in Iraq and Syria. It has carried out violent attacks in several nations.

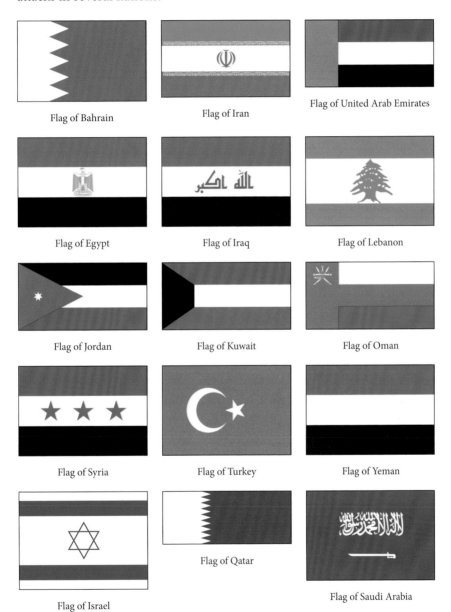

Flag of Bahrain

Flag of Iran

Flag of United Arab Emirates

Flag of Egypt

Flag of Iraq

Flag of Lebanon

Flag of Jordan

Flag of Kuwait

Flag of Oman

Flag of Syria

Flag of Turkey

Flag of Yeman

Flag of Israel

Flag of Qatar

Flag of Saudi Arabia

THE MIDDLE EAST

ISRAEL

ISRAEL: THE BIG PICTURE

Israel occupies a small section of the Middle East along the eastern shore of the Mediterranean Sea, between Egypt and Lebanon. The area has historic importance to those of Jewish, Muslim, and Christian faiths, especially the city of Jerusalem. Israel encompasses most of the Biblical Holy Land and most Jews, even those who do not live there, consider it their homeland.

Modern Israel's existence is a point of contention and conflict. After World War II, the United Nations (UN) divided Palestine into separate Jewish and Arab states. Arabs rejected the agreement, but Israel became a country in 1948. A series of wars resulted in Israeli occupation of the Sinai Peninsula, the Gaza strip, the Golan Heights, and the West Bank. Since then, those lands have been returned to Egypt, Syria, and Jordan. Violent clashes continue to occur frequently between Palestinian Arabs and Israelis.

MEET THE PEOPLE OF ISRAEL

Israel's population is about 75% Jewish and 25% non-Jewish. About three quarters of the Jews are Israeli-born, while the remaining one quarter come mainly from Europe and America. Israel has laws that allow almost any Jewish person to immigrate, receive temporary housing, and receive job training. Since 1948, about 3 million Jews have moved to Israel from other countries, many to escape persecution. Although the Jews share a common heritage, they represent a variety of ethnic groups and religious branches.

Most non-Jewish people in Israel are Arabs. Many of these are Palestinians who remained on family farms after the Arab-Israeli War in 1948–1949. They live in separate Arab neighborhoods and limit contact with Jews.

The nation's official languages are Hebrew, spoken by most Jews, and Arabic, spoken by the Arab minority. English is commonly used as well. Jews who emigrated from Russia speak Russian and some from Europe speak a Germanic language called *Yiddish*.

Overwhelmingly, the Israeli people live in urban areas. The western region along the Mediterranean is the country's most crowded area, while the deserts of the south are the least populated.

LAND, WATER, AND CLIMATE IN ISRAEL

Land

Israel, one of the world's smaller nations, is roughly the size of New Jersey. Its low coastal plains rise to mountains in the central part of the country. In the south lies the Negev desert and to the east is the Rift Valley.

Most of Israel's population, industry, and agriculture can be found in the Coastal Plain of the west. It includes fertile farming

Fast Facts

Capital:
Jerusalem

Size:
154th in the world

Area:
12,906 sq miles
(33,426 sq km)

Coastline:
170 miles (274 km)

Highest Point:
Mount Meron 3,963 feet
(1,208 m)

Lowest Point:
Dead Sea -1,338 feet
(-408 m)

Population:
8 million

Official Languages:
Hebrew, Arabic

Currency:
New Israeli shekels

National Anthem:
"Hatikvah" (The Hope)

National Symbol:
Star of David, menorah

areas, a broad stream, coastline, and many important cities. Inland, the Judeo-Galilean Highlands run north to south and include Israel's highest peak—Mount Meron at three quarters of a mile high (1208 meters). Most of Israel's Arab population live in this mountainous region. It includes the city of Nazareth, Israel's largest Arab center, as well as Jerusalem. The Rift Valley, a flat lowland with steep edges, is the world's lowest land area. It lies below sea level and includes the Dead Sea, the Jordan River, and the Sea of Galilee. The dry, sparsely populated Negev Desert region is used mainly to graze livestock.

Water

Israel's Sea of Galilee is an important freshwater source. The Dead Sea, on the other hand, is the second saltiest body of water in the world. The two are connected by the Jordan River, which flows through the Sea of Galilee and empties into the Dead Sea. These bodies of water form part of Israel's eastern border with Syria and Jordan.

Climate

Israel has a temperate climate with some hot, dry weather in the southern and eastern desert areas. Higher altitudes generally experience cooler temperatures. Summer temperatures can reach 120 °F near the Dead Sea but are less extreme in other regions. Winter temperatures average around 60 °F depending on the region. In spring and summer, sandstorms may occur brought on by desert winds called *khamsin*. Rainfall varies from over 42 inches (107 cm) per year in Upper Galilee to 1 inch (2.54 cm) per year in the southern Negev Desert. Some hilly regions receive snow in winter. Israel experiences regular droughts and occasional earthquakes.

EVERYDAY LIFE IN ISRAEL

Despite political and religious clashes with Palestinian Arabs, Israelis generally enjoy long lives and high incomes. The standard of living is similar to that in some European countries. Excellent health care contributes to Israel's rank among the longest life expectancies in the world.

Map of Israel

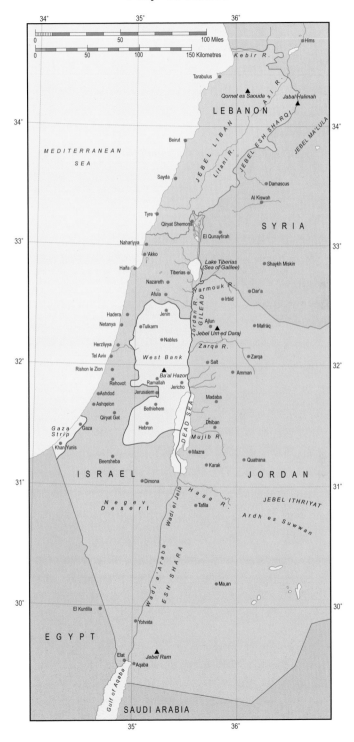

City Life

Almost all Israelis (92%) live in cities. The city of Tel Aviv has a population of 3.6 million, while Haifa and the capital city of Jerusalem have around 1 million residents. Israeli cities blend historic buildings from ancient times with modern high-rise apartments and office buildings. Because the cities have grown very quickly, some conveniences such as roads and city services have not kept up. Cities also face problems from traffic congestion and pollution.

Israel's most holy city, important to Jews, Muslims, and Christians, is Jerusalem. Jerusalem's Old City consists of the historically important area that was occupied during biblical times. The section of the city called West Jerusalem is a modern urban center inhabited mainly by Jews. East Jerusalem was not initially part of Israel, but Israel captured it in 1967. It is inhabited mainly by Arabs.

Other important cities include Tel Aviv, a commercial center, and Haifa, a port city. Israel also began building cities in less populated areas in the 1950's in hopes of attracting industry and providing lower-cost housing for immigrants.

Country Life

Israeli Jews living in rural areas often form a *kibbutz*, or cooperative community. Members of a kibbutz work in exchange for food, housing, education, and health care. They share property, which may include farmland or industrial resources.

Food and Drink

In Israel, most restaurants, hotels, and public buildings serve only *kosher* foods, those that follow Jewish laws for preparation. Some non-kosher restaurants do exist, along with fast-food restaurants and those that serve Western foods. Israeli food includes traditional European Jewish dishes, such as chicken soup, chopped liver, and gefilte fish. It also includes popular Middle Eastern dishes like *falafel*, deep-fried chickpea patties. Many Israelis drink Turkish coffee, cola, beer, and wine, though Muslims do not drink alcohol.

Arts

Israeli artists tend to follow the traditions of their ethnic group in all forms of artistic expression. Some have blended the diversity of Israeli culture into a new artistic style. Much of the subject matter pulls from Jewish history and religion as well as modern social and political problems.

Israel is home to many museums, orchestras, and dance companies. It has one of the world's highest rates of books published per person. Some Israeli authors have won international acclaim, including 1966 Nobel Prize-winner Shmuel Yosef Agnon.

Education

Israelis value education highly, providing free schooling and requiring attendance for all children up to age 16. As a result, almost all Israelis can read and write, putting the national literacy rate at about 98%. The government funds both Jewish schools, which use the Hebrew language, and Arab/Druse schools, which teach in Arabic. Druses make up a small population of Israelis who speak Arabic and follow an offshoot of Islam. Schools cater to their students by teaching religion and history geared toward their culture.

The grades and school divisions are very similar to those in the United States. After age 18, education is no longer free, but Israel's many universities are well-respected.

Religion

In addition to the 75% of the population who are Jewish, Israel is also home to Muslim (18%) and Christian (2%) populations, as well as followers of some other minor religions. The government guarantees religious freedom to members of all faiths. The overwhelmingly Jewish population varies in how strictly they observe traditional laws of Judaism. Orthodox Jews are the strictest and many believe the government should follow Jewish principles. Other branches observe fewer Jewish laws, or adapt them to fit modern culture. Some Jews do not follow Jewish laws at all. They favor a limited role of religion in politics.

JUDAISM

Judaism, the ancient religion of the Jewish people, is the world's first *monotheistic* religion—one that centers on a single God. The Jews consider themselves a chosen people, set apart by God to live in covenant, or promise, with him. Judaism is a complete way of life, encompassing religion, culture, heritage, and even the Hebrew language. Today, about 15 million people follow Judaism.

History

Judaism began with the patriarch, or founding father, Abraham around 2,000 BCE. The Old Testament of the Bible tells of Abraham's encounter with God and God's promise to make Abraham and his offspring a great nation in the land of Canaan. Abraham's grandson, Jacob, also encountered God, who changed Jacob's name to Israel. From then on, the Jews also called themselves Israelites. After a time of famine, the Israelites left Canaan to move to Egypt. They were enslaved there.

The story of Judaism's beginning is recorded in the Torah, the first five books of the Old Testament that Jews consider the Law. Jewish tradition ascribes these five books (also called the Pentateuch) to Moses. According to the book of Exodus, Moses met with God in the form of a burning bush in the wilderness. He followed God's command to free the Hebrew people from slavery in Egypt. Later, God met with Moses again, on Mount Sinai, and gave him the Ten Commandments. These laws, recorded in the book of Exodus, are as follows:

"You shall have no other gods before me.

"You shall not make for yourself a carved image, or any likeness of anything that is in heaven above, or that is in the earth beneath, or that is in the water under the earth...

"You shall not take the name of the Lord your God in vain...

"Remember the Sabbath day, to keep it holy. Six days you shall labor, and do all your work, but the seventh day is a Sabbath to the Lord your God. On it you shall not do any work...

"Honor your father and your mother...

"You shall not murder.

"You shall not commit adultery.
"You shall not steal.
"You shall not bear false witness against your neighbor.
"You shall not covet..."

Beliefs

Judaism involves practicing religious rituals found in the Scriptures and also following scriptural rules for an ethical life. The Hebrew Bible consists of the Torah plus other books called the Prophets and the Writings. They contain Jewish history and moral teachings. Around 70 CE, Jewish scholars began recording additional laws that had been passed on orally. These laws were collected in the Mishnah around 200 CE and later writings, called the Gemara, interpret and comment on the laws. Together, the Mishna and the Gemara make up the Talmud.

Jews believe that God will one day send a Messiah to bring peace and justice to the world. The Old Testament book of Isaiah describes the Messiah as an anointed ruler who will reconcile the Jews with God. People with a Jewish heritage who believe that the Messiah already came to Earth as Jesus Christ are called Messianic Jews.

Branches

Judaism encompasses many branches that differ in beliefs and practices. Orthodox Judaism is one of the most popular branches, and also one of the strictest and most traditional. Its followers believe that God revealed his law (both the Torah and the Talmud) directly to Moses and still observe all aspects of that traditional law. It affects the way Orthodox Jews dress, what they eat, and how often they pray. They also strictly obey the rule of doing no work on the Sabbath, or Shabbat. This includes cooking, driving, and carrying money. In Modern Orthodoxy, these rules are relaxed somewhat to allow followers to participate in the general culture. The Hasidic sect of Orthodox Jews follows Eastern European traditions of dress.

Another branch of Judaism, Reform Judaism, teaches that the Bible came from God but the Talmud came from humans. Followers focus on living morally rather than performing strict traditional rituals. In Conservative Judaism, followers believe that the Bible and the Talmud came from God, but that rituals can be adapted to fit the times. A rabbi, or Jewish teacher, decides which laws can be altered. One of Judaism's newest branches, Reconstructionist Judaism, views Judaism as more a culture than a religion. Followers reject the idea that God chose the Jewish people as his own and they believe that rituals and customs can change as society sees fit.

Worship

Each Jewish synagogue, or house of worship, is headed by a rabbi and no higher central authority exists at the head of the religion. Rabbis study at seminaries run by their branch of Judaism. While rabbis once simply taught the law, today they perform a variety of roles, like giving sermons and providing counseling. Except for Orthodox Jews, women as well as men can be rabbis.

Synagogues, sometimes referred to as temples, often include community resources such as schools, social halls, athletic facilities, lecture halls, and cultural centers. Jewish children usually attend Hebrew school to learn the Hebrew language and Jewish history. Synagogues are built to face the holy city of Jerusalem. They contain an ark, or chest, at the front of the sanctuary. It contains the scrolls of the Torah. An electric light or oil lamp hangs above the ark to represent God's eternal presence.

Worship services at a synagogue must include at least 10 people, or a *minyan*. Worshippers read from the Torah, chant prayers from the *siddur* prayer book, and listen to a sermon. Often, a cantor chants prayers or leads a choir. A cantor has been trained in voice, Hebrew language, and traditional chanting. Specific details about the service depend on the branch of Judaism. Some branches allow women to lead the service, while others do not. In Orthodox synagogues, men and women do not sit together, but are separated by a barrier called a *mehiza*. Services may be entirely in Hebrew, or a combination of Hebrew and the local language. Some synagogues offer services daily, while others only provide Sabbath and holiday services.

Holy Days

Holidays make up an important part of the Jewish faith. The Sabbath, or seventh day of the week, is a holy day reserved for rest. It commemorates

God's creation of the world and his rest on the seventh day. The Sabbath begins at sundown on Friday and continues through sunset on Saturday. Jews attend synagogue on the Sabbath and also worship in the home by lighting candles, saying prayers, and sharing a special meal. Observing the Sabbath is the only Jewish ritual required in the Ten Commandments.

Other than the Sabbath, the holiest days for Jews are Rosh Hashanah and Yom Kippur, called the High Holidays. The Jewish New Year of Rosh Hashanah is celebrated for two days in September or October during the Jewish month of Tishri. It is a time to repent of sins, or wrongdoing, and ask God for forgiveness. At the synagogue, Jews sound a ram's horn, called a *shofar*, to begin the observance. They enjoy a festive meal to usher in the New Year. Ten days later, the Days of Judgment come to a close on Yom Kippur. This solemn holiday involves fasting, prayer, and confessing sins.

Jews also observe pilgrimage festivals. In ancient times, these festivals included a pilgrimage, or journey, to Jerusalem. Each festival commemorates an aspect of the Jews' escape from Egypt and coincides with a seasonal harvest. Passover, or Pesah, occurs during the barley harvest in March or April. It celebrates the time when God struck down the first-born of all Egyptian families, but passed over the Jewish households. Jews remember this event by sharing a meal called the Seder in their homes. The Seder includes many symbolic foods, such as unleavened bread called *matzo*. When the Jewish people escaped from slavery in Egypt, they left in such a hurry that God told them not to add yeast to their bread dough. They had to bake the unleavened bread into something like crackers.

Fifty days after Passover comes the Pentecost, or Shavuot, festival. It commemorates the day God gave the Torah to the Jews and coincides with the harvest of first fruits. The third pilgrimage festival, Sukkot, begins five days after Yom Kippur. It lasts seven days and coincides with the autumn harvest. Sukkot is also called the Feast of Tabernacles or the Feast of Booths, because the Jewish people lived in huts in the wilderness after leaving Egypt. In memory of this, Jews build small huts (booths) for Sukkot. Many also celebrate the completion of reading through the Torah in a year in some synagogues.

Jews celebrate many other holidays throughout the year. Hanukkah, or the Festival of Lights, occurs during December. During this eight-day celebration, Jews remember an important victory in 165 BCE. At that time, a group of Jews called the Maccabees fought against the Syrians to protect their faith. During the fight, an important lamp in the Jewish Temple ran out of oil but God miraculously kept the lamp burning for eight days. Today, Jews remember this event by lighting candles on a *menorah*, a special candleholder for seven candles. They also read the Torah, sing songs, play games, and give gifts.

On Purim, celebrated in February or March, Jews remember the events recorded in the book of Esther. It tells of the Persian Queen Esther, a Jew, who helped thwart a plot to kill all Jews.

In addition to joyous holidays, Jews also observe solemn days of fasting. For example, Tishah be-Av reminds Jews of when the Temple was destroyed by Babylonians in 586 BCE and again by Romans in 70 CE.

Customs and Ceremonies

Most Jews observe *kosher* dietary laws, meaning they are ritually correct. The laws come from the Bible, which some interpret as divine commandments and others observe as cultural habit. Kosher laws prohibit Jews from eating, or even storing, meat and milk products together. Jews will wait several hours after consuming meat before eating milk products. In many Jewish homes, this law means owning two refrigerators and two stoves to keep meat and milk separate. Jews only eat meat that has been butchered according to *shehitah*, a quick and less painful ritual slaughter that includes a blessing over the animal. Kosher laws forbid pork and shellfish.

Jewish people celebrate the birth of a child with a *simhat bat* for baby girls or a *bris bat* for baby boys. At the age of 13, children become full members of the Jewish community. They celebrate with a ceremony called a *bar mitzvah* (for boys) or *bat mitzvah* (for girls) in which the honoree reads from the Torah. A festive party usually follows. A Jewish wedding involves a ceremony performed under a *huppa*, or canopy, followed by the bride and groom stomping on a glass to break it. At these fun occasions,

Jewish people often wish one another "Mazel tov!" which means *good fortune* or *congratulations*.

Upon a person's death, Jews also observe certain rituals. They have the body buried, usually within about a day. Then, the family begins shiva, a week-long period of deep mourning. For the next 11 months, mourners continue to recite a prayer called the Kaddish. Once this period ends, Jews remember the deceased person each year on the anniversary of the death by lighting a candle. This yearly memorial is called *yahrzeit*.

Influence

Judaism shares roots with two of the world's major religions—Christianity and Islam. Christians and Jews share the same Old Testament of the Bible, though the Jewish Scriptures include some apocryphal writings and the Talmud, while Christian Scriptures include the New Testament. Christianity was founded by followers of Jesus Christ, himself a Jew. Early Christians were mainly Jews and Greeks who believed Jesus to be the awaited Messiah. Today, Christians and Jews share a belief in some common religious history and theology, but disagree about whether or not Jesus was the Messiah.

Muslims, also have common roots with Judaism. Abraham had a son named Ishmael before he and his wife had their son Isaac. While Isaac went on to become father to Jacob (Israel) and the Jewish nation, Ishmael was exiled. Muhammad, who emerged in Arabia in the 600's CE, proclaimed faith in the same God of Abraham, a God that Muslims call Allah. Muslims believe that Allah sent many prophets, from Adam, the first man, to Ishmael, Abraham's exiled son, and finally Muhammad. Today, disputes over claims to holy lands in Palestine and Israel have led to ongoing conflicts between Arabs and Jews.

Persecution

The Jewish people have faced different forms of persecution over thousands of years. As far back as about 600 BCE, the Jews were taken captive by Egypt until, according to the Bible, they followed Moses to freedom.

More recently, Jews faced a devastating *genocide*, or systematic murder of an ethnic group, during World War II. Nazi dictator Adolf Hitler oversaw the murder of about 6 million Jewish men, women, and children—over two-thirds of Europe's Jewish population. Prior to the war, Jews faced increasing *anti-Semitism*, or prejudice against Jews. Their rights were slowly stripped away and they were confined to neighborhoods called ghettoes. Then, Nazi soldiers began sending Jews to concentration camps, where they performed hard labor or were executed, often in mass gas chambers.

ISRAEL'S GOVERNMENT

The State of Israel is a parliamentary democracy with a president and a prime minister. It consists of six districts, called *mehozot*. Although the capital is Jerusalem, much political activity, including location of foreign embassies, occurs in Tel Aviv. The state was formed in 1948 through a mandate by the League of Nations under British administration. The act was not approved by all nations and many Arab nations still refuse to acknowledge the existence of Israel.

Israel has no formal constitution, but other documents serve as an outline for independence and government. These include the Declaration of Establishment, the Basic Laws of Israel, the Nationality Law, and the Law of Return. The legal system follows some principles of English common law and separate religious laws exist for Jews, Christians, and Muslims.

The parliament, or legislative body, of Israel is called the Knesset. Its 120 members are elected by popular vote to serve 4-year terms. They indirectly elect the president, and one Knesset member becomes prime minister. Israel's president serves one seven-year term and is basically a figurehead. Israeli citizens age 18 or older can vote in elections. They do not choose individual candidates; rather, they vote for a group of candidates from a single political party. The number of seats awarded to each political party reflects the percentage of votes received. Voters previously elected the prime minister directly, but that practice changed after 2001.

Israel maintains a large military, a costly but necessary investment due to ongoing conflicts. It has an army, navy, and air force of about 141,000. All men enter the military at age 18 and must serve for three years. Unmarried Jewish women also serve for two years. After that time, men and women serve annually in reserve forces.

THE ECONOMY OF ISRAEL

Israel has an economy based on advanced technology. It produces and exports high-tech equipment, pharmaceuticals, and cut diamonds. It imports oil, grains, raw materials, and military equipment. The nation imports more than it exports, but makes up for the deficit with a robust tourism industry and foreign investments. Its Gross Domestic Product (GDP), a measure of all the goods and services produced in a year, is the world's 56th largest. Israel's main trade partner is the United States, but it also trades goods with many other nations.

Agriculture

Before becoming an independent nation, Israel had a larger agricultural industry. Today, it accounts for very little (2%) of the nation's GDP and employs 2% of the workforce. The use of modern machinery has replaced the need for many agricultural workers. About one fourth of Israel's land, irrigated by water drawn from the Jordan River, is used for agriculture. Israeli farmers grow citrus, vegetables, and cotton. They also raise cattle and poultry. The government oversees agricultural activity, but farmers own their own land. Arabs generally own private farms while Jews work together in a kibbutz. Israel produces enough food to feed its population, with some exports making up for the imports it requires.

Natural Resources

Israel has stores of magnesium, potash, copper ore, natural gas, and some other resources. Drawing minerals, including table salt, from the Dead Sea is an important industry. However, Israel has almost no energy resources, such as coal, oil, gas, or hydroelectric power. It must, therefore, import almost all of its crude oil and coal needs.

Manufacturing

Manufacturing in Israel produces a variety of goods and accounts for one quarter of Israel's GDP. These include electronics, chemicals, machinery, metal products, processed foods, textiles, and clothing. Israel imports diamonds, cuts them with high-tech tools, and resells them. Much of Israel's manufacturing occurs in Tel Aviv and Haifa.

Services

Services make up about 72% of Israel's economy and employ about three fourths of the labor force. Many of these workers are employed by the Israeli government, which also owns many businesses. They help provide the large immigrant population with services related to housing, education, and vocational training. Many service workers are employed by the tourist industry as well, which includes restaurants and hotels.

Transportation

Thanks to Israel's large military investments, the country has a well-developed transportation system it uses to move troops and equipment. Cities have public buses and railways, but most middle- and upper-class Israelis own automobiles. Some have automobiles provided by their employer. The country has international airports near Tel Aviv, Elat, and Haifa, where the Israeli airline El Al operates. Haifa, Ashdod, and Elat have major shipping ports.

Communication

Like all high-tech nations, Israel has well-developed communications systems. It publishes many newspapers in Hebrew, Arabic, English, Russian, and other languages. A government-run corporation provides television and radio stations, in addition to the commercial stations that are also available.

ISRAEL'S HISTORY

Ancient History

Israel began as the Holy Land where the Jewish nation developed. From, 2000–1500 BCE, Abraham, his son Isaac, and his grandson Jacob settled in the land of Canaan, until Jacob and his descendants migrated to Egypt due a famine in the land. Eventually, the Israelites became Egyptian slaves.

In the 13th century BCE, Moses led the people out of Egypt and back to the Land of Israel. During their journey, they received the Ten Commandments.

During the next two centuries, the Israelites conquered most of Israel and went from being nomads to farmers and craftsmen. Periods of peace and times of war followed, during which the people were led by "judges," persons chosen for their leadership qualities.

Jewish Monarchy

The first king, Saul (about 1020 BCE), was followed by a full monarchy under his successor, David. King David (ca. 1004–965 BCE) established Israel as a strong nation by military expeditions and a number of alliances with nearby kingdoms. David's son Solomon (ca. 965–930 BCE) further strengthened the kingdom. During Solomon's reign, the Jews built a Temple in Jerusalem, which became the center of the Jewish people's national and religious life.

Divided Kingdom

After Solomon's death (930 BCE), the ten northern tribes broke away from the whole of Israel, dividing the country into a northern kingdom, Israel, and a southern kingdom, Judah.

The Northern Kingdom, with its capital Samaria, lasted more than 200 years under 19 kings, while the Southern Kingdom, with its capital Jerusalem, lasted for 350 years with an equal number of kings. The Assyrians conquered Israel in 722 BCE and removed all the people. The Babylonians conquered Judah in 586 BCE. While some Jews remained in the land, many of the Jews in the Southern Kingdom were exiled to Babylonia, which followed the destruction of the First Temple. After Persia conquered Babylon, some Jewish exiles returned to Israel in 539 BCE, under the reign of Cyrus the Great, and rebuilt their temple.

The land of Israel was ruled by various kingdoms for the next 400 years, including the Persians, Alexander the Great, the Hasmoneans, and in 63 BCE, the Romans conquered the land under Pompey.

Roman Rule

After Pompey conquered the land, the Romans appointed rulers who gave the Jews some autonomy to worship and follow their Jewish traditions. During Roman rule, Jesus Christ was born and began his ministry. His followers were called Christians.

In 70 AD, after a revolt by some Jews, the Romans destroyed Jerusalem. They removed the Jews from the land, which marked the beginning of the Jewish Diaspora, the dispersion of the Jews out of the land of Israel.

Other Rulers

By the end of the 4th century, following Emperor Constantine's adoption of Christianity (313 CE) and the founding of the Byzantine Empire, the Land of Israel became a predominantly Christian country. The Jews were deprived of their former autonomy, their right to hold public positions, and were forbidden to enter Jerusalem except to mourn the destruction of the Temple one day a year.

The Arabs conquered the land four years after the death of Muhammad (632) and ruled more than four centuries. At the outset of Arab rule, Jewish settlement in Jerusalem was resumed, and the Jewish community lived under "protection," the status of non-Muslims under Arab rule.

However, Arabs introduced restrictions against non-Arabs (717), which changed the Jews' ability to engage in their religious observances. By the end of the 11th century, the Jewish community in the land was much smaller and had lost its organizational and religious cohesiveness.

For the next 200 years, Crusaders dominated the country following an appeal by Pope Urban II to go to the country and recover the Holy

Land. The Crusaders extended their power over the rest of the country through treaties and agreements following military victories.

The Muslim army under Saladin (1187) overthrew the Crusaders and the Jews were again accorded some freedom, including the right to live in Jerusalem. Crusader authority ended when they were defeated in 1291 by the Mamluks, a Muslim military class that came to power in Egypt.

In 1517, the Ottomans conquered the land and ruled for 400 years.

Ottoman rule ended in 1917 when the British conquered the land and the British pledged support for a "Jewish national home in Palestine." The British ruled the land until 1948.

View of Masada, in the Judaean Desert

A New State

When World War I began in 1914, about 85,000 Jews lived in Palestine, making up 12% of the population. European Jews facing persecution began to desire a homeland in Palestine, land they believed God promised them. The British government, hoping to gain wartime support from Jewish leaders in the United Kingdom and the United States, supported this desire. However, the British government also promised independence to Arabs in the Middle East, in order to gain their support in the war against the Ottomans. Arab leaders interpreted this promise to include Palestine.

When the war ended in 1918, the British government had a problem. It controlled Palestine as a territory, but had been charged with establishing a Jewish homeland. Jews saw this as an invitation to immigrate to Palestine. Arabs saw it as an invasion of their long-held lands. The friction increased when Jews fleeing Nazi persecution during World War II came to Palestine in large numbers. As the Jews continued coming, the Palestinian Arabs revolted against the British, and the British attempted to reduce tensions by limiting the number of Jews allowed into the country.

In an effort to reach peace, the United Nations (UN) proposed dividing the land into an Arab state of Palestine and a Jewish state of Israel. The disputed city of Jerusalem would fall under international control. The plan appealed to Palestinian Jews but not the Arabs. Israel became an independent nation on May 14, 1948, but peace did not follow. Fighting began immediately. Israel won these battles and occupied regions of Egypt, Syria, and Jordan. Many Arabs fled the Israeli-held areas while 150,000 others remained. The warring nations attempted to reach peace, but formal treaties were never signed, because the Arab nations refused to acknowledge Israel's right to exist.

Conflict Continues

In the 1950's, Egypt provided assistance to Palestinian Arabs who invaded Israel from the Egyptian-controlled part of Palestine, the Gaza Strip. Egypt also refused Israeli ships passage through the Suez Canal. In response, Israel attacked and took control of Egypt's Sinai Peninsula and Gaza Strip. The United Kingdom and France joined Israel in the attack. The UN intervened by sending a peacekeeping force to the disputed area.

Egyptian President Gamal Abdel Nasser demanded the UN remove its force from Egyptian lands, which it did in May 1967. Immediately, Nasser sent Egyptian troops into the Sinai and closed an important strait to Israeli ships. Israel responded with a surprise air strike on June 5. War broke out as Syria, Jordan, and Iraq joined Egypt in the fight. However, Israel's air and ground forces overcame the Arabs. The UN stepped in after six days to arrange a cease-fire, thus giving rise to the name the Six-Day War.

After the Six-Day War, Israel held onto Syria's Golan Heights, Jordan's West Bank, and Jerusalem. Israel vowed to keep troops in the conquered lands where 1 million Palestinian Arabs lived until they recognized Israel's right to exist.

Smaller skirmishes continued for years. Israelis and Egyptians fought along borders. Palestinians formed a resistance group called the Palestinian Liberation Organization (PLO) that launched guerilla attacks against Israel. War erupted once again in 1973 when Egypt and Syria launched an attack on Israel on Yom Kippur, the holiest Jewish day. The rivals fought for about three weeks before calling for a cease-fire. Although Israel won the war and gained even more territory, it was economically costly and many Israelis died.

Steps toward Peace

Prime Minister Golda Meir resigned in 1974 over complaints about how her government had handled the Yom Kippur War. Israel became more dependent on economic help from the United States. For the first time, Israel's Labor Party lost control of the government to the Likud Party. Its leader, Menachem Begin, became prime minister.

In 1977, Begin agreed to meet with Egyptian President Anwar el-Sadat and U.S. President Jimmy Carter, upon the announcement that el-Sadat wanted to negotiate a peace treaty. The leaders met at Camp David in the United States, giving rise to an agreement called the Camp David Accords. It began with Egypt and Israel signing a peace treaty in 1979. The following year, the two nations exchanged diplomats. Finally, Israel withdrew from the Sinai Peninsula in 1982. Although the Camp David Accords helped establish peace between Egypt and Israel, it did little to reach the greater goal of peace throughout the Middle East.

Modern Developments

Israel's conflicts continued in the 1980's. After several years of attacks by PLO guerillas, Israel invaded Lebanon to drive them out. Both Israel and the PLO later withdrew troops from Lebanon.

While the Israeli government became divided between the Labor Party and the Likud Party, with neither gaining a majority influence, Palestinians began uprisings throughout the Gaza Strip and the West Bank. This *intifada* (uprising) often turned violent. During the years of conflict, a new Islamist organization called Hamas began to replace the PLO in leading the Palestinian resistance movement. Meanwhile, the Israeli government attempted to accommodate hundreds of thousands of Jewish immigrants by housing them in occupied territories.

In 1991, during the Persian Gulf War between Iraq and several other countries, Iraq fired missiles at Israel. That same year, Middle Eastern nations met for peace talks, though the PLO did not participate. Two years later, the PLO and Israel agreed to work toward peace. The two recognized one another officially and signed an agreement. The PLO renounced terrorism, recognized Israel as a state, and declared its own state in the West Bank and the Gaza Strip. Israel turned over the Gaza Strip and the West Bank to Palestinian control and withdrew its troops. In 1994, Israel and Jordan officially ended the war that had been in existence between them for 47 years.

Some Israelis disagreed with these decisions and protested. They wanted Israel to retain all of its historic territory. In 1995, an Israeli university student assassinated Prime Minister Yitzhak Rabin. The following year, Benjamin Netanyahu, who criticized Rabin's peace agreements with the PLO, was elected prime minister. In direct contrast with Rabin's promise to limit Jewish settlements in occupied territories, Netanyahu expanded settlements in the West Bank and East Jerusalem. Tensions between Israel and Palestine rose once again. The two made occasional moves toward peace, but often violated terms or failed to follow through on promises.

Ehud Barak succeeded Netanyahu in 1999 and attempted to repair relationships with Palestine. Barak met with Palestinian leader Yasser Arafat, once again at Camp David, but the two were unable to agree on some key issues. For example, both Muslims and Jews sought control over the Temple Mount, a holy site, in Jerusalem. The Temple Mount holds significance for both Jews and Muslims. The Muslims hold sacred the Dome of the Rock Mosque on the Mount and the Jews revere the land that held the Jewish temple which the Romans destroyed in 70 CE.

As Palestinians rose up once again, Israel responded, and back-and-forth attacks continued. Hamas, which does not recognize Israel as a state, gained power in Palestinian elections in 2006. As a result, allies of Israel, including the United States, refused to deal with Palestine. Hamas seized the Gaza Strip while Fatah, a rival Palestinian group, took control of the West Bank. Ongoing violence in Gaza resulted in hundreds of deaths, mostly Palestinian. Israel also engaged in fighting with Lebanon once again, when the radical Islamist group Hezbollah captured two Israeli soldiers in 2006.

Today, protesting, violence, and political changes continue in Israel and its surrounding countries. In Palestine, Hamas and Fatah have formed a joint government, but continue to clash with Israel. Netanyahu became prime minister of Israel once again in 2009. Fighting continues between Israel and Hamas, mainly in the Gaza Strip.

Flag of Israel

SAUDI ARABIA

SAUDI ARABIA: THE BIG PICTURE

Saudi Arabia, the birthplace of Islam, is home to the two holiest Muslim shrines—Mecca and Medina. Saudi Arabia is also famous for its thriving oil industry. Though the country consists mainly of deserts, this large Middle Eastern nation is quite wealthy and attracts workers from around the world.

Once a land of simple mud houses, dirt roads, and camel caravans, Saudi Arabia is now a modern economic power. Paved roads, modern transportation, and high-rise buildings have all become the norm, thanks to the nation's vast reserves of petroleum and the development of the oil industry. Despite many modern conveniences, however, Saudi Arabia maintains many traditional practices. It is a kingdom ruled by a king and is a strictly Muslim nation.

Located on the Arabian Peninsula, Saudi Arabia is the 13th largest nation in the world and the largest in the Middle East. Its neighbors include Jordan, Iraq, and Kuwait to the north, the United Arab Emirates, Qatar, and Bahrain to the east, and Oman and Yemen to the south. It has coastlines along the Red Sea in the west and the Persian Gulf (or Arabian Gulf) in the east. Its capital city Riyadh is its largest city.

MEET THE PEOPLE OF SAUDI ARABIA

Almost all (90%) of Saudi Arabia's population are Arab, though that includes a mix of races and ethnicities. The other 10% of people are mainly Afro-Asian. In the past, Arabs brought many blacks from Africa to Saudi Arabia as slaves. They later became free and intermarried with people of other backgrounds. Some people descend from African, Indonesian, and Indian Muslims who came to the country as pilgrims. The nation has a large community of expatriates, or those living and working outside of their home country. Accounting for about a third of Saudi Arabia's population, these foreigners represent a variety of ethnicities and cultures.

Almost everyone speaks Arabic, the official language. However, schools teach English because foreigners and business people use it frequently.

LAND, WATER, AND CLIMATE IN SAUDI ARABIA

Land

Most of Saudi Arabia's terrain is sandy desert that slopes downward from higher land in the west to lower lands in the east. The Hejaz and Asir regions along the coast of the Red Sea consist of mountains that reach

Fast Facts

Capital:
Riyadh

Size:
13th in the world

Area:
1,335,755 sq miles
(3,459,590 sq km)

Coastline:
1,640 miles (2639 km)

Highest Point:
Jabal Sawda 10,279 feet
(3,133 m)

Lowest Point:
Persian Gulf 0 feet (0 m)

Population:
27.8 million

Official Language:
Arabic

Currency:
Saudi riyals

National Anthem:
"Aash Al Maleek" (Long Live Our Beloved King)

National Symbol:
palm tree above two crossed swords

over 9,000 feet (2,743 meters) above sea level. They taper down to a Central Plateau that is barren except for scattered fertile *oases*, isolated areas of water in the desert. The rocky expanse of the Syrian Desert and the sandy dunes of An Nafud lie to the North of the Central Plateau. To the south, 250,000 square miles (647,500 square km) of Saudi Arabia is covered by the Rub al Khali, or Empty Quarter. This windy desert has no permanent inhabitants, though nomads graze their herds there in the spring. Saudi Arabia's low, flat east coast, where petroleum deposits are most abundant, has given rise to large cities. The natural springs have also allowed agricultural settlements to thrive there.

Dust storm in Saudi Arabia

Water

Saudi Arabia is the largest country in the world without a river. However, it has long coastlines along the Persian Gulf and the Red Sea. It also has access to the Suez Canal, which connects the Red Sea to the Mediterranean Sea. Water from infrequent rainstorms sometimes collects in dry valleys but evaporates or soaks into the ground quickly.

Climate

Saudi Arabia experiences great temperature extremes. Overall, it has a harsh desert climate with frequent sand and dust storms, called *sumoom*. The temperatures are generally hot all year, averaging over 90° F during the day in coastal regions during the summers. Inland, temperatures can reach 120° F, though the climate there is less humid and nights are cooler. Occasionally, parts of Saudi Arabia experience temperatures below freezing.

The only region to receive significant rainfall is Asir, in the southwest. There, seasonal winds called *monsoons* bring up to 20 inches (51 cm) of rain per year while the rest of the country receives less than 4 inches (10 cm) per year. Despite having many volcanoes, such as Harrat Rahat, Harrat Khaybar, Harrat Lunayyir, and Jabal Yar, few have shown any activity in the past few centuries.

EVERYDAY LIFE IN SAUDI ARABIA

Less than 100 years ago, most Saudis lived in rural areas and worked as farmers, herders, or traders. The country has changed dramatically, however, since the beginning of the oil industry in the mid-1900's. People have moved to urban areas where they work in many types of service and manufacturing jobs. The government has used oil profits to improve education, transportation, and communication throughout the country. Today, Saudis enjoy improved housing with many modern conveniences, even in rural areas.

Family Life

In Saudi families, the father is considered the head of the household. His wife may have a large say in running the household, but women have traditionally had limited freedom and opportunities outside the home. Society's treatment of women is slowly starting to improve, however. More and more women receive an education and work outside the home. They hold a variety of jobs, but are still limited by rules that prohibit them from driving and that restrict their travel.

City Life

Many large, modern cities exist in Saudi Arabia. The capital, Riyadh, is home to over 6 million people. Jeddah has a population of 4 million and Mecca, Medina, and Ad Dammam all have populations over 1 million.

Country Life

Saudi Arabia's small rural population lives in farm villages or small settlements around desert oases. Their homes might be made of stone or mud. Some herders, called nomads or Bedouins, constantly follow their flocks through deserts to find water and pastureland. These nomads live in traditional goat hair tents and meet at local markets to trade and to socialize. Rural Saudis generally live very simple lives.

Recreation

Saudis enjoy spending time socializing with family and friends. Since the 1980's, public movie theaters have been banned, though people watch television and videos at home. Men enjoy modern sports, such as basketball, soccer, and volleyball, as well as the traditional sports of camel and horse racing. Saudis celebrate the formation of their country on September 23rd each year.

Clothing

Muslims living in Saudi Arabia have two main concerns when it comes to clothing: Shari'ah law and the climate. Shari'ah law dictates that Muslims must dress according to standards of decency. That means nothing tight, see-through, or very flashy. Women generally cover their entire bodies except for the hands and face with a long robe called an *abaya*. Some cover their entire body, wearing a veil over their face. Men usually wear a *thawb*, an ankle-length garment, along with a jacket or cloak. The desert climate also dictates how Saudis dress. Men wear a *ghutra*, or head covering, to protect against wind and sun. It is usually a piece of red and white cloth held in place by a cord.

Food and Drink

Saudis enjoy a typical Middle Eastern diet of bread, rice, lamb, dates, and dairy products. They drink coffee and tea. Their Islamic faith prohibits eating pork and drinking alcohol. In cities, Saudis can find a wide variety of foods grown locally and imported from around the world.

Education

The Saudi government offers, but does not require, free education to all citizens. In the past, the first public schools only taught boys, but now about 80% of children, both boys and girls, attend primary school. About

95% of Saudis can read and write, though slightly more males than females are literate.

Religion

Saudi Arabia is a strictly Muslim country, dominated by Sunni Muslims. About 10–15% of the Muslims are Shi'ite rather than Sunni. Every Saudi citizen is Muslim and most follow a conservative form of Sunni called Wahhabism. This means that they not only study and strive to follow Islamic principles, but they encourage others to do the same. This results in a society that emphasizes conformity. A religious police force even helps ensure that people follow rules for dress and behavior.

The nation's large community of expatriates represents a variety of faiths. However, the government restricts any public expression of faith that is not Sunni Islam, and non-Muslims are not allowed to become Saudi citizens. Non-Muslim places of worship are prohibited.

The cities of Mecca and Medina play an important part in the history of Islam. The Prophet Muhammad was born in Mecca, and he formed the first Islamic community in Medina. Millions of Muslims visit these cities every year as part of a religious pilgrimage, or journey. Saudi Arabia has created religious charities in recent decades to build mosques and religious schools in other countries.

ISLAM

Islam is a major world religion based on the teachings of the Prophet Muhammad, who preached in Arabia in the 600's CE. The word *Islam* is Arabic for *surrender*, because Muslims, or those who practice Islam, surrender to the will of Allah (God). Muslims believe in Allah as the sole creator, sustainer, and restorer of the world. They believe he has made his will known through sacred scriptures called the Qur'an (or Koran), which Allah revealed to his messenger, Muhammad. According to Islam, Muhammad was the last in a series of prophets that includes Adam, Noah, Abraham, Moses, Solomon, and Jesus.

Muhammad was born in Mecca, and he formed the first Islamic community in Medina. Millions of Muslims visit these cities every year as part of a religious pilgrimage, or journey. Today, Islam is the world's second largest religion, with followers all over the world.

History of Islam

Around 570 CE, the people of the Arabian Peninsula followed religions that worshipped many gods. Muhammad was born in Mecca at this time. While there, he received the first chapters of the Qur'an, what he believed was the word-for-word revelation of God, delivered by the archangel Gabriel. These first chapters, or *suras*, focus on spiritual and moral teachings along with teachings about the Day of Judgment. Muhammad began teaching belief in one God who would someday judge the world.

In 622, wealthy leaders in Mecca drove Muhammad and his followers out of the city. They fled on a journey, called the Hijrah, to Medina where they began a Muslim community. There, Muhammad received further suras of the Qur'an that deal with social principles and living in an orderly community. Once the community grew large enough, Muhammad led them militarily back to Mecca, where they captured the city in 630. Muslim rule spread to almost the whole Arabian Peninsula by the time of Muhammad's death in 632.

The *caliphs*, or Muslim leaders, who then came to power spread the Muslim Empire from Spain to India. A caliph in 661 established the capital in Damascus, Syria but it was moved to Baghdad, Iraq in 762. Despite these changes, Mecca and Medina remained important Muslim cities, as they are to this day.

Islam spread rapidly throughout the Middle East and into parts of Africa, Europe, India, China, and eastern Asia. By the early 2000's, more than 1.5 billion people worldwide identified as Muslim.

Islamic Beliefs

Muslims believe, above all, in *tawhid*, or the oneness of God. They believe in one God who created and rules over the universe. He is the all-knowing lawgiver and judge who restores life after death. Muslims believe in heaven and hell. Islam also teaches that God reveals himself to man through prophets, and includes Adam, Abraham, Moses, David, and Jesus among the 25 prophets mentioned by name. Therefore, Muslims do not see their religion as new, but as ancient, beginning with Adam and carrying the same message through all the prophets since. However, Muslims reject the Christian belief in the trinity, or the three-part nature of God.

Islam names Muhammad as the final prophet. As a *rasul*, or *messenger*, Muhammad is considered the most important type of prophet because God revealed to him a book to guide humanity. According to Islam, people attain salvation by following the books of God's messengers and by living a morally good life.

In addition to the written words of the Qur'an, Muslims also follow the example of the Prophet Muhammad, as interpretted in writings known as Hadith. These writings, which contain Muhammad's words and deeds, differ somewhat among groups of Muslims such as the Sunnis and the Shiites. However, all Muslims agree that they should follow the *Sunnah*, or *well-trodden path*, of Muhammad. Together, the Qur'an and the Sunnah form the primary sources of Islamic law.

Two centuries after Muhammad's death, two additional foundational principles arose in Islam. *Ijma*, or *consensus*, came about in the 800's as a way to establish common points of agreement in Islam. Later, the principle of *ijtihad*, or *individual thought*, arose as a somewhat controversial way to find solutions to new problems. Ijtihad led to conflicting opinions and interpretations of Islam, so the Sunnis did away with it almost completely while the Shiites continued to use it.

Many aspects of daily life for Muslims are dictated by Shari'ah law, the Islamic law. It draws mainly from the Qur'an and the Sunnah, but also takes into account the agreement of Muslim scholars. It classifies actions into five categories: obligatory (required), recommended, neutral, disapproved, and forbidden. The obligatory actions include most religious duties, like the Five Pillars. Those that Shari'ah law forbids include adultery, gambling, cheating, eating pork, consuming alcohol, and lending money at interest. The Qur'an outlines strict punishments for breaking laws.

Mecca is the holiest city in Islam

Worship and Practices

Muslims consider any act of obedience to God a form of worship. Muslims practice formal acts of worship called the Five Pillars of Islam. These include shahadah, prayer, almsgiving, fasting, and pilgrimage.

Shahadah consists of two statements that form the basis of the Islamic faith. The first, "I bear witness that there is no God but Allah," proclaims belief in just one God. The second, "I bear witness that Muhammad is the Messenger of Allah."

The Muslim call to prayer, or salat, occurs five times a day. A *muezzin*, or person who serves as a caller, announces prayer times just before dawn, at midday, in midafternoon, just after sunset, and at night. Believers wash their hands, face, and feet and then face Mecca in Saudi Arabia. They might gather to pray in a house of worship, called a *mosque*, or just stop to pray wherever they are. The prayer ritual involves standing, kneeling, bowing, raising hands, reciting verses from the Qur'an, and repeating, "God is greatest." The men pray at the front of the group and women pray separately behind them or to the side. On Fridays, a leader called an imam, recites two short sermons. Muslims believe that praying formally several times a day demonstrates devotion to God and protects against disobedience.

Almsgiving, or *zakat,* is an act of recognizing God's ownership of all things. Muslims give a percentage of their wealth to the needy once a year. In addition, they may give a voluntary gift called *sadaqah.* These contributions usually go to mosques, Islamic centers, or welfare organizations.

During the month of Ramadan, the ninth month of the Islamic calendar, Muslims fast. This means they refrain from eating, drinking, and smoking during daylight hours. The fasting continues for about 30 days and allows Muslims to reflect on spiritual matters and practice self-restraint. Those excused from fasting include the sick, injured, elderly, and pregnant. Instead, these people try to provide food for the poor. At the end of Ramadan, Muslims give their alms to the poor.

Pilgrimage, which is a journey called hajj, occurs in the 12th month of the Islamic calendar. All Muslims are required by the Qur'an to journey to Mecca at least once in their lives if they are able. Over several days, Muslims honor the prophet Abraham, his wife Hagar, and their son the prophet Ishmael. They visit the Kaaba, the first house of worship, which they believe Abraham and Ishmael built. The Kaaba is a cube-shaped building around which the Great Mosque in Mecca was later built. Worshipers wear special garments, called *ihram,* and walk around the Kaaba seven times. Many pilgrims perform additional rites of worship while in Mecca.

Muslims celebrate the two major holidays of Id al-Fitr (the Feast of Fast-Breaking) and Id al-Ad-ha (the Feast of the Sacrifice). Id al-Fitr is a feast that celebrates the end of Ramadan fasting. On Id al-Ad-ha, Muslims often sacrifice an animal and share the meat with the poor. Muslims celebrate the birthday of Muhammad by praying, reading the Qur'an, and reciting commemorative stories and poems.

In daily life, Islam teaches followers to practice several virtues, such as kindness, honesty, respect,

A mosque in Cairo, Egypt

charity, hard work, generosity, and honor. Muslims are to respect their parents, care for orphans and widows, and help the poor. They should never refuse a request for help.

Islam Today

About one fifth of the world's Muslims live in the Middle East, but every country has Muslims living in it. Bangladesh, India, Indonesia, and Pakistan have the largest populations of Muslims but countries in the Middle East and northern Africa have the highest percentage of Muslims.

Muslims fall into three main groups: Sunni, Shi'ah, and Kharijites. The Sunni, to which the vast majority of Muslims belong, follow a strict interpretation of Islamic law. They favor traditional interpretations of the law rather than more permissive modern interpretations. The next largest group of Muslims, the Shi'ah, call themselves Shi'ites. The Shi'ites split from the Sunni just after the death of Muhammad, due to a disagreement over who was his rightful successor. The Sunnis believe Abu Bakr, one of Muhammad's earliest converts, and his faithful aide and companion, should lead the Muslim community. The Shi'ites believe that Ali ibn Abi Talib, Muhammad's cousin and son-in-law, should lead the Muslim community. In 657, a group of Shi'ites broke away and formed the smallest division of Islam, the Kharijites. They had been followers of Ali who began following a slightly different interpretation of Islamic law.

Health Care

Although Saudi Arabia's health care spending is among the lowest in the world, the nation has a very low death rate. It also has a low rate of obesity among adults.

SAUDI ARABIA'S GOVERNMENT

Separate territories united in 1932 to become the Kingdom of Saudi Arabia. It is a monarchy, or kingdom, ruled by the Al Saud family. The king, who is also prime minister, serves as both chief of state and head of the government. He also leads the nation in spiritual matters. The king is followed by the Heir Apparent Crown Prince, who is usually his oldest son. A Council of Ministers, appointed by the king, serves as a cabinet and usually includes many royal family members. In 2006 the king established a committee of Saudi princes to help select future kings.

The nation has a Basic Law of Government, a type of constitution, issued by royal decree in 1992. It provides a framework for the government based on the Qur'an and the teachings of the Prophet Muhammad. Only males are granted suffrage, or rights of citizenship, once they reach the age of 21. The king appoints members to a 150-seat legislative council. In 2013, this Consultative Council included 30 women. The Council advises the king and proposes new laws, but the king has the final say in all matters. He can overrule the Council and dismiss members at will.

The legal system, called Shari'ah law, is based on Islamic principles. Many laws remain unwritten and depend on the way a judge interprets Shari'ah. Other codes exist for areas such as traffic and trade that are not covered by Shari'ah law. Saudi Arabia has no political parties. The main influences on government, besides the royal family, are gas companies and religious groups.

The nation consists of 13 provinces. Each has a governor and a council of government officials, all appointed by the king. Military service is voluntary, but prohibited for women. Saudi Arabia has an army, navy, air force, and air defense forces.

THE ECONOMY OF SAUDI ARABIA

Saudi Arabia's economy is dominated by oil. It is the world's largest producer and exporter of petroleum, and possesses about 16% of the world's petroleum reserves. This has made Saudi Arabia the 15th richest country in the world based on Gross Domestic Product (GDP), a measurement of all goods and products produced in a year. Oil prices spiked in the 1970's, contributing to the nation's wealth, but Saudis realize that prices fluctuate and oil reserves won't last forever. Therefore, they have been working to develop other industries.

Saudi Arabia imports machinery, food products, chemicals, motor vehicles, and textiles, mostly from China, the United States, and India. A huge portion of the Saudi labor force consists of expatriates.

Agriculture

Because Saudi Arabia is mostly dry desert, only 1% of the land is used for agriculture, accounting for only 2% of the nation's GDP. Farmers produce wheat, barley, tomatoes, melons, dates, and citrus. They raise cattle, goats, and sheep for meat and dairy, and raise chickens

The sands of Rub al Khali

for meat and eggs. Modern technology has helped improve agriculture, but Saudi Arabia must still import much of its food needs.

Forestry and Fishing

Less than 1% of Saudi Arabia's land consists of forest. The fishing industry is small, focusing mainly on shrimp in the Persian Gulf.

Natural Resources

Saudi Arabia has abundant stores of petroleum and natural gas. It also has deposits of iron ore, gold, lead, silver, zinc, and copper. The petroleum industry accounts for almost half of the nation's entire GDP, and 90% of its exports. It exports petroleum products mainly to China, Japan, the United States, South Korea, and India. The state owns the oil industry and other major industries. It has an influential role in OPEC, the Organization of Petroleum Exporting Countries.

The nation lacks adequate freshwater resources. Most of the water used for irrigation comes from a huge underground reservoir that originates in

Turkey. Drinking water in cities and towns comes from saltwater that has been treated in plants—a process called desalination.

Services

Almost 80% of the Saudi labor force work in service industries. Tourism accounts for a large part of this sector, with many religious pilgrims visiting Mecca each year.

Transportation

Saudi Arabia's transportation networks are well developed. Paved roads cover most areas, and railways connect major cities. Saudi Arabian Airlines, owned and operated by the government, has several national and international airports. Major ports, which deal mainly with oil, include Ras Tanura and Ad Dammam on the Persian Gulf and Jiddah and Yanbu on the Red Sea.

Communication

The Saudi government owns and operates all local radio and television stations, but many households enjoy foreign TV stations via satellite. The newspapers, published mainly in Arabic with some in English, are privately owned. Saudis have widespread access to telephones, cellular phone networks, and the Internet.

SAUDI ARABIA'S HISTORY

The land that is now Saudi Arabia has a long history of division among different dominant people groups. About a century ago, the Ottoman Empire loosely controlled the eastern and western regions, while various local families ruled the central region. Abd al-Aziz ibn Saud unified the separate regions and established the Kingdom of Saudi Arabia in 1932. Shortly thereafter, this once-poor nation developed its oil industry and quickly modernized. It is still ruled by the Al Saud family and has grown to become quite wealthy.

Ancient History

Long ago, people living in the area that is now Saudi Arabia learned to live in the harsh, dry climate. They settled in oases where water allowed for some farming, or they followed their herds from place to place to find water and pasture. Domestication of the camel allowed people to travel further across the desert and transport goods.

At the convergence of Europe, Africa, and Asia, Saudi Arabia's location gave rise to centers of trade. Early kingdoms that arose around these trade centers include the kingdom of Saba (or Sheba) around 700 BCE and the Nabatean kingdom around 400 BCE.

The Birth of Islam

Around 570 CE, the people of the Arabian Peninsula followed religions that recognized many gods. In the northwest, Christians and Jews worshiped one God. The Prophet Muhammad was born in Mecca at this time. He believed he received revelation from Allah and began teaching belief in one God who would some day judge the world. In 622, wealthy leaders in Mecca drove Muhammad and his followers out of the city. They made a journey, called the Hijrah, to Medina where they began a Muslim community. Once the community grew large enough, Muhammad led them back to Mecca, where they captured the city in 630. Muslim armies spread Islam to almost the whole Arabian Peninsula by the time of Muhammad's death in 632.

The *caliphs*, or Muslim leaders, who then came to power spread the Muslim Empire even further, from Spain to India. A caliph in 661 established the capital in Damascus, Syria, but it was moved to Baghdad, Iraq in 762.

Desert camels

Despite these changes, Mecca and Medina remained important Muslim cities, as they are to this day.

By the 1500's, the Ottoman Empire gained control of eastern and western Saudi Arabia. The central portion, called Najd, was isolated by mountains and deserts. It remained independent and under the control of local nomadic tribes.

The Saud Dynasty

One of these tribes became the Saud dynasty and controlled an area near what is now Riyadh sometime around 1500. This family of rulers remained somewhat uninfluential until the mid-1700's. At that time, their leader Muhammad ibn Saud began to spread a stricter interpretation of Islamic law. Along with religious leader Muhammad ibn Abd al-Wahhab, he turned their city of Dariyah into a center of Islamic teaching. There, people learned to follow the Qur'an and the example of the Prophet Muhammad. Muhammad ibn Saud sent missionaries out to other parts of Najd to convert nomadic peoples and villagers.

By the early 1800's, Saudi influence and control had spread throughout the west coast of the peninsula, including the cities of Mecca and Medina. The army of the Saudi rulers moved into Iraq and Syria. Their progression was slowed somewhat when Egyptian forces captured and destroyed Dariyah in 1818 and had the Saudi ruler executed. Within a few years, the Saud family regained control and moved the capital to nearby Riyadh. The Saud family leaders briefly had to flee to Kuwait in 1891 when the Al Rashid family captured Riyadh.

Founding Saudi Arabia

The Saud family recaptured Riyadh in 1902 under the military leadership of Abd al-Aziz ibn Saud, who had fled to Kuwait earlier. Over the next 25 years, this leader, who became known as Ibn Saud, helped his family regain control of their ancestral lands. His forces consisted of former Bedouins, or nomads, who had converted to conservative Wahhabi beliefs about Islam. Their success coincided with a revival of Wahhabi influence.

In 1921, they defeated the Al Rashid family. In 1932, Ibn Saud named the lands under his control the Kingdom of Saudi Arabia.

Ibn Saud's new kingdom consisted mainly of poor farmers and nomads who lived simple, traditional lifestyles. This all began to change in 1933, when the new government allowed an American oil company to look for petroleum in Saudi Arabia. Within years, several oil companies discovered major petroleum deposits under the desert sands and waters of the Persian Gulf.

After World War II ended in 1945, oil production began in earnest. The Arabian American Oil Company (Aramco) formed as an alliance of various American oil companies working in cooperation with the Saudi government. Aramco extracted and processed the petroleum, paying the government a portion of the profits.

With this newfound wealth, Ibn Saud's government began building roads, schools, and hospitals. Life in Saudi Arabia improved as the government invested in social and economic programs. In 1953, Ibn Saud died. His sons Saud and Faisal attempted to continue their father's modernization of the country, but they spent money unwisely and disagreed with one

Ruins of Al-'Ula

another. At first, the elder brother, Saud, became king, and Faisal became prime minister. However, they exchanged power over the years as Saud turned over control, then Faisal resigned, then a council of royal family members and religious leaders convinced the ailing Saud to give up the throne to Faisal.

By the late 1950's, Saudi Arabia faced serious economic problems. Added to this problem was the threat of war with Egypt. In 1962, military leaders in what is now Yemen overthrew their royal government. Egypt supported the rebels and moved its forces into Yemen. Saudi Arabia, however, supported the royal government. The tensions came to an end in 1967, when Egypt withdrew from Yemen.

International Conflicts

In the late 1960's, oil profits allowed the Saudi government to continue developing the nation's infrastructure. The nation also became more involved in world affairs. King Faisal sent troops to Jordan and Syria during their Six-Day War with Israel in 1967. Muslims opposed the Jewish occupation of portions of Israel called Palestine, which included the holy city of Jerusalem. The Saudi troops never actually participated in combat, though, and Israel took control of much new territory.

Just a few years later, Saudi Arabia again became involved in war with Israel. When the Yom Kippur War broke out in 1973, the Saudi government placed an embargo, or restriction, on oil exports. They refused to export oil to countries supporting Israel, which included the United States, and reduced the amount of oil they sold to neutral countries. That year, the Saudi government also began taking control of its oil industry from Aramco. By 1988, this transition was complete, with the formation of the Saudi Arabian Oil Company (Saudi Aramco).

The sharp rise in oil prices in the mid-1970's brought great wealth to Saudi Arabia. The government invested in new projects and repaired relationships with the United States. During this period of wealth and progress, King Faisal was assassinated by one of his nephews. In 1975, Faisal's half-brother Khalid became king and prime minister of Saudi Arabia. He was succeeded by his half-brother Fahd in 1982. Together, Khalid and Fahd continued Faisal's political and economic policies. However, declining oil prices cut into the nation's income and forced them to invest in developing other industries.

Conflict came to Saudi Arabia once again in 1990, when Iraqi forces invaded nearby Kuwait. The Saudi government feared Iraq would next invade the Saudi oil fields. Many nations opposed Iraq's occupation of Kuwait. In 1991, the allied forces of Saudi Arabia, Egypt, Syria, the United States, and other countries entered the Persian Gulf War, in an effort to drive Iraq out of Kuwait. Saudi Arabia served as a staging ground for the international forces, largely consisting of U.S. troops and equipment. Although the allies were successful in overcoming Iraq, the war had a negative impact on Saudi Arabia. Saudis had borne almost the entire cost of the war, forcing the nation to cut back on spending in other areas. It also led to anti-American sentiment across the nation.

As U.S. troops continued to remain in Saudi Arabia after the war, resentment among Saudis increased. Millionaire Saudi Osama bin Laden led a terrorist organization called al-Qaeda that launched the 2001 attacks against the United States in New York City and near Washington, D.C. After overthrowing the Iraqi government in 2003, U.S. troops withdrew from Saudi Arabia. In 2011, they killed bin Laden who had been in hiding in Pakistan.

Saudi Arabia Today

In 2005, King Fahd died after years of declining health. His half-brother Abdullah took the throne. That year the government allowed Saudi men to vote in the country's first municipal elections. Women voted in the 2015 elections.

Flag of Saudi Arabia

AFRICA

AFRICA: THE BIG PICTURE

Africa is not a country or a single region but an entire continent, the world's second largest continent at approximately 18.9 million square miles (48.7 million square km). Africa borders the Atlantic Ocean to the west, the Mediterranean Sea to the north, and the Red Sea and Indian Ocean to the east. At its southern tip, the Cape of Good Hope or Cape Agulhas, the Atlantic and Indian Oceans meet. Africa was once joined to Asia by the Sinai Peninsula, but the construction of the Suez Canal cut through that land bridge.

Africa's northernmost country is Tunisia and the furthest south is South Africa. Somalia reaches the furthest east and Senegal is the furthest west. The largest country in Africa is Algeria and the smallest is Seychelles, an island nation. The largest of Africa's island nations is Madagascar, off the east coast. Nigeria is the continent's most heavily populated country. Africa has 54 countries in all, including Egypt, Libya, Sudan, Kenya, Angola, Ghana, and Zimbabwe.

Africa's largest country, Algeria

Africa lies across both the Equator and the prime meridian, which places it in all four hemispheres. Because most of the land falls between the Tropic of Cancer and the Tropic of Capricorn, it has a tropical climate. One of Africa's most distinct features, the Sahara, stretches across almost all of northern Africa, creating the world's largest desert. Africa is also home to a wide range of tropical rain forests, widespread plateaus, grasslands, mountains, and coastal plains, as well as the world's longest river—the Nile.

A satellite photo shows the extent of the western Sahara

MEET THE PEOPLE OF AFRICA

Although Africa is the world's second-largest continent, it is home to only about 14% of the people in the world, making it underpopulated for its size. Most of Africa's population (85%) live south of the Sahara in a region called sub-Saharan

Fast Facts

Largest country:
Algeria (1,479,946 sq miles) (3,833,042 million sq km)

Smallest country:
Seychelles (283 sq miles) (733 sq km)

Largest city:
Lagos, Nigeria (population 11,400,000)

Population:
1.1 billion

Highest Point:
Mount Kilimanjaro 19,340 feet (5,895 m)

Lowest Point:
Lake Assal -508 feet (-155 m)

Highest Recorded Temperature:
131 °F (Kebili, Tunisia)

Lowest Recorded Temperature:
-11 °F (Ifrane, Morocco)

Primary language:
Arabic

Africa. Africa is also home to a diverse animal population. Large mammals such as elephants, giraffes, lions, zebras, and many others live in Africa. A variety of wildlife live throughout the continent's different climate and vegetation zones.

Across the continent, Africans represent hundreds of different ethnic groups, each with their own language, customs, and way of life. This diversity has made it difficult for some African nations to become unified. Historic national boundaries drawn up by Europeans often do not reflect the settlement patterns of ethnic groups. Adding to Africa's problems is the fact that it has the least developed economy of any continent (except Antarctica), despite having a great wealth of natural resources.

For thousands of years, Africans worked and lived in poor agricultural societies, as many continue to do today. However, the continent also gave rise to great civilizations, such as ancient Egypt and the Aksum Empire. In the 7th century, the Muslim Empire spread throughout northern Africa, bringing Arabic language and culture. Beginning in the late 1400's, European traders began exporting gold, ivory, and slaves from Africa. In a rush to exploit the continent's resources, Africa was carved up among colonial powers of Europe. This colonization had long-lasting impacts on the people, their cultures,

Lions on a reserve in Zimbabwe

and the development of nations in Africa. Not until the mid-1900's did most nations gain independence. Since then, many countries have struggled to develop stable governments and strong economies. The continent also faces problems of poverty, famine, disease, and violence.

Population

Because of Africa's vast deserts, thick rainforests, and barren grass-lands, its 1.1 billion people mainly crowd into a few areas, while other areas remain almost completely unpopulated. Highly populated areas include the Nile River Valley, one of the Earth's most heavily populated regions, as well as the Mediterranean coast, the west coast of Nigeria, Africa's southern coast, and the African Great Lakes region of eastern Africa. Rwanda and Burundi have the highest population densities among African countries. About one-third of African countries have fewer than 5 million people.

Despite having plenty of land, Africa faces overpopulation as its population grows more rapidly than any other region in the world. Its birth rate and death rate are both very high, and improved health care has led to a young, growing population. Some estimates predict that Africa's population will reach 2.3 billion by 2050. Life expectancy in Africa is low overall (about 58 years compared with 79 years for Americans); however, this number varies greatly by country. People in Nigeria and Mozambique have very low life expectancies, at around 52 years, while those in Libya and Tunisia enjoy life expectancies of about 75 years.

Many factors contribute to the high death rate and low life expectancy in Africa. Areas around the Sahara regularly experience famine, malnutrition, and starvation. Many countries depend on aid from other nations to feed their population. Warfare has caused millions of deaths and has interrupted health care and foreign aid in many countries. Disease is also a widespread problem in Africa, especially the HIV/AIDS virus and malaria.

Nighttime lights show the dense population of the Nile River Valley

African Peoples

Africa has a long history of various people groups, representing

283

different ethnicities, races, and cultures. People today sometimes refer to the descendants of Africa's original inhabitants as *black* or *black African,* but those terms are very inadequate. People whose ancestors come from west and sub-Saharan Africa are ethnically very diverse. They generally prefer to be called by their national identity, such as Ethiopian, or their ethnicity, such as Maasai. In the north, most Africans are Arabs.

Patterns of African physical and cultural diversity have become complicated due to migration, intermarriage, and colonization. Ethnic groups identify themselves according to common history, culture, language, religion, and way of life. Even within each group, one may find a variety of customs and spoken dialects.

Today, Africa's largest ethnic groups include central Africa's Igbo and Yoruba, eastern Africa's Kikuyu, and southern Africa's Zulu. Many Pygmy groups inhabit the forests of the Congo River Basin in central Africa. They have traditionally lived as hunters and gatherers who traded with nearby agricultural communities. Because the term Pygmy comes from a Greek word meaning "short," many people consider it an insult. They prefer using names of individual ethnic groups, such as Aka, Mbuti, Efe, and Twa.

Some of the world's most ancient cultures remain in small numbers in Namibia, Botswana, and South Africa. These include the Nama people, descendants of the Khoikhoi, and also the San. Their similar languages include unique clicking sounds.

Arabs came to Africa in the early 600's CE as part of the Muslim Empire. They settled mainly in Egypt, Sudan, and along the Mediterranean coast, but their influence has since spread throughout northern Africa. Also inhabiting northern Africa, though much longer than the Arabs, are the Berbers. They speak Tamazight and the name Berber comes from the Greek language meaning *non-Greek speaker.* Today, these people often prefer the term Amazigh by which to identify themselves.

Colonialism in the 1600's brought waves of European peoples to Africa, mainly British, Dutch, and French, who settled along the Mediterranean coast and in South Africa. Although Asian populations began migrating to Madagascar 2,000 years ago, they came in greater numbers during the 1800's. Many came from India and settled in southern and eastern Africa.

Language

Scholars have determined that Africans speak over 1,500 distinct languages, though their knowledge of this area remains incomplete. Adding to the difficulty is the fact that many languages have no *indigenous*, or *native*, forms of writing, but are only oral. About a quarter of the world's languages are spoken only in Africa. The most widespread African languages are Arabic, Swahili, and Hausa. African languages fall into four broad families: Niger-Congo, Nilo-Saharan, Afro-Asiatic, and Khoisan.

The Niger-Congo family of languages is the most widespread. It includes nine major branches that are spoken through most of central and southern Africa, one of which is Swahili. The Nilo-Saharan family of languages includes widely scattered, and inadequately researched, languages. The Afro-Asiatic languages blend influences from Arabic, Egyptian, Berber, and other languages. People living throughout northern and eastern Africa speak a variety of Afro-Asiatic languages. The Khoisan family of languages, which includes clicking sounds, is limited to aboriginal peoples of southern Africa and two small ethnic groups in Tanzania. It is completely unrelated to other African languages. In some parts of Madagascar, Africans speak another family of languages called Austronesian.

European colonialism brought additional language influences to Africa. Some nations today have adopted European languages as their official language. For example, English is the official language of Ghana, Zimbabwe, and Nigeria. French is the official language of the Republic of the Congo, Senegal, and Niger. And Portuguese is the official language of Angola. Having an official language, however, does not mean that everyone in the country uses, or even understands, it. English and French have become more widespread through formal education and business. In southern Africa, many people speak Afrikaans, a blend of Dutch and other languages.

Religion

Africa has many followers of the world's most popular religions—Christianity and Islam. In general, northern Africans tend to be Muslim, where Islam is often the state religion, and those in the south tend to be Christian. However, hundreds of other religions exist among the various ethnic groups, especially those in sub-Saharan Africa. These various religions are animist and include an awareness of spirits, often present in natural objects, as well as witch doctors and other spiritual leaders. They explain creation of the world and the people group's origin, as well as concepts of life and death, right and wrong, and reasons for suffering. Often, these principles are related through myths, legends, folktales, and riddles. Some religions are more complex than others, but most include some rituals, rites, or ceremonies, such as the recognition of passing from childhood to adulthood.

ANIMISM

Animism originated among tribal peoples thousands of years ago, and is generally defined as spirit worship. Animism promotes the belief that spiritual beings take interest in humans and act to help or harm them—most often to harm them. Hence, people seek to offer sacrifices (often at great cost) to appease these spirits so they will not harm them. Animists often live in great fear of the spirit's powers.

Some tribes with more developed beliefs around animism have spiritual leaders called *shamans*, who communicate with the spirits and act as go-betweens through rituals. In many people groups, ordinary people perform rituals in an effort to influence spirits. They might seek a good harvest or a successful hunt. If they experience unexplained hardships, they might consult a shaman.

Across cultures, the spirits of animism take different forms. Often, people believe spirits can inhabit rivers, rocks, the sun, and other objects. Spirits can be eternal, such as angels, or mortal, such as witches. Some spirits are kind and helpful, but others take the form of evil ghosts, monsters, or demons. Spirits do not work together, and none have complete control of events, so they are not gods.

CHRISTIANITY

Christianity, the world's most popular religion, is based on the life and teachings of Jesus Christ. In fact, the word *Christian* means *follower of Christ*. Christians believe that Jesus of Nazareth, who lived 2,000 years ago, was the Son of God. They believe that he was fully human yet fully God, and that he rose from the dead after being *crucified*, or nailed to a cross.

Christianity shares common roots with Judaism. Christians believe in the Old Testament of the Bible, which tells of God's creation of the universe, man's sin, the growth of the nation of Israel, and God's prophets.

The New Testament of the Bible, which Christians also believe, tells of the life and death of Jesus as well as the spread of the early Christian church. According to Scripture, Jesus was a Jew who lived in Israel. At about the age of 30, he began a ministry that included many miracles. As his following grew, so did opposition. After three years of ministry, the Roman government crucified Jesus. Christians believe he rose from the dead three days later, interacted with believers and witnesses, and then ascended to heaven. They believe that Jesus' sacrifice allows all believers to receive forgiveness for sins and enjoy an eternal home in heaven.

A famous sculpture of Jesus and his mother, Mary, after his crucifixion

After Jesus' death and resurrection, his followers spread Christianity throughout the eastern Mediterranean and beyond. It became strongest among Europeans and subsequently Americans and Australians. Today, Christianity has spread to almost every nation on Earth. Some nations, like Vatican City, Romania, and Papua New Guinea, have almost 100% Christian populations. In some nations, branches of Christianity have become the state religion. It is growing most rapidly in Africa and Asia. Today, over 2 billion people around the world are Christians.

History of the Church

For hundreds of years, the Jewish people awaited the Messiah, God's anointed one. Christians believe that this Messiah came as a baby born in Bethlehem around the year 4 BCE. There, Jesus was born to parents Mary and Joseph, Jews from Nazareth. According to the Bible, his virgin birth fulfilled a prophecy.

As an adult, Jesus preached and performed miracles throughout Galilee, north of Judea. He often criticized the Jewish authorities of the time and many dismissed him as a *heretic*, or one who speaks against the established religion. Among his followers, Jesus became known as the *Christ*, the Greek word for Messiah. Jesus was eventually arrested and killed, but his followers believe he rose from the dead. They spread the message of salvation through belief in Jesus and established churches throughout the Roman Empire.

Although Christianity spread quickly, the Roman government often opposed it. Some emperors had Christians arrested or killed. The Roman Colosseum may have been used as a site where Christians were murdered for sport. It became an honor for Christians to become *martyrs*, or those who suffered or died for their faith.

In the early 300's, Roman Emperor Constantine legalized the practice of Christianity. He converted to Christianity himself. In an effort to unify Chris-

Ruins of the ancient Colosseum
in Rome, Italy

tian beliefs, Constantine called together church leaders, called bishops, at the Council of Nicaea. Together, they established foundational beliefs of Christianity, such as the *divinity* of Jesus, or the state of being God. From that point on, the bishop of Constantinople (now Istanbul, Turkey) became head of the Greek-speaking Christians in the eastern Roman Empire while the bishop of Rome, called the pope, led the Latin-speaking Christians in the western Roman Empire.

After the fall of the Roman Empire, the Eastern Orthodox Church, which grew out of Constantinople, continued to spread through eastern Europe and Russia. The Western Church built grand cathedrals throughout western Europe. The Western Church, under the authority of the pope, became the Roman Catholic Church in about 1054.

Salisbury Cathedral in England
was completed in 1258 CE

By the early 1500's, the Christian church in Europe had become very wealthy, powerful, and corrupt. During a time called the Reformation, Europeans protested against the current state of the church and called for changes. They wanted Christianity to follow the Bible more closely, rather than following influential church leaders. The branches of the Christian church that arose during this time became known as Protestant Churches, because they protested against Catholic doctrine and practices. They include Lutheranism, the Reformed tradition, the Radical Reformation, and the Church of England.

Lutheranism arose based on the teachings of German theologian Martin Luther. In 1517, he exposed corruption in the Catholic Church and turned people back to a belief in salvation only through God's grace. The Reformed tradition began in Switzerland under the leadership of John Calvin, who expanded on Luther's ideas. The Church of England was established in the 1530's by King Henry VIII of England for reasons more personal than theological. King Henry wanted to *annul*, or cancel, his marriage to Catherine of Aragon, but the pope refused. An angry King Henry then stripped the pope of authority in England, and made himself head of a new church.

The Modern Christian Church

Today, almost all Christians associate themselves with one of four main groups: Roman Catholics, Eastern Orthodox, Anglicans, or Protestants. Each group includes several subgroups called *denominations*. Other Christians, who do not fall into these four main groups, number about 300 million.

The Roman Catholic Church, which underwent large-scale changes after the Protestant Reformation in the 1500's, now makes up the world's largest Christian church with over 1 billion members. It is headed by the pope, who leads from Vatican City in Italy. Roman Catholics believe that the pope is *infallible*, meaning he cannot make any mistake when speaking about Christian beliefs. The Catholic hierarchy of pope, cardinals, archbishops, bishops, priests, and laypeople has resulted in one of the most unified groups of Christians.

The Eastern Orthodox Church has continued under the leadership of the Patriarch of Constantinople, an honored bishop, and resembles the Catholic Church in many ways. It has about 275 million members, mainly throughout eastern Europe, Greece, the Middle East, and Russia.

Anglican Churches arose out of the Church of England and are sometimes grouped with Protestant churches. They consider England's Archbishop of Canterbury their spiritual leader, but each church is governed by its own bishop. Worldwide, the Anglican Churches have about 85 million members.

Protestant Churches differ most from the other three main groups. They do not follow the leadership of a pope or bishop and they hold different beliefs about authority, doctrine, and worship. They base their beliefs strictly on the Bible and the teachings of some reformers such as Martin Luther. The Protestant Church includes Lutherans, Baptists, Presbyterians, Pentecostals, Methodists, Amish, Mennonites, and many other groups.

Regardless of the group, all Christians stand firm on the belief that salvation comes through Jesus. They differ on the interpretations of less significant doctrines.

Christian Beliefs

In addition to beliefs about Jesus, Christians have other generally-accepted doctrines of their faith. It is a monotheistic religion, meaning they believe in just one God. However, Christians believe in the *trinity*, or the three-fold nature of God. They believe God includes the Father, who created the universe, the Son, who came to Earth as Jesus, and the Holy Spirit, who remains active within believers.

Christians believe that all humans sin, or do wrong, by following their own evil desires rather than God's will. This creates separation between man and God. Therefore, God saved humanity from sin by sacrificing Jesus. Jesus' resurrection represents God's victory over sin and spiritual death. Christians believe that one day Jesus will return to judge the living and the dead.

The Bible contains the basis for Christian teaching and beliefs. The Old Testament tells the history of God's work on Earth before Jesus' birth. The New Testament tells of Jesus' birth and the events that followed. The Gospels (the books of Matthew, Mark, Luke, and John) tell of Jesus' birth, life, ministry, death, and resurrection. The book of Acts tells how Jesus' followers continued his work and grew the early Christian church. Several books called Epistles contain instructions in the form of letters. They were written by early Christian leaders. The final book, Revelation, prophecies the end of the world and the return of Jesus. Christians believe that all Scripture is "God-breathed," meaning it is the perfect word of God, recorded by man. Early in church history, Christians decided which writings would be accepted as canon, or Biblical truth, and which would not. The Catholic and Eastern Orthodox Churches accept as canon some Jewish writings called the Apocrypha, but other Christian churches do not.

Over the years, other writings have become important to Christians, though they are not considered Scripture inspired by God. The Apostles' Creed, dating back to the late 100's CE, and the Nicene Creed, written in 325, reaffirm basic Christian beliefs. Worshipers in many churches often recite these creeds during services. Some church services include catechisms, which are question-and-answer recitations that outline basic religious doctrines. In the 300's, Saint Augustine wrote about experiencing God's grace. In the 1200's, Saint Thomas Aquinas wrote to explain Christian doctrine. Both have become classic works among Christians.

Worship and Practices

Most Christians, no matter their denomination, observe certain sacraments, or sacred rituals, as part of their worship and expression of faith. Some believe they will receive salvation through the sacraments, while others regard them as reminders of the salvation that only comes through faith in Jesus. Christian churches vary in the number and nature of sacraments they observe, but all include the sacraments of baptism and Communion.

Before Jesus began his ministry on Earth, his cousin John prepared people by *baptizing* them, or dunking them in water. This symbolized their repentance from sin and profession of faith in God. Jesus himself was baptized. Today, some churches baptize people by sprinkling or pouring water over their head. Others, like the Baptists, immerse a person completely in water. Christians disagree about whether a person should be baptized as an infant or wait until they make the decision as an adult.

Christians also observe the sacrament of Communion. In different churches, this may be called Holy Communion, the Lord's Supper, or the Eucharist. It involves eating bread (or a cracker) and drinking wine (or grape juice). This solemn practice reminds Christians of Jesus' body and blood, which he sacrificed for their sins. During Jesus' final meal with his apostles, he shared bread and wine, calling them his body and his blood, and instructed the apostles to continue doing this in remembrance of him.

In the Catholic and Eastern Orthodox Churches, believers follow five additional sacraments. *Penance* (or confession) involves confessing one's sins to a priest to receive forgiveness. *Confirmation* (or mysteries of chrismation) involves membership in the church or commitment to a Christian life. Individuals generally choose either *ordination* (becoming a member of the clergy) or *marriage* as their role in life. Finally, *anointing of the sick* (or holy unction) involves praying for an ill or dying person and pouring holy oil on them.

Most Christians gather for church services on Sundays. The service usually includes singing, prayer, reading from the Bible, and a sermon that includes teaching about Christian belief or everyday life. In *liturgical* churches, the worship service follows an elaborate set form, called the *liturgy*. Christians also celebrate Christmas, the observation of Jesus' birth, on December 25th, and Easter, the celebration of his resurrection, in March or April.

LAND, WATER, AND CLIMATE IN AFRICA

Covering about one-fifth of the Earth's land surface, Africa stretches 5,000 miles (8,000 km) from north to south and 4,600 miles (7,400 km) from east to west. Most of the land is relatively flat, with a low plateau covering most of northern, western, and central Africa (called Low Africa) and a higher flat region across most of eastern and southern Africa (called High Africa). Africa's highest peak, Mount Kilimanjaro, rises 19,308 feet (5885 meters) in Tanzania.

Low Africa

Low Africa ranges from about .1 to .4 miles (150 to 610 meters) above sea level. It includes coastal plains, the Sahara Desert, and the river basins of the Nile and Congo Rivers. Parts of Algeria, Morocco, and Tunisia rise toward mountains, such as the Atlas Mountains along the Mediterranean coast. A narrow strip of coastal lowland follows much of the coastline and can consist of farmland, forest, desert, or swampland. Moving inland, the Sahara Desert dominates most of northern Africa.

The river systems of low Africa create their own land regions. The Niger and other rivers flow through forests and grasslands south of the Sahara. The Nile River creates a strip of very fertile farmland throughout its flat basin, but also a huge southern swamp called the Sudd. The Congo Basin, surrounding the Congo River and its tributaries, is covered mainly in tropical rain forest.

High Africa

While still relatively flat, High Africa rises about .6 miles (910 meters) above sea level. The Great Rift Valley stretches from Eritrea to Mozambique. This formation consists of long, steep-sided valleys running parallel to one another. The region contains rich volcanic soil, good for farming, and three main lakes. To the east lie grassy plains where wild animals roam and herders graze their livestock. The rolling grassland of the south is used for farming or pasture. It also holds stores of gold and diamonds. The coasts of the south and east consist of sandy beaches, farmland, and swamps. About 240 miles (386 km) east of the African mainland lies the island nation of Madagascar. Its central peaks rise to over 1.7 miles (2,700 meters) above sea level.

Vegetation Zones

About 40% of Africa is covered in desert, including the world's largest desert, the Sahara. This region of sand, gravel, rocks, and boulders covers about 6 million square miles (15.5 million square km). It contains just a few scattered oases and the fertile Nile Valley. Other important African deserts are the Namib in the southwest and the Kalahari in the south central region.

Another 40% of Africa's land is covered in grasslands called *savannas*. These consist of tall grasses, thorny bushes, and few trees.

Less than one-fifth of Africa contains forests, most of which are tropical rain forests. They grow in the Congo Basin, parts of western Africa, and Madagascar.

Water

Africa is home to the world's longest river, the Nile, which flows 4,160 miles (6,695 km) from east-central Africa to the Mediterranean Sea. Two other major rivers, the Congo and Niger, empty into the Atlantic Ocean. In eastern Africa, the Limpopo and Zambezi Rivers flow to the Indian Ocean. Many tourists visit the famous Victoria Falls on the Zambezi River between Zambia and Zimbabwe.

The rapids and waterfalls in many of Africa's rivers make them difficult to navigate by boat, but provide a great source of hydroelectric power. The river deltas provide rich soil for farming and great sites for fishing.

Most of Africa's lakes lie in the long, deep valleys of the east. One of these, Lake Tanganyika, is more than 4,700 feet (1,432 meters) deep. Lake Victoria, in Tanzania and Uganda, is the world's second-largest freshwater lake.

Climate

The vast size of the African continent makes for a variety of climate zones. However, most of Africa is quite warm or hot and only the humidity and precipitation vary from one region to another. About 90% of Africa lies within the tropical zone between the Tropic of Cancer and the Tropic of Capricorn. Temperatures do not vary greatly from one season to another, but do tend to vary greatly from day to night.

The Sahara has the highest temperatures, as well as the greatest range of temperatures. Summer days usually reach 115 °F while winter nights can drop to around 50 °F. Somalia is also one of the hottest parts of Africa, while South Africa and parts of the northwest are the coolest. Mountain regions often see frost and snow.

Africa generally receives too much or too little rainfall. Too much rainfall can wash away crops and soil. It also creates wet, humid conditions that breed dangerous insects. Too little rainfall can lead to crop failure and famine. Many African farmers, unsure of how much rain to expect, plant a variety of crops and hope that at least some will thrive.

One or two rainy seasons per year can bring anywhere from more than 100 inches (254 cm) per year on the west coast to less than 10 inches (25.4 cm) per year in the deserts. Prolonged periods of drought have caused widespread famine and starvation, especially in Ethiopia and parts of southern Africa. The forests of the Congo Basin, in contrast, receive rainfall all year.

EVERYDAY LIFE
IN NORTHERN AFRICA

Africa's northernmost countries, Mauritania, Morocco, Algeria, Tunisia, Libya, and Egypt, share a common way of life. Their history involves Arabs from the Muslim Empire moving into northern Africa in the 600's. As a result, these nations are Islamic and the people speak Arabic. Nearby nations of Europe and the Middle East strongly influence life in northern Africa. Some minorities in this region include the Arabic-speaking Christians of Egypt, called Copts, as well as Muslim ethnic minorities like the Amazigh.

Family Life

Islamic traditions and beliefs dominate home life in northern Africa. Men are allowed to have more than one wife, a practice called *polygyny*, in all countries except Tunisia. Arranged marriages, in which parents choose their child's spouse, have decreased in recent years, but still occur frequently. The family of the bride traditionally gives the family of the groom a *dowry*, or payment, though this is also becoming less common.

Extended families, including grandparents, aunts, uncles, and cousins, often live together in one home. In urban areas, small apartments may only have room for parents, children, and grandparents. Living together with extended family gives North Africans security, financial help, and social interaction. The role of women in the family has traditionally been to stay home and care for the family. This is often true of older women and those in rural areas, but today more and more urban women are leaving the home for education and to work.

City Life

Overall, Africa is the least urbanized continent in the world. However, in northern Africa about half of the population live in urban areas. The largest include Cairo, Egypt; Tripoli, Libya; Algiers, Algeria; and Casablanca, Morocco. Cities contain large *mosques* (Muslim temples) and *suqs* (outdoor markets). Buildings combine European and Islamic architectural styles and cities often blend ancient and modern structures. Older sections of cities have winding, narrow roads and small, crowded buildings, while newer sections have multi-lane boulevards and tall, modern buildings.

City workers often hold professional office jobs, such as those in banking or government. They earn more money than rural people and enjoy a higher standard of living. Health care, education, and other services are better in the city than in the country. Most cities also have slum areas, with substandard housing, inadequate sanitation, and limited public services.

Country Life

The farmers of northern Africa often tend small plots of land using traditional tools and practices. Often, the land does not produce enough to support a family, and they must seek work elsewhere to survive. In some areas, the government or wealthy landowners run larger farms that use modern machinery. A small percentage of rural North Africans live a nomadic lifestyle in which they move from place to place following their herds of camels, goats, or sheep. These nomads are called Bedouins.

Rural Africans often construct homes out of thick adobe, or mud brick, with flat roofs. The homes have only simple furnishings and few modern conveniences. Electrical power often comes from a generator.

Food and Drink

North African cuisine centers on grains such as flat breads and *couscous*, a labor-intensive preparation of wheat berries and flour. Fruits and vegetables also make up a large part of many meals. North Africans tend to enjoy meat, which is very expensive, only on special occasions. Muslims do not eat pork, but do eat chicken, goat, and lamb. Fish is also popular, especially now that refrigerated trucks can deliver seafood from the coast areas to the interior. Islam also prohibits alcohol, but North Africans drink plenty of coffee, tea, soft drinks, and juice.

Clothing

Urban dwellers in North Africa look very similar to Europeans and North Americans in the way they dress. Often, the only difference is the head coverings worn by women to conform to Muslim laws. Sometimes they also cover their face with a veil. More and more, women and men in cities are beginning to wear traditional clothing, which has remained common in rural areas. This consists of long, loose robes for men, along with a turban or skullcap. Women wear long, simple dresses with a shawl and possibly baggy trousers. They also cover their head and sometimes their face.

Education

Education has traditionally been very limited in North Africa. Some people attend elementary school while only religious scholars continue their studies. European colonialism brought more formal schooling, but it was usually reserved for European children and the children of important African leaders. As a result, the literacy rate today is about 66%. More city dwellers than country dwellers, and more men than women, can read and write.

In modern times, the countries of North Africa have worked to improve education. They have built more schools, including some well-respected universities. However, the population is growing quickly, and towns cannot build schools fast enough to keep up. Also, education is becoming more and more expensive, and qualified teachers are in short supply. In rural areas, children have to travel long distances by foot to get to school. Often, they drop out of school to help their families or to work.

EVERYDAY LIFE IN SOUTHERN AFRICA

Life in sub-Saharan Africa, the nations south of the Sahara, is much more rural and traditional than life in North Africa. Families often work the land as farmers, and many face the challenges of famine, poverty, and disease. Africa's great mineral wealth is concentrated in this part of the continent, but it is largely controlled by the European minority.

Family Life

Loyalty and cooperation in African families spread from parents to children to extended family members. Relatives often live together in tight-knit communities, where they share chores, finances, and important decisions. Usually, families of both the bride and groom must consent before a marriage can occur. The groom's family provides valuable gifts, called *bridewealth*, to the family of the bride to show that they value her and her family. Most ethnic groups also allow men to have more than one wife, a practice called *polygyny*. A husband must provide a home, livestock, household goods, and equal attention to each of his wives.

Some ethnic groups organize extended families into *lineages* and larger *clans*. Each member of the clan is believed to have descended from a common ancestor. Therefore, they are often not permitted to intermarry. Clans provide families with a sense of identity, often represented by symbols called *totems*. They also provide security and support for all members.

City Life

Only about a third of sub-Saharan Africans live in cities, though the number varies depending on the country. Angola, Djibouti, Gabon, Liberia, the Republic of the Congo, and South Africa have larger urban populations than other sub-Saharan countries. As people move to urban areas in increasing numbers, many cities have grown to have populations of more than a million. The largest of these include Cape Town and Johannesburg, South Africa; Addis Ababa, Ethiopia; Dar es Salaam, Tanzania; Kinshasa, Democratic Republic of the Congo; Lagos, Nigeria; and Nairobi, Kenya.

The cities of sub-Saharan Africa offer modern buildings, well-paying jobs, and modern conveniences that are scarce in rural areas. Better schools and medical facilities also add to the higher standard of living. The cities often blend high-rise apartments and office buildings with the small, crowded homes, winding streets, and open air markets of older, unplanned neighborhoods.

Because of the rapid population growth and movement to urban areas, cities have had difficulty accommodating everyone. Many cities experience housing shortages and inadequate public services, such as water, sewage, electricity, and transportation. Many unemployed adults also live in the cities.

Country Life

In sub-Saharan Africa, about 65% of the population live in rural villages, much like their ancestors did. Large or small, the villages usually consist of a close-knit community of people from the same ethnic group

Cape Town, South Africa

who share the same language and customs. Many of the villagers are often related to one another by birth or marriage. A king, chief, or group of elders may provide guidance for the people of the village, but they hold little real political power.

Homes are simple structures clustered around a central square where villagers congregate. There they socialize and take part in ceremonies and celebrations. Larger villages may include a school, some shops, and a medical clinic. The type of homes in each village depends on the resources available and the tradition of the people. Many homes are made of mud brick walls with straw roofs. Wealthier residents might have homes with concrete walls and sheet-metal roofs. Muslims often build their homes around a private courtyard, where women can work without outsiders seeing them.

Many villages operate around an agricultural way of life that their ancestors have followed for hundreds of years. They raise crops and livestock, farming the land with traditional tools and methods. Because the soil is often very poor, an entire village may move every few years to more fertile lands. Once the soil has rested for several years, the farmers can move back and grow crops once again. Africa's growing population has made this practice, called *shifting cultivation*, more and more difficult. As a result, many farmers are forced to continue working land that has deteriorating soil. In some parts of South Africa, Kenya, and Zimbabwe, farmers use modern machinery and agricultural practices.

Sub-Saharan farmers grow a variety of crops based on their climate and needs. In grassland areas, they often grow peanuts, corn, millet, and sorghum. In wetter areas, they grow bananas, cassava, rice, and yams. In addition to these food crops that feed their families, farmers also grow *cash crops* to sell. They can grow and sell coffee, cacao, cotton, and other crops to pay for school fees, taxes, and medical care. They also buy consumer goods like kerosene, batteries, and canned foods. Almost all farmers also raise chickens, and some raise goats and sheep.

Both men and women work long hours on family farms. Women also spend much of their time gathering firewood, grinding grain, and obtaining water. Often, young girls walk long distances to collect clean water for their families, a daily practice that keeps them from attending school. Many organizations have worked to bring water pumps and wells to villages to help solve this problem and improve life for villagers.

Other than those living along the Nile River, farmers do not irrigate their crops. Instead, they depend on seasonal rains. This means the life of the entire village follows seasonal patterns of hard work and little food in the spring, and plentiful food and leisure time after the harvest.

When the long, hard days of planting, tending, and harvesting crops are over, villagers work together to build or repair homes or clear new land. They also socialize and share food. Community ceremonies are a time of coming together, enjoying entertainment, and marking important life events. Villagers gather in the central square to commemorate the first rain of the season, the harvest, births, marriages, deaths, and the passage from childhood to adulthood.

Upon reaching adulthood, many young men leave their village temporarily or permanently. They go off seeking education, or work as miners or laborers. Once they earn some money, they may return to their village to marry. While the young men are gone, women perform the heavy farm work.

Other communities follow a life of nomadic herding, following cattle from place to place, rather than agriculture. The Dinka, Fulani, Maasai, and Turkana peoples, along with others, follow a long tradition of herding cattle. They walk the same routes their ancestors did, as their sheep, goats, or camels graze. Livestock provide food and other resources as well as indicate a person's wealth and social status. Herders can trade live animals, meat, milk, or skins for grain and other resources. Usually, the men of the community tend the herds while the women perform household chores. Nomadic peoples might live in animal skin tents or, like the Maasai, build small homes out of brush, mud, and manure.

Food and Drink

Most sub-Saharan Africans in both cities and villages follow a diet that includes one large evening meal and only light snacks at other times. Meals are a social time, with people often sharing one large bowl of food.

They sit on the floor and scoop from the bowl with fingers or pieces of bread. Usually, men and boys eat separately from women and girls.

The most common foods are rice, cassava (a root vegetable), corn porridge, and yams. In warmer climates, plantains, a kind of banana, are eaten fried, boiled, baked, grilled, or dried and ground into flour. Families that raise livestock also enjoy milk, cheese, and a yogurt-like dairy product. Because meat and fish are expensive, they are reserved for special occasions. Many Africans enjoy beer made from honey or grain, as well as wine made from palm tree sap.

In some parts of sub-Saharan Africa, periods of drought lead to famine and death from starvation. Even when food is available, many Africans suffer malnutrition because of the lack of variety.

Clothing

Sub-Saharan African clothing tends to be simple, loose, and colorful. Men often wear a long robe or tunic with loose trousers. Sometimes they cover their head with a turban or cap. Herders might wear leather garments made from the skin of their cattle. Women wrap a long cloth into a dress. They might wear a scarf or turban on their head or, in the Muslim tradition, cover their face with a veil. In many ethnic groups, men and women wear lots of brightly-colored jewelry.

Education

Traditional education in sub-Saharan Africa involved parents teaching their children ways of life. Some older children took on the role of an apprentice to learn a trade like weaving, metalworking, woodcarving, or pottery making. When Muslims arrived from the Middle East, they established schools to teach Arabic and science. Later, Christian missionaries taught literacy skills to Africans.

By the 1900's, European colonial powers began establishing schools, so Africans could take on jobs with more responsibilities. Since then, African governments have taken over building schools and extending educational opportunities. Though the number of Africans attending school is greater than ever, a large number remain illiterate. The literacy rates range from 80% in Kenya, Namibia, South Africa, and Zimbabwe to less than 30% in Burkina Faso, Mali, and Niger. Many areas lack school buildings, resources, and qualified teachers. Children often attend school only seasonally, or drop out after just a few years, because their families need help on the farm, or need the additional money that working children can provide.

AFRICAN CULTURE

Art in Africa began in ancient times as a form of communication or religious expression. Artwork often consisted of objects with everyday or ceremonial uses. The oldest forms of art include cave paintings and engravings that date back thousands of years. Egypt retains many of Africa's oldest sculptures, from small clay figures to the Great Sphinx, which is 4,500 years old. In sub-Saharan Africa, the Nok culture created *terra-cotta*, or baked clay, sculptures of people and animals about 2,500 years ago. They also engaged in ironworking, as evidenced by the furnaces they left behind.

More recently, peoples across Africa began working with brass around the 1100's. In West Africa, the Yoruba created brass weapons, tools, and works of art, while artists in Nigeria crafted lifelike brass heads.

Fine Arts

African art centers on a conceptualized version of the human body. Masks and figures do not look realistic, but highlight certain features that the artists value. Oftentimes, the artwork takes place right on the human body. Africans from various ethnic groups might use hairstyle, jewelry, or body painting as a form of expression. In Sudan, the Nuer people cut patterns of scars into the faces of men to show strength and maturity.

Male and female artists differ in their traditional roles and medium. Men often use hard materials, such as wood, stone, metal, and bone, to make religious or ceremonial objects. Women, in contrast, tend to use softer materials to make objects with everyday functions, like baskets, mats, and clothing. Both males and females often work with leather, pottery, and weaving.

Artwork usually reflects the region and its resources. In West Africa, hardwood forests give rise to woodcarving, and everyday tools made from wood. In grassland or desert areas, artists work with stone, bone, clay, leather, and fiber. Art from northern Africa reflects the Islamic influence of that region. Artists there have become known for metalwork, glassware, and working in textiles.

Many traditional African art forms declined during and after the time of European colonialism. The introduction of Christianity drew artists away from traditional African religions. Access to manufactured consumer goods replaced traditional handmade artifacts.

Architecture

In many rural cultures, women serve the role of primary homebuilder, while men tend to cattle. They use whatever resources are available in their environment. Tuareg women of North Africa use animal skins to construct tents. These structures are lightweight and easy to transport as the group travels from one grazing area to another. In east Africa, the Maasai pile branches into a loaf-shaped structure held together with mud, grass, and manure. The Ndebele of southern Africa build homes of mud plaster, which they then decorate with paintings.

In cities of the north, architecture reflects the influence of the Muslim Empire.

14th century buildings in Cairo, Egypt

Dance and Music

African artists often combine performance art, such as music and dance, with visual art, such as the display of objects. Performances often play an important part of ceremonies such as funerals or the installation of a new chief. Dancers might move carved masks rhythmically to the sound of music, or musicians might relay messages from ancestors embodied by a mask.

Music is a form of entertainment, a method of storytelling, and an element of labor in Africa. At concerts or religious gatherings, choruses perform with or without musical accompaniment. In Senegal and other western countries, a *griot*, or storyteller, plays music while reciting ancestral history. Even while working in fields and villages, some Africans sing to maintain the rhythm of their work.

African musicians often use a variety of drums to provide a clear, steady beat. Other instruments provide a melody. These include string and wind instruments like flutes, horns, harps, and xylophones. African music has influenced many modern styles, such as pop music, jazz, and calypso.

Literature

Much of Africa's oldest literature comes from an oral tradition. Long before they had systems of writing, different groups passed stories from one generation to the next orally. Often, oral literature makes up an important part of religious ceremonies. Africans tell histories, fables, and riddles, and even sing songs, to preserve their history and teach moral lessons.

Some African cultures developed their own writing system, or adopted one from another culture. Nearly 5,000 years ago, the ancient Egyptians developed a form of writing called hieroglyphics. In Ethiopia, a religious script called *Ge'ez* developed around 300 CE. Since the mid-600's, North Africans have used the Arabic script brought from the Middle East.

Today, most modern writers in Africa use the languages of their former colonial powers—English, French, or Portuguese. However, many write in sub-Saharan African languages. Modern writers have earned international acclaim for novels, plays, and poetry that often deal with colonialism and the condition of modern-day Africa.

AFRICA'S WILDLIFE

Africa is famous around the world for its great variety of wild animals. It has more species of hoofed mammals, and more species of freshwater fish, than any other continent. The animal population varies by region, depending on the environment. Herds of giraffes, zebras, elephants, rhinoceroses, buffaloes, wildebeests, and a variety of other kinds of antelope roam the grasslands. They give rise to populations of more than 60 species of large predators, such as lions, cheetahs, hyenas, jackals, leopards, and wild dogs. A variety of baboons, chimpanzees, and gorillas, as well as 45 species of monkeys, live in the forests. Crocodiles and hippopotamuses live in wet areas of rivers and swamps. Snakes live throughout the continent, including

Burchell's zebra drink from a pool
in Mkhuze Game Reserve, South Africa

the venomous mamba and vipers. Africa is also home to a variety of bird species, including ostriches, flamingos, pelicans, and storks.

Today, many of Africa's animals exist in smaller numbers and areas than in the past. Part of this change may be due to natural changes in the environment, but much of it is due to human activity. People have destroyed many natural environments to build farms or cities. They have also over-hunted many species of animal. The black rhinoceros, gorilla, and elephant have all become endangered and are now protected.

Governments in most African countries have taken steps to protect animals and their environments. They have established conservation areas and national parks where hunting is prohibited. Tourists who visit these areas contribute to conservation efforts. The most famous national park in Africa is probably Tanzania's Serengeti. It covers some 5,700 square miles (14,700 square km) and is home to huge, migrating herds of plains animals.

In some areas, hunters can take part in *safaris*, or regulated hunting expeditions. However, illegal hunting, called *poaching*, is a major problem throughout parts of Africa. Nations around the world have created laws to help stop the sale of poached animal parts. Some of these, like the horn of the black rhino, are valued in some countries for

Foraging baboons in Tsavo
West National Park, Kenya

supposed healing powers. Governments hope that eliminating the market for elephant, gorilla, and rhino parts will stop the poaching.

African elephants in Botswana

For those Africans living in rural areas, conservation laws have created challenges. Farmers and herders compete with animals for land. Many people hunt wild animals for meat to survive. New laws aimed at protecting animals have infringed on the traditional way of life for many people groups.

Giraffes in the Okavanga Delta, Botswana

Africa is also home to a wide variety of plant life. Many factors determine which plants grow in an area, including temperature, rainfall, and soil type. In the rain forests of western and central Africa, hundreds of tree species grow. Tropical coasts and swamps give rise to Mangrove trees, with their distinct tangles of above-ground roots. Hearty plants that can survive periods of drought grow in the grasslands. These include the unusual baobab trees as well as the easily-recognized acacia trees.

Plants in Africa have grown to withstand droughts as well as fire. Dry conditions give rise to frequent wildfires. In addition, farmers often use fire to clear land for farming. This practice, combined with overgrazing livestock, has damaged much of the plant life and soil in parts of Africa. Land that was once grassland has become dry, sandy desert.

Africa has many plants and animals that have been introduced from other regions. Some have brought

Impala in Kruger National Park,
South Africa

Cheetah in Wabi Sands Game Reserve, South Africa

many benefits but others have been harmful. Important food crops like bananas, cassava, and corn plus cash crops like cacao beans and tea all came from other continents. Asians first domesticated camels, which are now used throughout parts of Africa for transportation of people and goods. Pine trees from Mexico provide timber and paper; eucalyptus trees from Australia are used for firewood and construction. However, eucalyptus trees pull water away from other native plants. A pond plant called water hyacinth, from South America, has spread to rivers and lakes where it crowds out fish and makes boating impossible. In Lake Victoria, Nile perch provide food for people, but at 200 pounds each they dominate other fish species.

THE ECONOMY OF AFRICA

Because Africa consists of 54 different countries, it has varied economies. Factors such as politics, history, and natural resources affect the economies of the various countries. South Africa, Egypt, Algeria, Nigeria, and Morocco have the continent's largest economies. Except for these and a few other northern countries, Africa's countries have underdeveloped economies. Although the continent is rich in natural resources, more than 60% of people in Africa work as farmers or herders earning just enough to provide their families with basic necessities.

The economies of most African nations underwent two major changes in the 1900's. The first came in the form of colonial rule in the first half of the century. This brought improvements to transportation and communication. It also introduced wage labor to African economies. As colonial powers developed just two or three major agricultural products in a territory, they left each territory vulnerable to price fluctuations. A nation depending on exports of just peanuts and copper suffers greatly when peanut and copper prices fall.

The second change to African economies came in the second half of the century as newly independent nations became industrialized. Often borrowing money from foreign countries, African nations overbuilt their industrial needs. This left them with unused resources and huge debts.

One measure of a nation's economy is *per capita* income, which divides the total income of all people by the total population. However, due to the rapidly growing population across Africa, this measure comes out extremely low, averaging about $650 across the continent, compared to about $54,000 in the United States. In the early 2000's, more than 30 African countries had per capita incomes of less than $500.

Agriculture

Incredibly, just 6% of Africa's land is used for agriculture, but it produces an average of 30–60% of each nation's gross domestic product (GDP), a measure of all the goods and services produced in a country. It also accounts for about 30% of exports. Egypt, Ethiopia, Nigeria, South Africa, and Sudan have the largest areas of farmland in Africa.

African farmers produce both *staple crops*, those used to feed the local population, and *export crops* or *cash crops*, those sold as exports. Staple crops include grains such as corn, millet, rice, sorghum, and wheat. Other staple crops are cassava, potatoes, yams, legumes (peas, peanuts, and beans), fruits and vegetables. The most important export crops are cacao, coffee, cotton, kola nuts, palm oil, sugar, tea, and tobacco. In general, small family-owned farms grow staple crops while large plantations owned by governments, companies, or wealthy individuals grow export crops.

Across the continent, varying climates and soil conditions allow for cultivation of different crops. Often times, extended droughts lead to crop failure and famine. Even when crops are plentiful, farmers have difficulty keeping up with the population. Unable to pay for food imports, some countries have come to rely on food aid from foreign countries.

Farmers also raise livestock, mainly cattle, sheep, and goats, for meat. Only a small number are used for hides or skins, though wool production is a larger industry in South Africa. Except in a few countries, livestock do not produce enough milk and milk products to meet local needs. Poultry production has nearly doubled since the 1960's in nations across Africa. The tsetse fly poses a challenge to livestock farmers, as it transmits a fatal disease among some species of livestock.

Mining

Africa's great mineral wealth has given rise to a large mining industry. In addition to producing oil and natural gas, Africa has large reserves of chromium, cobalt, gold, manganese, phosphates, platinum, uranium, and vanadium. The Republic of South Africa has the most developed mining industry, producing the most gold in the world. Botswana is the world's leading diamond producer.

Despite its rich mineral resources, much of Africa does not benefit from the wealth it produces. Mining employs few workers compared with agriculture and services and is expensive. Many companies are owned by foreign investors rather than by Africans. In addition, mineral prices can fluctuate greatly on the global market. In many cases, mineral wealth has even contributed to major problems across Africa. Mining creates pollution, such as that in the Niger River Delta due to the petroleum industry. Illegal trade of resources such as diamonds has helped finance civil war and terrorism, especially in Sierra Leone. In response, the United Nations has tried to prohibit the trade of so-called *blood diamonds*.

Manufacturing

Growth of the manufacturing sector of the economy has come slowly to Africa. In colonial times, only those nations with large European populations developed significant manufacturing industries. These nations include Algeria, Kenya, Zimbabwe, and South Africa. The next nations to develop manufacturing industries were those that gained independence early, such as Egypt. In general, most African nations now have small industries to produce consumer goods they once needed to import, including processed foods, beverages, and textiles.

Services

Like most nations, African nations include public sector services, or those provided by the government, and private sector services, or those provided by individuals and corporations. However, much of the private sector in Africa consists of small-scale businesses that do not follow formal steps for licensing, paying taxes, and such. In fact, this undocumented sector of business makes up nearly half of the GDP in many nations.

For many African nations, tourism is a leading source of income and service industry employment. Foreign tourists visit historical sites in Egypt, game reserves in Kenya, and natural wonders of Tanzania, among other countries. In response, the countries have developed extensive hotels, restaurants, shopping centers, and other services to cater to tourists.

Transportation

Most African nations, with the exception of South Africa, Nigeria, and the Democratic Republic of the Congo, have poorly developed systems of transportation. Only one fourth of the roads are paved and few people own automobiles. Many Africans, especially those living in urban areas, rely on public transportation such as buses and taxis to get around. Otherwise, they walk or ride bikes. In some regions, people use donkeys or camels to carry people and goods.

Every country in Africa has at least one large airport, with well-developed air industries in Algeria, Egypt, Ethiopia, Kenya, Morocco, and South Africa. The continent has a relatively smooth coastline with few natural harbors, but coastal countries are working to improve shipping facilities.

Communication

Communication systems in Africa have improved greatly over the past two decades. However, many areas remain inadequate. Television and phone services are unavailable in most rural areas, though cellular phone access is growing. Nations produce several newspapers but radio remains the most widespread form of communication. Only urban areas provide access to motion pictures, computers and the Internet. The entire population of Africa has fewer Internet users than New York City. Most are concentrated in South Africa and the cities of western and northern Africa.

AFRICA'S HISTORY

Ancient History (7,000–3,500 BCE)

In different parts of the continent, civilizations developed around agricultural centers. Prior to that, people hunted, fished, gathered food, and moved from place to place. Growing crops and raising livestock allowed them to form permanent communities. This improved access to food allowed the population to grow and spread.

Ancient Egypt (3,500–500 BCE)

The earliest civilization in Africa, and one of the oldest in the world, began in the Nile Valley's fertile plains. There, farmers grew sorghum and other crops. Small farming communities grew into larger states. Eventually, two states emerged as the most powerful—Egypt and Nubia. Egypt developed into an upper kingdom and a lower kingdom. Around 3,500 BCE, King Menes of Upper Egypt unified the two and took the title *pharaoh*. He established a system of *dynasty*, or family, rule that lasted for the next 3,000 years among 30 dynasties.

Kush Civilization (1080 BCE–350 CE)

In Nubia, the Kush civilization arose around 1000 BCE and paralleled the Egyptian civilization in many ways. At times, the two neighbors exchanged goods and ideas. At other times, they battled for control of the region. Kush ruled Egypt from 750 to 660 BCE, but was later conquered itself by the kingdom of Aksum.

Greek and Roman Rule (332–639 CE)

A series of foreign invaders, including Assyrians, Libyans, and Persians, conquered and ruled Egypt from about 1085 BCE until the 300's BCE. At that time, Alexander the Great of Macedonia expanded the Greek Empire through Egypt and beyond. One of his generals, Ptolemy, became king of Egypt. His dynasty continued to rule until 30 BCE, when the Roman Empire took over the Greek lands. Roman rule in Egypt lasted until 639 CE.

Aksum Kingdom (100–600)

Meanwhile, a powerful kingdom arose in Ethiopia around 100 CE and lasted for several hundred years. This kingdom of Aksum emerged in a fertile region of the Ethiopian highlands. It controlled trade through the Red Sea and in 350 conquered the Kush. The kingdom came to an end in the 600's once Muslim traders gained economic control.

Rise of Christianity (300's)

Before 100 CE, Christianity came to Africa from Asia. It spread throughout Egypt and parts of northern Africa as far as Morocco. Egypt, Ethiopia, and Nubia became major Christian centers. In Egypt, the Christian church took the name Copt, or the Coptic Church. In Ethiopia, King Ezana of Aksum established Christianity as the state religion after his own conversion in 333.

Beginning in the 600's, Arab conquests into Africa brought Islamic influence and led to a decline in Christianity. The Coptic Church in Egypt shrunk to just a small portion of the population, but has survived to this day. By about 1056, almost all of northern Africa had been converted to Islam. Only Ethiopia remained a nation with most of its population following Christianity. Not until the 1400's did Christianity spread to sub-Saharan Africa through European missionaries.

Islamic Empire (late 700's)

Islam began in the Middle East in the early 600's based on the teachings of the Prophet Muhammad. Upon his death, followers of Islam quickly conquered nearby regions and spread Islam. By the late 700's, this Muslim Empire stretched from Central Asia through northern Africa and to Spain.

As Arabs settled in North Africa, Muslim influence grew. The Berbers converted to Islam and helped spread it along their trade routes to Ghana, Mali, Songhai, and south of the Sahara. Meanwhile, traders along the Nile spread Islam to Somalia, Eritrea, and Ethiopia. There, they traded with Arab Muslims across the Red Sea, while some Muslims settled in coastal towns in Africa.

With the spread of Islam, African nations became more connected with the rest of the world. In 970, Islamic universities were established in northern Africa to teach religion, science, math, philosophy, and history. Islamic principles permeated all aspects of life in much of northern Africa, for the first time uniting people with a common language and culture.

West African Empires (700–1600's)

While the northern kingdoms began to fall to foreign invaders and adopt Islam, powerful kingdoms began to arise in western Africa south of the Sahara. The first of these was Ghana, founded by the Soninke people around 700. With extensive grain harvests and iron-producing abilities, the Soninke people amassed great wealth and political influence. They traded wheat and iron with southern states for gold. Then, they traded gold to Arab merchants for other goods. Ghana became a great empire until conflicts and climate change led to its downfall around 1000.

AFRICAN EMPIRES

Ghana Empire

Beginning in the 300's CE, the Soninke people of West Africa founded an empire called Ghana. Although the name is borne by a modern-day country in West Africa, the Ghana Empire was not located in what is now Ghana. It was further north in parts of what are now Mauritania and Mali.

The Soninke people called their land Wagadu and believed it was founded by a magician named Dinga. Its kings supposedly descended from

Dinga. They built their power, wealth, and influence through trade. They grew grains and raised cattle, which they traded with sub-Saharan African peoples for gold, ivory, and slaves. When Arab traders began visiting the region in the 700's, they paid a high price for these goods. In return, the Arabs gave the people of the Ghana Empire books, salt, textiles, and tools. As the empire grew, its capital, Kumbi Saleh, became one of the largest cities in West Africa, with approximately 30,000 inhabitants.

The Ghana Empire conquered nearby people and lands. The king required payments, called *tribute*, from each province, adding to the kingdom's wealth. Ghana's army enforced the king's laws and policed trade routes. However, in 1076, Berbers from Morocco invaded and took control of Kumbi Saleh. By the late 1000's, outer provinces declared independence, and the empire crumbled. Although the Soninke never ruled again, some joined King Sumanguru in the province of Soso and conquered the remaining territories of Ghana.

As Ghana declined, nearby Mali increased in size and wealth. By the 1200's, it had become the largest and richest empire in Africa. Its capital city, Niani, became a major trade center, while its largest city, Timbuktu, grew to a population of about 50,000. The university in Mali drew scholars from across the Islamic world. Around the 1400's, Mali began to suffer from political conflicts and invasions. By the early 1600's, the empire ceased to exist.

AFRICAN EMPIRES

Sundiata Keita

In the early 1200's, the Soso kingdom threatened the small kingdom of Kangaba in what is now Mali. Kangaba's King Sudiata Keita and his army of Malinke people fought back and conquered King Sumanguru and his Soso army in 1235. Sundiata continued to expand his kingdom, which became the Mali Empire. Located on important trade routes, and controlling major gold fields, the Mali Empire became one of ancient Africa's largest and wealthiest empires. As its ruler, Sundiata blended new Islamic influences with traditional African beliefs. He was seen as magical by his followers in ancient times and is still revered as a hero among the Malinke people today.

Mali Empire

From 1235 until about 1500, the Mali Empire flourished in West Africa. It arose from the conquests of King Sundiata Keita, who began with just the small kingdom of Malinke people called Kangaba. As they fought with other small states for control of the declining Ghana Empire's lands, the kingdom grew. At its height, the Mali Empire controlled an area that includes the modern-day countries of Gambia, Guinea, Mali, Senegal, Burkina Faso, Mauritania, and Niger.

Under the leadership of Mansa Musa from 1312 to 1337, the Mali Empire achieved its height of power. Islam spread throughout the empire. The city of Timbuktu became a famous destination for scholars of Islam and law. Education and trade flourished, and even farmers and herders prospered. They traded with Africans from south of the Sahara, and with Arabs from the east. Although many people in the Mali Empire maintained their traditional African spiritual beliefs, Muslims rose to power as the governing class. Between about 1400 and 1500, the Mali Empire fell to the Songhai people.

Mansa Musa

Also known as Kankan Moussa, this king of the Mali Empire ruled during its heyday of the early 1300's. His great-uncle Sundiata Keita had founded the empire, and Mansa Musa expanded it. Under his leadership, the Mali Empire became the primary political and cultural power of West Africa. He conquered the important trading cities of Gao, Walata, and Timbuktu and turned Timbuktu into a world-renowned center of learning.

In 1324, Mansa Mousa packed up thousands of his people and loaded hundreds of camels with gold and gifts to head to the Muslim holy city of Mecca. There he learned more about Islam, which he spread throughout his kingdom. He brought back scholars and architects, who taught Muslim principles and built Muslim houses of worship, called *mosques*. He spread the Muslim religion throughout his empire in West Africa. Upon Mansa Musa's death, his son Mansa Magha I became king.

Part of the Mali empire, known as Songhai, continued to thrive. Its capital city, Gao, became a major center of trade along the Niger River. Trade and learning flourished among the Songhai people until a 1591 invasion from Morocco weakened the empire. By the early 1600's, the last of the great empires of West Africa, including the Songhai, disappeared.

AFRICAN EMPIRES

Songhai Empire

The Songhai people existed as a culture for hundreds of years before rising to power in West Africa. Beginning sometime around the 700's, they formed towns near the present-day border of Mali and Niger. By the 1000's, their towns had become a kingdom called Kaw-Kaw with its center in Gao, an important trading city. As the nearby Mali Empire declined, the Songhai people grew their kingdom of Kaw-Kaw into a large and wealthy empire, known as the Songhai Empire.

The Songhai people traded with Europeans and Asians to build their wealth and power. Soon, the empire stretched from what is now central Nigeria all the way to the Atlantic Ocean. It conquered all the lands previously controlled by the Mali Empire, and made Gao its capital city.

The Songhai Empire had two exceptional kings who contributed most to its strength. King Sunni Ali, who reigned from 1464 to 1492, led his army in conquering Timbuktu and Djenne, two important trading cities. King Askia Muhammad, or Askia the Great, succeeded him in 1493. A strict Muslim, Askia spread Islam and expanded trade. He governed the kingdom according to the laws of Islam. In 1528, his son replaced him as king. The Songhai Empire declined after losing the Battle of Tondibi to Moroccan invaders in 1591.

City-State Kingdoms (1000–1500's)

On Africa's east coast, independent states arose around individual cities and their surrounding region. Perched between the rich African interior and the Arab merchants across the Red Sea, these city-states became prosperous trade communities. They exported gold, copper, ivory, grain, iron, timber, and other products to traders from the Middle East, China, India, and Indonesia. In return, they imported silk, cotton cloth, glass, and porcelain. These coastal people, descended from Africans and Arabs, were called *Swahili*, from the Arabic word meaning *coast*.

Manda, Mogadishu, Mombasa, Kilwa, Pate, and Zanzibar became the largest of these city-states. All along the east coast of Africa, city-states remained independent and dominated trade. Occasionally, neighboring city-states clashed. In 1503, the Portuguese attacked Zanzibar in an attempt to take control of trade in the Indian Ocean. Two years later, they destroyed Kilwa. With the invasion of European powers, the Swahili civilization began to decline.

Southern and Central African Kingdoms (1100's–1700's)

States and kingdoms also arose around the resources of southern and central Africa. In the 1100's, the Kingdom of Zimbabwe developed in southern Africa's fertile plains. Its land was rich in gold, iron, tin, copper, and granite. Inhabitants built the city of Great Zimbabwe with granite walls and buildings, the ruins of which form a tourist attraction today. The Kingdom declined in the 1400's due to overpopulation and reduced trade.

In central Africa, several kingdoms emerged, one of which was the Kongo kingdom in the 1400's. Its capital in Mbanza Kongo (now in the Democratic Republic of the Congo) was home to a well-developed central government. The Kongo kingdom was among the first states in central Africa to interact with European countries. At first, Portuguese traders explored the gold trade in Ghana and the Kongo kingdom and established ports for trade. However, they increasingly traded in slaves rather than gold. The slave trade, in addition to internal conflicts and wars with neighbors, led to the collapse of the Kongo kingdom in the early 1700's.

The Atlantic Slave Trade (1400's)

Slavery had existed in Africa before the arrival of Europeans, but on a much smaller scale. In biblical times, the pharaohs of Egypt enslaved the Israelites. Warring city-states sometimes enslaved their conquered neighbors. Africans sent slaves to Europe and Asia long before the Portuguese arrived on the west coast.

However, the Atlantic slave trade that arose between Portugal, Britain, the United States, and other countries became the largest forced migration of people in all of history. Somewhere between 10 and 12 million Africans were enslaved and transported to the Americas over the course of about 400 years. Europeans and Americans transported them across the ocean and sold them as plantation or mine workers. Africans themselves took part in the slave trade, with some merchants and rulers growing rich by assisting the Europeans. The Ashanti kingdom in Ghana, for example, became wealthy by taking part in the slave trade.

A monument in Tanzania serves as a memorial to captured slaves

The Atlantic slave trade had devastating and long-lasting effects on Africa. It disrupted the economy, led to depopulation of the youngest and healthiest people, and led to warfare. African nations missed out on years of important growth and development as they fought against slave traders and saw their people taken away. Those who supported the slave trade contributed to racist stereotypes against Africans.

Dutch East India Company (1652)

As European military and technology became more advanced, their interest in Africa increased. With a greater ability to travel long distances overseas and conquer native peoples, European merchants, explorers, and missionaries flocked to the continent. By the late 1800's, European governments began launching full-scale colonial invasions.

The Portuguese led the way beginning in the 1400's, seizing cities along the east and west coasts and establishing trading posts. The Dutch followed in the late 1500's and began to challenge Portugal for control of the African trade in slaves, gold, ivory, and other goods. The Dutch government established the Dutch East India Company, a merchant organization with broad governmental and military powers. It set up a station in 1652 at Africa's southernmost point, the Cape of Good Hope, to supply Dutch ships as they traveled around the continent to reach Asia. The post grew into a colony called Cape Town, where Dutch and other Europeans settled. These settlers became known as *Afrikaners*.

In 1814, the United Kingdom took control of the Cape from the Dutch, leading to intense rivalries. The situation escalated between the Afrikaners and the British when diamonds were discovered in 1867 and gold was discovered in 1886.

By that point, the British had already founded the colony of Sierra Leone in West Africa and was infiltrating Zanzibar on the east coast. Despite its colonizing efforts, the United Kingdom outlawed slave trading in 1807 and it opposed the African slave trade.

The French also competed with the Dutch for control of African trade. In 1677, the French captured the Dutch post at Goree, a West African island off the coast of Senegal and hub of slave trading. France also had colonies on the Islands of Mauritius and Reunion in the Indian Ocean, where slaves from east Africa worked on plantations. It controlled a trading post at the mouth of the Senegal River and later colonized Algeria in 1830.

Suez Canal (1869)

As European trade spread throughout Africa and the Middle East, it became clear that a waterway connecting the Red Sea and the Mediterranean Sea would greatly improve shipping and transportation. The ideal site for such a canal was the narrow Isthmus of Suez, a 75-mile (121 km) strip of land across Egypt.

In 1854, French engineer Ferdinand de Lesseps obtained permission from his friend Said Pasha, the ruler of Egypt, to build the Suez Canal. The agreement, however, favored the French far above the Egyptians. Egypt's government went into debt to purchase shares of the canal that went unsold in France. Egypt also supplied much of the labor and paid its costs. France was given full permission to operate the canal until 1968, one hundred years after its completion.

Just seven years after the canal's opening, Egypt's government was forced to sell its shares to the United Kingdom to pay off its debt. The United Kingdom then occupied Egypt, mainly to protect its large interest in the canal. For decades, the British used control of the Suez Canal to limit its enemies during times of war. In 1922, Egypt gained independence from the United Kingdom, but still British troops remained to control the canal zone. Although British troops left Egypt in 1956 as part of an agreement, they later joined Israel and France in an attempt to overthrow Egypt's president and reclaim the canal. Their efforts were stopped by the United States, the Soviet Union, and many other nations. In 1957, the Suez Canal returned to Egyptian control.

European Colonialism (1880's–1950's)

By the 1880's, European merchants had established a widespread presence throughout much of Africa. They requested political and military support from their governments in the areas where they operated. However, the European governments had been fighting for years over political control of Africa, resulting in intense rivalries. To help put an end to the conflicts caused by this "scramble for Africa," leaders of European nations met in 1884 at the Berlin Conference in Germany. Their goal was to establish boundaries and rules among colonial powers to prevent war over land claims in Africa. They did not include any Africans in the conference.

Without regard for existing boundaries based on national, ethnic, or religious tradition, the Berlin Conference divided almost all of the African continent among European powers. Only Ethiopia, who defeated Italian forces, and Liberia remained independent. The rest of the continent fell under the colonial control of Belgium, France, Germany, Italy, Portugal, Spain, and the United Kingdom.

In a few instances, European colonial powers peacefully established agreements with African leaders. In many others, Africans rose up violently against European invaders. The British faced violent revolts in Nigeria and Ghana, while western and northern Africans fought back against the French, and Africans in Tanzania and Namibia resisted the Germans. However, by the mid-1920's, European colonial powers had a firm grasp on most of Africa.

Resistance efforts, and then life under colonial rule, took a harsh toll on Africans. Many millions died fighting in wars against the Europeans, and more then labored to death on colonial plantations. King Leopold II of Belgium was especially brutal to Africans in what is now the Democratic Republic of the Congo, causing several million Africans to die.

All aspects of life across Africa changed under European colonialism. Christianity and Islam both grew. People moved into growing urban centers, and education became more formalized. Social life, religion, work, and politics all changed. Many Africans, educated by Christian missionaries, spoke out against colonialism and sought higher education, even if it meant moving overseas.

African Independence (1951–1994)

Although Africans had been protesting colonial rule since the early 1900's, it wasn't until the end of World War II in 1945 that the movement really gained momentum. The United Nations helped Libya gain

Woman carrying a pot on her head

independence peacefully in 1951. Five years later, Morocco, Sudan, and Tunisia followed in suit. However, not all independence movements were peaceful. The Africans of Algeria revolted against the French in a violent conflict that lasted eight years and cost Algerians about 1 million lives. Finally, the nation became independent in 1962.

Independence came to the west coast of Africa beginning in 1957, with the liberation of the Gold Coast from the United Kingdom. The nation then changed its name to Ghana, after the once-great kingdom in that region. The United Kingdom also lost its control of Kenya in 1963, partly due to a 1952 revolt called *Mau Mau*. Most eastern and western colonies once under the control of France, Belgium, and the United Kingdom had become free by the mid-1960's. Other areas had a longer struggle for independence.

In Guinea-Bissau, on Africa's west coast, the Portuguese fought against uprisings until 1974 when they finally granted the country its independence. The Portuguese also hung onto Angola and Mozambique until 1975. In other parts of southern Africa, the United Kingdom finally gave up control of its colony Rhodesia, which became the independent nation of Zimbabwe in 1980. In 1990, South Africa ceased its illegal control of nearby Namibia, which became an independent country.

The final step in ending European colonialism in Africa came with the end of *apartheid* in South Africa. For centuries, apartheid in South Africa meant strict segregation of whites and blacks and complete political control by the white minority. In 1994, South Africa transitioned to an integrated democracy with black leaders.

Africa Today

Independence has not been a magic bullet for most African nations. In the absence of dominant European military powers, many countries fell into conflict. Civil wars broke out in many countries, as people from various ethnic groups attempted to gain control of their new nation. In many cases, military officers overthrew the civilian government to establish a dictatorship. While most African nations have now established democratic governments, they are often ineffective and corrupt. Economic decline has added to the problems, as prices for African goods such as coffee and cocoa have fallen around the globe. Many African nations carry large debts to foreign nations that hinder their ability to spend money on health, education, and public works.

Many African nations continue to struggle against disease and warfare. The AIDS epidemic has devastated areas of sub-Saharan Africa, leading to millions of deaths and orphaned children. The highly-contagious and deadly Ebola virus has also killed thousands of Africans since outbreaks began in the 1970's. In some parts of Africa, vicious civil wars have claimed millions of lives and have disrupted economic and political development. In 1994, militants from the ethnic Hutu group in Rwanda murdered hundreds of thousands of Tutsi, another ethnic group with whom they shared the country. They also murdered many fellow Hutus whom they saw as too moderate. The Democratic Republic of the Congo ended its five-year civil war in 2003, but violence between ethnic groups continues. The conflict has led to the spread of disease and malnutrition, resulting in over 5 million deaths.

Today, several organizations have formed to help African nations overcome these challenges. Their goal is often *pan-Africanism*, a movement to unite separate countries and form stronger economic and political powers. The Economic Community of West African States, the Southern African Development Community, and the Arab Maghreb Union all work to form strong economic partnerships across Africa. In 2002, an association of African states formed the African Union (AU) to promote cooperation among nations, strengthen good governments, and promote peace.

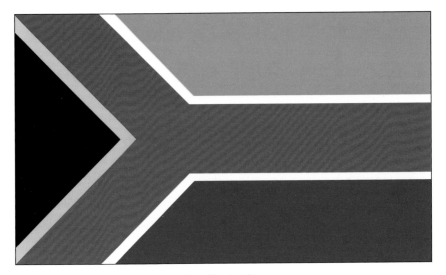

Flag of South Africa

PACIFIC ISLANDS

PACIFIC ISLANDS: THE BIG PICTURE

Volcanic activity and coral formations in the South Pacific Ocean have created tens of thousands of scattered islands between Asia and South America. Known largely as Oceania, the region includes the large islands of New Guinea and New Zealand and the continent of Australia. Part of Oceania, called the Pacific Islands, consists of 20,000 to 30,000 islands that are not closely associated with any nearby continent. Some of the largest nations in the Pacific Islands include New Zealand, Papua New Guinea, French Polynesia, Kiribati, Fiji, Tuvalu, New Caledonia, Tonga, Nauru, the Marshall Islands, and the Solomon Islands.

Spanning 300,000 square miles (777,000 square km) of land and millions of square miles of ocean, the Pacific Islands consist of independent countries, associated states, and dependent states. The islands range from large, mountainous forests to low, sandy *atolls*, or coral reef formations. Climates vary from hot beaches to snowy mountain peaks. New Guinea and New Zealand make up about 90% of the land, while some other islands are no more than small outcroppings of rock in the ocean. New Guinea, the world's second largest island, is divided between the nations of Papua New Guinea, in the east, and Indonesia, in the west.

The Pacific Islands fall into three main regions, based on geography and ethnicity of the inhabitants. Melanesia includes the islands just northeast of Australia. Micronesia lies further north, across the Equator from

Melanesia, in a small arc east of the Philippines. Further east, the large triangle of Polynesia stretches as far as Hawaii in the north, New Zealand to the southwest, and Easter Island to the east. These islands are more widely scattered than those in Melanesia and Micronesia.

The island of Bora Bora

People first came to the Pacific Islands from Southeast Asia thousands of years ago. They inhabited most islands in the region, where they developed varied and complex cultures. In the 1500's, Europeans arrived in the area, bringing capitalism, Christianity, European culture, and disease. By the 1800's, much of Oceania had fallen under the colonial control of European countries, Japan, and the United States.

Since the 1960's, most islands have become independent or self-governing. Today, about 19 million people inhabit the Pacific Islands, mainly on New Guinea, Fiji, Hawaii, and New Zealand. Many speak and understand English and French, the languages of the colonial powers that once ruled. France has maintained its territories of French Polynesia, New Caledonia, Wallis, and Futuna. The United States also continues to administer American Samoa, the Commonwealth of the Northern Marianas, and Guam. Chile owns Easter Island and Indonesia controls its half of New Guinea.

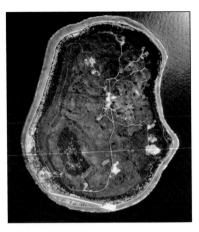

The island of Nauru, one of the world's smallest countries

MEET THE PEOPLE OF THE PACIFIC ISLANDS

The people of the Pacific Islands represent a wide range of backgrounds, ethnicities, and cultures. The second most populous country, New Zealand, is made up of a majority of people of European descent. Excluding New Zealand, however, people of European descent make up less than one-tenth of the population of the Pacific Islands. Of the large indigenous, or native population, about three-fourths are Melanesians, one-sixth are Polynesians, and one-twentieth are Micronesians.

Historians believe that the first settlers came to the Pacific Islands from Southeast Asia, southern China, and Taiwan. Thousands of years ago, they sailed or crossed now-submerged land bridges. While settlers developed their own distinct cultures on different islands, they often interacted and traded with one another. Early peoples developed societies around farming, fishing, and handicrafts.

In 1831, Jules Dumont d'Urville, a French explorer, divided the region and its people into three groups: Melanesia, Micronesia, and Polynesia. He based this classification on his observations of the geography, culture, and ethnic background of the people at the time. Although these lines have become increasingly blurred over time, and were never totally clear to begin with, the names have remained. In many cases, the classifications have become part of the local political, cultural, and artistic identity.

Melanesia

Melanesia comes from the Greek words meaning *black islands*, and was the name given to the southwestern islands inhabited mainly by

Map of the Pacific Islands

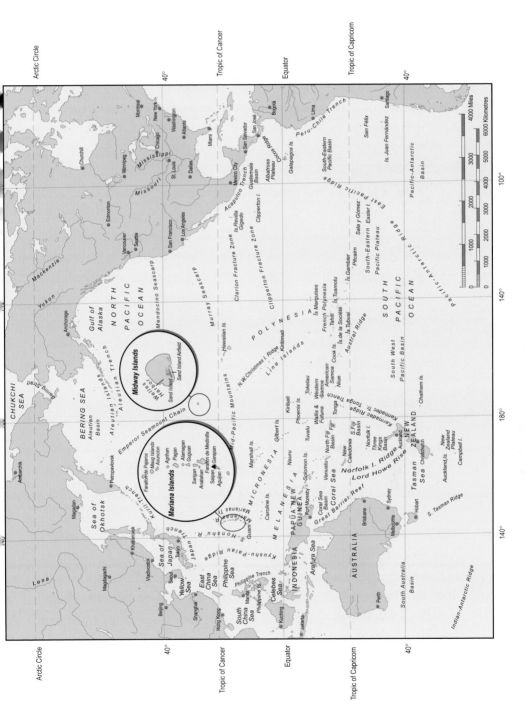

dark-skinned peoples. These islands, generally south of the Equator, now include the nations of Papua New Guinea, the Solomon Islands, Vanuatu, and Fiji, as well as the French territory New Caledonia. Of these, Fiji, as the furthest east, tends to have more in common with the islands of Polynesia. The societies of Melanesia are frequently dominated by *big man systems*, or communities informally led by wealthy, influential men who are relatively equal in status.

Micronesia

Micronesia stems from the Greek words meaning *tiny islands*, and consists of low-lying coral formations north of the Equator. With more than 2,000 separate islands, it includes Guam, the Commonwealth of the Northern Marianas, the Federated States of Micronesia, Nauru, Palau, and the Republics of Kiribati and of the Marshall Islands. Politically, the islands are divided between those that were colonized by the United States and those that were not. It has both societies that are *hierarchical*, meaning that some people have higher status than others, and societies that are *egalitarian*, meaning that people are basically equal.

Polynesia

Polynesia comes from the Greek words meaning *many islands*, and stretches across the largest area of the South Pacific. Its easternmost point is Easter Island, more than 4,000 miles (6,437 km) east of New Zealand. From north to south, it stretches 5,000 miles miles (8,047 km) from Midway Island in the north to New Zealand in the south. Included in this vast area are American Samoa, the Cook Islands, French Polynesia, Hawaii, New Zealand, Niue, Samoa, Tokelau, Tonga, Tuvalu, Wallis, and Futuna. Because the islands are so widespread, historians and scientists believe they were the most recently settled. People from Fiji, Samoa, and Tonga relied on advanced navigation and seafaring knowledge to reach the far-flung islands of Polynesia. Many societies in Polynesia are hierarchical, with a chief or king leading. In some cultures, women can become chiefs, but they rely on a male *talking chief* as spokesperson.

Other Groups

In addition to these indigenous groups, the Pacific Islands are home to many migrant groups that settled among the islands since the late 1800's. Americans, Chinese, Europeans, Filipinos, and Japanese have developed communities in Micronesia. Chinese also live throughout Polynesia in significant numbers. People from Asia and Europe have settled throughout much of Melanesia and the French live in French Polynesia and New Caledonia in large numbers. New Zealanders mainly descend from Great Britain and the population of Fiji is largely descended from India.

Languages

Across the many different islands, inhabitants speak hundreds of distinct languages. However, almost all people understand some English or French, one of which is the official language of almost every island. Many also speak Chinese, Hindi, or Japanese. Melanesians have the greatest diversity of language, with over 850 languages spoken in just Papua New Guinea. Micronesia has about 15 spoken languages and Polynesia has about 30. In areas where people speak many different languages, they often communicate with one another through common, cobbled-together languages called *pidgin languages*. Fiji, Hawaii, French Polynesia, Nauru, Papua New Guinea, the Solomon Islands, and Vanuatu all use this type of simplified, mixed language.

Religion

Today, most people in the Pacific Islands follow the Christian faith, though some blend Christianity with traditional beliefs and practices. Before Europeans arrived and spread Christianity, indigenous peoples followed a number of different religions. All included belief in gods or spirits and developed creation stories and tales of the relationship between the gods and people. Almost all involved honoring ancestors, a practice which remains widespread today. Since the late 1800's, Christianity has been the dominant religion throughout the region, though many other faiths also exist. Many Asian populations observe Buddhism, while most of Fiji's

Indian population is Hindu. Other Pacific Islanders are Muslim, Sikh, or followers of the Baha'i Faith.

LAND, WATER, AND CLIMATE IN THE PACIFIC ISLANDS

The Pacific Islands fall into two main categories: the high islands and the low islands. The high islands, formed by volcanic activity, rise from low, flat coastlines to rugged interior mountains and valleys. Some islands are themselves volcanoes, many of which are active. The variety of eco-logical areas on the high islands gives rise to diverse plant and animal life.

A high island in the Marquesas

The low islands, in contrast, are *coral reef* formations. Tiny sea ani-mals called coral leave behind their conglomerated skeletons to form these low islands. Most only rise a few feet above sea level and they often have a circular shape. A coral reef island that surrounds a lagoon is called an atoll. Many of the islands of Kiribati, Tokelau, Tuvalu, and the Marshall Islands are atolls. Occasionally, movements of the earth's crust raise some atolls higher than usual.

The Pacific Islands lie almost entirely in the tropics, which means they have warm, consistent weather year-round. Average temperatures range from the low 60's °F to the low 80's °F, with warmer temperatures closer to the Equator. Areas of high elevation, such as the tall mountains in Hawaii, New Guinea, and New Zealand have snow cover all year round.

Most Pacific Islands experience a wet season from December through May in the south or May through

An atoll in the Marshall Islands

December in the north, which can bring more than 150 inches (381 cm) of rain per year. It also brings powerful cyclones, hurricanes, and typhoons. Floods occur frequently, especially across low atolls, as water levels rise and waves surge. Sometimes, underwater earthquakes cause huge, destructive ocean waves called *tsunamis*. The climate of the Pacific Islands is also affected by an intermittent seasonal condition called *El Niño*. This can include droughts, heavy rainfall, flooding, changes in sea level, and even cyclones or typhoons.

A tropical cyclone over the island of Fiji

EVERYDAY LIFE IN THE PACIFIC ISLANDS

Life in many Pacific Island cultures has changed little in hundreds of years. Many people enjoy the same types of housing, food, and clothing that their ancestors did. Everyday interactions follow traditional codes of conduct, such as the *faʻa Samoa* (Samoan way) or the *te katei ni Kiribati* (Kiribati custom). These traditional customs regulate behavior in families and communities.

The city of Noumea in New Caledonia

City Life

Some areas of the Pacific Islands include large, modern cities. Among these are Auckland and Christchurch, New Zealand; Honolulu, Hawaii; Noumea, New Caledonia; Papeete, French Polynesia; Port Moresby, Papua New Guinea; and Suva, Fiji. These and other cities began as colonial settlements, military stations, or missionary posts.

Country Life

Although most people live in small agricultural or fishing villages, some of the Pacific Islands' larger villages have kept their small-town feel. Villagers know one another well and often have common relatives. Depending on the location, Pacific Islanders living in rural villages may or may not have easy access to cities. Those living in Papua New Guinea's highlands are especially isolated.

Food

Like many other cultures around the world, those in the Pacific Islands find identity and a sense of community around shared foods. Traditional foods include a variety of local fruits and vegetables. The coconut palm tree, which grows throughout the Pacific Islands, provides locals with coconut meat (the white, fleshy part) and tree sap, which is used to make drinks, sugar, and vinegar. Other popular crops include bananas, yams, and a variety of fruits and roots from plants like the breadfruit tree, the pandanus tree, taro, sago palm, and Polynesian arrowroot. Sweet potatoes are also popular, though scientists don't know when or how they arrived in the Pacific Islands from South America. Other plants brought from faraway lands include the cassava and pineapple.

Pacific Islanders eat plenty of fish and seafood, but traditionally eat little meat. Some cultures celebrate special feasts by including pork. Today, islanders eat meat, including chicken and beef, more often. Some continue to cook in earth ovens, pits dug in the earth and filled with heated stones.

Pacific Islanders brew a fermented drink called *kava* from the kava plant. Some also chew *betel nuts* (seeds of palm trees) as a stimulant, much like a strong cup of coffee.

Clothing

Pacific Islanders today dress similarly to people in Europe and the United States. Especially in more urban areas, men and women wear pants and shirts or women wear dresses. In general, fashion tends to be modest for both men and women.

Traditional clothing still exists in some areas. This often includes loose, brightly-colored material for both men and women or garments made from local resources. To make tapa cloth for skirts, men and women in Fiji, Samoa, and Tonga peel the inner bark from paper mulberry trees, soak it, and then beat it with wooden clubs. They wear their tapa cloth skirts for performances and special occasions. In Kiribati, islanders make dance skirts out of coconut fiber and woven pandanus leaves. Some islanders wear cotton or lightweight *muumuus* (loose dresses), *sulus* (loose skirts), or *aloha shirts* (brightly colored buttoned shirts).

Arts

Much of the traditional art of the Pacific Islands served a practical purpose. Performance art, such as music and dance, did more than just entertain audiences. It was used to preserve history and genealogy, or to record important events and relationships. Artisans also created pottery, sculpture, weaving, and woodcarving to serve as everyday tools and objects. Canoes and masks also served practical purposes.

Recreation

Pacific Islanders love to celebrate. Festivals and feasts occur regularly to celebrate holidays, birthdays, weddings, funerals, and even the opening of new buildings. Many include music and dancing. The Festival of Pacific Arts celebrates the variety of cultures and art forms by gathering artists on a different island every four years.

Islanders also enjoy a variety of traditional and modern sports. Boxing, canoe racing, surfing, and wrestling all existed before Europeans arrived and continue to be practiced today. Canoe racing has grown in popularity since the 1970's, with the competition culminating in the South Pacific games every four years. Europeans introduced Pacific Islanders to basketball, cricket, rugby, soccer, and volleyball, which are all popular.

Education

Many of the Pacific Islands' first schools were started by Christian missionaries as religious institutions. Today, all island nations have elementary and secondary schools, and some have colleges and universities. However, many children stop attending school after the elementary level. Few finish high school or attend college or university. Therefore, literacy rates vary throughout the region. Fiji, Hawaii, Papua New Guinea, and New Zealand all have high literacy rates as well as large universities.

THE ECONOMY OF THE PACIFIC ISLANDS

The Pacific Islands generally have developing economies focused on agriculture, fishing, and services. Mining is important on some islands as well, though, in general, mineral resources are scarce. The region's greatest resource is the Pacific Ocean, which provides transportation, food, offshore oil and gas resources, and sand and gravel for construction. American military bases in Guam, Hawaii, and the Marshall Islands also contribute much to the economies of those areas. Tourism is a major industry throughout most of the Pacific Islands. Hawaii and New Zealand have considerable manufacturing industries.

Islanders often grow their own food, and earn income by informally selling crops of betel nut, coconut, sweet potato, and yams, as well as fish and handicrafts. Many have family members who live overseas and send money back to them. Most countries receive formal aid from Australia, Canada, Japan, the United Kingdom, the United States, and other countries. Organizations such as the United Nations, the European Union, and the Asian Development Bank also support nations of the Pacific Islands.

Agriculture and Fishing

On most small islands, farmers only grow enough to support their own families. Native people own much of their own farmland, except in Hawaii, New Caledonia, and New Zealand. Only the larger islands have enough pasture to raise significant numbers of pigs, cattle, and chicken. Almost every island grows coconuts, one of the region's main exports. Pacific Islanders produce a variety of goods from the coconut palm tree.

Dried coconut meat, called copra, remains a top export. The trees also provide timber, and their coconut oil can be used for many products, including fuel.

On low islands that have poorer soil and less rainfall, farmers grow breadfruit, pandanus, and taro. Farmers on high islands take advantage of the fertile soil and plentiful rainfall to grow a wide variety of crops, including mango, pineapple, sugar cane, sweet potatoes, taro, and yams. Other plants, such as paper mulberry and ti plants, provide fiber for weaving and crafts. Cocoa and coffee are major exports from New Guinea, as is timber from the islands of Melanesia.

On all islands except New Zealand and Hawaii, fishing is an important part of local subsistence, or survival. The Solomon Islands, Kiribati, and Fiji also have commercial fishing industries.

Mining and Manufacturing

In addition to off-shore oil and gas deposits, the Pacific Islands have some deposits of copper, gold, nickel, iron, manganese, and chromium, particularly on the high islands. New Caledonia and New Guinea mine gold and nickel while Papua New Guinea has oil fields. Phosphate was once an important mineral mined on many raised atolls, but has been almost completely depleted by Australia, New Zealand, and the United Kingdom's mining efforts.

Some islands have manufacturing industries in urban areas. They produce cardboard, clothes, cooking oil, packaged foods, and soap, among other goods. Many foreign businesses establish industries in areas of the Pacific that are tax-free zones.

Tourism

The natural beauty and year-round warm climate attract many tourists to the Pacific Islands. Service industries in the Cook Islands, Fiji, French Polynesia, Guam, Hawaii, New Zealand, Samoa, and other

A beach on the island of Fiji

areas depend on income from tourism to survive. Although this industry is important, it also threatens the area's resources and traditional ways of life. Some people groups want to limit tourism for these reasons.

Transportation

Pacific Islanders have always relied heavily on sea transport. Traditionally, this meant using canoes, some of which could carry hundreds of passengers. Some islanders continue to use canoes today, outfitted with either a sail or motor. Industries also use sea transport, though not canoes, to ship food, raw materials, and manufactured goods.

Bicycles became popular in the early 1900's and since then, improved roads have led to an increased use of automobiles. Most nations also have access to local or regional airlines.

Communication

Communication among widespread islands in the Pacific improved with the introduction of radio in the 1920's. In recent decades, satellites improved communication still further. Today, many islanders use cell phones to communicate. Those in urban areas have Internet access.

Over the water bungalows in Tahiti

THE PACIFIC ISLANDS' HISTORY

Early Cultures

The South Pacific has a long ancient history of human settlement, specifically Australia, New Guinea, and a few islands of Melanesia. However, due to the need for advanced navigational equipment and knowledge, much of the area remained the world's last unsettled human habitat. Sometime around 6,000 years ago, migrants from Southeast Asia, China, and Taiwan explored and settled the islands reaching eastward. They were some of the world's earliest skilled navigators and their descendants now make up much of the population of the Pacific Islands.

European Explorers

The first Europeans to explore the Pacific Islands came from the east. Spaniard Vasco Núñez de Balboa sighted the eastern Pacific Ocean from Panama in 1513. Eight years later, Portuguese explorer Ferdinand Magellan sailed west to Guam. From then on, Europeans began sailing the South Pacific in search of new lands that could bring wealth and knowledge.

Dutch explorer Abel Janszoon Tasman landed in New Zealand in 1642. Other Dutch and French explorers followed. In the late 1700's, British naval officer Captain James Cook sailed throughout the South Pacific, creating accurate maps that included Hawaii and New Caledonia.

Missionaries, Traders, and Settlers

As early as 1668, Roman Catholic missionaries settled in Guam and the Northern Marianas. However, it wasn't until the early 1800's that missionaries spread to the rest of the Pacific Islands. The missionaries converted islanders to Christianity and also trained them to help spread this new faith throughout the islands.

Meanwhile, settlers and traders also spread throughout the Pacific Islands in the 1800's. These were mainly Europeans and Americans who established large plantations on which to grow coconuts, coffee, pineapples, or sugar cane. Along with them came *blackbirders*, or slave traders,

Bungalows and beaches in Bora Bora

who kidnapped native islanders to be sold as slaves in Australia and South America. The settlers also brought with them diseases to which the islanders had no resistance. Epidemics spread quickly, and greatly reduced the populations of some islands.

Colonial Rule

European and American powers quickly staked their claims on Pacific Islands, and by the late 1800's, the entire region had been colonized. Spain controlled part of Micronesia, but its defeat in the 1898 Spanish-American War meant that its holdings went to Germany and the United States. Germany also held land in Nauru, New Guinea, and the Samoan Islands. The United States controlled the rest of the Samoan Islands as well as Hawaii. France controlled New Caledonia and French Polynesia. It shared Vanuatu with the United Kingdom, which itself held Fiji, Kiribati, Tuvalu, Papua, the southern Solomons, and Tonga.

World War I affected power in the South Pacific somewhat, with Germany losing its lands after its defeat in the war. Japan took possession of German holdings in Micronesia, New Zealand took over its Samoan

Islands, and Australia gained northeastern New Guinea. These changes in control and struggles for power took place without regard for the desires of native islanders. They had little or no say in the governments that took possession of their lands. In some cases, island leaders cooperated with colonial powers in order to achieve their own agendas.

World War II

After World War I, Japan's power in the Pacific grew. In 1941, during World War II, it attacked a U.S. naval base in Hawaii. This surprise attack at Pearl Harbor brought the war to the Pacific. The U.S. military and its allies responded by chasing the Japanese off islands across the Pacific. After many battles, Japan surrendered in 1945 and lost control of its Pacific colonies.

NUCLEAR TESTING

A major factor in Japan's surrender was the use of nuclear weapons by the United States. After the war ended, the U.S. and U.K. militaries continued to develop nuclear weapons, testing them in the islands of the Pacific. Several Pacific Islands experienced nuclear weapons tests, including parts of the Marshall Islands, Kiritimati Atoll, Malden Island, and Johnston Island in Polynesia.

Nuclear testing off Bikini Atoll in 1946

Nuclear testing caused serious problems in the Pacific Islands. Native islanders in some areas had to flee their homes. Anyone exposed to the resulting radiation, including islanders and military personnel, faced illnesses like cancer. In 1963, several nations signed a treaty to stop above-ground nuclear tests, and the United States and the United Kingdom ceased nuclear operations in the Pacific. France, however, did not sign the treaty, and conducted hundreds of nuclear weapons tests in French Polynesia. Islanders protested the testing, and colonial rule, throughout the 1970's and 1980's. They banned nuclear testing with the 1985 South Pacific Nuclear-Free Zone Treaty in 1985, but France continued testing nuclear weapons in the Pacific until 1996.

Alliances and Independence

Pacific Islanders began gaining varying levels of independence in 1962. The United Kingdom granted full independence to its colonies: Fiji and Tonga in 1970, the southern Solomon Islands and Tuvalu in 1978, Kiribati in 1979, and Vanuatu (which had been held jointly with France) in 1980. New Zealand granted the Cook Islands self-government in 1965, but continued to handle the islands' international affairs by request. It also granted the island of Niue self-government in 1974.

Some areas, however, were not deemed ready by the United Nations to receive full independence after World War II. The UN established four trust territories that were administered by different nations until they received independence. New Zealand governed Samoa until 1962. Australia, the United Kingdom, and New Zealand governed Nauru until 1968. Australia governed New Guinea, which became part of the self-governing territory of Papua New Guinea in 1973, which then became independent in 1975.

The United States also governed a trust territory that included the Mariana Islands, the Marshall Islands, the Federated States of Micronesia, and Palau. Between 1986 and 1994, the United States established different political ties with its territories. Some became fully independent nations that the United States agreed to defend in case of attack. Others became commonwealths or, in the case of Guam, a territory.

The Pacific Islands Today

Since the 1990's, the Pacific Islands have worked to forge new identities under democratic independence while still maintaining traditional cultures. Leaders have formed international associations to improve cooperation and security. Some groups have stopped referring to themselves as *Poly-*, *Mela-*, or *Micro-* and simply call themselves *Nesians* as an indication of unity.

Flag of Micronesia

Flag of Melanesia

Flag of Polynesia

NEW ZEALAND

NEW ZEALAND: THE BIG PICTURE

Located in the South Pacific Ocean about 1,000 miles (1,609 km) southeast of Australia, New Zealand consists of two main islands—the North and South Islands—and many other small islands. As one of the world's most remote lands, even some of New Zealand's own islands are located hundreds of miles from the main group. The indigenous people of New Zealand, the Maori, call the land Aotearoa.

New Zealand boasts beautiful and diverse scenery, including active volcanoes, glacier lakes, mountains, valleys, caves, waterfalls, and beaches. Its isolation has also given rise to unique plant and animal life, like the flightless kiwi bird, which only lives in New Zealand. This national symbol has given rise to the nickname *kiwis* for New Zealanders.

As part of Polynesia, New Zealand was first settled by Polynesians who sailed from the eastern Pacific, possibly around the 1200's. Their descendants, called Maori, became the first inhabitants. During the 1800's, British immigrants came to New Zealand. In 1840, it became part of the British Empire.

The nation gained its full independence from the United Kingdom in 1947, after existing as a crown colony, a self-governing colony, and a dominion since 1840. Today, New Zealand is a constitutional monarchy with its capital in Wellington, on the North Island. Its largest city, Auckland, is also located on the North Island.

MEET THE PEOPLE OF NEW ZEALAND

New Zealand's indigenous people group, the Maori, make up about 14% of the population. Another 71% of the people are European. Other New Zealanders mainly come from the Pacific Islands and Asia. Until the arrival of Europeans, the Maori of New Zealand had no name for themselves. They eventually began using Maori, meaning *normal*, to distinguish themselves from *Pakeha*, or white European settlers.

Around 1769, when Captain James Cook of the British navy visited the country, the Maori numbered about 100,000. The population declined quickly after that due to diseases brought by the Europeans and warfare among themselves and with the Europeans. By 1896, about 42,000 Maori remained. Around that same time, the European population, many of whom had been born in New Zealand, had grown to about 772,000. Since the 1950's, the population of immigrants from the Pacific Islands and Asia has increased.

Nine out of ten New Zealanders speak English and many are multi-lingual. Almost all Maori speak English, and only about one-fourth of them also speak Maori. Other primary languages in New Zealand include Samoan, Hindi, and Mandarin Chinese. In 2006, New Zealand Sign Language was added as an official language.

Fast Facts

Capital:
Wellington

Size:
76th in the world

Area:
166,347 sq miles
(430,837 sq km)

Coastline:
9,404 miles (15,134 km)

Highest Point:
Aoraki-Mount Cook
12,316 feet (3,754 m)

Lowest Point:
Pacific Ocean 0 feet (0 m)

Population:
4.4 million

Official Languages:
English, Maori, New Zealand Sign Language

Currency:
New Zealand dollars

NZ$

National Anthem:
"God Defend New Zealand" and "God Save the Queen"

National Symbol:
Southern Cross constellation; kiwi (bird)

345

LAND, WATER, AND CLIMATE IN NEW ZEALAND

New Zealand measures about 1,000 miles (1,609 km) from north to south and 280 miles (451 km) from east to west, giving it almost the same land area as Colorado. Its many harbors and fjords (inlets) give it a very long coastline for a country this size. In New Zealand, there is no place that's further than 80 miles (129 km) from the coast. The North Island and South Island, separated by the 16-mile (26 km) wide Cook Strait, make up 99% of the country's area.

Overall, New Zealand has a temperate climate that varies greatly from region to region. It has frequent, though usually not severe, earthquakes, and plenty of volcanic activity. The nation is located in the Ring of Fire, an area of seismic activity around the Pacific Ocean that experiences frequent earthquakes and volcanic activity. On North Island, Ruapehu last erupted in 2007 and has a history of large eruptions.

New Zealand in comparison with the United States

Other active volcanoes include Taranaki, Okataina, Raoul Island, Tongariro, and White Island. Disastrous earthquakes struck in Napier and Hastings in 1931 and in Christchurch in 2010–2011. New Zealanders feel about 100 earthquakes per year.

Land

New Zealand's North Island consists mainly of forested lowlands in the north that serve as an agricultural area. The central part of the island is

Map of New Zealand

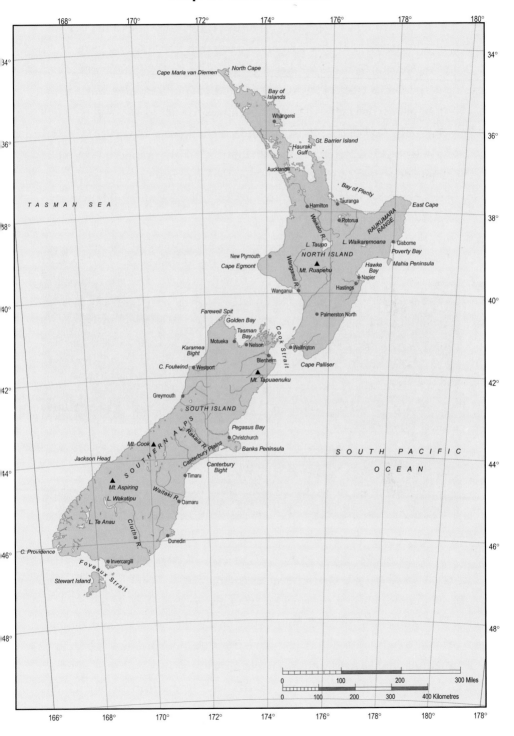

mountainous, with volcanoes, hot springs, and geysers. Its highest peak is the volcanic Mount Ruapehu at 9,175 feet (2,797 meters). To the east and south lie rugged hills that farmers use to graze livestock and grow fruits and vegetables.

The South Island consists mainly of the Southern Alps and narrow coastal plains. Its extensive mountain ranges rise above 10,000 feet (3,048 meters) in many places. New Zealand's highest peak, Mount Cook, rises 12,316 feet (3,754 meters) in the Southern Alps. The Southern Alps alone contain more than 360 glaciers, or dense bodies of moving ice. The Tasman Glacier, New Zealand's largest, stretches 18 miles (29 km) as it flows down the eastern slopes of Mount Cook.

Mount Cook, New Zealand's highest peak

A small section of nearly flat land along the east-central coast, called the Canterbury Plains, provides an area for growing grains.

Among New Zealand's many smaller islands, Stewart Island is home to many fishermen and the Chatham Islands are inhabited mostly by Maori fishermen and sheep farmers. People also live year-round on Campbell Island. New Zealand has many islands with no permanent population, including the Antipodes Islands, the Auckland Islands, the Bounty Islands, the Kermadec Islands, the Snares Islands, Solander Island, and the Three Kings Islands.

Water

Glacial activity has formed many rivers, lakes, and waterfalls across New Zealand. Melting glacier ice also feeds many rivers that flow from the mountainous interior outward. They are generally too rough to navigate, but provide hydroelectric power. The longest river, the Waikato, flows 264 miles (425 km) on the North Island. The largest lake, Lake Taupo, is also located on the North Island. Its 234 square miles (606 square km) serve as a great fishing and vacation destination. On the South Island, Sutherland Falls drops 1,904 feet (580 meters).

Fox Glacier

Climate

New Zealand's climate is generally mild and moist, but altitude and the ocean cause regional differences. Breezes off the Pacific bring warm air in the winter and cool air in the summer, keeping the country from extremes. Winters average about 35 °F to 53 °F and summers average about 59 °F to 69°F. Because of its location south of the Equator, New Zealand's seasons are opposite those in the Northern Hemisphere.

Peaks of Fiordland National Park

The South Island is cooler than the North Island. It has a rainy west coast and a drier east coast. On the North Island, the northern tip tends to be warm and humid year-round while the central plateau has hot, sunny summers and cold, somewhat snowy winters. Snow and ice cover New Zealand's mountains year-round.

The mountains also affect the amount of rainfall on the North and South Islands. Moist western winds off the ocean bring up to 80 inches (203 cm) or more per year to the west coasts. Milford Sound, on the South Island, averages 260 inches (660 cm) of rain per year. The east coasts, in contrast, remain protected from the winds by the mountains. They stay much drier, with some areas averaging less than 20 inches (50 cm) of rain a year.

EVERYDAY LIFE IN NEW ZEALAND

City Life

Almost three-quarters of New Zealanders live on the North Island, and about 90% of the population lives in cities. The largest of these are

Almost a third of the population lives in Auckland

Auckland, with a population of 1.3 million, and the capital city Wellington, with a population of 383,000. Owner-occupied single-family homes have been popular, but as more people move to cities, apartment complexes are becoming more popular.

Country Life

New Zealand's countryside is scattered with small towns of up to 10,000 people. They generally work in agriculture, raising livestock and growing crops. In the north, farmers generally raise dairy cattle. Further south, beef cattle and sheep are more common. Many farmers grow grapes in vineyards to produce New Zealand wine.

Wellington, New Zealand

Recreation

New Zealanders love sports and recreation. Rugby Union, a form of rugby football, and cricket are popular sports, as is horse racing. New Zealand's varied terrain and climate make possible many outdoor pursuits, such as mountain climbing, hiking, skiing, surfing, and boating. People also enjoy fishing and hunting.

Education

The nation has a high literacy rate, with education required for all children ages 6 to 16. The state funds public schools. Some private schools, often sponsored by churches, also exist. Students who cannot attend school because of distance or special needs can learn through Wellington's Correspondence School. It provides long-distance learning to these students and other children and adults who wish to study courses that are not offered locally. The nation has eight universities, many technical and professional institutions, and *wananga*, which provide higher education that emphasizes the Maori language and culture.

Religion

New Zealand has no official religion, and about 40% of New Zealanders do not identify with any religion. Christians make up about 44% of the population and Hindus 2%. Many other religions exist among small populations and some New Zealanders claim more than one religious affiliation.

351

NEW ZEALAND'S GOVERNMENT

Since gaining full independence from the United Kingdom in 1947, New Zealand has been a constitutional monarchy, based on the British model. However, it did enjoy some form of independence since 1907, and took several small steps to become fully independent over time. The nation consists of 16 regions and one territory (the Chatham Islands). In addition, the Cook Islands, Niue, and Tokelau are dependent areas. It claims part of Antarctica, called the Ross Dependency, but many other nations do not recognize land claims in Antarctica. New Zealand belongs to the Commonwealth of Nations, a group of independent countries that once existed under the government of the United Kingdom.

The formal chief of state is the British monarch, who appoints a governor-general to serve as a representative for a five-year term. New Zealand also has a head of government, a prime minister who is usually leader of the majority party in the legislature and is appointed by the governor-general. The country has one House of Representatives, called Parliament, with about 120 members. Of these, 70 are elected directly (some of which are specifically Maori seats) and 50 are elected by proportional representation vote. This means that the most popular parties get seats based on the percentage of votes they receive. Parliament members serve three-year terms. In addition, a Cabinet consists of Parliament members appointed by the governor-general upon the recommendation of the prime minister. Together, the prime minister and the Cabinet make up what is called the *Government*. The Government proposes new legislation, on which Parliament votes.

New Zealand does not have a formal written constitution. Instead, it operates under a combination of statutes, or various laws, and convention or *precedent*, which is just how things have traditionally been done. In 1962, the nation instituted an ombudsman, an officer from Parliament who investigates complaints regarding government corruption.

In 1893, New Zealand became the first country in the world to allow all its female citizens to vote. Today, the nation has a high level of women in government, including past prime ministers. All citizens and permanent residents age 18 and older can vote in general elections.

New Zealand has a Supreme Court consisting of a chief justice and four other judges. It also has several lower courts as well as courts that serve special functions, like the Environment Court and Maori Land Court.

Military service is voluntary for those age 17 and older. The country maintains a fairly small New Zealand Defence Force, consisting of an army, navy, and air force. It mainly takes part in overseas peacekeeping efforts.

NEW ZEALAND CULTURE

British, Maori, and Polynesian influences have blended to create a unique New Zealand culture. The country has many museums, including its national museum, Te Papa Tongarewa. The New Zealand Historic Places Trust works to preserve archaeological, historic, and cultural sites. Every other year, New Zealanders come together at the Te Matatini festival to celebrate Maori culture. For six days, they enjoy song and dance performances called *kapa haka*.

The nation has taken great steps to encourage development of the arts. An agency called Creative New Zealand funds programs in theater, music, dance, opera, and literature. A special fund compensates authors for the lost royalties due to people borrowing books from libraries rather than purchasing them. The government also supports a national orchestra and the motion-picture industry.

New Zealand has produced many famous artists, performers, and writers since the early 1900's. Traditional Maori woodcarvings and tattoos are also unique art forms.

The cuisine of New Zealand also combines the nation's very different influences—British cooking and local ingredients. In the British tradition, New Zealanders enjoy beef, mutton, and venison in various forms such as steaks, sausages, and meat pies. The vast Pacific waters also provide a variety of seafood. Increasingly, however, more and more New Zealanders are becoming vegetarians. Dairy products like milk, cheese, and ice cream abound, as well as whipped cream that fills the popular meringue dessert *pavlova*. New Zealanders often drink coffee, tea, beer, and wine.

NEW ZEALAND'S WILDLIFE

Before the arrival of Europeans and the ancestors of the Maori, New Zealand's wildlife developed in virtual isolation. These include several types of beetles, flies, and moths, along with geckos, skinks, and frogs. The ancient tuatara, a reptile similar to an iguana, also makes its home in New Zealand. Coastal and wetland birds live year-round, or migrate to and from the islands. The native kiwi, unable to fly, remains there all year and lives only in New Zealand. The large moa bird was hunted to extinction by the Maori. Other than its aquatic mammals (dolphins, seals, and whales), New Zealand only has one native mammal—bats.

Over the years, settlers have introduced many other animals to New Zealand. The Maori brought dogs and a type of rat. Europeans brought wild deer and rabbits as well as livestock (cattle, pigs, and sheep). Australians introduced wallabies and brush-tailed possums. While these new species brought variety and new sources of food to the islands, they also caused some native species to become endangered.

Thousands of years ago, rain forests covered almost all of New Zealand. As the climate cooled, those plants that could withstand frost became more abundant. Especially in higher elevations, forests of broad-leaf and cone-bearing trees arose. Today's forests include kauri trees, beech trees, and other species that have been introduced since about 1900. Among New Zealand's native plants, about nine-tenths grow only in New Zealand.

THE ECONOMY OF NEW ZEALAND

New Zealand has a developed, though fairly small, economy. During the late 1800's and early 1900's, it enjoyed a standard of living that was among the highest in the world, thanks to its agricultural exports. However, its rate of growth after the mid-1900's was one of the slowest among developed nations. This was due in part to higher taxes on agricultural exports and the slow-growing economy of its trade partner the United Kingdom. In response, New Zealand has invested in growing other industries and exporting new products, like wine and paper products. Its main trade partners are China, Australia, the United States, and Japan.

Once very involved in the economy, New Zealand's government has recently moved away from intervening in many economic areas. Some of these areas include social security, banking, insurance, the Post Office, and tax incentives for farmers and manufacturing exporters.

Agriculture

New Zealand's agricultural industry has grown within a complex economy. Europeans imported specialized grasses and fertilizer to improve lands for grazing flocks. Large-scale milk production required processing plants for butter, cheese, and other products as well as exporting infrastructure. Wool, lamb meat, and other agricultural products required a similar support system of finance, construction, transportation, processing, land improvement, and trade.

Today, dairy farming remains popular, but other industries, such as paper and wood products, fishing, deer farming, and winemaking, have increased. Farmers raise chickens for meat and eggs, and they grow apples, barley, grapes, kiwi fruit, onions, potatoes, and wheat. Agriculture accounts for just 4% of the nation's GDP.

Mineral and Energy Resources

New Zealand's mineral resources are somewhat poor compared with its biological ones (plants, animals, and sea life). Although it has a wide variety of minerals, only a few exist in quantities sufficient for mining. These include gold, coal, iron ore, limestone, marble, and construction materials. It has some natural gas reserves but also imports petroleum and petroleum products from other countries. New Zealand has done much to take advantage of its extensive hydroelectric power, but as demand for energy has increased, other energy sources have become important. Its two main islands are linked by underwater cables to allow industries and people on the North Island to use surplus hydroelectric power from the South Island. The nation also captures power from wind and from underground steam in volcanic areas.

Manufacturing

Manufacturing contributes about a quarter of New Zealand's economy. Many of the nation's manufactured goods come from its agriculture, forestry, and fishing industries. It produces dairy products, meat, paper, and wood. Factories, generally based in Auckland, produce machinery, textiles, and transportation equipment.

Services

Almost 70% of New Zealand's economy comes from service industries, and three-quarters of employees work in services. Tourism is a leading industry, as people from around the world visit New Zealand. Foreign students have also been coming to New Zealand in increasing numbers to study in language schools and in universities.

Transportation

Despite rugged conditions, New Zealand's roads are well-developed, and almost all inhabited areas are accessible. Most of the bigger cities developed around important shipping ports, which are still active today. Ferries service the route across the Cook Strait. Travel by rail is somewhat limited and slow for passengers, but is efficient for transporting goods. All major cities have air service, and three of these—Auckland, Christchurch, and Wellington—have international airports.

Communication

New Zealanders have more cellular phones than landlines and most of the population has access to the Internet. The nation has several newspapers, radio stations, and television broadcasts, some of which use the Maori language.

NEW ZEALAND'S HISTORY

As one of the world's most recently settled nations, New Zealand has a relatively short history. Settlement began around 1200 with a group of Polynesians later known as Maori. They remained isolated for several hundred years until Europeans arrived in the early 1800's. These two cultures formed a unique and complex society, with New Zealand becoming a British colony in 1840. The British and the Maori alternated between cooperation and conflict, as they clashed over land and authority. Although the nation became fully independent from the United Kingdom in 1947, the more powerful British continued to force the Maori to the margins of society. In the 1990's, New Zealand's government made several agreements with the Maori. They granted certain tribes land, money, and formal apologies for unfair treatment in the past.

The Maori Arrive (1200 CE)

Sometime in the early 13th century, voyagers from eastern Polynesia and the central Pacific reached the uninhabited islands of New Zealand. They likely sailed large canoes outfitted with food, plants for cultivation, dogs, and even a few rats. Several ships likely perished on the long and dangerous journey, but even one double-hulled craft could have held enough people to produce the Maori population that European explorers later encountered.

The early civilizations primarily settled in hunting and fishing villages along the warm coasts of the North Island. They hunted the flightless moa birds and grew limited amounts of crops. Among these were the *kumara* (sweet potatoes), taro, and yams they had brought. Later, the Maori moved inland where they built more developed villages and improved agriculture. They also used more bone, wood, and stone artifacts.

The Maori called their land *Aotearoa*, meaning *the land of the long white cloud*. They had no name for themselves, however, until European settlers arrived. They had not viewed themselves as a single nation or people group but as members of tribes known as *hapu* or *iwi*. The tribes often fought with one another and kept separate territories.

European Explorers (1642–1769)

In 1642, Dutch explorer Abel Janszoon Tasman set off from Indonesia. He and his crew searched for a mythical southern land, riches, and trade routes. They became the first Europeans to sight New Zealand as they approached the west coast of the South Island. With their ship anchored in a large open bay, Tasman and his crew sighted some Maori who rowed two canoes out to the large ship. The Maori blew a horn and shouted. Tasman and his crew did the same in return. However, neither party understood the other. The next day, a short battle broke out in which the Maori killed four of Tasman's crew. Tasman left the area without ever making land. His maps remained incomplete and he recommended the land be left alone, as it held no valuable source of trade and its inhabitants were dangerous.

For over one hundred years, European explorers did leave New Zealand alone. Then, in 1769, British naval captain James Cook landed in New Zealand on a journey of exploration and scientific discovery. At this point, approximately 100,000 Maori occupied the islands of New Zealand. Cook and his crew treated them with caution, but some violent confrontations erupted.

Over the course of six and a half months, Cook and his crew sailed entirely around both main islands of New Zealand. The journey provided thorough maps, charts, and illustrations of the area. Cook later made two more voyages to explore New Zealand.

Following Cook, French explorers voyaged to New Zealand. They named newly discovered islands and landmarks and also clashed with the Maori. In 1769, Jean Francois de Surville explored eastern New Guinea and New Zealand. Marion du Fresne arrived in 1772 but was killed, along with 24 crew members, by Maori. In response, the remaining French crew attacked and killed about 250 Maori. This dangerous interaction kept Europeans away from the islands for another 20 years.

European Immigration (late 1700's–early 1800's)

In the late 1700's, Europeans once again returned to New Zealand for economic and religious purposes. Australians from the British colony of New South Wales hunted seals and whales off the coast of New Zealand.

Humpback whale

They also traded for timber and New Zealand flax, a type of plant. Soon, the demand for seal fur drove hunters from America, Britain, and other countries to join the Australians. Within about 20 years, the industry collapsed due to overhunting.

The whaling industry, in contrast, continued to grow. Deep sea whalers in search of sperm whales stopped in New Zealand ports for fresh water and food. Offshore hunters of right whales remained closer to the main islands. They established communities in New Zealand, erecting buildings, planting crops, and marrying Maori women. By the late 1830's, several hundred Europeans lived in these whaling communities along New Zealand's coasts. They produced oil rendered from whale blubber and used baleen (thin plates from the whales' mouths) to make corsets and parasols.

At the same time, European traders also sought New Zealand flax from the Maori. They used this plant fiber to make rope. They traded for Kauri timber, which they used for furniture, housing, and shipbuilding.

The Maori became involved in many aspects of the new industries arising in New Zealand. They supplied, transported, and sold timber and flax.

They joined whaling crews, or worked at shore camps. Some Maori, like chief Te Pahi, visited British colonies in Australia. There they learned from Europeans, and obtained valuable goods for trade, such as pigs and potatoes. They also obtained firearms, which they had not owned previously. Some Maori tribes used these new weapons to attack enemy tribes. A bloody war broke out in the early 1800's when Chief Hongi Hika of the north attempted to overpower weaker tribes by using European weapons. Although the Maori also conflicted with Europeans, these skirmishes were usually small, isolated events, due to cultural misunderstandings. In general, the Maori cooperated with the Europeans in order to keep new wealth-building industries intact.

Christian missionaries also settled in New Zealand in the early 1800's. Anglican, Catholic, Methodist, and other groups established missions across the islands. They taught the Maori, and attempted to convert them to Christianity. By the 1840's, many Maori had converted, possibly because of the practical benefits of associating with European Christians.

Treaty of Waitangi (1839)

Settlers, traders, missionaries, and Maori all coexisted in a society without a legal government. Often, their interactions were peaceful, but sometimes disputes broke out. As lawless conditions arose and various nations competed for control, the British government came to the forefront. In 1835, British representatives and Maori leaders, known as the Confederation of Chiefs of the United Tribes of New Zealand, signed an agreement. It declared New Zealand an independent nation, granted the Maori sovereignty (self-determination), and established the British monarch as the country's protector.

Just two years later, Edward Gibbon Wakefield began buying land in New Zealand in an effort to promote British colonization. He formed the New Zealand Company and established settlements at Wellington, Wanganui, New Plymouth, and Nelson. Leaders from other groups began to do the same. Sometimes, these land deals involved violent clashes with the Maori.

In an effort to restore order and prevent the growth of the New Zealand Company, the British government sent William Hobson to New

Zealand. Hobson tried to persuade the Maori chiefs to give up their sovereignty. As a representative of the British government, Hobson declared the boundaries of the British colony in New South Wales, Australia extended to include New Zealand. He also declared an end to private land purchases in New Zealand.

Hobson and some local missionaries drafted the Treaty of Waitangi in 1840. It turned authority of Maori lands over to the British. In return, the Maori gained property, rights as British subjects, and British protection. Although 500 Maori chiefs signed the treaty, translation from English to Maori led to misunderstandings. The Maori thought they had retained the right to govern themselves, but the English version of the treaty called for the Maori to give up their sovereignty completely. In addition, Hobson had rushed the treaty into effect, in order to hinder the New Zealand Company, without gaining signatures from all Maori leaders. Whether or not their leaders had signed the treaty, all Maori were included in its terms.

Hobson became the administrator for the islands and moved the seat of government to Auckland. There, a community of Europeans settled but relied on the largely Maori population for food and other necessities. In 1841, the British government separated New Zealand from its colony in New South Wales, Australia. It became a crown colony with Hobson as governor.

As British rule became more formalized in New Zealand, conflicts with the Maori continued. The Maori became upset over loss of land and power to the British. Clashes between the two groups became more and more violent. In the mid-1840's, the first chief who had signed the Treaty of Waitangi and his Ngapuhi tribe protested by cutting down the British flagpole in the Bay of Islands. Four times they cut down the flagpole and four times the British rebuilt it. Finally, the protests became violent, as the Ngapuhi attacked the town and settlers fled. British soldiers from New South Wales were sent to defend the town. They fought with the Ngapuhi until a peace settlement was reached a short time later.

By 1851, the European population in New Zealand had grown to over 26,700. Colonists from Britain, Germany, Scandinavia, the Czech Republic,

Kaukau sheep grazing in Wellington, New Zealand

and other countries established settlements. About a third settled in Auckland, a third settled elsewhere on the North Island, and a third settled on the South Island.

The following year, the British government granted the colony of New Zealand a constitution. It established a General Assembly, a House of Representatives, and a Legislative Council. This way, the diversity of the European settlers could be represented by the government. However, representation was limited to men who owned property. Since the Maori owned land as a group, rather than as individuals, they were excluded from participating in the new government.

New Zealand Wars (1860–1872)

As the population of European colonists increased, so, too, did the demand for Maori land. The Maori fought with the Europeans over land disputes. They also became divided over whether or not to sell land to the Europeans, and ended up fighting among themselves as well.

Full-scale war broke out over a disputed land claim at the mouth of the Waitara River in north Taranaki. At that time, in 1859, Thomas Gore

Brown was the governor of New Zealand. He purchased the land from a minor Maori chief who claimed to own it. However, a senior Maori chief, Wiremu Kingi, also claimed ownership of the land. His tribe refused to recognize the sale of the land and they pulled out the stakes surveyors had planted. Brown declared a state of *martial law*, or military rule, in the area. He sent in troops who seized a Maori fort built on the disputed land. Maori from around the area joined Kingi in fighting against the government troops in a conflict called the Taranaki War.

In 1863, another large-scale conflict broke out between the colonial government and the Maori. Governor George Grey was upset that the Maori had established a king, and that they planned to stop selling land to the British government. He also suspected the Maori of planning an attack on Auckland. With the support of settlers who sought fertile grazing lands in the Waikato region, Grey ordered an invasion of Waikato in 1863. The Maori fought back, often defeating the British in battles and inflicting many casualties. After fighting battles that ranged across several regions, the British conquered the Maori and took control of the Waikato land.

Fighting continued on a smaller scale for the next several years. A religious movement called Pai Marire and two notable Maori warriors encouraged the Maori to continue fighting against the British to preserve their land and their culture. Those who took up arms against the British were declared rebels and were punished. The colonial government seized 3 million acres of their land. They also rewarded the Maori who helped fight on the side of the British. For example, the government reserved four seats in the House of Representatives for Maori.

In 1865, the colonial government began converting collective Maori lands into individual claims. Rather than allowing the Maori to own land as an entire tribe, as was their custom, the government issued individual titles. In the end, most Maori land ended up in the hands of European settlers. Maori communities suffered economic and social decline as they retreated to the harsh, isolated regions of the country.

During the mid-1800's, the South Island avoided most of the conflict occurring in the north. It developed a thriving sheep farming industry, in which wool became a major export. Wealthy farmers dominated politics and social life on the South Island. In 1861, prospectors discovered gold on the South Island and a gold rush followed. Mining towns cropped up in Otago and Canterbury, transforming these struggling settlements into prosperous provinces. In 1867, gold was discovered on the North Island as well. As European miners flocked to New Zealand, gold became the leading export.

Despite the growing mining industry and the newfound ability to refrigerate dairy products for export, New Zealand fell into economic depression in the 1870's. The New Zealand Wars had cost the government greatly and gold profits were shrinking. The government had gone into heavy debt to finance mining operations and development projects to support the growing population. The depression lasted until the 1890's.

Around that time, a new political party won control of Parliament and formed a new government. Under the leadership of Richard John Seddon, the government carried out social reforms, including extending women the right to vote in 1893. For the first time in its history, New Zealand had a stable, nationwide political party, called the Liberal Party. New Zealanders began to establish an identity separate from their European ancestors. In 1907, they requested and were granted *dominion*, or the right to become a self-governing country, within the British Empire.

World War I (1914–1918)

When the British went to war against Germany, New Zealand supported the British by sending 100,000 troops. However, New Zealanders despaired when the government made military service mandatory and the casualty rate rose to about one in seven among New Zealand soldiers. New Zealand's troops, which included Maori soldiers, gained a reputation as determined fighters. New Zealand's military first occupied German Samoa in the South Pacific. Then they joined Australian and Egyptian troops in an attempt to occupy a region of Turkey known as the Gallipoli Peninsula. Later in the war, they fought in France.

Once the war ended in 1918, New Zealand enjoyed a brief economic boom. Electric power expanded throughout the country and automobiles became more widely available. This prosperity continued until prices on exports dropped in 1921. By 1929, New Zealand entered the Great Depression, a worldwide economic downturn. Tens of thousands of New Zealanders lost their jobs. Those living in big cities began to riot as living conditions worsened.

The government responded by investing in public works projects, such as building railroads and planting forests. Workers lived in camps and received small wages. In 1935, the newly powerful Labour Party increased these efforts. It also raised wages and introduced a widespread social security system.

World War II (1939–1945)

Once again, the United Kingdom went to war against Germany in 1939 and once again, New Zealand joined them. The New Zealand government required mandatory military service, sending troops mainly to the Middle East and Europe. Along with Maori soldiers who joined them, New Zealanders fought valiantly, this time as pilots as well as ground troops.

The war came closer to home for New Zealanders in 1941, when Japan entered on the side of Germany. New Zealanders feared the Japanese would invade their country. With British power focused halfway around the world, New Zealand came to depend on the United States for military support in the South Pacific. As a result of the thousands of American troops stationed in New Zealand or stopping at its ports, American culture spread through the country.

Waitangi Tribunal (1975)

After the war ended, New Zealand entered a time of economic stability. The standard of living improved as the government invested in housing, employment, and education. Many Maori, who had traditionally lived in rural areas, began moving to cities. While this move allowed them greater education and employment opportunities, it also separated them from their traditional way of life.

In 1975, the Maori organized a march from the northern part of the North Island to the capital in Wellington. They protested the government's violation of the Treaty of Waitangi, which Maori had argued since the 1840's. In response, the government established the Waitangi Tribunal, a group of Maori and Pakeha (non-Maori) members to launch an inquiry into the Maori claims of British violations. The group eventually investigated claims dating all the way back to 1840. They also proposed possible settlements to make up for abuses by the British government. As a result, New Zealand's government has issued formal apologies to several Maori tribes and has returned land and made financial payments.

Rainbow Warrior (1985)

In the 1980's, New Zealand took a stand against controversial world events. In 1981, New Zealanders protested *apartheid*, or racial segregation, in South Africa when that country's rugby team visited New Zealand on tour.

In 1984, the nation began to protest use of nuclear weapons. Prime Minister David Lange banned ships carrying nuclear weapons from its ports. This decision caused a rift with New Zealand's military ally, the United States, which resulted in the suspension of U.S. military duties in New Zealand. The nation also protested France's continued testing of nuclear weapons in the South Pacific. In 1985, the French bombed a ship in Auckland Harbour. The ship, called the *Rainbow Warrior*, had been intended for use in protests against nuclear testing. Although the French apologized for sinking the ship, they prevented their agents from serving out prison terms in New Zealand.

New Zealand Today

The nation continues to oppose nuclear weapons, having signed a 1996 UN resolution to ban nuclear weapons from the Southern Hemisphere.

The government has shifted many areas of the economy to privately owned, and less regulated, free-market economies. It has also imposed a goods and services tax that has increased the price of most consumer goods. As these changes did little to improve the economy, New Zealanders voted the Labour Party out of office in 1990 and replaced it with the

National Party. They also voted in 1992 to reform the election system in the country.

Flag of New Zealand

AUSTRALIA: THE BIG PICTURE

The Commonwealth of Australia is the only country that is also a continent. This island nation lies between the Indian Ocean and the South Pacific Ocean in the Southern Hemisphere and includes the smaller island of Tasmania. Its nearest neighbors across the seas are Papua New Guinea, Indonesia, and New Zealand. People refer to Australia as the land "down under" and its name comes from the Latin *australis*, meaning *southern*.

This large country consists mainly of a vast interior desert called the Outback. The north has a hot, tropical climate, and the south has a more temperate climate, with warm summers and cool winters. Therefore, the population of Australia is concentrated on the eastern and southern coasts. Its capital, Canberra, is located in the southeast between the larger cities of Sydney and Melbourne. Much of Australia remains practically uninhabited, due to the hot, dry climate. However, the country is home to a wide assortment of unique and unusual animals. These include the kangaroo, koala, platypus, and wombat, among others.

The nation gained its independence from the United Kingdom on January 1, 1901. Having existed first as a British colony, the country has many British customs. However, immigration since the 1950's has resulted in a more multicultural atmosphere. Before the more recent arrival of the Europeans, Australia was inhabited by Aboriginal people.

MEET THE PEOPLE OF AUSTRALIA

Australia's immigrant population began as mostly English and Irish. After World War II, its government encouraged Europeans, many of whom were left homeless by the war, to come to Australia. By the mid-1900's, millions of immigrants came to Australia in search of jobs, a higher standard of living, and a clean environment. Mainly Europeans came at first; later, the number of Asian immigrants increased. More recently, immigrants have come from New Zealand and Southeast Asia. Australia's population is now about 30% foreign-born.

Today, about a quarter of Australians are of Australian descent, and another quarter are English. The rest of the population are a variety of European, Chinese, Indian, and other ethnicities. About one percent of the population is native Aboriginal, but that population is growing after a period of decline.

Most Australians (about 90%) live in urban areas, mainly along the southern and eastern coasts. The rest live mainly along the northeast and southwest coasts. Sydney and Melbourne, on the southeast coast, have populations over 4 million each. Other large cities include Brisbane, Perth, Adelaide, and the capital city Canberra. Although Canberra is not as large as the others, it is Australia's largest inland city, lying about 80 miles (129 km) from the coast.

Fast Facts

Capital:
Canberra

Size:
6th in the world

Area:
4,773,560 sq miles
(12,363,464 sq km)

Coastline:
16,007 miles (25,761 km)

Highest Point:
Mount Kosciuszko
7,313 feet (2,229 m)

Lowest Point:
Lake Eyre -49 feet (-15 m)

Population:
23 million

Official Language:
English

Currency:
Australian dollars

AUD

National Anthem:
"Advance Australia Fair"

National Symbol:
Southern Cross constellation (five, seven-pointed stars)

About three-quarters of Australians speak English, the official language, as their primary language. English is widely understood by almost all Australians. It differs from British or American English in accent and vocabulary. Some words that describe plants and animals unique to Australia, like *kangaroo* and *koala*, come from Aboriginal people. Aboriginal languages, which once numbered in the hundreds, have been going extinct since about 1950. The remaining Aboriginal languages have very few speakers. Other languages spoken by small populations include Mandarin, Italian, Arabic, Greek, Cantonese, and Vietnamese.

Aboriginal people, once persecuted by European immigrants and the Australian government, have experienced a revival of culture and identity. Their population has quadrupled in the past 30 years or so, and government support and recognition increased as well during that time. Until the late 1960's, most Aboriginals lived in rural areas, often on government reserves. Some lived in tribal societies that maintained traditional ways, while others worked on ranches. Since then, most Aboriginal people have moved to cities in search of education, jobs, and a higher standard of living. Aboriginal art and music has become a treasured part of Australian culture.

LAND, WATER, AND CLIMATE IN AUSTRALIA

As the world's sixth-largest country and smallest continent, Australia is slightly smaller than the United States. It measures about 2,485 miles (3,999 km) from east to west and about 1,988 miles (3,199 km) from north to south. Although it is surrounded by water, geographers refer to it as a continent rather than as an island because of its great size. About 124 miles (200 km) off the southeastern coast lies the smaller island of Tasmania. It was once connected to the mainland until rising ocean levels covered the land bridge. Overall, Australia is a very flat and very dry continent.

Land

Australia consists mainly of a low plateau with widespread deserts. The east coast contains some mountains and the southeast is a fertile plain.

Map of Australia

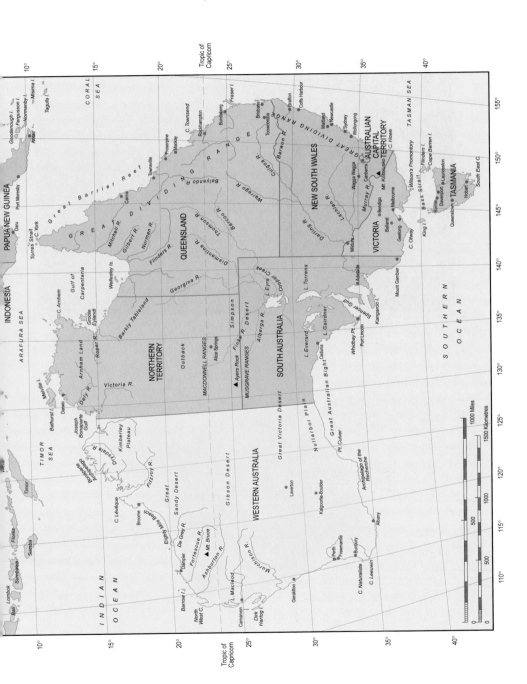

Three Sisters formation in the Blue Mountains

Its terrain can be classified into three main regions: the Eastern Highlands, the Central Lowlands, and the Western Plateau.

The Eastern Highlands stretch from Cape York Peninsula in the north to the south coast of Tasmania. This region is Australia's highest in elevation, with just a narrow plain along the Pacific coast. This flat stretch of sandy beaches and rocky cliffs receives more rain than anywhere else in the country. The Eastern Highlands consist of low mountain ranges, along with high plateaus, gorges, hills, and valleys. Much of the land is covered in grass or forests, and its fertile soils are used for agriculture.

Australia's highest point, Mount Kosciuszko, is located here in the Snowy Mountains, part of the

Australia compared to the United States

Australian Alps. This group of mountain ranges is covered in snow each winter, attracting skiers to the region.

The Australian Outback

Further west lie the Central Lowlands, Australia's lowest, flattest region. Infrequent rains create several rivers that flow through the region, but most of the time the riverbeds remain dry. The land is generally too dry and hot for farming, but farmers in the southern part can grow wheat. The rest of the land, covered in coarse grass and shrubs, is used to graze livestock. The region also contains a sandy desert in the west and Australia's lowest point, Lake Eyre, in the southwest. Its largest cities are mining towns of about 30,000 people. Vast stretches of uninhabited land are called the Outback, or the bush.

Australia's largest land region, the Western Plateau, covers the western two-thirds of the continent. It is slightly higher than the Central Lowlands, but still very flat. The central part of this region is covered in deserts. Deserts give way to grasslands closer to the coasts. Where heavy rains fall in the far north and far south, farmers raise crops. In the arid central area, they graze livestock on the grass and shrubs. The region is home to Ayers Rock. This formation, also called Uluru, is sacred for Aboriginal people and attracts many tourists.

Ayers Rock is an inselberg, or island mountain

Water

In a hot, dry land covered with many deserts, Australia's water is a vital resource. The country has an extensive coastline, many rivers, and a few lakes that people use for drinking, farming, and transportation. In many areas, hydroelectric plants convert the energy of moving water to electricity. Tasmania gets almost all of its electricity this way.

Plentiful water also exists underground throughout the country, but it is usually too salty for drinking or irrigation. In some areas, livestock can drink the water. Some large cattle ranches supply their livestock with water supplied by underground wells. When underground water is trapped under pressure, it creates *artesian* springs and wells. This means that water gushes out through any opening without needing to be pumped to the surface. In eastern Australia, the Great Artesian Basin contains a huge store of salty underground water trapped under pressure by a rock formation.

Australia's rainy season occurs during summer in the north and winter in the south. Heavy rains during these times cause often-dry rivers to swell. Outside of the rainy season, many lakes and rivers dry up. The longest permanent river is the Murray, which winds 1,609 miles (2,590 km) from the Snowy Mountains to Adelaide in the southwest. The Darling River is a bit longer at 1,702 miles (2,739 km), but it dries up each winter. In summer, it feeds the Murray River with rainwater from the Eastern Highlands. Australians have built dams and reservoirs on all major rivers to store the water for year-round drinking and irrigation.

Australia has no permanent natural lakes. *Playas*, or dry beds of salt or clay, fill with water after heavy rains. Some playas dry out seasonally

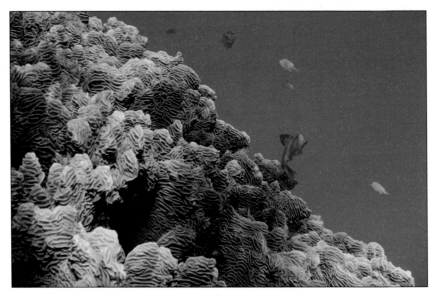

A section of the Great Barrier Reef

while others remain dry for years at a time. The playas are most common in the south and west. In addition, Australia has some artificially created lakes, which serve as huge reservoirs.

One of Australia's most unique features and popular tourist attractions is the Great Barrier Reef. Underwater creatures called coral cling together and leave behind their tiny skeletons after dying. Millions of these tiny creatures have created chains of islands and underwater formations that stretch through the warm waters of the Pacific Ocean. The Great Barrier Reef is protected as an environmental treasure, but swimmers and divers can visit and enjoy the beautiful sea life it attracts.

Climate

Australia's climate is generally arid, meaning it receives little precipitation. The only drier continent is Antarctica. The south and east are temperate, meaning they have warm summers and cool winters. Some parts of the south have occasional frosts, but only the mountains and the interior of Tasmania receive accumulated snowfall. The northern third is considered tropical, so it is hot year-round.

The coastal areas receive the most rainfall, with as much as 150 inches (381 cm) per year. Further inland, the driest two-thirds of the country receive less than 20 inches (51 cm) per year, with the driest third receiving less than 10 inches (25 cm). Except for parts of the southeast coast and Tasmania, which receive rainfall year-round, Australia's precipitation is very seasonal. As a result, irrigation is necessary to grow crops in almost all regions. Much of the continent is too dry to graze livestock.

Because it is located south of the Equator, Australia's seasons are opposite those in the Northern Hemisphere. The south experiences four distinct seasons, with a cool, wet winter from June to August and a hot, dry summer from December to February. The tropical north doesn't have such variations in temperature, as it is hot year-round. It has a wet season from November to April that serves as a summer and a dry season the other half of the year.

In summer, temperatures in Australia regularly exceed 100 °F. Without much cloud cover to retain the heat, however, temperatures drop quite a bit at night. Heat waves are common and dangerous.

The combination of a hot, arid climate with heavy seasonal rains causes regular weather extremes. The long dry season often leads to droughts across the continent. Water conservation has helped people, animals, and crops survive this yearly drought, but sometimes even the wet season has periods without rainfall. The dry, brittle grasses create ideal conditions for dangerous wildfires, which often spread across parts of the country. During the wet season, floods often occur. Australia also experiences seasonal cyclones along the coast. In 1974, one such storm nearly destroyed the city of Darwin on the north coast.

EVERYDAY LIFE IN AUSTRALIA

Australians are proud to have forged a modern society in a harsh land. They began as a colony of convicts and oppressed native peoples to become a developed, multicultural nation with its own unique personality. Australians tend to be very relaxed and casual, greeting one another with the informal "G'day" (good day). They often drink beer and gamble, though the government has tried to limit these pastimes. The nation celebrates many public holidays, making the long weekend a regular occurrence.

Ways of life in Australia do not differ much from one region to another, but differ quite a bit from urban to rural areas. The nation has an increasing gap between those with education, employment, and wealth and those without. However, the nation does not have the extreme poverty seen in other developed countries.

City Life

Almost 88% of Australians live on 1% of the most developed land, making it one of the world's most urbanized countries. About seven out of ten Australians live in cities with populations over 100,000. The largest of these by far are Sydney and Melbourne, with over 4 million people each. Other major cities include the state capitals—Brisbane, Perth, Adelaide, and Hobart. The federal capital, Canberra, is relatively small in comparison but still home to about 350,000 people. In each of the six states, the capital city serves as a political, commercial, industrial, and cultural hub.

The Sydney skyline

These cities became the largest in their respective states and were chosen as capitals because of their many advantages. They are all the oldest or one of the oldest settlements in their state. All are located by the mouth of a river close to an ocean harbor. The rivers provide drinking water while the harbors allow for transportation and immigration.

Australian cities feature modern high-rise office buildings, usually located in the oldest section of town near the water. Stores, theaters, and restaurants also fill the city centers. Extending outward from the business district lie the suburbs, where many city-dwellers live. These neighborhoods consist mainly of single-family homes. Most families own their own home, which often includes a garden and a wide porch. In Queensland, older wooden homes sit above the ground on poles called *stumps*.

Like all major cities, those in Australia have their advantages and disadvantages. Urban areas offer a variety of government and commercial services, cultural institutions, shopping centers, and recreational facilities. Schools and employers are plentiful. However, crowds of people and automobiles cause traffic jams and air pollution. Crime tends to be higher in cities than in rural areas.

Country Life

Australia's rural areas are often referred to as the Outback (in the continent's interior) or the bush (any other wilderness area). Large areas of desert and some mountains are completely uninhabited. The largest settlements are scattered mining towns. Elsewhere, huge cattle ranches, called *stations*, stretch up to thousands of square miles. Usually, banks, investment firms, or companies own the stations, though individuals and families may own shares. Anywhere from about 15 to 50 people might live on a station, with a few others living in scattered outlying cottages. Life there is very isolated as the nearest town is often more than 100 miles (160 km) away. A station often consists of a central compound of homes, an office, garages, a machine shop, a butchery, a shearing shed, and an airstrip. Families that can afford to own a light airplane use that to reach the nearest towns. Those who don't own airplanes must drive often-unpaved roads, limiting their trips to a few per year.

Australians living in rural areas have limited access to cultural and educational institutions and government services. They have a higher rate of unemployment than those in urban areas due to a lack of local employment. They also endure seasonal natural disasters such as droughts, floods, and bushfires. However, rural Australians have developed a sense of community through traditional fairs, festivals, and sports competitions. They have their own political party, called the National Party, and tend to vote conservatively. Many families own their own farms and live comfortably in homes that have electricity and often air conditioning.

Recreation

Many Australians enjoy a variety of outdoor sports or hiking. They take part in water sports, like skin diving, surfing, swimming, and boating. Many play individual sports, like golf and tennis, along with team sports.

Basketball and netball are popular team sports. Netball, a game that involves throwing and catching a ball to score in a goal, is especially popular among women.

Australian athletes have attained worldwide acclaim in tennis, golf, swimming, track and field, rowing, cycling, yachting, and surfing. The nation competes in the Olympic Games and is often among the top medal-winning countries. Its most successful Olympians have been swimmers.

Important holidays include ANZAC Day (Australian and New Zealand Army Corps), marking the Australian military effort in Gallipoli in 1915, Australia Day, which marks the arrival of the British in 1788, and the birthday of the British monarch. Annual festivals include concerts, fireworks, art displays, sports, and parades.

Education

Australia's national government develops guidelines for education, but states and territories create their own laws under these guidelines. The federal government provides some funding to states and territories, but mainly funds higher education. Most students attend primary and secondary schools run by the state, and nearly one-third attend private schools, which are mainly Roman Catholic.

School attendance is mandatory for children ages 6 to 15 (16 in Tasmania). About three-fourths of students complete 12 years of schooling.

The overall literacy rate of the nation is high, but varies considerably by region. In the Northern Territory, less than half of all students complete grade 12 while almost all students in the Australian Capital Territory do. Those who leave school before age 17 usually enroll in a vocational program or enter the workforce full-time.

Special services exist to support Aboriginal children and adults as well as those living in remote areas. Some students who live in very remote areas attend *schools of the air*, correspondence schools that operate by mail or, more recently, over the Internet. Students complete primary and secondary school from home, under the supervision of teachers with whom they communicate over two-way radios, computers, televisions, and fax machines.

The federal government funds more than 40 universities and colleges. Students pay fees to cover part of the cost of their education and the government pays the rest. Australia's few private universities charge much higher tuition fees. Most students who go on to attend universities do so in their home states.

Religion

Australia has no official state religion as the constitution forbids it. The constitution does guarantee religious freedom. More than two-thirds of Australians are Christian, with 30% representing a variety of Protestant religions and another 25% who are Catholic. The Anglican Church, which began in England, is the largest of the Protestant denominations. Australia also has small percentages of Orthodox, Buddhists, and Muslims, which have increased sharply since the late 1900's, along with small groups of Jews and Hindus. Religious affiliation tends to reflect the backgrounds of immigrants. The Aboriginal population has its own spiritual belief system, which greatly influences everyday life.

Health Care

Australians have a relatively high life expectancy, good nutrition, and favorable living conditions compared with the rest of the world. Those living in remote areas benefit from the Royal Flying Doctor Service, which provides emergency medical care. Some Aboriginal communities in the Outback suffer from the effects of poor living conditions, which include trachoma, leprosy, and tuberculosis.

AUSTRALIA'S GOVERNMENT

Australia is a parliamentary democracy, based somewhat on the British model. Its Constitution went into effect upon its independence from the United Kingdom in 1901 and has since been amended several times. The British monarch is the official chief of state, represented by a governor-general. The prime minister serves as the head of government.

The prime minister is the leader of the majority party. He or she nominates members of Parliament to serve as Cabinet members. The prime minister also recommends a governor-general to be appointed by the British monarch. The Australian Parliament consists of a Senate and a House of Representatives. The 76 Senators represent the states and territories equally. They serve six-year terms. The 150 members of the House of Representatives each represent an electoral district. They serve three-year terms.

Australia has six states and ten territories. The six states are New South Wales, Queensland, South Australia, Tasmania, Victoria, and Western Australia. Of the ten territories, the Australian Capital Territory and the Northern Territory are on the mainland of the continent and generally function as states with slightly differing government bodies. Norfolk Island has been granted limited self-government. The seven other territories, governed through an administrator, are the Ashmore and Cartier Islands, the Australian Antarctic Territory, Christmas Island, the Cocos (Keeling) Islands, the Jervis Bay Territory, the Territory of Heard Island and the McDonald Islands.

The Australian Defense Force (ADF) consists of the Australian Army, the Royal Australian Navy (which includes a Naval Aviation Force), the Royal Australian Air Force, and the Joint Operations Command. Both males and females can voluntarily serve in the military at age 17.

AUSTRALIAN CULTURE

Australia's state and federal governments have done much to support art and culture. Capital cities have art galleries, museums, and performing arts centers. Government funding helps support opera, theater, and dance companies, as well as individual artists and performers.

Architecture

European immigrants of the 1800's brought with them Georgian and Victorian styles of architecture. Originating in England, these styles were adapted to Australia's hot climate with the addition of wide *verandas*, or porches. Today, these types of structures are often preserved as historic buildings.

Australia's modern architecture reflects an international style. Concrete, steel, and glass skyscrapers rise from all of the large cities. In 1973,

Victorian-era architecture of the Hotel Shamrock in Bendigo

The famous Sydney Opera House

Danish architect Jørn Utzon designed the unique Sydney Opera House to look like a series of sails.

Literature

Australia's earliest literature began in the oral tradition of the Aboriginal peoples. They used storytelling and song to entertain, instruct, and reveal spiritual truths. The arrival of Europeans largely destroyed this tradition, replacing it with their own style of literature. Stories of colonists' lives, and novels set in this exotic new locale, became popular in the mid-1800's.

Visual Arts

Today, some Australian artists continue the long tradition of Aboriginal art forms, including rock painting, rock carving, bark painting, sand sculpture, wood sculpture, and body decoration. Some of these, such as the painted wooden boomerang, have become popular souvenirs for tourists.

Performing Arts

Australia has several dance companies, including the world-renowned Australian Ballet. The Bangarra Dance Theater, which draws from ancient traditions of Australia's indigenous peoples, performed in the opening ceremonies of the 2000 Summer Olympic Games. States also have their own professional symphony orchestras.

Australian music draws from both the Aboriginal and European traditions. A characteristic instrument of the Aborigines, the didgeridoo, makes a low, drone sound. European influence has brought musical styles from classical to pop to opera.

Theater and Film

Each state has its own company of professional actors who perform classical and modern plays year-round. Filmmaking began in Australia with its first feature film in 1906, but the industry nearly died out in the 1930's due to competition from the United Kingdom and the United States. Since the 1960's, however, the industry has rebounded to produce some of the world's most well-known actors and directors.

Food and Drink

The Australian diet is based largely on European influence and the prevalence of available meat. Large cattle stations across the country have made beef the most popular meat. Australians also enjoy poultry, pork, lamb, and mutton. Barbecues (called "the barbie") are an essential part of Australian cooking. Traditional Aboriginal cuisine includes kangaroo, wombat, turtle, eel, emu, snake, and witchetty grubs (larvae of the ghost moth). Australians love vegemite, a salty yeast extract that is a staple in the Australian diet.

British customs have long influenced Australian food choices, and immigration from mainland Europe since the 1950's has brought Italian, Greek, and other styles of cooking. The more recent influx of Asian immigrants has brought an abundance of Chinese restaurants, along with Indian, Japanese, Thai, and Vietnamese cooking influences.

Older Australians tend to drink tea, in the British tradition, while younger Australians tend to prefer coffee. Since the mid-1900's, coffee consumption has more than tripled. Beer is a popular drink, but it is becoming overshadowed by the growing wine industry in Australia.

AUSTRALIA'S WILDLIFE

Isolated from the rest of the world for thousands of years, Australia developed a unique array of native plants and animals. Some of these, like the kangaroo and the emu, became national symbols. Later, people introduced new species that have thrived on, and even threatened, the continent. Since European settlement, some 20 mammal species have become extinct, along with 20 bird species. Many other animal species have become endangered, including

Koala

50 mammals, 30 amphibians, 50 reptiles, and 50 birds.

Animals

Australia is well-known for its unique and wide assortment of *marsupials*. This group of mammals give birth to underdeveloped young, who then mature in a pouch on the mother's abdomen. Marsupials include kangaroos, koalas, wallabies, and wombats, but Australia has about 200 different species of marsupials that live all over the country. Outside of Australia, marsupials are much less common, living only in parts of North and South America and other islands near Australia.

Kangaroo

Two of Australia's strangest animals are the platypus and the echidna. The platypus, which lives only in

Echidna

Australia, looks a bit like a beaver with a duck's bill. The echidna, which lives only in Australia and New Guinea, resembles a cross between a porcupine and an anteater. These two odd mammals are the only ones in the world that lay eggs instead of giving birth to live young.

Australia also has a variety of over 700 species of native birds. Two of these, the emu and the cassowary, are quite large and cannot fly. Australians across the country recognize the loud, harsh call of the kookaburra. In addition to many brightly-colored cockatoos, parakeets, and other parrots, Australia is home to the world's only black swans.

A thorny devil lizard

The country's native reptiles include over 140 species of snakes and hundreds of lizards. Many of the snakes are venomous, like the deadly taipans, death adders, and tiger snakes. Though some of the lizards may look intimidating, none of them are venomous. In addition, Australia has 190 species of frogs and around 100,000 insects and spiders. Many of the spiders are poisonous and can be deadly to humans. The large saltwater crocodile has been known to eat humans.

Plants

Several types of plants and trees have adapted to Australia's harsh climate, providing food and shelter for people and animals. The acacia tree, of which Australia has over 700 species, grows as shrubs in dry areas and as trees in areas of heavier rainfall. Acacia trees, which Australians call *wattles*, are the most common trees across the country. They often grow brightly colored flowers and bear their seeds in pods.

Australia also has about 500 species of eucalyptuses, which they call *gum trees*. This widespread plant provides the only food koalas eat. Its

Boab trees in the Outback

leathery leaves contain a fragrant oil that is highly flammable. Among the tallest trees in the world, the eucalyptus once grew only in Australia and some nearby islands.

Acacia tree in the Outback

The unusual boab tree has a characteristic swollen trunk and root-like limbs. Australia also grows many types of palms, shrubs, and grasses, as well as a few pines. While wildflowers bloom only rarely, a heavy rain can bring thousands of desert plants into bloom.

Introduced Species

Very few mammals lived in Australia before the first settlers arrived. These included the marsupials along with bats, mice, rats, platypuses, and echidnas. The Aborigines brought a type of dog called a *dingo*. Today, wild dingoes are Australia's main predators. Later, European settlers brought a wide array of domesticated animals and livestock, including cats, cattle, deer, foxes, goats, hogs, horses, rabbits, sheep, camels, and water buffaloes. They also brought a variety of birds and plants. Since then, many introduced species have escaped or been released into the wild where they have become pests. Domestic cats threaten native birds and other small animals. Wild rabbits have damaged crops and grazing lands. At one point, the rabbit problem became so serious that Australian officials purposely introduced diseases to control the rabbit population. Other pests include camels, cane toads, and water buffaloes.

THE ECONOMY OF AUSTRALIA

Australia differs from most other developed countries because its wealth comes mainly from agriculture and mining, not manufacturing. Australia produces, processes, and exports crops, livestock, wool, and mineral resources. As a result, it has become one of the richest nations in the world. In the past several decades, services have grown to become a more important sector of Australia's economy.

Australia is the world's largest exporter of coal, accounting for almost a third of global coal exports. It also exports iron ore, gold, meat, wool, wheat, machinery, and transportation equipment. Australia imports computers, office equipment, crude oil, electrical appliances, medicine, and petroleum. Its main trade partners are China, Japan, South Korea, Singapore, Germany, and the United States.

Agriculture

Although farmland covers about half of the country, it produces less than 4% of the GDP and employs a similarly low percentage of workers. The agricultural industry relies heavily on machines, so a small number of workers are able to feed the entire nation. In general, Australia's soils are poor and require the addition of several nutrients. The arid climate means irrigation is critical in most agricultural areas.

Farmers grow wheat, barley, sugarcane, and fruits on less than 10% of the farmland. Every state grows wheat, the country's leading grain crop. The majority of the land is used to graze cattle and sheep. Farmers also raise poultry and hogs. These animals produce meat, eggs, dairy products,

A caravan of camels in Northern Australia

and wool. Australia is the top wool producer in the world, providing about a third of the global total. However, collapsing wool prices in the 1990's have hurt this industry. Many old farms have been revived by Australia's growing wine industry. Farmers grow grapes and make wine in all Australian states. The nation has recently become one of the world's top wine producers.

Forestry and Fishing

Australia's forests cover about one-fifth of the continent and are concentrated in the Eastern Highlands and coastal areas where rainfall is heaviest. Eucalyptus trees dominate the forests, but their extremely hard wood limits their usefulness. Australians use and export some eucalyptus paper, floorboards, and furniture. Tree farms grow softer timber, like Monterey pines, that have been imported.

The nation has a small but profitable fishing industry based in the coastal waters. Shellfish like lobsters and scallops make up most of the commercial catch, along with sardines and tuna. Oysters also provide food and pearls. Australia has a growing aquaculture industry, which raises water plants and animals for sale.

Mineral and Energy Resources

Although Australia has rich mineral resources, many deposits lie far from major cities. Mining is expensive because companies must construct roads or railways to transport minerals to factories as well as housing for workers and their families. Therefore, Australia has depended heavily on foreign investors to finance mining operations.

Since the 1800's, Australia has mined and exported large amounts of copper, tin, gold, silver, lead, and zinc. More recently, it has discovered and begun mining bauxite, coal, iron ore, uranium, nickel, tungsten, rare earth elements, mineral sands, lead, zinc, diamonds, opals, natural gas, and petroleum. Australia is a leading producer of many mineral resources.

Much of Australia's electric power comes from thermal stations that depend on the nation's vast coal reserves. Some dams provide hydroelectric power, but in general unpredictable river volumes limit this option. The exception is Tasmania, which has rugged terrain and regular rainfall. It produces almost all of its required electricity from hydroelectric plants. Solar and wind energy are promising, but underdeveloped, energy resources in Australia.

Manufacturing

Australia is unusual among developed nations in that it imports more manufactured goods than it exports. Although the nation can produce most of the consumer goods it requires, it depends on trade with other countries to obtain producer goods, like machinery and construction equipment. Most of Australia's manufacturing deals with mining, industrial equipment, transportation equipment, food processing, chemicals, and steel. It accounts for 30% of the nation's GDP. More than half of the nation's manufactured goods, and half of its factory workers, come from the industrial areas around Sydney and Melbourne.

Services

About two-thirds of the GDP, and 75% of the labor force, work in the services sector. These include community, social, personal, business, and financial services. The nation's many natural attractions bring millions of foreign tourists every year. Foreigners visit wildlife sanctuaries, beaches, the Great Barrier Reef, the Australian Alps, and Uluru, contributing to restaurant, hotel, retail, and transportation industries. The growth of tourism is limited by the distance and expense of traveling from North America and Europe. However, plenty of tourists visit from nearby New Zealand, the Pacific Islands, China, Japan, and Southeast Asia.

Transportation

In such a large, widespread country, reliable transportation is important to families, businesses, and government services. Almost all families own automobiles, as paved roads connect coastal cities and some of the larger inland cities. In the Outback, many roads are unpaved and roadside services are limited. Therefore, many Australians depend on air travel in the interior. Ranchers, traveling doctors, and others use light aircraft to travel the Outback. Large cities have international commercial airports. Trucks, railroads, and ships haul freight from one city to another or from remote farms and mines to processing plants in cities. Foreign ships carry most of Australia's international exports.

Communication

The Australian government owns, at least in part, the postal and telephone systems. Independent government agencies, like the Australian Postal Corporation, run these systems. Almost all homes, except in the Outback, have telephones, and cell phone usage has increased dramatically since the mid-1990's. In the isolated Outback, people communicate via two-way radio where they do not have cellular phone service or, increasingly, they use the Internet.

Almost all Australian families also own at least one television and a radio. Many own computers and have Internet service. The nation publishes dozens of newspapers, including some in foreign languages.

AUSTRALIA'S HISTORY

Australia's history can be divided into two distinct and widely separated settlements of people groups. The first, that of the Australian Aborigines, remained relatively unchanged until the second, that of Europeans, began just 200 or so years ago. European settlement brought a wave of change that modernized the continent and led to its current status as one of the world's most developed nations.

EARLY AUSTRALIAN HISTORY

Scientists and historians believe the first people came to Australia from the islands of Southeast Asia. At that time, lower sea levels would have provided more land bridges, though they may have used watercraft as well. The first settlers arrived in the northern part of the continent. They likely followed the coastline around Australia and then moved inland, following rivers. Settlements spread to all reaches of the continent, including Tasmania, which was connected by a now-submerged land bridge until sea levels rose and Tasmania became an isolated island.

In the past 3,000 years or so, the Aboriginal population increased and the dingo, a wild dog, appeared on the continent. The Aborigines developed complex societies and spiritual systems, though they did not advance from the societal stage of hunting and gathering and using simple technologies. They grew no crops and had no domesticated animals other than the dingo. As nomadic people, each group traveled within its own territory to hunt, fish, and gather food, without forming permanent settlements. Although they did not plant crops, they managed the land by setting fire to the dry grasses. This allowed for new growth, which they could eat or would attract animals for them to hunt. It also made traveling by foot easier. In one area, Aboriginal people built dams to trap eels and aid fishing.

Aboriginal peoples used stone, shell, bone, wood, and fiber to create tools and weapons. They also had an extensive cross-continental system of trade, in which they used shells, stone, tools, and *pituri*, a nicotine-bearing desert plant. Their societies had leaders and complex laws. Separate groups interacted with one another to trade and share news and ideas. Aborigines also produced artwork, using *ocher*, a mixture of clay and iron oxide.

The Aborigines and their ancestors hold a spiritual belief called *the Dreaming*. It includes concepts of creation, mythic beings, human beginnings, divine power, and rules for social life. Aboriginal peoples interacted with the spiritual world through dreams, rituals, myths, dances, and objects. Some of these traditions have been preserved into modern times.

By the time Europeans arrived in the late 1700's, Aboriginal peoples had successfully adapted to the entire continent, from hot, damp tropical rainforests to extremely dry deserts. They spoke more than 200 different languages and numbered somewhere in the hundreds of thousands. Although they had a rich culture of art, spirituality, language, social structure, and knowledge of the land, the Aborigines were dismissed by Europeans as primitive. As a result, they were oppressed and discriminated against until just recently.

EARLY MODERN HISTORY

Asian Fishing Fleets

Around 1700, Asian fishing fleets began sailing boats called *perahus* from Makassar to Australia. Seasonal winds called monsoons blew them to Australia, where they stayed for several months until changing winds blew them back home. These interactions, mainly on the northwestern coasts, brought new influences to the Aborigines. Although the relationship with the perahus continued, a stronger influence came to Australia, beginning a few decades later.

European Explorers

Europeans had long believed in a vast southern landmass they called *Terra Australis Incognita*, meaning *Unknown Southland*. In 1606, Dutch explorer Willem Jansz and Spanish navigator Luis Vaez de Torres both sailed separate expeditions along the north coast of the continent. Jansz and his crew came ashore but clashed violently with the Aboriginal people, whom he called "barbarians."

The Dutch continued to explore the continent for the next hundred years. Captain Abel Tasman sailed along the coast of Tasmania in 1642, claiming it for the Netherlands. He later charted the north coast of Australia, naming it New Holland.

The Dutch gave up interest in Australia after finding the land harsh and uninviting, with violent natives and a lack of natural treasures. In 1688, English navigator William Dampier visited the northwestern coast where he mapped the land and recorded descriptions of the plants, animals, and people. Like the Dutch, he found the land wholly unappealing.

In 1768, the British sent Captain James Cook on an expedition to Tahiti with secret instructions to claim the great southern continent for Britain. After sailing from

A replica of James Cook's ship the Endeavor

Tahiti and around New Zealand, Cook and his crew arrived on the southeast coast of Australia in 1770. This more temperate region left a better impression on Cook and his crew than previous explorers had found in the northwest. They traveled north along the coast and struck part of the Great Barrier Reef. After repairing the ship, they continued as far north as Cape York, and claimed the east coast for Britain, which Cook named New South Wales. Cook brought back a report of favorable lands, suitable for farming and livestock. Neither he nor the British government concerned themselves with the Aboriginal land management system.

British Settlements

In 1788, Britain sent its First Fleet to Australia—a convoy of 11 ships carrying convicts and soldiers. The British government sent convicts to colonies. This removed criminals from British society and overcrowded jails and built up British settlements around the world. Australia seemed an ideal location for a new *penal* colony, or one used to house criminals. It was far enough from Britain to discourage return and it had land suitable for agriculture. British officials felt that convicts could start over in the new colony and lead productive lives.

The First Fleet brought about 1,000 people to Botany Bay, of which 750 were convicts and their families. However, the summer conditions were not nearly as hospitable as Cook had found there in autumn. The group settled further north in what is now Sydney. The settlers desperately needed fresh food to fight off the effects of scurvy, a vitamin deficiency disease. They struggled against starvation for about two years, until supply ships had returned and crops began to grow.

The town of Sydney developed in a somewhat disorderly layout. Settlers got their water from a small stream called Tank Stream. Government officers settled on the east side of the stream, while the convicts and their families settled on the west side. Military officers and soldiers settled to the south. Although officials later tried to establish a more orderly town inland in Parramatta, Sydney continued to grow and thrive.

The British convicts were mainly working-class laborers who quickly began building their neighborhoods. Though they didn't own the land, they lived and worked on it with little interference from the British soldiers. The colony did not resemble a jail in any way. Convicts lived in homes with their families where they raised children. They built roads, bridges, and buildings and ran businesses. Sydney grew into a town much like any small village in England.

Encounters between these first settlers and the Aboriginal people varied. Sometimes they learned from one another and interacted peacefully, and at other times they stole from one another and acted violently. Captain Arthur Phillip, who was the officer in charge, tried to work for peace and understanding between the Europeans and the Aborigines. After a period of generally positive relations, the Aboriginal people become upset with losing their land to Europeans. Crowded out of their coastal lands, some had trouble obtaining enough food. In addition, disease, which was likely smallpox, spread quickly among the Aboriginal people and killed great numbers of their population.

British settlements quickly expanded into other areas of Australia, including Norfolk Island and Tasmania. Philip and his marines left in 1792 and were replaced by the New South Wales Corps. This British regiment took economic control of the colony, becoming very powerful and trading in rum as currency. In an effort to control the rum trade and the power of the corps, the British government appointed sea captain William Bligh as governor in 1806. Bligh sternly proclaimed British ownership of most of the land in Sydney. With tensions rising over property rights and other issues, members of the New South Wales Corps attacked Bligh's home, arrested him, and took control of the government. The British regained control under Governor Lachlan Macquarie, who brought his own troops to replace the New South Wales Corps, in 1809.

Macquarie led with a much gentler hand than Bligh. He granted colonists and convicts ownership of their existing lands, and allowed for the continued trade in rum. He also developed new towns, and ordered construction of bridges, roads, a hospital, a bank, and a church. He treated convicts and *emancipists* (pardoned convicts) very well, allowing the latter to travel and work in government service. Many free colonists and British officers criticized Macquarie's liberal treatment of convicts and emancipists. He was later recalled to England and the government enforced stricter guidelines for convicts in Australia.

Australia's population grew quickly in the early 1800's. Tens of thousands of convicts arrived and provided forced labor for the development of new towns. Meanwhile, the first wave of convicts had children who were now raising free families of their own. Free immigrants continued to arrive from Europe, attracted by free land and cheap labor from convicts. The British government also assisted particular populations in moving to Australia. These included skilled workers, who were needed to work in the new settlements, and single women, who were needed as domestic workers. By 1850, Australia's population had grown to about half a million people.

Opposition arose over the transport of convicts to Australia and their assignment as forced laborers to wealthy free colonists. In 1840, the British government stopped convict transport to New South Wales, but continued it elsewhere in eastern Australia until 1853. Some Australians became upset at the loss of cheap labor. Many were ashamed that their thriving new colony had gained a reputation as a corrupt land overrun by unruly convicts. Convict transport resumed in Western Australia from 1850 to 1868, as settlements in that region required cheap labor.

Mapping the Continent

As Europeans first settled the east and west coasts of Australia, they did not know for certain whether the land was one large landmass or separate islands. Portions of the north and south coasts remained uncharted. French and British explorers competed to discover and claim new lands in Australia. With growing cattle and wool industries, both sought lands suitable for grazing.

In the early 1800's, British explorers Matthew Flinders and George Bass explored the southern coast. They proved that Tasmania (then called Van Diemen's Land) was indeed an island. Flinders became the first European to sail completely around the entire continent, discovering that it truly was one huge landmass. He suggested the name *Australia*, which Governor Macquarie adopted for the continent.

During this time of discovery, European explorers often relied heavily on help from Aboriginal guides. The Aborigines served as guides, found food and water, and communicated with other Aboriginal groups they encountered. Often, these guides were not acknowledged in the historical records of the explorers.

In 1813, Australian settlers journeyed across the Blue Mountains west of Sydney. They brought back news of good grazing land in the continent's interior. As ranchers moved their flocks into this land, the grazing destroyed the native pastures. The animals couldn't eat the tough, prickly weeds that grew up in place of the grass, so ranchers continually sought new grazing lands. This great need to support Australia's fastest-growing sector of the economy led to more exploration of the continent's interior.

British explorers spread out to the north and south. They followed inland rivers to the west. They discovered the interior contained little but dry desert. Exploration by land and by river was dangerous and difficult. In 1848, Prussian explorer Friedrich Wilhelm Ludwig Leichhardt disappeared without a trace, along with six companions and 300 animals, in an attempt to be the first to cross the continent from east to west. However, this period of exploration led to new settlements that became major cities, and forged land routes from one region to another.

The Early Colonies

As ranchers and *graziers*, people who raise sheep, spread into the newly explored interior, the government attempted to limit their land holdings. The English market for fine wool had grown, and graziers had brought many sheep to Australia and had bred many more. They moved further and further from the reaches of government, as they followed their flocks to new grazing land. In 1826, the governor declared limits on the land that could be settled. Graziers who went beyond these limits and settled illegally were called *squatters*. Soon the squatters had occupied so much illegal territory that the government was forced to grant annual licenses, allowing them to use the land.

At first, the British government awarded land to deserving individuals for just a small fee. They thought it would encourage reform among convicts, and foster agriculture. However, reformers soon convinced the government to charge higher prices for land and use the profits to help desirable immigrants come to Australia. In 1831, the British government instituted these changes under the Ripon Regulations. However, they made no distinction between plots of land, selling fertile and poor, steep and flat all at the same price. Due to the price increase and the rise of squatters, the demand for land fell.

Meanwhile, the British had established four new official colonies. Modern-day Tasmania, then called Van Diemen's Land, became a colony separate from New South Wales in 1825. It established successful farming and grazing enterprises along with overseas trade. Although it suffered a depression when Britain stopped transporting convicts for cheap labor, Tasmania became self-governing in 1856.

Western Australia, established in 1829, almost didn't survive. Its free immigrants found the land unsuitable for farming and lacked laborers. The colonists finally convinced the British government to send convicts as cheap labor, which stabilized the economy.

In 1836, a London banker bought a large tract of land that became South Australia. Rather than using convicts, he sold land to free immigrants. He appointed a board of commissioners to oversee land sales. When the new colony faced bankruptcy in 1841, the British government took over completely.

The colony of Victoria was established in 1851 after squatters who had spread out from Melbourne and Sydney overran the territory and demanded separation from New South Wales.

Settlement did not come without conflict in Australia. The Aborigines at first attempted to bring Europeans into their culture and legal systems. However, the Europeans generally saw the Aborigines as an inferior race who had no claim to the land. The official stance of the British government was to establish friendly relations with the Aboriginal people and protect them. However, this order was followed to wildly varying degrees. Governors like Macquarie, some colonists, and missionaries treated the Aborigines with respect. They offered education and land grants. However, other authorities sometimes revoked land ownership when the Aboriginal land became desirable to Europeans. Especially in the frontier, squatters took land from Aborigines without compensation. These conflicts sometimes led to violent clashes and bloody massacres. Although the Aboriginal warriors fought bravely and mounted clever attacks, they were no match for Europeans on horseback with rapid-fire rifles.

Aboriginal societies crumbled as the people suffered disease, attacks, starvation, and isolation. Many Aborigines became dependent on alcohol, which became a major problem. Others clung to the remaining opportunities, working on European cattle ranches or retreating to the outskirts of towns.

Discovery of Gold

In 1851, prospectors found major gold deposits in New South Wales and Victoria. A gold rush immediately followed, as Australians flocked to Victoria in search of riches. Men left jobs and families behind, leaving the city of Melbourne practically deserted. By early 1852, miners and their families also began arriving from overseas. Chinese miners who arrived faced fierce racism from Europeans.

At first, individual miners panned for gold in streams and dug shafts. Later, companies used heavy equipment to dig deep mines into the earth. Tent towns cropped up around mining areas. The government charged a huge fee for miners' licenses and punished those caught mining without one. This led to protests that erupted in violence in Eureka. After 30 miners and 6 soldiers died in the fighting there, the government revised its rights for miners.

Prospectors later discovered gold fields in Queensland, Tasmania, South Australia, and Western Australia. This boom brought new settlers to Western Australia, but the effects of the gold rush were not all positive. Men abandoned their wives and children, and colonies like South Australia experienced a population decline. People worried that those who acquired sudden wealth would destroy the morals of their society. Eventually, the gold rush improved life in Australia. Farmers found new markets for wool and meat, infrastructure grew up around mining towns, providing additional jobs. In addition to gold, mining industries sprung up around discoveries of coal, copper, tin, shale oil, diamonds, silver, lead, and opals.

Becoming a Nation

By the 1850's, Australia had grown considerably in wealth and in its free population. Colonists demanded freedom to self-govern, and the British government took steps to comply with the request. Colonies set up constitutions and governing bodies, while Britain handled defense and foreign affairs. After 1858, all adult males in several Colonies could vote for their Assemblies. In 1894, women gained the right to vote, making Australia the second nation to grant women voting rights (after New Zealand).

From the 1860's to the 1890's, unsuccessful gold miners turned their attention toward farming. The colonial governments attempted to redistribute land held by squatters. It sold off blocks of land under the provision that the owners live on and farm their plot. Oftentimes, this effort failed as the new owners had little agricultural knowledge or experience and the land was often unsuitable for farming. In addition, squatters prevented the new owners from taking legal possession of the land.

As the government replotted land and invested in irrigation to solve these problems, explorers continued to probe the interior of the continent. Still a dangerous undertaking, explorers managed to cross the continent from east to west in 1856 and from south to north in 1861. At that time, an Overland Telegraph line ran from Port Augusta in the south to Port Darwin in the north. Explorers began to focus their attention on exploring the country between this telegraph line and the settled areas of Western Australia. Their findings opened up new areas for grazing.

Meanwhile, all of Australia's capital cities (Sydney, Hobart, Brisbane, Perth, Melbourne, Adelaide, and Darwin) grew in size and importance. Sydney and Melbourne rivaled one another for the title of largest city. The development of mass transit, such as trams and trolleys, allowed the urban population to spread further into the suburbs. Workers no longer had to live close enough to work to walk. Middle-class families bought detached houses on large suburban blocks. Colonial governments scrambled to support their growing, spreading populations. They made great efforts to bring clean water to city dwellers and to carry sewage away. One by one, cities improved roads and footpaths and obtained gas lighting for streets. At the end of the 1800's, cities began switching from gas to electric street lighting.

From 1850 to 1901, more than 1.3 million immigrants came to Australia. Most came from the United Kingdom, Ireland, and other parts of Europe. Australians generally welcomed and encouraged immigration, except that from China and the Pacific Islands. Anti-Chinese attitudes that had persisted since the gold boom led to a ban on Chinese immigrants in the 1850's. In addition, the government outlawed importing labor from the Pacific Islands. This measure was in part a response to the complaint that plantation owners were treating Islanders as slave laborers and in part an effort to limit non-European immigration.

Women also faced difficult conditions in Australia during this time. The male population far outnumbered the female population, especially in rural areas. Women had few opportunities for work outside the home, and the available jobs demanded long, difficult hours for low pay. Women had to depend on husbands or fathers to support them. Those whose husbands abandoned them for the mine fields or other reasons usually fell into poverty. Families tended to be large, with about seven children, and it was almost impossible for a woman to support her children on her own.

Men and children also faced difficult working conditions in most unskilled jobs. Along with women, they worked long hours for low wages. Workplaces were hot and crowded with little fresh air. Companies had no safeguards for operating heavy machinery, so accidents occurred frequently. Workers had no social security or unemployment benefits. In 1873, Victoria became the first colony to regulate working conditions and outlaw the employment of children. It also established a minimum wage for different positions. Other colonies followed suit.

In 1869, Tasmania made school attendance mandatory for children. Up until that point, children in rural and urban areas regularly missed classes to work.

The discovery of gold in the 1850's and 1860's had set off a long boom, or period of strong economic growth, in Australia. The population more than tripled and overseas investors put money into mining projects and other businesses. Agriculture continued to grow as graziers found new grazing lands and water sources and technology improved. Farmers and graziers began using wire fences, shearing machines, and refrigeration to improve processes. South Australia became a major producer of wheat. Manufacturing industries rose up around the need to process food and minerals. They also provided goods for the demands of the growing population. Towns became better connected by waterways, roads, railways, and telegraph lines.

The Depression of the 1890's

The boom years came to an end in the late 1880's. Pastures became overcrowded, forcing animals to compete for food. In addition, wild rabbits plagued many parts of the country, stripping the ground bare and leading to soil erosion. A series of drought years led to crop failures. Even the new railroads caused problems as engineers had used different *gauges*, or track sizes, from one state to another, preventing easy transportation between states. Wool prices fell, and debt to foreign investors reached an all-time high. The United Kingdom itself faced financial problems and pulled out of many projects in Australia, leading to unemployment. By the 1890's, a full-blown depression had spread to all parts of the continent except Western Australia, which continued to ride a gold boom.

The depression revealed underlying problems in Australia's banking and labor systems. With too many banks and too little regulation, the banks did not have enough cash to cover the many withdrawals during the depression. Labor unions, which had existed for decades, continued to fight for workers' rights. However, with unemployment so high, strikes were unsuccessful. Whenever union members went on strike to protest working conditions, employers easily hired many out-of-work laborers in their place. Employers formed associations to fight back against the demands of unions.

Female social activists rose up in the 1880's and 1890's to lead the fight for women's rights. They sought equal voting rights, land ownership, education, and employment opportunities. In many cases, the Australian government complied with the women's requests. It amended divorce laws that had been unfair toward women, introduced universal education, and granted women the right to vote.

Despite the problems brought on by the depression, Australia began to see itself as a more unified nation, rather than a collection of fiercely independent colonies. The telegraph and railroad had brought them closer together.

Outside factors also contributed to feelings of Australian nationalism. As France and Germany established colonies in the Pacific region, Australians felt the common need to protect themselves and their land.

Increasingly global markets made it necessary for the colonies to unify their approach to trade and tariffs.

Independence

Some Australians wanted to sever ties completely with the United Kingdom and become a unified democracy, while those at the other end of the spectrum wanted the colonies to become provinces of the United Kingdom. Five-time premier of New South Wales, Sir Henry Parkes, helped Australians land somewhere in the middle as a federation. This meant that the separate colonies would establish one federal government, but maintain ties with the United Kingdom in some matters. After several meetings, drafts of the Constitution, and votes, Australians presented their plan for government to the British Parliament in 1900. The Parliament and Queen Victoria approved the Constitution, and the Commonwealth of Australia came into being on January 1, 1901.

The new Constitution allowed the federal government to raise revenue through taxes. It established two houses in Parliament, based on the model of the United States Congress. It created a high court and the position of governor general to represent the interests of the United Kingdom. The Constitution established the national capital of Canberra in New South Wales. Australians would retain their status as British citizens and the monarch would continue as head of state. At first, Western Australia did not take part in the meetings because officials there thought becoming a federation would hurt its economy. However, after the Constitution was presented to the British Parliament, Western Australia voted for the federation.

Although injustice toward Aboriginal people continued under the new government, many improvements also took place in Australian society in the early 1900's. The economy recovered, and production of wheat, wool, and other products increased. The government enacted social programs, such as pensions for the elderly and sick, workers' compensation for those injured on the job, and a maternity allowance for white women who gave birth to children.

MODERN HISTORY

World War I (1914–1918)

The United Kingdom's declaration of war on Germany in 1914 automatically involved Australia in the war. Australians eagerly supported the war effort. Tens of thousands of men enlisted in the Australian and New Zealand Army Corps (ANZAC) and were sent to train in Egypt. The Australian navy also got involved, sinking a German ship off the Cocos Islands in 1914. The ANZAC earned recognition for its fighting in the Gallipoli Peninsula of Turkey. Although they lost 8,000 Australians, 2,700 New Zealanders, and suffered a military failure, the effort established them as legendary fighters. To this day, Australians celebrate ANZAC Day each year to commemorate this military effort. After Gallipoli, the ANZAC troops fought mainly on the Western Front in Europe until the end of the war.

The war had a negative impact on the home front in Australia. Workers were unhappy as prices rose, wages stayed stagnant, and jobs were cut. Australians of German descent faced discrimination and oppression, with many sent to internment camps where they were held as virtual prisoners until after the war ended. Australian officials changed many German place names to English or Aboriginal ones.

With patriotism low and anti-war sentiments high, military enrollment dropped. The federal government proposed *conscription*, or compulsory military service, to maintain the Australian Imperial Force (AIF), but the proposal was defeated on two separate occasions.

By the end of the war, Australia had suffered the highest casualty rate of any British force with 60,000 killed and 156,000 wounded or captured. Australia entered a period of economic depression that lasted until about 1936. During that time, many political and social changes took place in the country.

New political parties rose to power, and industrial development increased dramatically. Australia instituted programs to help returning servicemen and servicewomen acclimate to civilian life. These programs included education, vocational training, loans, and government employment. Just as these soldiers began to reenter society, a worldwide influenza epidemic came to Australia. In 1919, about 12,000 Australians died as a result of the contagious disease.

In the 1920's, immigration surged once again after many British and other Europeans were left homeless by the war. American influence spread across the country in the form of new forms of entertainment by radio programs and motion pictures. Aboriginal people and their white supporters organized associations and protests that advocated for Aboriginal rights. With the return of soldiers from the war, some state governments took back land from Aborigines and gave it to whites to farm. Some cities moved Aborigines to camps far-removed from the city centers. Perhaps worst of all, the government continued a decades-long program of child removal in which Aboriginal children were often taken from their parents.

The worldwide Depression that began in 1929 hit Australians hard. Prices on exports dropped significantly and about a third of workers lost their jobs. Families lost their homes and became reliant on soup kitchens to eat. The Australian government had difficulty supporting its people through this crisis, as it could barely keep up with its debt payments from the years of expansion. Australia began to recover from the Depression along with the rest of the world in 1933. By 1939, unemployment had dropped to about 10%.

World War II (1939–1945)

In 1939, Australia entered World War II on the side of the Allies (including the United Kingdom,) having already been warned that the United Kingdom would be unable to help defend Australia. The government formed the Second AIF and reintroduced conscription for home defense. The Second AIF departed to fight in North Africa and Greece. In 1941, however, Japanese aggression in the Pacific brought the war to Australia's doorstep. The Japanese launched air raids against Darwin and sent submarines into Sydney Harbour. The Australian prime minister recalled the Second AIF to defend the country, while simultaneously making plans to evacuate if necessary.

Australia reached out to the United States military, which had entered the Pacific fight against Japan. Together, the two forces drove Japan out of Australian territory. The Japanese surrendered in 1945 and an Australian representative attended the formalities. Despite the victory, Australia once again suffered heavy losses in the war. Many soldiers died of malaria fighting in the tropical jungles of the Pacific Islands. Thousands of Australians, including female nurses, were taken as prisoners of war. They suffered hard labor, deplorable conditions, and execution in prisoner camps. Meanwhile, Japanese prisoners of war held at Cowra in New South Wales attempted a mass escape in which 230 Japanese and 4 Australians were killed.

During the war, Australian women served as nurses or in auxiliary roles in the military, and also served on the home front. They worked on farms and in factories, filling in positions vacated by men. For the first time, they received wages equal to those of men.

The end of the war brought further social changes to Australia. Manufacturing increased, the status of women in the workplace improved, and multicultural immigration slowly resumed. Once again, the government provided returning servicemen with land, tuition assistance, pensions, and medical care.

At first, Australian officials welcomed only British immigrants, but its White Australia policy crumbled as immigrants from mainland Europe arrived in the hundreds of thousands between 1947 and 1960. With the increased population and increased manufacturing, the economy grew rapidly. Wool and agricultural prices rose and the government expanded social welfare programs. The government brought several industries, such as telecommunications, air transportation, and coal production, under its control, but many citizens resisted these changes.

During the Cold War of the 1950's, when democratic and Communist nations became hostile toward one another, some Australians feared Communist influences. However, an attempt to outlaw the Communist Party was deemed unconstitutional. Australia signed a defense treaty with New Zealand and the United States in 1951 in anticipation of Communist aggression. When Communist uprisings broke out in Asia, Australia sent troops to the Korean War (1950–1953).

In spite of Cold War tensions, Australian society in the 1950's and 1960's grew in positive directions. Cities spread as the population continued to grow. In the strong economy, Australians bought homes, had children, and worked well-paying jobs. Australian art and culture flourished in many areas.

The 1960's to the 1990's

The post-war economic boom continued into the 1960's. The end of the White Australia policy brought immigrants from Europe, Asia, and the Middle East who added to the population and the work force. Technology transformed the nation, and Australia became a truly modern, multicultural country.

By the 1980's, an increasing number of Australian workers held *white-collar jobs*, or those in business and professional positions, rather than *blue-collar jobs* in factories. They enjoyed weekends and evenings off, vacation time, and higher pay. This generation had greater educational and economic opportunities than previous ones. However, they also experienced slowed economic growth, along with the fall of marriage rates, birth rates, and homeownership. More women began to work outside the home, as the feminist movement of the 1960's and 1970's led to political and labor reforms.

Along with public movements for women's rights came increasing awareness and support of Aboriginal rights. Aborigines demanded equal pay and land rights. In 1962, they finally gained the right to vote in national elections and were included in the national census for the first time in 1971.

In 1965, Australia became involved in the Vietnam War on the side of the anti-communists of the South and the United States. The government introduced a form of conscription that sent troops to fight overseas. Many Australians opposed this conscription and the war in general. New government leadership in 1971 abolished conscription and pulled Australian troops out of Vietnam.

In 1998 and 1999, Australia came close to changing its government to a republic, with a president instead of the British monarch as head of state. However, the change was rejected by voters.

The 2000's

Liberal Party leader John Howard led the Australian government from 1996 to 2007. He made economic reforms and promoted traditional family and social values. He opposed multiculturalism policies and disagreed with the acknowledgement and apology for wrongs done to Aboriginal people. He also took a hard stance against refugees landing in Australia.

Prolonged periods of drought in the early 2000's prompted legislation concerning climate change. Environmental problems continued, however, with widespread bushfires that devastated southern Victoria in 2009 and then major flooding in eastern Australia in 2010–2011.

An increasing number of refugees from the Middle East and Indonesia challenged Australia's strict stance on refugees. The government made arrangements to rehome most people seeking asylum in Papua New Guinea and Cambodia.

Flag of Australia

ANTARCTICA

ANTARCTICA

ANTARCTICA: THE BIG PICTURE

The world's fifth-largest continent, Antarctica lies across the South Pole, completely covered by a vast sheet of ice. At nearly 8.8 million square miles (22.8 million square km), the continent is almost circular in shape, except for the prominent Antarctic Peninsula, which reaches toward the southern tip of South America, and two large indentations of the Ross Sea and Weddell Sea.

The smaller portion, or that "pinched" by the Ross and Weddell Seas, is called West Antarctica or the Andean province, and the larger portion is called East Antarctica or the Gondwana province. The two regions are separated not only by longitude but by a 1,900-mile (3058 km) stretch of mountains called the Transantarctic Mountains. East Antarctica consists mainly of a high, flat plateau, while West Antarctica is more mountainous. Antarctica's true size is often distorted by map projections that show it stretching from the west coast of the Americas as far east as Australia. In reality, the continent is only about 25% larger than Europe.

A global view of Antarctica shows its true size in relation to southern Africa and Madagascar

Antarctica's land is 98% covered in ice, which averages 1.5 miles (2.4 km) thick across the continent. The ice sometimes flows as glaciers advance or retreat. It also clings to the coast and floats in seas where it *calves*, or breaks, into icebergs. The vast ice and cold temperatures mean that very little plant and animal life exists inland. The surrounding sea, however, is home to a variety of wildlife. Antarctica has no permanent human residents, but scientists occupy research stations and tourists visit for brief periods. In 1959, the Antarctic Treaty established that the continent would not be owned by any nation or used for military purposes, but would remain an international science base.

Access by sea and exploration on land have been so challenging that little was known about the continent until modern aviation and satellite technology arose. It was first sighted in 1820 and inland exploration began in the early 1900's. Many geographic locations are named after Antarctica's early explorers.

LAND, WATER, AND CLIMATE IN ANTARCTICA

Like other continents, Antarctica is covered in mountains, valleys, lakes, and rivers. However, unlike other continents, it is also covered in a sheet of ice and snow

Fast Facts

Extremes of Antarctica:

Coldest continent
lowest recorded temperature: -128.6 °F

Driest continent
average 2 inches of precipitation per year

Windiest continent
gusts of 155 miles (250 km) per hour or more

Highest continent
average elevation of 7,500 feet (2,286 meters)

Iciest continent
holds 90% of the world's ice

that's over a mile thick (2 km) in most places. Antarctica doesn't receive much precipitation. In fact, it's the world's largest desert. The little precipitation it does receive, however, has been accumulating for thousands of years because temperatures hardly ever rise above freezing.

Land

Antarctica is quite mountainous and contains several volcanoes. Its highest point, Vinson Massif in the Ellsworth Mountains, rises 16,066 feet (4,897 meters). Several ranges of mountains make up the Transantarctic chain, which crosses the entire continent. The S-shaped mountain chain of the Antarctic Peninsula is actually a continuation of the Andes Mountains of South America.

Antarctica's highest peak, Vinson Massif

Antarctica's most active volcano, Mount Erebus, rises 12,447 feet (3,794 meters) on Ross Island. Another active volcano is Deception Island in the South Shetland Islands. It erupted between 1967 and 1970, destroying British and Chilean research stations nearby. Today, scientists closely monitor Mount Erebus, which is home to Antarctica's largest research station, McMurdo Station. Antarctica also has many dormant volcanoes.

Ice

Over 7 million cubic miles (18.1 million square km) of ice cover the Antarctic continent, reaching out into the Southern Ocean. This represents about 70% of all the fresh water on Earth. At its thickest, the ice measures 15,700 feet (4,785 meters) deep. The crushing weight of that much ice forces it to flow outward, toward the ocean.

Map of Antarctica

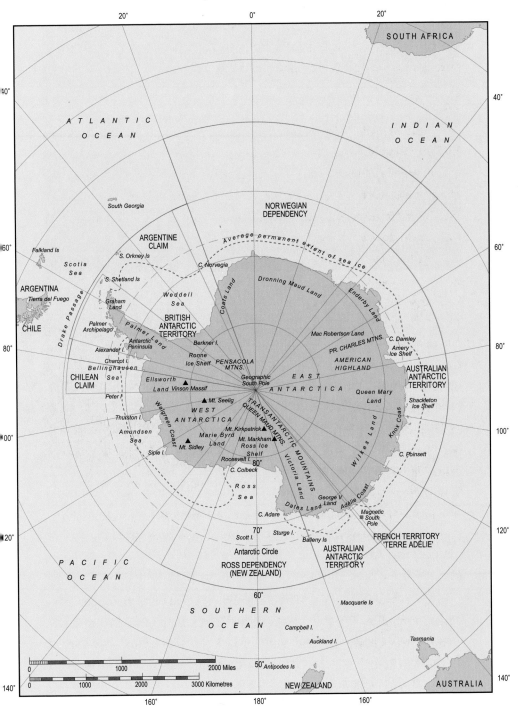

Icebergs floating off the coast of Antarctica

The Transantarctic Mountains separate the ice into two huge ice sheets. The East Antarctic ice sheet is larger, thicker, colder, and slower moving than the West Antarctic ice sheet. It covers 90% of the continent, including the South Pole, and receives less than 1 inch (2.5 cm) of snowfall per year. The West Antarctic ice sheet flows more quickly due to slightly higher temperatures and flatter underlying terrain. If the ice in the West Antarctic ice sheet melted, it would flood the area, leaving just a few small islands peeking out. If the larger East Antarctic ice sheet melted, it would affect sea level around the world and flood coastal cities.

In the center of the continent, ice moves at a slow pace of just a few feet per year. As it approaches the coast, it speeds up to hundreds of feet per year. These faster-moving glaciers can be up to 250 miles (402 km) long and 30 miles (48 km) wide. As they move at up to 2.5 miles (4 km) per year, the ice cracks and forms deep crevasses. At the coast, the ice breaks off, or calves, into icebergs that float on the ocean. Icebergs from Antarctica are the largest in the world. In 2000, a piece of the Ross Ice Shelf broke away and formed the largest ever recorded iceberg at 4,200 square miles (10,800 square km). As icebergs float out to the warmer open ocean, they melt.

Water

The Southern Ocean surrounds Antarctica to about 50° south latitude. There, a large, circular current flows from east to west around the continent. Beyond that lie the Atlantic, Pacific, and Indian Oceans. Where the oceans meet, the cold waters of the Antarctic mix with warmer, saltier waters of the more northern oceans.

Antarctica has two main seas, the Ross and the Weddell, at opposite ends of the Transantarctic Mountains. The Ross Sea contains the world's largest mass of floating ice, called the Ross Ice Shelf, which reaches up to 2,300 feet (701 meters) thick at the coast.

In winter, the waters of the Southern Ocean freeze into *sea ice*, a sheet of salty ice. In warmer temperatures, the sea ice breaks up into *floes* that float and push up against the shore driven on by wind and waves. Often, the floes stick together in a thick mass called *pack ice* that can extend as far as 1,000 miles (1,610 km) from the coast. Pack ice made early exploration of Antarctica by boat difficult.

Climate

The entire Antarctic continent is extremely cold and dry, though the coast is slightly warmer and moister than the interior. Some coastal areas

Sea ice forms near an iceberg in the Bellinghausen Sea

receive up to 24 inches (61 cm) of snow per year, in contrast with about 1 inch (2.5 cm) in the interior. Parts of West Antarctica and the Antarctic Peninsula receive several feet of snow per year.

Winter lasts from May through September in Antarctica. Because of the tilt of the Earth, most of the continent experiences total darkness for several months. Temperatures range from -94 °F to -40 °F inland and from -22 °F to -5 °F along the coast. In summer, Antarctica sees several weeks of round-the-clock daylight. Temperatures rise to -31 °F to 5 °F inland and reach about 32 °F along the coast.

Antarctica's strong, cold winds add to the bitter cold. Air sweeps across the inland plateau at an average speed of 44 miles (71 km) per hour. Just like desert winds blow sand into dunes, the Antarctic winds blow snow into rippled dunes called *sastrugi*. These sastrugi measure up to 6 feet (2 meters) tall. On the coast, winds whipping off the ocean can gust 120 miles (193 km) per hour or more.

ANTARCTICA'S WILDLIFE

Antarctica was not always a lifeless desert of snow. Once part of a landmass that included Africa, Australia, India, and South America, it had a much warmer climate. Scientists have found fossilized remains of trees, dinosaurs, and small mammals that once inhabited Antarctica.

Today, few living things can survive the frigid interior of the continent, but a variety of life exists along the coasts and in the ocean waters. Antarctica's most prevalent plants are mosses that cling to rocks along the coast. On the northern part of the Antarctic Peninsula, two other types of plants grow—a hearty grass and a short, bunchy herb. Small organisms called algae grow on snow, on ice, and in water. Similar organisms, called lichens, cling to rocks like moss. Antarctica's largest year-round land animal is a ½-inch (1.2 cm) fly called a wingless midge. These and other lice, mites, and ticks cling to seals, birds, or clumps of moss to avoid freezing.

The abundant wildlife of the Southern Ocean begins with small, shrimplike creatures called *krill*. This plentiful creature feeds on tiny floating organisms and itself provides food for several larger animals. In addition to krill, Antarctic sea animals eat squid and about 100 different kinds of fish.

In summer, a large variety of whales migrate to Antarctica. The blue whale, the earth's largest animal, at up to 100 feet (30 meters) long, feeds on tiny krill. Fin whales, humpback whales, minke whales, right whales, and sei whales also eat krill. Fish-eating whales include southern bottlenose whales, southern fourtooth whales, and sperm whales along with killer whales (or *orcas*), which also prey upon seals, penguins, and other whales.

Antarctic fur seals

Arctic seals spend most of their time in the water and come onshore to nest. The southern elephant seal, at up to 16 feet (5 meters) long, is the largest. It feeds on squid, as do the Ross and Weddell seals. Smaller seals, like the Antarctic fur seals and crabeater seals, eat krill. Leopard seals hunt other seals, as well as penguins.

International laws protect whales and Antarctic fur seals today. These animals were once hunted to dangerous levels in the 1800's and early 1900's. Hunters sought fur from seals and valuable blubber from whales. Today, killing these animals is prohibited or greatly restricted.

Antarctica is also home to a variety of birds. The flightless penguin is the most well-known of these. They live close to the water where they feed on fish and krill. With webbed feet and powerful breasts, penguins are built to swim, but waddle awkwardly on land. Oftentimes, penguins flop on their belly and use their wings to help them slide along the ice and snow. Their small, densely packed feathers keep them warm and dry.

Emperor penguins, at three feet tall, are the largest penguins in the world. They are also the only ones that breed on the continent during the harsh winter. Female Emperor penguins lay a single egg and then return to the ocean to feed. For several months, in temperatures as low as -80 °F, the male penguins care for the eggs and the chicks, until the females return. Other Antarctic penguins include the Adélie, which are most common, chinstrap, gentoo, king, macaroni, and rockhopper.

In summer, more than 40 kinds of flying birds migrate to Antarctica. They nest on land but spend most of their time diving for food in the waters offshore. These birds include albatrosses, prions, petrels, gulls, skuas, terns, and others.

Adélie penguins

Antarctica's History

Long before the continent was discovered, Antarctica already had a name. Ancient Greek philosophers imagined a landmass at the southern end of the world that was needed to balance the northern lands. Sometime in the 100's CE, Ptolemy named this unknown landmass *Antarctica*, meaning *opposite the bear*, because of a bear-shaped constellation in the northern sky. As far back as 650 CE, Maori legend tells of New Zealanders sailing a canoe as far south as the frozen ocean. Throughout the Middle Ages and the Renaissance, European geographers guessed at a huge continent at the South Pole. In the late 1700's, Captain James Cook sailed around the globe proving that if a southern continent existed, it must be smaller than imagined and lie below about 70° south latitude. By 1820, explorers from Russia, England, and the United States all claimed to be the first to see Antarctica.

Throughout the 1800's, explorers and hunters from many nations sailed the Southern Ocean. They hunted fur seals and whales, charted the coastline around the continent, and claimed lands for their respective countries. Improved technology and navigational techniques, along with increasing ambition to conquer the South Pole, led to the "heroic era" of the early 1900's.

Explorers such as Englishmen Robert F. Scott and Ernest Shackleton began inland expeditions in which they disembarked their ships, established base camps, and explored the continent. This approach involved the dangerous prospect of spending the winter on the continent until a ship could return in the spring. The early explorers experimented, sometimes miserably, with using sledges, automobiles, dogs, and ponies to traverse the ice and snow. These British expeditions set out mainly from the Ross Sea. In an early attempt to reach the South Pole, which is approximately 800 miles (1290 km) from the coast of the Ross Sea, Shackleton and a small party of men came within 97 miles (156 km) in 1909. Though they could have pushed on to reach the pole, they felt certain that their remaining provisions would not allow them to make it back to base alive.

An intense race to reach the pole began in 1910. Robert Scott and his British party set out from the Ross Sea, walking across the ice and snow while pulling their supplies on sledges. Meanwhile, a Norwegian party led by Roald Amundsen had also set out from the Ross Sea just three weeks prior to Scott and his party. These excellent skiers and trained dog handlers encountered exceptional weather. Their 52 dogs dragged sleds and allowed them to move quickly across the continent. On December 14, 1911, they raised the Norwegian flag at the South Pole. Even more remarkable, they returned back to their base alive after the 99-day journey.

Meanwhile, Scott and his party trudged on toward the pole only to discover a Norwegian flag. They were five weeks too late. On the return journey, the party became pinned down by blizzards. Unable to leave their tent and continue their trek, they used up their meager resources of food and fuel. Eventually, Scott and his four companions froze to death.

With the South Pole attained and the heroic age drawing to a close, Ernest Shackleton returned south to make one more attempt at achieving greatness in Antarctica. In 1914, he set off to cross the entire Antarctic continent. However, his expedition met with one disaster after another and became one of the great survival tales of history. Shackleton's ship, the *Endurance*, was immediately trapped in ice in the Weddell Sea and dragged further from shore by strong ocean currents under the ice. After 10 months of aimless drifting, the ship was crushed by ice and sank. Shackleton and his 27 men rescued three small lifeboats and set up camp on the pack ice. After another five months of drifting in the Weddell Sea, the ice began to break apart in the warm weather. The men took to the boats and sailed to Elephant Island in the South Shetland Islands. From there, Shackleton and five others sailed for help to South Georgia island where they hoped to find a whaling station. Amazingly, the men survived the 800-mile (1290 km) journey across some of the most treacherous seas in the world, but arrived on the wrong side of the island. Exhausted, starving, and underequipped, Shackleton and two of the men crossed the entire uncharted glacial interior of the island on foot to reach the whaling station on the other side. From there, they led the rescue of their companions on the other side of South Georgia and made four attempts before they succeeded in rescuing the rest of their party from Elephant Island. All 28 men survived the ordeal.

Aerial exploration of Antarctica began in 1928 when Australian Sir Hubert Wilkins flew over outer parts of the continent. One year later, American Richard E. Byrd flew over the South Pole as part of a three-year exploration of the interior. In 1935, American Lincoln Ellsworth and English-born Herbert Hollick-Kenyon attempted the first flight across the entire continent. After four stops, bad weather, and a shortage of fuel, they finished the journey on foot.

The U.S. launched the largest exploration yet in 1946 and 1947. Byrd led 4,700 men, 13 ships, and 23 airplanes and helicopters in Operation Highjump. This exploration discovered much new land and documented previously unexplored areas.

From July 1, 1957 to December 31, 1958, scientists around the globe worked together to make observations and share findings. They called it the International Geophysical Year (or IGY). Knowledge of Antarctica increased rapidly as 12 different countries established over 50 scientific stations on and around the continent. They studied earthquakes, gravity, magnetism, oceanography, geology, meteorology, glaciology, and solar activity. During that time, British geologist Vivian Fuchs set out to achieve what Ernest Shackleton had attempted over 40 years earlier—a land crossing of the entire continent. Fuchs and his team departed from the Weddell Sea with dogsleds and snow tractors. At the South Pole, they met up with New Zealand explorer Sir Edmund Hillary and his team. Hillary's team had left supply depots to lead the men from the pole to McMurdo Sound in the Ross Sea. Fuchs completed the first Antarctic land crossing of 2,158 miles (3493 km) in about three months.

During the IGY, seven of the twelve countries that built research stations claimed Antarctic land as their own. They divided the continent into slices from the center, like a pie. However, the United States and many other nations refused to recognize these claims. In 1959, officials from the 12 countries signed the Antarctic Treaty, which froze existing land claims and prohibited future ones. They agreed to only use Antarctica for peaceful purposes, such as research and tourism. The agreement requires scientists to share the results of their studies. It also prohibits military forces and outlaws the use of nuclear weapons and the disposal of radioactive waste. Since then, many other nations joined the treaty. They signed an updated agreement in 1991, called the Madrid Protocol, that reaffirms the use of the continent for peaceful and scientific advancement. It includes stricter environmental regulations.

Today, many different countries maintain over 40 year-round scientific stations in Antarctica. The largest of these, McMurdo Station, is home to about 1,200 scientists in the summer and 250 in the winter. During the long, dark, frigid winter, powerful ships called icebreakers plow through the ice to deliver supplies. When the weather permits, airplanes and helicopters can land at the station. McMurdo in turn supplies other, harder-to-reach stations, like South Pole Station. It uses cargo planes equipped with skis to deliver supplies to the winter crew of about 12 at the South Pole.

McMurdo Station on Ross Island

Current research on Antarctica focuses on environmental issues. Scientists study the *ozone*, a layer of protective atmosphere that has been thinning over Antarctica. Their findings resulted in the Montreal Protocol in 1987, which banned the use of a chemical that leads to ozone loss. They also seek to answer questions about climate change and global warming. In 2007, scientists from around the world launched the International Polar Year, in which they focused on assessing the condition of polar regions and determining how global warming might be affecting them.

Since the late 1990's, Antarctica has increased in popularity as a tourist destination. This presents new challenges, as scientists hope to preserve the natural environment while the human population increases.

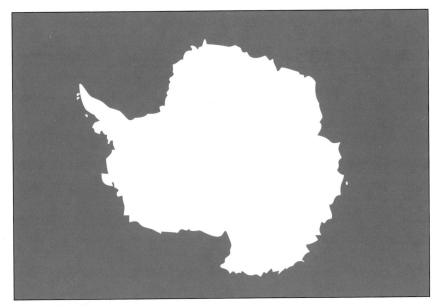

Flag of Antarctica

References

ASIA | CHINA

"China". *Encyclopaedia Britannica. Encyclopaedia Britannica Online.* Encyclopaedia Britannica Inc., 2015. Web. May 2015.

"China." *National Geographic Kids.* National Geographic Society. Web. May 2015.

"China." *The World Factbook.* Central Intelligence Agency. Web. May 2015.

DK find out! Dorling Kindersley. Web. May 2015.

Edmonds, Richard Louis, and Richard J. Smith. "China." *World Book Online InfoFinder.* World Book, 2015. Web. 11 May 2015.

World Wildlife Fund. Web. May 2015.

"China." *Encyclopaedia Britannica. Encyclopaedia Britannica Online.* Encyclopaedia Britannica Inc., 2015. Web. June 2015.

Cline, Erin M. "Confucianism." *World Book Online InfoFinder.* World Book, 2015. Web. 8 June 2015.

DK find out! Dorling Kindersley. Web. June 2015.

Lun yu. Confucius.org. Web. June 2015.

"Chinese Communist Party." *Encyclopaedia Britannica. Encyclopaedia Britannica Online.* Encyclopaedia Britannica Inc., 2015. Web. June 2015.

"Karl Marx." *History.com.* A+E Networks, 2009. Web. June 2015.

"Long March." *History.com.* A+E Networks, 2009. Web. June 2015.

"Vladimir Lenin." *History.com.* A+E Networks, 2009. Web. June 2015.

Vontz, Thomas S. "Communism." *World Book Online InfoFinder.* World Book, 2015. Web. 9 June 2015.

ASIA | NORTH KOREA

"Korea." *Factmonster.* Pearson Education. Web. June 2015.

"North Korea." *Encyclopaedia Britannica. Encyclopaedia Britannica Online.* Encyclopaedia Britannica Inc., 2015. Web. June 2015.

"North Korea." *The World Factbook.* Central Intelligence Agency. Web. June 2015.

Oh, Bonnie Bongwan Cho, and John K. C. Oh. "Korea, North." *World Book Online InfoFinder.* World Book, 2015. Web. 12 June 2015.

Armstrong, Charles K. "Korean War." *World Book Online InfoFinder.* World Book, 2015. Web. 2 July 2015.

"Korean War." *Factmonster.* Pearson Education. Web. July 2015.

"Korean War." *History.com.* A+E Networks, 2009. Web. July 2015.

ASIA | SOUTH KOREA

"Korea, South." *Factmonster.* Pearson Education. Web. June 2015.

"South Korea." *Encyclopaedia Britannica. Encyclopaedia Britannica Online.* Encyclopaedia Britannica Inc., 2015. Web. June 2015.

"South Korea." *The World Factbook.* Central Intelligence Agency. Web. June 2015.

Oh, Bonnie Bongwan Cho, and John K. C. Oh. "Korea, South." *World Book Online InfoFinder.* World Book, 2015. Web. 12 June 2015.

ASIA | JAPAN

Allinson, Gary D. "Japan." *World Book Online InfoFinder.* World Book, 2015. Web. 3 July 2015.

"Japan." *Encyclopaedia Britannica. Encyclopaedia Britannica Online.* Encyclopaedia Britannica Inc., 2015. Web. 03 Jul. 2015.

"Japan." *Factmonster.* Pearson Education. Web. July 2015.

"Japan." *The World Factbook*. Central Intelligence Agency. Web. July 2015.

Rambelli, Fabio. "Shinto." *World Book Online InfoFinder*. World Book, 2015. Web. 12 July 2015.

"Shinto." *British Broadcasting Corporation*. BBC Online. Web. 12 Jul. 2015.

ASIA | RUSSIA

"Karl Marx." *History.com*. A+E Networks, 2009. Web. June 2015.

Raleigh, Donald J. "Russia." *World Book Online InfoFinder*. World Book, 2015. Web. 15 July 2015.

"Russia". *Encyclopaedia Britannica. Encyclopaedia Britannica Online*. Encyclopaedia Britannica Inc., 2015. Web. 15 Jul. 2015 <http://www.britannica.com/place/Russia>.

"Russia." *The World Factbook*. Central Intelligence Agency. Web. June 2015.

"Vladimir Lenin." *History.com*. A+E Networks, 2009. Web. June 2015.

Vontz, Thomas S. "Communism." *World Book Online InfoFinder*. World Book, 2015. Web. 9 June 2015.

SOUTHEAST ASIA

"Southeast Asia." Fact Monster. © 2000–2013 Pearson Education, publishing as Fact Monster. 27 Jul. 2015 <http://www.factmonster.com/encyclopedia/world/southeast-asia.html>.

Temple, Frederick T. "Southeast Asia." *World Book Online InfoFinder*. World Book, 2015. Web. 27 July 2015.

The World Factbook. Central Intelligence Agency. Web. July 2015.

SOUTHEAST ASIA | VIETNAM

Pelley, Patricia M. "Vietnam." *World Book Online InfoFinder*. World Book, 2015. Web. 29 July 2015.

"Vietnam." *Encyclopaedia Britannica. Encyclopaedia Britannica Online*. Encyclopaedia Britannica Inc., 2015. Web. 29 Jul. 2015 <http://www.britannica.com/place/Vietnam>.

"Vietnam." *Factmonster*. Pearson Education. Web. July 2015.

"Vietnam." *The World Factbook*. Central Intelligence Agency. Web. July 2015.

Gilbert, Marc Jason. "Vietnam War." *World Book Online InfoFinder*. World Book, 2015. Web. 3 Dec. 2015.

"Vietnam War." *Encyclopaedia Britannica. Encyclopaedia Britannica Online*. Encyclopaedia Britannica Inc., 2015. Web. 03 Dec. 2015 <http://www.britannica.com/event/Vietnam-War>.

SOUTH ASIA | INDIA

"India." *Encyclopaedia Britannica. Encyclopaedia Britannica Online*. Encyclopaedia Britannica Inc., 2015. Web. 25 Sep. 2015 <http://www.britannica.com/place/India>.

"India." *The World Factbook*. Central Intelligence Agency. Web. September 2015.

Lal, Vinay, and Anil Lal. "India." World Book Online InfoFinder. World Book, 2015. Web. 25 Sept. 2015.

McGovern, James. "Teresa, Mother." *World Book Online InfoFinder*. World Book, 2015. Web. 6 Oct. 2015.

"Mohandas Karamchand Gandhi." *Encyclopaedia Britannica. Encyclopaedia Britannica Online*. Encyclopaedia Britannica Inc., 2015. Web. 03 Oct. 2015 <http://www.britannica.com/biography/ Mohandas-Karamchand-Gandhi>.

"Hinduism." *Encyclopaedia Britannica. Encyclopaedia Britannica Online*. Encyclopaedia Britannica Inc., 2015. Web. 9 Oct. 2015 <http://www.britannica.com/topic/Hinduism>.

Ramey, Steven W. "Hinduism." *World Book Online InfoFinder*. World Book, 2015. Web. 9 Oct. 2015.

Jhutti-Johal, Jagbir Kaur. "Sikhism." *World Book Online InfoFinder*. World Book, 2015. Web. 9 Oct. 2015.

"Sikhism." *Encyclopaedia Britannica. Encyclopaedia Britannica Online*. Encyclopaedia Britannica Inc., 2015. Web. 9 Oct. 2015 <http://www.britannica.com/topic/Sikhism>.

THE MIDDLE EAST

CIA World Factbook <https://www.cia.gov/library/publications/the-world-factbook/geos/kn.html>

Cuno, Kenneth M. "Middle East." *World Book Online InfoFinder.* World Book, 2015. Web. 10 Oct. 2015.

"Middle East." *Encyclopaedia Britannica. Encyclopaedia Britannica Online.* Encyclopaedia Britannica Inc., 2015. Web. 10 Oct. 2015 <http://www.britannica.com/place/Middle-East>.

"Egypt." *The World Factbook.* Central Intelligence Agency. Web. November 2015.

"Islam." *Encyclopaedia Britannica. Encyclopaedia Britannica Online.* Encyclopaedia Britannica Inc., 2015. Web. 01 Nov. 2015 <http://www.britannica.com/topic/Islam>.

"Saudi Arabia." *The World Factbook.* Central Intelligence Agency. Web. November 2015.

Takim, Liyakat. "Islam." *World Book Online InfoFinder.* World Book, 2015. Web. 3 Nov. 2015.

THE MIDDLE EAST | ISRAEL

"Israel." *Encyclopaedia Britannica. Encyclopaedia Britannica Online.* Encyclopaedia Britannica Inc., 2015. Web. 145 Oct. 2015 <http://www.britannica.com/place/Israel>.

"Israel." *The World Factbook.* Central Intelligence Agency. Web. October 2015.

Reich, Bernard. "Israel." *World Book Online InfoFinder.* World Book, 2015. Web. 14 Oct. 2015.

Berenbaum, Michael. "Holocaust." *World Book Online InfoFinder.* World Book, 2015. Web. 11 Oct. 2015.

"Judaism." *Encyclopaedia Britannica. Encyclopaedia Britannica Online.* Encyclopaedia Britannica Inc., 2015. Web. 10 Oct. 2015 <http://www.britannica.com/topic/Judaism>.

Magid, Shaul. "Judaism." *World Book Online InfoFinder.* World Book, 2015. Web. 10 Oct. 2015.

Takim, Liyakat. "Islam." *World Book Online InfoFinder.* World Book, 2015. Web. 11 Oct. 2015.

Exodus 20:3-17 https://www.biblegateway.com/passage/?search=Exodus%2020&version=ESV

THE MIDDLE EAST | SAUDI ARABIA

Doumato, Eleanor Abdella. "Saudi Arabia." *World Book Online InfoFinder.* World Book, 2015. Web. 15 Oct. 2015.

"Saudi Arabia." *Encyclopaedia Britannica. Encyclopaedia Britannica Online.* Encyclopaedia Britannica Inc., 2015. Web. 12 Oct. 2015 <http://www.britannica.com/place/Saudi-Arabia>.

"Saudi Arabia." *The World Factbook.* Central Intelligence Agency. Web. October 2015.

AFRICA

"Africa." *Encyclopaedia Britannica. Encyclopaedia Britannica Online.* Encyclopaedia Britannica Inc., 2015. Web. 16 Oct. 2015 <http://www.britannica.com/place/Africa>.

CIA World Factbook https://www.cia.gov/library/publications/the-world-factbook/geos/kn.html>

Desanker, Paul V., Peri M. Klemm, Kenneth J. Perkins, Kwesi Kwaa Prah, and Paul Tiyambe Zeleza. "Africa." *World Book Online InfoFinder.* World Book, 2015. Web. 16 Oct. 2015.

Russell, Mona L. "Suez Canal." *World Book Online InfoFinder.* World Book, 2015. Web. 18 Oct. 2015.

"animism". *Encyclopaedia Britannica. Encyclopaedia Britannica Online.* Encyclopaedia Britannica Inc., 2015. Web. 20 Oct. 2015 <http://www.britannica.com/topic/animism>.

Fratkin, Elliot. "Animism." *World Book Online InfoFinder.* World Book, 2015. Web. 21 Oct. 2015.

MacDonald, Kevin C. "Ghana Empire." *World Book Online InfoFinder.* World Book, 2015. Web. 21 Oct. 2015.

MacDonald, Kevin C. "Mali Empire." *World Book Online InfoFinder.* World Book, 2015. Web. 21 Oct. 2015.

MacDonald, Kevin C. "Mansa Musa." *World Book Online InfoFinder.* World Book, 2015. Web. 21 Oct. 2015.

MacDonald, Kevin C. "Songhai Empire." *World Book Online InfoFinder.* World Book, 2015. Web. 21 Oct. 2015.

MacDonald, Kevin C. "Sundiata Keita." *World Book Online InfoFinder.* World Book, 2015. Web. 21 Oct. 2015.

THE PACIFIC | PACIFIC ISLANDS

CIA World Factbook <https://www.cia.gov/library/publications/the-world-factbook/geos/kn.html>

"Pacific Islands." *Encyclopaedia Britannica. Encyclopaedia Britannica Online.* Encyclopaedia Britannica Inc., 2015. Web. 21 Oct. 2015 <http://www.britannica.com/place/Pacific-Islands>.

Teaiwa, Katerina Martina. "Pacific Islands." *World Book Online InfoFinder.* World Book, 2015. Web. 21 Oct. 2015.

"Christianity." *Encyclopaedia Britannica. Encyclopaedia Britannica Online.* Encyclopaedia Britannica Inc., 2015. Web. 21 Oct. 2015 <http://www.britannica.com/topic/Christianity>.

Williams, Peter W. "Christianity." *World Book Online InfoFinder.* World Book, 2015. Web. 21 Oct. 2015.

THE PACIFIC | NEW ZEALAND

Byrnes, Giselle M. "New Zealand." *World Book Online InfoFinder.* World Book, 2015. Web. 23 Oct. 2015.

Byrnes, Giselle M. "New Zealand, History of." *World Book Online InfoFinder.* World Book, 2015. Web. 23 Oct. 2015.

"New Zealand." *Encyclopaedia Britannica. Encyclopaedia Britannica Online.* Encyclopaedia Britannica Inc., 2015. Web. 21 Oct. 2015 <http://www.britannica.com/place/New-Zealand>.

"New Zealand." *The World Factbook.* Central Intelligence Agency. Web. October 2015.

THE PACIFIC | AUSTRALIA

"Australia." *Encyclopaedia Britannica. Encyclopaedia Britannica Online.* Encyclopaedia Britannica Inc., 2015. Web. 24 Oct. 2015 <http://www.britannica.com/place/Australia>.

"Australian Aborigine." *Encyclopaedia Britannica. Encyclopaedia Britannica Online.* Encyclopaedia Britannica Inc., 2015. Web. 24 Oct. 2015 <http://www.britannica.com/topic/Australian-Aborigine>.

"Australia." *The World Factbook.* Central Intelligence Agency. Web. October 2015.

Carter, David. "Australia." *World Book Online InfoFinder.* World Book, 2015. Web. 24 Oct. 2015.

Darian-Smith, Kate, and Grace Karskens. "Australia, History of." *World Book Online InfoFinder.* World Book, 2015. Web. 24 Oct. 2015.

http://www.australia.gov.au/about-government/how-government-works/state-and-territory-government

ANTARCTICA

"Antarctica." *Encyclopaedia Britannica. Encyclopaedia Britannica Online.* Encyclopaedia Britannica Inc., 2015. Web. 22 Oct. 2015 <http://www.britannica.com/place/Antarctica>.

"Antarctica." *The World Factbook.* Central Intelligence Agency. Web. October 2015.

Bindschadler, Robert. "Antarctica." *World Book Online InfoFinder.* World Book, 2015. Web. 22 Oct. 2015.

DK find out! Dorling Kindersley. Web. October 2015.

"Sir Ernest Henry Shackleton." *Encyclopaedia Britannica. Encyclopaedia Britannica Online.* Encyclopaedia Britannica Inc., 2015. Web. 22 Oct. 2015 <http://www.britannica.com/biography/Ernest-Henry-Shackleton>.

Photo Credits

ASIA | SOUTH KOREA

"Sunset" by Carmine.shot at https://www.flickr.com/photos/xingty/22411629183/ licensed under CC BY 2.0, cropped from original

"Cheonggye Stream" by Kimmo Räisänen at https://www.flickr.com/photos/kim-momurmu/7090802091/ licensed under CC BY 2.0

Seoul night skyline photograph by Kim Daram at https://www.flickr.com/photos/43566645@N03/635000752/ licensed under CC BY 2.0

"Gwangju World Cup Stadium" by Michael Howe-Ely at https://www.flickr.com/photos/114305793@N07/12716827665/in/photostream/ licensed under CC BY 2.0

"청자_거북이_모양_주자" by the National Museum of Korea, available at https://en.wikipedia.org/wiki/File:청자_거북이_모양_주자.jpg and licensed under the Korea Open Government License Type 1: Attribution

"Korea Busan Cityscape 01" by Gilad Rom at https://commons.wikimedia.org/wiki/File:Korea-Busan-Cityscape-01.jpg licensed under CC BY 2.0, enhanced from original

ASIA | JAPAN

"Lotus Flower" by Yoshikazu TAKADA at https://www.flickr.com/photos/yoshikazut/20617478921/ licensed under CC BY 2.0, cropped from original

"Shinto Statues" by James Trosh at https://www.flickr.com/photos/troshy/3082564313/ licensed under CC BY 2.0

Tokyo's Metropolitan Government Building photograph by t.ohashi at https://www.flickr.com/photos/t-ohashi/4358902563/ licensed under CC BY 2.0

"金閣寺 / Temple of the Golden Pavilion" by Freedom II Andres at https://www.flickr.com/photos/freedomiiphotography/7453049028/ licensed under CC BY 2.0

"Park @ Naritasan Shinshoji Temple @ Narita" by Guilhem Vellut at https://www.flickr.com/photos/o_0/15262295771/ licensed under CC BY 2.0, cropped from original

"bad luck" by J3SSL33 at https://www.flickr.com/photos/eelssej_/486414113/ licensed under CC BY 2.0, cropped from original

"Lotus (Ueno Zoo, Tokyo, Japan)" by t-mizo at https://www.flickr.com/photos/tmizo/6013495844/ licensed under CC BY 2.0, cropped from original

"Statue of Duke Masashige Kusunoki / 楠正成公像" by Toshihiro Gamo at https://www.flickr.com/photos/dakiny/8342652424/ licensed under CC BY 2.0

"Narita-san - Gakudo Hall" by Shizuka Sama at https://www.flickr.com/photos/97607404@N02/9067449583/ licensed under CC BY 2.0

"imperial palace gardens" by Mike Haw at https://www.flickr.com/photos/guyfromva/2629493953/ licensed under CC BY 2.0

ASIA | RUSSIA

"The Church of the Saviour on Spilled Blood" by Jorge Láscar at https://www.flickr.com/photos/jlascar/20956466968/ licensed under CC BY 2.0, cropped from original

"Amazing Sarychev Volcano - as seen from space" by NASA at https://www.flickr.com/photos/gsfc/3660169591/ licensed under CC BY 2.0, enhanced from original

"Vue sur la petite ceinture de Moscou" by Oscar W. Rasson at https://www.flickr.com/photos/papaorhum/13290709784/ licensed under CC BY 2.0

Saints Peter and Paul Cathedral photograph by ninara at https://www.flickr.com/photos/ninara/19928241923/ licensed under CC BY 2.0

"St Basil's Cathedral" by Dominique at https://www.flickr.com/photos/malinki/2337503596/ licensed under CC BY 2.0, cropped from original

SOUTHEAST ASIA

SOUTHEAST ASIA | VIETNAM

SOUTH ASIA | INDIA